D1540033

FORT UNION
AND THE
WINNING
OF THE
SOUTHWEST

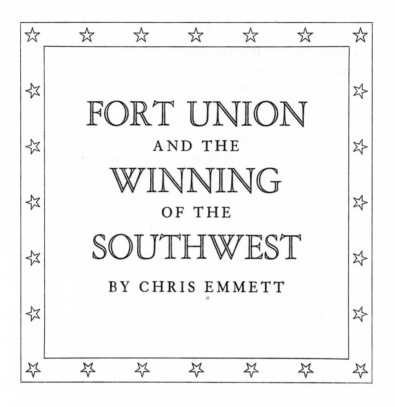

FORT UNION

AND THE

WINNING

OF THE

SOUTHWEST

BY CHRIS EMMETT

UNIVERSITY OF OKLAHOMA PRESS : NORMAN

o
CHS.
F
58B
E46

BY CHRIS EMMETT

Fort Union and the Winning of the Southwest (Norman, 1965)
In the Path of Events with Colonel Martin Lalor Crimmins
(Waco, Texas, 1959)
Shanghai Pierce: A Fair Likeness (Norman, 1953)
Give 'Way to the Right (San Antonio, 1931)
The General and the Poet (San Antonio, 1930)
Texas As It Was Then (San Antonio, 1930)
Texas Camel Tales (San Antonio, 1929)

F588
E46

LIBRARY OF CONGRESS CATALOG CARD NUMBER: 64–20769

Copyright 1965 by the University of Oklahoma Press,
Publishing Division of the University.
Composed and printed at Norman, Oklahoma, U.S.A.,
by the University of Oklahoma Press. First edition.

DEACCESSIONED BY
CHICAGO HISTORICAL SOCIETY
PRINTED COLLECTIONS

DEDICATED TO THE MEMORY OF

JAMES WEST ARROTT

SAPELLO, NEW MEXICO,

transplanted Pennsylvanian, whose interest
in New Mexico history has wrought incalculably
for the verity of the West, paving the way
for students to interpret a confused
but glamorous amalgamation
of three peoples.

Baker & Taylor Nov.1965 5⁰⁰

FOREWORD, BY W. S. WALLACE

"I am well enough acquainted with my country to know . . . ." (Honorable Richard H. Weightman of New Mexico, vindicatory of the character of the people of that country.

THE GREAT TREK into the West during the nineteenth century uprooted families, changed the proprietorship of the land, and began a new era in the history of the United States. From discontented freeholders in New England and the Ohio country to the land-starved planters of the South, an ever increasing stream culminating in a torrent of humanity crossed the Father of Waters and pointed the prows of their prairie schooners toward every nook and cranny of the Great West.

However, it should be remembered that the westward movement was preceded by a Spanish northern movement. The Spanish penetration of the West resulted in a great impact. It was responsible for the conquest of the southern part of the entire region, and its influence on the history of the West is indelible. The livestock of the Spaniards was the beginning of the cattle and sheep industry, and the introduction of the horse increased the spatial mobility of the Indians. The significance of these facts cannot be overestimated. Today, the Spaniards comprise, perhaps, as much as 20 per cent of the population of the southern portion of the West. Their architecture, mingled with that of the Indian pueblos, is widely used, and the place names of the West from states down to the smallest land forms are largely the result of the Spanish influence.

The northern movement of the Spaniards and Mexicans into what is now the southern portion of the western United States required

vii

225 years before it reached as far north as western New Mexico. These were years of slow and torturous progress, often deterred by the changing vanity of the kings of Spain and the rebellious Pueblo Indians. Between the beginning of the Coronado expedition and the arrival of Rivera in present-day western Colorado, a new province for the Spanish empire had been carved from the lower stretches of the North American continent.

North-south travel in the West by the Spaniards dates from the time of Coronado (1540), and was continued by a number of clerical, commercial, and military leaders. Juan María Rivera (1765), the Domínguez-Escalante expedition of 1776, and Juan Bautista de Anza in 1779 were particularly notable for their travels in the western areas south of the forty-second parallel.

The Spanish frontier in the Four Corners was never pushed farther north. This was probably due to the decline of Spanish power throughout the empire as a result of the increasing pressure of England and, later on, Napoleonic France. Spain's failure in this respect occurred just at the moment when a dynamic United States, with colorful Mountain Men in the vanguard, arrived on the scene, with trappers and traders eager to turn untapped resources into operations that meant profit and power for themselves as well as for the young nation.

As early as 1739 or 1740 the French Mallett brothers made a trading expedition from Illinois to Santa Fe. By 1825, contact of the traders from the Mississippi with the land that is now New Mexico had expanded to such a point that Congress began to show an interest in what was going on.

The later years of the eighteenth century and those of the first part of the nineteenth were years in which an essentially northern, Indo-European population was to initiate contact with an Ibero-Indian population. For the most part this contact was not altogether a pleasant experience. Differences in religious, political, and social institutions were great. However, the acquisitive instincts of American merchants, the desire for American goods by the people of the Spanish Southwest, and the ever expanding frontier of the United States were sufficient inducements to broaden and increase the intercourse between eastern North America and the Spanish states.

The inevitability of the eventual domination by the United States of the southwestern portion of this country is brought out in the following pages. The instrument used finally to achieve this was the military. And the story of the military operations concerning the Southwest is the story of Fort Union.

Few casual readers of American history are even remotely aware of Fort Union and its history. Many would probably confuse it with another Fort Union on the headwaters of the Missouri, also important, but not as decisive in its influence on the history of the West as the Fort Union in New Mexico.

The founding of Fort Union marked the beginning of the final stages of United States penetration into the Southwest.

The vast amount of research involved in preparing a history of Fort Union could not have been readily achieved as recently as ten years ago. Neglected almost to the point of being totally forgotten, it would eventually have been lost in the haze of unrecorded history had it not been for the zealous collecting interests of the late James W. Arrott.

As so often happens in gathering great private collections, Mr. Arrott with little more than idle curiosity about the remains of Fort Union, which happened to be located a few miles from his ranch, many years ago began to buy an occasional book about the fort and to make mental notes of the hearsay concerning it. At the time of this first interest in the fort he was engaged in business and industrial activities in Pittsburgh, Pennsylvania, and only managed to visit New Mexico for short and infrequent periods. In some respects the attributes that made him a successful industrialist were helpful in organizing what was to become the Arrott Collection. His forceful yet considerate insistence on doing any job thoroughly and properly was invaluable to him when he retired from active business and turned the full power of his talents on Fort Union.

It has been his goal to bring together into one organic whole a file consisting of every available document pertinent to Fort Union. His success has been little short of amazing. For several years he retained a research assistant at the National Archives in Washington to ferret out every possible document involving Fort Union. In Pittsburgh his long-time and devoted private secretary, Mrs. L. E. Lewis, maintained an office furnished with microfilm equipment where she made transcriptions and handled the physical preparation of new additions to the files of the collection. These additions were sent to the Arrott ranch where they were inserted in their chronological positions in the files. In addition to the National Archives, documents in other depositories throughout the country were examined. Separate and distinct from the documentary aspects of the collection was the continuous acquisition of books, pamphlets, maps, photographs, and microfilms—all pertinent to Fort Union and the general military history of the Southwest.

Chris Emmett is the first and only researcher to have unrestricted access to Mr. Arrott's collection. Beginning in the Fall of 1956, he set up his headquarters at Rodgers Library, New Mexico Highlands University, Las Vegas, New Mexico, and devoted all his time and energy for two years to research for this volume. He was given complete freedom to make use of anything in the Arrott Collection, which at that time was still housed at the Arrott ranch.

Working with Mr. Emmett on this volume has been truly a rewarding experience. This present volume is based on Mr. Emmett's draft manuscript of some three thousand typewritten pages, which has been bound and placed in Rodgers Library.

Fort Union today is a National Monument, created by act of Congress in 1954. Extensive ruins remain, and the National Park Service has undertaken to stabilize them. A museum has been built to house mementoes of the fort and to display interpretive material relating to the history of the fort and its role in the development of the Southwest.

Rescued from near oblivion, this venerable old military establishment is once again bustling with activity. No longer do the commands of drill sergeants and the noise from the wagon shops echo out across the beautiful Fort Union Valley. Today, cars disgorge tourists and students in steadily increasing numbers from all sections of the country. They come to see the always colorful, always interesting Fort Union.

W. S. WALLACE, Librarian
Rodgers Library
New Mexico Highlands University

Las Vegas, New Mexico
October 28, 1964

CONTENTS

ILLUSTRATIONS

MAPS

ABBREVIATIONS USED IN FOOTNOTES

AC: Arrott Collection on Fort Union,
     New Mexico Highlands University, Las Vegas, N.M.

AG: Adjutant General.

AAG: Assistant Adjutant General.

AAAG: Acting Assistant Adjutant General.

AGO: Adjutant General's Office.

GO: General Orders.

MB: Militia Book.

NA: National Archives, Washington, D.C.

RG: Record Group (in NA).

SO: Special Orders.

FORT UNION
AND THE
WINNING
OF THE
SOUTHWEST

CHAPTER ONE

"THE HOLES IN THE PRAIRIE"

A WAIL went out of Santa Fe, New Mexico. The *St. Louis Republic,* ever ready to further the cause of Missourians in the West, echoed the "plight of the abandoned city": "Santa Fe is dull—dull in the superlative degree. The headquarters of the army have been removed from here to a place where are said to be some holes of water in the prairie (and here called 'Holes in the Prairie,') somewhere north of Barclay's fort. Money seems to have taken its flight. The glory of Santa Fe has departed, I fear me, forever."[1]

Out at the Holes in the Prairie there was real cause for discontent, but as the cause there was physical inconvenience, not economic, the sufferers accepted their plight with insouciance. The Holes in the Prairie had been transformed overnight "into a tent city." The only two women in the city, "wives of Colonel Alexander and Major E. S. Sibley," had taken shelter under "double-canvas, cotton houses" adjacent to each other. The third woman to arrive, coming with a belated contingent following in the wake of Sumner's command, was Kittie Bowen, wife of Captain Isaac Bowen, chief of the Subsistence Department. When Kittie arrived on August 20, 1851, the two other women were "veterans." They had been at the Holes in the Prairie approximately a month. In fact, both Mrs. Alexander and Mrs. Sibley had been with Colonel Sumner's detachment all the way from the "States," even going into Santa Fe with the troops since Sumner could not make up his mind before reaching the Holes in the Prairie where he wanted to establish his headquarters. And at Santa Fe, Mrs. Sibley had found two letters addressed to Mrs. Kittie Bowen. With these

[1] Letter, dated September 27, 1851, quoted in Richard H. Weightman's speech of March 18, 1852.

3

two letters from Kittie's mother Mrs. Sibley greeted the new arrival "in the kindest manner."

The daughter's reply to her mother was prompt. She was "at last at our destination, safe in every particular, in health, and our goods in as good order as anything could possibly be after the hard journey they have had." Her destination was "a point one hundred miles nearer home than Santa Fe, located particularly with a view to extensive farming operations, and certainly it is well adapted—plenty of water, abundance of wood, and, to all appearances, a fertile valley, with mountains on two sides of us. The hills are close by, and timbered with pine, red or pitch pine, I believe: anyway, it makes good lumber and fine wood, and will not fail a supply in thousands of years."[2]

Mrs. Bowen was not only grateful to Mrs. Sibley for her thoughtfulness in bringing the letters from Santa Fe but sympathetic on account of the unnecessary traveling, since "she had come with Colonel Sumner and had to go to Santa Fe before he [Sumner] decided to locate (then make) the tedious trip back nearly all the way over the mountains." The unnecessary and tedious trip back over the mountains from Santa Fe to the Holes in the Prairie had resulted from inadequate information in the War Department and Colonel Sumner's inordinate zeal to further his military status, as well as age-old insoluble conflicts of the three peoples living in New Mexico.

As a forerunner of Mrs. Sibley's tedious trip over the mountains, to say nothing of momentous things to come thereafter, Order No. 41, dated at Fort Leavenworth, Kansas, March 12, 1851, relieved Brevet Colonel Edwin Vose Sumner from the command of the First Dragoons. The fact that such an order existed (although those privy to the information were admonished to "tell it not in Gath") came surreptitiously to Captain R. S. Ewell, commanding at Rayado, New Mexico, who, on April 27, 1851, availed himself of his information to give substance to the persistent rumor that Colonel Munroe was to be relieved of military command in New Mexico. Seventeen days after Brevet Colonel Sumner was relieved of his dragoon command,

---

[2] Arrott Collection (hereafter cited as AC). There are copies of Kittie Bowen's letters to her parents dealing with life at Fort Union after August 20, 1851.

Order No. 17 was issued from the Adjutant General's Office relieving Colonel Munroe from command of the Ninth Military Department. Again this order preceded official relay of communications
reaching Captain Richard S. Ewell, June 29, 1851, at Rayado. Three
days after publication of the order relieving Colonel Munroe, Secretary of War C. M. Conrad, dating his letter April 1, 1851, at Washington City, told Colonel Sumner that he had been "selected to take
the command of the Ninth Military Department" and that he should
"repair to it as early as practicable."

New Mexico was not untrodden ground to the new department
commander. By special request—almost on demand—Colonel Kearny
had caused Major Sumner, along with Captain Philip St. George
Cooke, to be attached to the Kearny Expedition in 1846. Sumner had
traveled in the wake of Kearny's invading army, stopping to camp at
Ocate[3] and again at a point called *Los Posos* by the Mexicans, but
better understood by the United States Army as the "Holes [of water]
in the Prairie." At the latter encampment Major Sumner found not
only the water holes but a spring. This oasis was northwest of Barclay's Fort, near the confluence of the Sapello and Mora rivers and
approximately twenty-seven miles from the village of Las Vegas.[4]
After leaving the Holes in the Prairie, Major Sumner traveled along
with the invading army until turned back by orders (west of the Río
del Norte) after being informed by Kit Carson that California was
in the possession of the United States army and navy. Retracing his
march, again through Santa Fe and *Los Posos,* he went back to the

[3] Later to be the site of General Sumner's experimental farm. The land was
owned by the United States consul, Manuel Alvarez, and leased to the government
for an army farm.

[4] Lieut. Col. W. H. Emory, *Notes of a Military Reconnoissance . . . Made in 1846–7
with the Advanced Guard of the "Army of the West,"* 30 Cong., 1 sess., *House
Ex. Doc. No. 41;* Kenyon Riddle, *Records and Maps of the Old Santa Fe Trail,* 91.
The following entry appears in Emory's account under the date of August 12, 1846:
"About 12 o'clock the advance was sounded, and the colonel with Sumner's command marched 20 miles [Coyote or Wolf Creek, where Fort Union was built in the
1850's] and halted in a beautiful valley of fine grass and pools of cool water. . . .
The stream . . . is a tributary of the Mora. . . . Six miles brought us to the first settlement we had seen in 775 miles [near Watrous, New Mexico]."

"States," made his way to Mexico, and helped General Scott land his army at Vera Cruz. There he was slightly wounded but remained with the army until after the capture of the City of Mexico. In July, 1848, he was commissioned lieutenant colonel of the First Dragoons, and on April 1, 1851, learned that he had been selected to take the command of the Ninth Military Department.

The Secretary of War immediately apprised the Lieutenant Colonel "that material changes ought to be made in that department both with a view of a more efficient protection of the country and to a diminution of expenses." He was, "immediately on assuming command, [to] revise the whole system of defense, to examine particularly whether the posts now occupied by the troops are the most suitable, and if not . . . make such changes as you may deem advisable." In the selection of posts he was to "be governed mainly by the following considerations, viz: 1st. The protection of New Mexico: 2d. The defense of the Mexican Territory, which we are bound to protect against the Indians within our borders: 3d. Economy and facility in supporting the troops, particularly in regard to forage, fuel and adaptation of the surrounding country to cultivation."

The War Department had been much troubled about the inefficiency of the Ninth Military Department and the conduct of the soldiers in the West; therefore, Secretary Conrad confided that he "had been induced to believe that both economy and efficiency of the service would be promoted by removing the troops out of the towns where they are stationed, and stationing them toward the frontier and nearer the Indians." Further, he was convinced that "no permanent peace can exist with the Indians . . . until they have been made to feel the power of our Arms." This, Sumner, with reluctance, interpreted as an order, "as early as practicable, [to] make an expedition against the Navajoes, and also one against the Utahs and Apaches, and [to] inflict upon them the severest chastisement." And he had the approval of the Secretary of War to retain the captives as hostages (not slaves, of course, even though some army officers had construed such an authorization to make slaves of their Indian captives) "for the faithful observance of any treaty that may be made with them."

6

As to "pacific arrangements with the Indians," the Lieutenant Colonel was to "act in concert with the Superintendent of Indian Affairs," who would be permitted to accompany expeditions and was to be "afforded every facility for the discharge of his duties." Particularly was Lieutenant Colonel Sumner admonished to scrutinize the administration of the departments of the Quartermaster and Subsistence and "rigidly enforce all regulations having reference to the economy of the service," including the discharge of all civilian employees "without inconvenience to the service." That was not all. Rations were to be reduced "without interfering with the health or comfort of the soldiers." This last would be brought about by planting "kitchen gardens." And as an evidence of confidence in the new commander, Conrad told him that he might "exercise a larger discretion than would be allowable were the communication between the Commander and the Department . . . more frequent and more rapid."

After receipt of the notice of his selection in April until May 26, 1851, Sumner busied himself collecting supplies and men, concentrating them at Fort Leavenworth. Misfortune befell him even before he set out on his westward march. Several days before his departure cholera made its appearance in the command, remaining with him until he reached the Arkansas River.[5] His loss of men was heavy —thirty-five soldiers and his surgeon, Dr. Kennedy,[6] dying at Soldier's Creek about 150 miles out of Leavenworth.

The death of Dr. Kennedy left the Lieutenant Colonel with but one physician attached to his command. This man, Dr. Tingley, "besides being unwell most of the time," lost his nerve as well as his health, and was left behind "at the new post on the Arkansas with orders to come on with Major Rucker who was following with the supply train." The doctor's health improved rapidly after Colonel

[5] Sumner to Jones, October 24, 1851, in Calhoun, *Official Correspondence,* 416.

[6] H. H. Green, the *Las Vegas Optic*'s "Old Fogy," member of Sumner's force and later a resident of Mora, says that the surgeon who died was "our eminent surgeon Doctor Reynolds." He wrote that the "demon cholera decimated our ranks at the rate of five men a day." See "The Optic's Old Fogy Taps the Cask of Remembrance and Draws Off the Wine of Reminiscence," *Las Vegas Daily Optic,* July 17, 1891, p. 2, col. 2; also in AC, "Fort Union, 1851," File 2.

Sumner departed; and thinking that the probability of survival was greater eastward than along the Santa Fe Trail to the west, he promptly got "well enough to return to the United States."

With one doctor dead on the Arkansas and another deserting eastward, Sumner welcomed "an amateur adventurer of fickle fortune amid the ups and downs of the fickle West." The newcomer was a "jolly young Irish doctor, of Dublin University, all life and soul"— Dr. Barney Barry—who had attached himself unbidden to Sumner's army. When he showed his papers "to our rugged Colonel he was immediately employed." And well it was that his services were available, for, after they had traveled about seventy-five miles, Captain John Pope, of the Topographical Corps, "was taken down with the fell disease at Pawnee Fork. There the jolly young Irish doctor plastered him with mustard from his neck to his heels until he resembled a bronze statue of George Washington, and although Pope complained that the remedy was worse than the disease it saved him for posterity and Stonewall Jackson at the Second Manassas, and there wiped him out forever."[7]

Sumner's march was impeded first by cholera and afterwards by the extraordinary drought. The onset of drought caused the Colonel to decide at Fort Mann not to take the Cimarron Cut-Off route, which was one hundred miles shorter, but to follow the Arkansas River by way of Bent's Fort since sufficient grass grew along the river to sustain his animals. At Big Timbers a "thoughtless young dragoon felt the severity of the 'stern old commander.' " The lad discovered an Indian tree-burial, the first any of the novice soldiers had seen; and as the body of the recently departed was wrapped in a comparatively new red blanket, the dragoon, with commendable agility, dislodged the corpse, thus disturbing the tranquility of Poor Lo in his passage into a higher realm. But just as the acquisitive dragoon was appropriating the blanket, Colonel Sumner espied him. Forthwith, for his "thoughtlessness," the dragoon was dismounted to begin his long walk from the Big Timbers to Las Vegas, during which time he had ample opportunity for thought.

[7] *Ibid.*

Upon arrival within the vicinity of Bent's Fort, Sumner again had his march interrupted. On the Arkansas River he found a large number of Indians collected from the various tribes. Sumner noted "some uneasiness . . . among the Cheyennes." The uneasiness took the form, as the troops marched past their village, of several shots being fired "toward the rear of my column." Brevet Lieutenant Colonel Hoffman warned Sumner that the Indians were "banding together," and he thought "they intended some act of hostility." Since Sumner did not interpret firing into the rear of his passing column as an act of hostility, he pressed forward until he found a suitable camping place, where the army bivouacked for the night. After having a night in which to cogitate the incident, Sumner aroused the camp at dawn and "marched back with my whole command." Before the village whence the shots were fired he "assembled a number of the chiefs and head men, and said to them I had come back to meet them, as friends or enemies, it was for them to say which, but they must say it immediately." The Indians "disclaimed all intention of hostility," whereupon Sumner resumed his march toward Santa Fe.[8]

After passing beyond Bent's Fort the contingent climbed Raton Mountain. And in Old Fogy's words, "it took us two days to let by ropes our train of 100 wagons down the rugged hill of Raton, whilst black-tailed deer stared at us in wonder from the neighboring crags, and thousands of graceful antelopes gazed, more in astonishment than fear, from the plains."

From Council Grove, with the exceptions of Fort Mann and Bent's Old Fort, Sumner's army had seen "no sign of cultivated humanity," nor was it to see any until after breaking camp made on the evening "of July 15, 1851 . . . at what was then known as *Los Posos.*"

Lieutenant Colonel Sumner had with him as a guest of the government the arch-enemy of Colonel Munroe, none other than the Honorable Richard H. Weightman, but recently denied a seat in Congress[9]

[8] Sumner to Jones, October 24, 1851, in Calhoun, *Official Correspondence,* 417; AC, "Fort Union, 1851," File 2, p. 48.

[9] He was denied a seat in Congress because of the passage of the New Mexico Territorial (instead of the State) Act.

and now returning to New Mexico as a "civil officer," a title he had acquired lately through appointment as Indian agent, a position he failed to fulfill after arriving in New Mexico. The authority for the free passage to New Mexico with Sumner had been given by Secretary of War Conrad. On that trip, according to the *Santa Fe Weekly Gazette,* Weightman, in conversations with Colonel Sumner, secretly communicated "lessons on things in New Mexico, day by day and league by league, from Saint Louis to Santa Fe," so that the Colonel was "cocked and primed before he reached Las Vegas; and it was at the Holes in the Prairie that the first explosion of his genius took place."[10]

The reverberations of Sumner's first "explosion of genius," fired after the "cocking and priming" of Weightman, were muffled for four more days after camp was broken at *Los Posos* while the Sumner detachment trudged the last one hundred miles to Santa Fe, arriving on the afternoon of July 19, 1851. During that eventful day Colonel Munroe, acting purely from the urgency of the situation and not in anticipation of Colonel Sumner's plans, took cognizance of a raid of a large body of Navahos "about Cibolletta, killing some persons and wounding others who were engaged in cutting hay near Covero." Although this raid was quite disquieting to Colonel Munroe since "the force at Cibolletta is not considered sufficient in the present emergency," still he ordered Colonel Howe, at Albuquerque, to report to Colonel Chandler "for temporary service," thereby initiating a Navaho war much to the liking of the incoming commander. Other than ordering Howe to "communicate with Colonel Chandler," Munroe gave no orders;[11] but in all probability this inaction was intentional, for late in that day Sumner arrived in Santa Fe with his relief detachment. Without a moment of hesitation he assumed command of the Ninth Military Department, posting Order No. 17, relieving—according to the gleeful expression of the sardonic Weightman—"*The Grand Caliph—The Last of the Three-tailed Pashaws!!*"[12]

[10] Issue of February 19, 1850, p. 3, col. 3.
[11] Laws to Howe, July 19, 1851, NA, RG 98, 9 Mil. Dept. Orders, Vol. 7, p. 210.
[12] Weightman's speech, p. 37.

Order No. 17 swept the Munroe regime clean. Besides assuming command of the Ninth Military Department, Colonel Sumner appointed his staff: Brevet Major D. C. Buell, Adjutant General's Department; Brevet Major C. S. Sibley, Quartermaster's Department; Captain Isaac Bowen, Subsistence Department; Major F. A. Cunningham, Pay Department; Brevet Captain John Pope, Topographical Engineer. Paragraph 11 of Order No. 17 disclosed the core of the "explosion of genius." It provided: "The Head Quarters and Principal Depot of the Department *are* transferred to the Moro River, and all military stores at this place (Santa Fe), will at once be removed to the point selected."

Abandonment of Santa Fe as headquarters of the Ninth Military Department was accompanied by orders to Colonel Alexander to remove his troops from Las Vegas and "proceed to Headquarters," and Captain Macrae's Infantry must "repair" to the same place, although the Lieutenant Colonel commanding could not designate a more definite location than "headquarters on the Moro River."

The capital city—The City Different (although it was not different in this from almost all other cities)—since the arrival of General Kearny had been luxuriating in army expenditures and employment of civilians. Order No. 17 brought this to an end by "the immediate discharge of all citizens employed in the Staff Department with the exception of those temporarily required with the moveable trains." To tighten the disbursement further, all military expenses had to be countersigned by the commander of the department before "being passed by the drawer." Even an officer might not purchase from the Subsistence Department more than at the rate of one ration for each member of his family, and this ration must be charged for, not at the cost at Fort Leavenworth, but with transportation costs added to Santa Fe. Then, after announcing these sweeping reforms, Sumner adopted Colonel Munroe's military gesture toward the raiding Navahos and announced that "the expedition into the Navajo Country will move on the 15th Proximo."[13]

[13] Orders No. 17, 9 Mil. Dept., Santa Fe, N. M., July 19, 1851; AC, "Fort Union, 1851," File 2, pp. 12–14.

Uppermost in his mind—so Sumner said—was the condition in Santa Fe, so "my first step was to break up the post in Santa Fe, *that Sink of vice and extravagance,* and remove the troops and public property." The best he would say of the Santa Feans was that "they have managed hitherto to live, in some way, from the extravagant expenditures of the Government." Thus he considered "the withdrawal of the troops from the towns as a matter of vital importance, both as regards discipline and economy." He found that "most of the troops in this territory have become in a high degree demoralized, and it can only be accounted for by the vicious associations in those towns." The "evils were so great," moreover, that he did not "expect to eradicate them entirely" until he could bring the troops together in considerable bodies for discipline and instruction.[14]

On the second day after Sumner's arrival in Santa Fe, Brevet Lieutenant L. H. Marshall, Third Infantry, was instructed to take charge of Company D and conduct it without delay "to the point selected for Department Head Qurs: on the Moro." Lieutenant McFerran, also of the Third Infantry, was to remain in Santa Fe "to superintend the removal of the subsistence stores," after which he, too, was "to repair" to headquarters.

Superintending the removal of stores, however, was not unattended with difficulties. Transportation was lacking, so thirty-two wagons employed by F. X. Aubrey in freight service on the Santa Fe Trail were pressed into the military service. So rough was the usage of this equipment that four thousand dollars' damage was done.[15] Action in the Quartermaster Department was forthcoming when the newly appointed Assistant Quartermaster Sibley relieved Captain Easton from his duties as depot and chief quartermaster in the department,[16] while Captain W. R. Shoemaker, military storekeeper, transferred the ordnance and ordnance stores to "the new depot of the Moro."

While Colonel Sumner was revamping the entire military establishment, Territorial Governor Calhoun, experiencing no sense of

[14] Sumner to Jones, October 24, 1851, in Calhoun, *Official Correspondence,* 416.
[15] 33 Cong., 1 sess., *Sen. Doc. No. 85.*
[16] NA, RG 93, SO and GO, 9 Mil. Dept. and Dept. of N. M., 1851–61, Vol. 27, p. 1.

loss by the removal of Colonel Munroe and hoping for better days under Sumner, took notice of the fact that "agitators are yet attempting to excite the Pueblo Indians by misrepresentations and outrages upon their rights," but he thought that "the arrival of our judges, and two of our Indian Agents, Weightman and Greiner [obviously he did not know that Weightman had no intention of accepting the Indian agency, and was merely getting free government transportation to New Mexico], will afford to the public considerable protection against the disorders designed by evil disposed persons." Retrospectively, he could say, "At one time the peril was great," but he found comfort in the evaluation of the present situation made by Colonel Céran St. Vrain, who "came in yesterday from Taos [July 24, 1851]" and reported the Jicarillas entirely quiet and said he knew of no recent depredations. However, the Navahos had "committed several murders and depredations during the month." They had "surprised a number of Mexicans, about the third of the month, who were in search of animals run off by them, killed eight men and wounded eleven others." Too, on the night Colonel Sumner was at the Holes in the Prairie, the Navahos killed three men near Laguna. "The murdered men were Americans, engaged in complying with the government contract for hay."[17]

Sumner, taking cognizance of the fact that Governor Calhoun was aware of the Indian disorders and that even Munroe had made a gesture of defending the inhabitants, three days after throwing the army into utter confusion by ordering removal to "a point on the Moro," reverted to his declaration that he would make an expedition into the Navaho country. Consequently, special orders went to Brevet Major L. P. Graham of the Second Dragoons, occupying the post at Abiquiu, to remove his company to Santo Domingo. He was to be there "at the latest by the 14th proximo [August, 1851] in order to move from there on the 15th with the expedition to the Navajo country." Graham's detachment was to "form a part of the Garrison of the post which will be established in the country."

---

[17] It was this same incident which caused Colonel Munroe to make his last gesture toward a Navaho campaign.

Between the twenty-third and twenty-fifth of July, Colonel Sumner was traveling from Santa Fe to Las Vegas with his army, which he found necessary to locate "east of Santa Fe and directly on the line of communication with Missouri, as this gives me more direct control over all the affairs of the Department."[18] While at Las Vegas he broke up the military post at Rayado, issuing Order No. 19 to that effect and requiring Captain R. S. Ewell "and all public stores of whatever description at that point . . . immediately moved to the Headquarters of the Department." In addition, the detachment "encamped near Rayado, under the command of Major Blake," and the detachment of infantry, Lieutenant I. C. Moore commanding, was to move "forthwith to Department Headquarters on the Moro."[19]

But this peremptory removal of the only troops stationed east of military headquarters, only then in process of being located on the Moro, brought forth objections from Lucien Maxwell.[20] Seeking to mollify the irrepressible Maxwell, Sumner revised his hasty order by suggesting to Captain Ewell that he might "leave a dragoon guard . . . consisting of one non-commissioned officer and fourteen privates at the Rayado with the necessary supplies for three months," provided, of course, that he could effect an economy through Maxwell's providing the detachment "with quarters and stabling, free from government expense." This condescension was made in view of the fact that Mr. Maxwell had offered to accompany Captain Pope, who was ordered to explore a new route between Rayado and Fort Leavenworth.

Sumner then ordered Brevet Colonel Edmund B. Alexander away from Las Vegas to the Mora River "to the previously selected point" —still without a name—to take command there upon arrival. This movement Colonel Alexander began on July 26, taking with him Companies F and K, First Dragoons, and Company G, Third Infantry. They arrived "near the Moro" late in the same day. In this

[18] Sumner to Bliss, August 3, 1851, NA, RG 98, 9 Mil. Dept. Orders, Vol. 7, pp. 225–26.

[19] Order No. 19, July 25, 1851, Sumner; AC, "Fort Union, 1851," File 2, p. 19.

[20] Owner of the so-called Maxwell Land Grant and the most influential man north of the Mora River and east of Taos if Kit Carson and Céran St. Vrain are excepted.

"vicinity" Colonel Alexander assumed command—thus establishing a post without a name, the headquarters of the Ninth Military Department. On the following day Colonel Alexander was relieved of the command at Las Vegas by "official evacuation and abandonment."

Although Alexander's new assignment had no official name, he made his July, 1851, post return by writing: "The post at Las Vegas, N. M. was abandoned on the 25th day of July, 1851, by Co's. F & K, 1st Dragoons, & Co. G, 3rd Infantry and the post *Fort Union* established on the evening of the same day."

Colonel Sumner, marching in Colonel Alexander's wake, made his camp on July 26 also "near the Moro." The following day, he too made a post return, which stated: "Co. D, 3d Infantry, left Santa Fe, N. M. on the 23rd and arrived at this post on the 27th of July, 1851. Detachments of recruits arrived at this post July 27th, 1851. Co's F & K 1st Dragoons transferred to Dragoon Company near this post." Evidently Sumner billeted at the dragoon camp before pushing on to the post he was establishing.

With supplies on the road to the Mora River, and the troops at both Fort Union and "near this point," Colonel Sumner began to take stock of his hasty removal from Santa Fe. At his new department headquarters he dated an order, "Fort Union, Near Moro River, New Mexico, July 31, 1851," taking notice of the shortage of water and asking General H. Stanton, deputy quartermaster general, to send him "implements for boring for water." He would be "much obliged" if the General would "send a set to Leavenworth, to be sent out the first opportunity." He had—so he announced—"selected a place for the General Depot and headquarters, but it does not exactly suit me, as there is not enough land for tillage, but it is the only place that will answer at all on this side of Santa Fe." He was much pleased, however, that his selection of new headquarters "would certainly effect a great reduction in expenses," but "he hoped to do more."

His hope to do more consisted, for the moment, of a "march into the Navajo Country on the 11th of next month."[21] But before he could march his army back westward again to chastise the Navahos, the

[21] NA, RG 98, 9 Mil. Dept. Orders, Vol. 7, pp. 219-20.

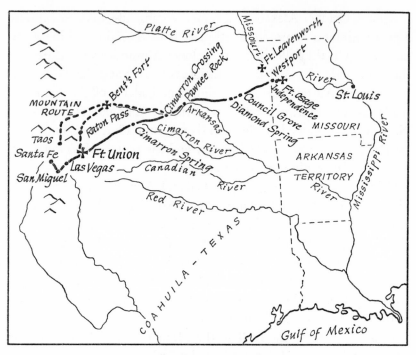

The Santa Fe Trail

Jicarillas and Comanches, renewing their annoyances along the Santa Fe Trail, had to be considered. Therefore, on August 1, he ordered Brevet Major James H. Carleton with his company "to cover and protect the Cimarron route to the Arkansas during the summer." With one day allowed for preparations, Carleton was to leave Fort Union "on the morning of the 3d inst., and make the usual marches to Fort Mackay." But Carleton, once away from Fort Union, was "not to be in a hurry. He was to remain a week at Fort Mackay, and "then move leisurely back, halting a day or two at a time" whenever he found good grass. His mission was to "intercept Indians." If they were peaceable, he was "to treat them with great kindness," but "if on the contrary, they are hostile toward you, or commit any serious depredations upon other travellers . . . pursue them at all hazards, till you inflict upon them a signal chastisement." Then, mixing morality and military expediency, he admonished Carleton: "It is of great

Gambling Saloon in Santa Fe, "that Sink of vice and extravagance."

Harper's Monthly, *April,* 1854

General Stephen Watts Kearny took possession of New Mexico
"without firing a gun or spilling a drop of blood."

Library of Congress

importance to keep everything quiet on this part of the frontier, during the operation in the Navajo country; and this can only be secured by kindness to the good and the prompt punishment of the bad." And, of course, concluded the apprehensive new commander, "On a service of this nature, much is left to your discretion, and if an unforeseen emergency should arise, I have no doubt but that your own judgment will dictate the proper course."

The fourth day in the new Department Headquarters brought the realization that he had "to send an express to Santa Fe—over 100 miles—for our mails." Therefore, he dispatched a plea to the Postmaster General for his "early attention to the appointment of J. W. Folger, the suttler of this post, as postmaster." Too, the postmaster should have the mail diverted six miles north of Barclay's Fort by way of Fort Union, a few miles farther than the then utilized route.[22] This brought him to a realization that no name had been officially given to the new headquarters, so he posted an order:

> HEADQUARTERS 9TH MILITARY DEPT.
> CAMP NEAR THE MORA, NEW MEXICO.
> August 2nd, 1851
> The Military Post established at this
> Point will be called FORT UNION.
> By Order of Bvt. Col. Sumner,
> D. C. Buell.

It was exactly fifty days later that the name of the new headquarters became known in Washington.

On the day following the official designation of the fort, writing now from "Headquarters, 9th Dept. *Fort Union, Near Moro River,*" in the elation of accomplishment which seemed to please him, he outlined his past two weeks' activities to Colonel Bliss, assistant adjutant general at headquarters of the Western Division in New Orleans, giving notice that he intended to "abandon Albuquerque, Abuiquiu [*sic*], Taos, and Socorro." In lieu of these posts, he would "establish two larger posts, one at Val Verde on the Rio Grande, and

---

[22] Sumner to Hall, NA, RG, 98, 9 Mil. Dept. Orders, Vol. 7, p. 224.

the other at some point in the mountains in the Utah and Apache Country." Then he reset his day of departure for his Navaho war for August 15, thus conforming to the original directions given to Major Graham to be at Santo Domingo not later than the fourteenth of August.[23] He would—so he said—"march . . . with 4 Companies of horse, 3 of Infantry, and one of Artillery." Furthermore, it was his intention to "establish a post of five companies in that country." He had already decided to send Major Backus to that western outpost. And in all his activities so far, "the intercourse between Col Munroe and myself had been of the most friendly nature." He could truthfully say, too, that the information he had received from the demoted Munroe "had been of great assistance . . . in forming my plans."

The general disruption of posts and living condition did not please the officers serving in New Mexico. Sumner took cognizance of this on July 31 in his first letter from Fort Union, suggesting to General Gibson the propriety of rescinding the "late order adding the transportation to the costs" of articles bought by officers, thinking "it made for better morale to let them have what they actually need for their own use at Leavenworth prices." He suggested this relaxation because he "had already taken effective measures to prevent all abuses in the sale of subsistence stores to officers." Too, he also had found "it is very expensive living here."[24]

As a part of the instructions given Sumner by Secretary of War Conrad regarding his duties when he should command in New Mexico, the Secretary made it clear that he would discountenance any disagreement with the Governor of New Mexico, who was ex-officio superintendent of Indian affairs. Explicitly, Sumner had been told: "In all negotiations and pacific arrangements with the Indians you will act in concert with the Superintendent of Indian Affairs in New Mexico, who you will allow to accompany you in expeditions into the Indian territory, if he should deem it proper to do so, and to

[23] On July 31, 1851, Sumner wrote General Stanton: "I shall march into the Navajo Country on the 11th of next month." NA, RG 98, 9 Mil. Dept. Orders, Vol. 7, pp. 219–20.

[24] Sumner to Gibson, July 31, 1851, NA, RG 98, 9 Mil. Dept. Orders, Vol. 7, p. 219.

whom you will afford every facility for the discharge of his duties." To make sure that there would be accord between the two officials, Commissioner of Indian Affairs L. Lea relayed to the governor also that "instructions to this end have been given to the officer in command of the army in New Mexico," adding that he trusted that nothing would be wanting on the Governor's part "in this important particular."

Despite these admonitions toward harmony and co-operation, Colonel Sumner moved the military forces from Santa Fe, leaving only a detachment under Lieutenant Colonel Brooks at Fort Marcy and failing to apprise the Governor of his intentions. His haste was based upon "economy," not harmony, and he was moving away from "sin"; however, it was common knowledge that Sumner's intention was to inflict an early signal chastisement upon the Navahos. This disrespect toward the Governor was the more blatant in that he had posted Order No. 17 at Fort Marcy the very day of his assumption of command, stating that the "expedition into the Navajo Country will move on the 15th Proximo." The Army and the *Nuevo Mejicanos* and even the Navahos themselves had learned of the Colonel's intentions, but official information had not been given the Governor. Sumner's attitude of "go-it-alone" was particularly offensive to the Governor since only recently Colonel Munroe had rebuffed a delegation of Navahos who had sought to make a new treaty. Governor Calhoun, consequently, knowing that the capital had but few troops to defend it and fearing a war from all sides, initiated an attempt at accord and co-ordination with Sumner by asking Colonel Brooks at Santa Fe whether or not the Colonel was clothed with authority to afford the superintendent and Indian agents with escorts and other facilities that might be necessary to enable them to discharge the duties imposed upon them by their positions.[25] Brooks, lacking orders, relayed the query to Sumner.

Four days later Sumner out-Munroed Munroe himself by the insolent observation "that the troops in this department will be prepared, at all times, for any service which the Government contem-

[25] Calhoun to Brooks, July 30, 1851, in Calhoun, *Official Correspondence*, 392.

plated, or its interests demand." In addition he stated: "No general authority, or orders, can be given to officers, to detach portions of their commands upon the discretional requisitions of the agents of the Indian Department . . .such demands might interfere with the specific service to which the troops had been assigned." Further, "The Government does not contemplate any display of Military force in the Indian country that is not made under the controll [*sic*] of Military authority." The Colonel would, however, "allow the superintendent of Indian Affairs or (Indian Agents,) to accompany him in the expedition which it *may* be necessary to make into the Indian Territory." Thus rebuffing Calhoun insolently, Sumner, the following day, posted Order No. 23, detailing his expedition into the West.

CHAPTER TWO

"NOT A PEPPER, NOR AN ONION, SHALL BE DISTURBED"

ALTHOUGH the removal of Colonel Munroe from command in New Mexico and the selection of E. V. Sumner to supplant him resulted immediately from Munroe's intransigence, still the New Mexico imbroglio had grown from many causes, some of major importance, some minor, but most anchored in racial incompatibilities of the three peoples attempting to occupy the region. Specific instances of intensification of antipathies—the Spanish for the Anglo-American, the Spanish for the Indian, and the Indian for both—culminated in a military domination in New Mexico which had its apogee in Colonel John Munroe. The "Munroe attitude" had been generated through a mutual distrust of the Mexicans and Anglo-Americans. Far toward the bottom of this distrust was the racial incompatibility which resulted in failure, then war, when Anglo-Americans were invited into Texas as colonists. War left the colonists with the infant Republic of Texas claiming a vast uninhabited expanse of theretofore Mexican territory encompassing the city of Santa Fe and terminating on the banks of the Río del Norte, as well as memories of the slaughter at the Alamo and the deception and murder of Fannin and his men at Goliad, while Mexicans rankled in the recollection of the defeat of their Napoleon of the West by Sam Houston at San Jacinto, with the consequent independence of Texas. For further cause for aversion Texans added their own ill-conceived and puerile effort to encompass New Mexican-claimed territory to the Río Grande and, instead, had to be content to know that "Texan-ears-for Armijo" had been nailed to Santa Fe's Palace of the Governors.

Then with a mixture of financial inability to support itself as an independent republic and an original desire and intention to be absorbed by the United States, Texas joined the Union, the United States accepting the incorporation knowing full well that Mexico would go to war over the loss of Texas and endeavor also to dispute Texas' claim to territory west to the Río Grande. On February 16, 1846, the Lone Star Republic came to an end; the flag of the United States was hoisted; and Mexico took the fatal step. In what the Republic of Texas thought would be a security move it caused to be written into the treaty of annexation this provision: "Questions of boundaries with other nations are to be adjusted by the United States."

On the part of the United States, plans had long been in existence. In the event of war with Mexico (And who had ever doubted that there would be war?), Mexico was to be invaded from three quarters. One army was to enter from Vera Cruz; another was to hold Texas as far as the Río Grande and later march southward to Monterrey and Chihuahua, while New Mexico was to be engulfed by an army going out from Missouri.

On April 23, President Peredes appeared in person before the Mexican Congress *with a pronunciamiento:* "From this day defensive war begins." On May 1, the Mexicans crossed the Río Grande. Out at Boca Chico, near Matamoros on the Texas side, the sound of cannon was heard. "The camp was wild with excitement," wrote Lieutenant U.S. Grant. "The war has begun." The news traveled west to Santa Fe. There was "joy and enthusiasm" among the Anglo-Americans, who had, with tongue in cheek, become Mexican citizens through naturalization. The mother country, now engaged in war, was extending her ever lengthening arm to embrace her wandering sons. On the other hand the United States expected aid from these transplanted sons in the coming struggle. The Taos and Santa Fe naturalization lists showed many one-time United States citizens, although some gave indications of their Mexican residence. On the rosters could be found Juan (John) Rowland, Carlos (Charles) Beaubien, Antoine and Louis Robidoux, and Christopher Carson. Another stalwart, whose name the Mexican clerk spelled euphoniously, became Dr. Ceran Sambrano instead of Céran St. Vrain. David Waldo was made to hail from "Efigenia," better known on the Atlantic seaboard as Virginia; and it was not uncommon for new arrivals from the east to have come from "Quintoqui," a passable attempt at Kentucky.[1]

Despite naturalization and constant association with *Nuevo Mejicanos,* ingrained distrust and discord abounded in the transplanted Americans. For example, Juan Rowland and his partner, William Workman, forfeited their Mexican citizenship when it became known to Governor Armijo that they had given aid and advice to members of the Texan–Santa Fe Expedition. Hearing that "the intermeddlers were to be shot on sight," they left for California, where distance and the intervention of years nullified the order.

Workman, however, was wholly unwilling to depart for the west until he had evened a score with one Juan B. Vigil, who Workman thought had taken "liberties with the truth." For scorekeeper he took along Charles Bent, another former United States citizen and foremost merchant of Taos, and when the angry Workman encountered the double-tongued *Nuevo Mejicano* on the plaza at Taos, he administered a horse-whipping, much to the amusement of American onlookers and the satisfaction of the wielder of the whip. Since the incident involved relations between a former United States citizen and his connection with Texas' effort to occupy her claimed territory and a New Mexico citizen, Charles Bent thought it of sufficient importance to detail it to the United States consul at Santa Fe.

Mr. M. Alvares: Taos, February 19, 1841.

      Sir:

I arrived heare last eavening without any axident, today about mid day Workman and myself called on Juan B. Vigil, I presented the coppy of the representation he made against us. I asked him after he had red it if it was a Coppy of the one he had made to the Governor, and he said it was. I then asked him how he dare make such false representations against us and he denied there being false. The word was hardly out of his Mouth, when Workman struck him with his whip, after whipping him a while with this he droped it and beate him with his fist untile I thought he had given him enough, whereupon I pulled him off. he run for life. he has been expecting this ever since

[1] Robert Glass Cleland, *This Reckless Breed of Men,* 209.

last eavening, for he said this morning that he had provided himself with a Boui Knife for any person that dare attack him, and suting the word to the action drue his Knife to exhibit. I suppose he forgot his Knife in time of neade.

I called on Mr. Lee this morning respecting what he had said against us in Santa Fe he denied the whole, and made many acknolidgements. He is a man you can't pin up he is a non Combatant. I preseume you will have a presentation of the whole affair from the other party Shortly . . . .[2]

Of those who had emigrated from the United States to Mexico, the Bent brothers were the most vocal against the Mexican government as the war came to New Mexico. They were former Virginians, but more recent residents of St. Louis, Missouri. Early in fur-trapping days they, together with Céran St. Vrain, had built Fort William, commonly called Bent's Fort, near the modern city of La Junta, Colorado. Céran St. Vrain moved to Taos, where he was soon joined by Charles Bent. To William Bent, who married Owl Woman of the Cheyennes, was left the management of Bent's Fort, while his brother and Céran St. Vrain (known as "Black Beard" to the Indians and "Seran Sambrano" to the Mexicans) freighted across the plains and operated stores and mills in Denver, Taos, and Santa Fe.

Charles Bent made his home at San Fernández de Taos, a few miles from the Taos Indian Pueblo. There he met and developed a perfect aversion for the village priest, Father Antonio José Martínez, who, because of his lust for money, was dubbed by Bent as "The Calf" (worshiper of the golden calf). Bent was aware of the fact that early in his residence in New Mexico Father Martínez had been instructed by the governor of New Mexico "to watch the Americans and intercept their correspondence," and when José Manuel Vigil, charged with delivering mail to Taos from Santa Fe, "lost" Bent's letters "in San Juan," Bent wrote: ". . . this I believe to be a ly, he no doubt delivered them to Martines."

During the last days of January, 1845, two letters came to Taos. Charles Bent was accorded the privilege of reading them. For this

[2] Letter in the Museum of New Mexico Library, Santa Fe.

confidence, he wrote his friend, he was "much obliged . . . for the nuse you communicate, all except the ellection of Polk. I am truly Sorry you could not insert with propriety that of Clay." He felt "fearfully that this election will cause difficulty with this and our Country."

Before New Mexicans knew that hostilities between the two countries were an actuality, rumors increased the tension. One new arrival in Taos, twenty-four-year-old Francis Preston Blair, Jr., celebrating his safe arrival from St. Louis in order to "improve his health," imbibed "several drams of Turley's select Taos Lightning known to be death to Indians and Hostile to Whites." It was not long until "the mob members (Padre Martinez . . . giving aid and comfort to the mob, some of whom are in Martinez employ) . . . attacked Blair and George." As a result, "Blair has three verry large Cutes in the head whether the Scule is affected or not we have not been able to acertain. . . . Blair was left for dead in a Hole of Water & Mud," and no authority acted "to put a stop to it." Bent confided to his friend Alvares that they were "no longer protected by the authoritys [and] we had better leave as Soon as possible, we are so fair [far] removed from any assistence which we [may expect] from elsewhare that it amounts to almost none attall."

In an unsigned paper he made known his political views to Alvares, evaluating the *Nuevo Mejicanos* as he wrote: ". . . thare is no Stability to theas people, they have no oppinion of thare one [own]   they are entirely governed by the powers that be, they are without exception the most Servile people that can be imagined. They are Compleately at the will of those in power let those be so Ignorant as may be   they dair not expres an oppinion to that of thar rules   they are not fit to be a free [people] they should be ruled by others than themselves . . . Whare thar is no Morality, Honesty or Patriotism of character that people are not fit for self Government   On the contrary every spesis of vise in this country is a recommendation to public office . . . thare is no confidences to be placed in them . . . with gold everything . . . can be accomplished . . . Vanity is thare predominant trate of character, they think themselves superior to all the world, besides in point of religion, honesty, valler, and tollerence   thare religion consistes intirely in actual Sham . . . they are taught to believe thare priests are the only Meadiators between the supriem being and themselves. . . . The Mexican Character is made up of Stypidity, Obstanacy, Ignorance—duplicity and vanity."

After unburdening himself of this vigorous expression of opinion, Charles Bent followed Céran St. Vrain and Folger down to Santa Fe, hoping but failing to join up with them en route to St. Louis. He was ready to leave Santa Fe for Independence on June 12 "with 20 men (a great many loffers)." Although he was not definitely informed, at Bent's Fort he "judged the war has Comenced (surmising this from the way the Indians were behaving) and no doubt they will kill all Mexicans They can."

The "great many loffers" who went along did not prevent the caravan from pulling into Westport one month later. There Bent and St. Vrain decided to continue their journey immediately to Fort Leavenworth, which they now were informed had been designated as headquarters for the rendezvous of the new United States Army of the West. Army officers who believed that the main chance lay with Scott and Zachary Taylor, who would invade Mexico direct, shrugged off participation in the contemplated campaign in the West, leaving that to men of lesser stature. In fact, so little was known of the West that soldiering there was looked upon as a grand adventure, not a military invasion. Those who knew the most about the plains were Missourians, boys who had heard the tales of Kit Carson and watched Céran St. Vrain load his wagons for the land of the buffalo, the wild Indian, and the "greaser." Consequently, when the President called for volunteers, Missourians flocked to the recruiting stations, where local aspirants, who hoped to ride into government political office after service with the bayonet, harangued the volunteers—mostly mere boys—into regiments.

Charles Bent and St. Vrain found at Fort Leavenworth a "political army." According to the custom of the time each company selected its own officers by popular acclaim. Political organization, however, did not exclude some men of military ability, notably Alexander W. Doniphan, Sterling Price, Congreve Jackson, David Waldo, John T.

Hughes, William Z. Angney, R. H. Weightman, Willard P. Hall, E. V. Sumner, and Philip St. George Cooke.

The Mantle of Distinction had fallen upon Stephen Watts Kearny; he was to command. The distinction, however, was not to his liking. He thought it was to be the Mantle of Obloquy. He longed to have his chance in the "main war." He was querulous from the beginning. Discovering that Philip St. George Cooke and Edwin V. Sumner were ordered south, he approached insubordination by demanding that these officers be reassigned to his command. He felt his inadequacy without his tried and true officers. Feeling no compunction, he made himself heard: he would "most respectfully urge—demand—(the interest of the Public Service admits of strong and respectful terms) that the 2 Comps. of my Regt.—Capts Sumner and Cooke . . . be ordered . . . to this Post [Fort Leavenworth] to follow on my trail to Santa Fe." Upon receipt of this dispatch the Secretary of War undertook to placate the presumptuous Colonel, called back the two officers "in the interest of the Public Service," and directed them to proceed with the Army of the West. To relieve Kearny's mind further and incidentally inflate his self-importance, the Secretary of War enclosed a copy of an order, dated June 3, 1846, authorizing Kearny to draw upon Missouri for one thousand more mounted men "for an additional force," should he need them.

That letter took Kearny into the confidence of the War Department: It disclosed that "the object of thus adding to your command is not, you will perceive, fully set forth in this letter, for the reason that it is deemed prudent that it should not at this time become a matter of public notoriety; but to you it is proper and necessary that it should be stated." The disclosure: "It has been decided by the President to be of the greatest importance in the pending war with Mexico to take the earliest possession of Upper California. [Up to that time none had thought of the war as other than to establish the Río Grande as the western limits of the newly annexed state, Texas.] ... An expedition with that in view is hereby ordered, and you are designated to command it. To enable you to be in sufficient force to conduct it successfully this additional force of a thousand mounted men has been provided to follow you in the direction of Santa Fe, to be under your orders, or the officer you may leave to command at Santa Fe."

Upon arriving at Fort Leavenworth, Charles Bent did not attempt to join the military forces; instead, accompanied by Céran St. Vrain, he went immediately to Colonel Kearny, relaying to him a conversation he had had with Governor Armijo just before his departure from Santa Fe. Armijo was expecting Urrea to march up the Río Grande to his relief if he were attacked from across the plains. Bent was "of the opinion that there can be no good feeling between Urrea and Armijo and if [Kearny] can get there in time, the services of the latter may be available against the former."[3] Bent then returned to St. Louis.

The convergence of recruits upon Fort Leavenworth began as, and continued to be, a lark. ". . . nearly all were mere boys . . ." Their "enthusiasm was immense, and crowds of ladies followed us to the steamer." There a parting shot was fired as a salute from an old cannon. At every town the salute was repeated "until at Jefferson City it burst and came near wrecking the boat."[4] This "burst of enthusiasm" quieted the boys down for a time, at least until they arrived at Fort Leavenworth. There the Ladies of Liberty deputed one Mrs. Cunningham "to present this flag to the volunteers from Clay County." This she did in a manner commensurate with "their willingness to sustain the honor of our common country" to "redress the indignities offered to its flag," and she would rather hear of them "failing in honorable warfare than to see [them] return sullied with crime or disgraced by cowardice."

[3] It is within the realm of probability that Bent suggested bribing Armijo and this was his way of indicating Armijo's susceptibility.

[4] Michael Ennis, of Company B, Laclede Rangers, reminiscing sixty years later in the St. Louis *Globe-Democrat*, July 2, 1905 (reprinted as Appendix E of *Doniphan's Expedition*, ed. by W. E. Connelley). The account of the journey from Fort Leavenworth to Santa Fe and incidents after arriving in Santa Fe is reconstructed from a variety of sources: Emory's *Notes of a Military Reconnoissance;* John T. Hughes' Diary and the reprint of his *Doniphan's Expedition* in Connelley's *Doniphan's Expedition;* the Journals of Abraham Robinson Johnston and Marcellus Ball Edwards in *Marching with the Army of the West, 1846–1848,* ed. by R. P. Bieber; and Philip St. George Cooke's *The Conquest of New Mexico and California.*

When the civilian bombast was over, 414 merchant wagons lined the trail following in the dust of the marching soldiers. One detachment of artillery was in a snarl within a hundred yards of its garrison. The harness on one of the teams pulled over the collars of the horses; they stopped, blocking the road while the gear was refitted. Ultimately, however, the harness was fitted, and, in an effort to return to the line of march, the teamster exhausted the horses "until they were struggling along in much disorder." They failed to find the road, however, from Fort Leavenworth to the Santa Fe Trail, so all they could do was "steer the course southwesterly." Colonel Doniphan himself missed the road and had to turn back with his command to find the route. Then someone had an idea: A messenger was sent back to Fort Leavenworth for a plow. The next day a furrow was cut at the intersection pointing toward New Mexico—and they were on their way at last.

Weightman's artillery company, largely composed of men of German extraction, became separated from their baggage and were forced to camp without it. The next morning the Germans showed signs of mutiny. They did not want to travel without breakfast. An officer with persuasive faculties talked them into going ahead with the promise that they "would be fed later," and they ate with "a great deal of noise . . . a continual vociferation." By the time they reached the plains, the fun of soldiering had diminished. Even Michael McEnnis' heavy curly beard failed to protect him from the sun, which "peeled the skin from our faces and necks in strips." On the ninth of July one of the messengers drowned attempting to cross a swollen stream. On July 29, Fitzpatrick, the mountaineer, came out from Fort Bent to tell Colonel Kearny that Governor Armijo had called his chief men together to deliberate on the means of defending Santa Fe and that Armijo was determined to make a vigorous defense. At Fort Bent a two-day rest was taken. Lieutenant De Courcy, with twenty men, was sent forward to ascertain the sentiment of the people at Taos. After three days of travel their three pack mules, with modern inclinations, staged a "lie-down" strike. "Neither gentle means nor the points of sabers had the least effect in inducing them to rise. Their term of service with Uncle Sam was out." So the men removed their shirts and drawers, filled them with flour and bacon, tying up the sleeves and legs, and took to the trail again.

At the Bent's Fort rest stop, a newcomer joined the camp, Francis P. Blair, Jr. He had had time for the "verry large Cutes in the head" to heal and to determine that his "Scule was not affected" by his recent tussel with Taos Lightning and the Martínez-inspired mob. At this point another noncombatant began to show his hand. Up to that time James Magoffin had merely "come along" with the Army of the West. He and his brother Samuel were rich United States—Chihuahua merchants, as well as friends of Senator Thomas H. Benton, the recognized votary of the West. If Colonel Kearny knew that there had been a conference between Magoffin, Benton, the Secretary of War, and the President of the United States before Magoffin's departure from Washington, he kept his counsel. Such a meeting had, in fact, taken place.[5]

Then at "Camp at Bent's Fort, on the Arkansas," on July 31, 1846, Colonel Kearny adopted the Mexican *modus operandi* and issued a "Proclamation to the Citizens of New Mexico":

> The undersigned enters New Mexico with a large military force, for the purpose of seeking union with and ameliorating the condition of its inhabitants. This is done under the instructions of his government, and with the assurance that he will be amply sustained in the accomplishment of this object. It is enjoined on the citizens of New Mexico to remain quietly at their homes, and to pursue their peaceful avocations. So long as they continue in such pursuits, they will not be interfered with by the American army, but will be respected and protected in their rights, both civil and religious.
>
> All who take up arms or encourage resistance against the govern-

[5] Thomas H. Benton, *Thirty Years' View*, II, 683: "At the time of the fitting out that expedition [Kearny's] there was a citizen of the United States, long resident in Mexico, on a visit of business at Washington City—his name was James Magoffin —a man of mind, of will, of generous temper, patriotic, and rich. He knew every man in New Mexico and his character, and all localities, and could be of infinite service to the invading force. Mr. Benton proposed to him to go with it: he agreed. Mr. Benton took him to the President and Secretary of War, who gladly availed themselves of his agreement to go with General Kearny. He went . . . ."

ment of the United States will be regarded as enemies, and will be treated accordingly.[6]

It was then determined by Colonel Kearny (more likely by James Magoffin) that the proclamation, to produce results, should be delivered into the hands of the Mexican authorities; consequently, he handed Philip St. George Cooke another proclamation, directed to "Don Manuel Armijo y Comdr Genl Santa Fe." This second pronouncement was considerably at variance from the previous statement to the citizens. It read:

> Head Qr. Army of the West
> Camp on the Arkansas at Bents Fort
> Aug 1st 1846

Sir: By the annexation of Texas to the United States, the Rio Grande from its mouth to its source forms at this time the Boundary between her & Mexico, & I come by orders of the Govt. to take possession of the Country, over a part of which you are now presiding as Governor—I come as a friend & with the disposition & intention to consider all Mexicans & others as friends who will remain quietly & peaceably at their homes & attend to their own affairs—such persons shall not be disturbed by anyone under my command either in their Persons, their Property or their Religion—I pledge myself for the fulfillment of this promise—I come to this part of the United States with a strong Military force & a stronger one is following us as a reinforcement of us. We have many more troops than sufficient to put down any opposition that you can possibly bring against us, & I therefore for the sake of humanity call upon you to submit to fate, & to meet me with the same feeling of Peace & friendship which I now entertain for & offer to you & to all those over whom you are Governor—If you do so, it will be greatly to your interest & that of all your Countrymen & for which you will receive their blessings & their prayers—Should you decide otherwise—determine upon resistance & oppose with troops, you can raise, against us, I then say, the blood which may follow will rest upon your head, & instead of the blessings of your Countrymen, you will receive their curses, for I shall consider all whom you bring in Arms against us enemies & will treat them accordingly.

[6] Emory, *Notes of a Military Reconnoissance,* 168.

31

I send this communication by Capt Cooke of my own Regt, & recommend him & his party of 12 Dragoons to your kindness & attention. All Exmo Senor Gobernador.[7]

Captain P. St. George Cooke, wishing to be "a fighting man," not a messenger, took umbrage at his new mission; especially was he displeased with the disclosure that "Mr. James Magoffin of Kentucky and Señor Gonzales of Chihuahua" had permission to accompany him. Both were "merchants of caravans," who were "rather singularly . . . now journeying to New Mexico and beyond." (Obviously, Cooke was not in the confidence of Kearny and Magoffin.)

Colonel Kearny sought to placate his would-be "fighting man" by stating that he " attached much importance" to the mission; that he had *"waited* for" Cooke, desiring that he should undertake delivery of the letter in preference to his chief of staff, and, in the event of fighting, Cooke "would undoubtedly return and meet him before it began." Being a soldier, Captain Cooke set off toward Santa Fe, observing that his "mission was, in fact, a pacific one." Furthermore, "The general had just issued a proclamation [annexing] all the territory east of the Rio Grande; the government thus adopting the old claim of Texas and thus manifestly, in a statesman's view, its bloodless process would lead to its confirmation in the treaty of peace, and the population would be saved the bitterness of passing *sub jugum."* He was not entirely satisfied, however, for "the difficulty of a half-measure remains; it cuts the isolated province in two! There must be an influential Micawber in the cabinet!" Obviously he doubted the candor of the Colonel.

On August 14, seven miles from the Mora [*Los Posos*], a Mexican lieutenant and three men, representing themselves as coming from Governor Armijo, approached the column and delivered a reply to the American demand received through Cooke and Magoffin: Armijo could not acknowledge the Río Grande as the western boundary of the United States. Furthermore, according to the lieutenant, the people of New Mexico had risen in arms against the invaders, and

[7] Cooke, *The Conquest of New Mexico and California*, 6–7.

the Governor was "bound by duty and inclination to put himself at the head of them." Significantly, however, Armijo's messenger relayed the Governor's desire to meet the Colonel "on the Mora" if the invader would tarry there. [Would he fight upon a chosen battlefield, or would he negotiate?]

The army came to a meadow (Las Vegas) where there was "an assemblage of mud houses covering a space of fifteen acres. The hills are covered with sheep and goats." A hungry soldier observed that there was "now a certainty of not starving even should reverse—await us." The *alcalde* came out "to visit" and inform the command that he was "a Mexican and had to obey the government but that he was pleased to see that the general's proclamation was so favorable to the people." There was a rumor that the army would be attacked as it entered a pass in the mountain a short distance from the town. Preparations were made for the contingency. It was discovered there was a shortage of ammunition, only about ten rounds per soldier having been issued. One thoughtful soldier noted that "this is a singular way to invade a country—without either ammunition or provisions." The army filed in a column of fours onto the Las Vegas plaza. The people, to the number of 150, had assembled. Just as Colonel Kearny appeared, in dashed Major Swords of the quartermaster department, Lieutenant Gilmer of the Engineers, and Captain R. H. Weightman. If there was to be serious opposition in the mountain pass, the Army of the West would not be lacking the support of Captain R. H. Weightman. He had remained behind at Bent's Fort to receive important mail from Washington, and having heard that there was to be a battle, "rode sixty miles during the night" to be in on "the Kill" and to help present Colonel Kearny with his brigadier's commission before the battle.

General Kearny halted the army. Having been so suddenly elevated, he would go to greater heights. Calling the *alcalde,* Don Juan de Dios Maes, he suggested they "mount one of the houses [pointing to one of the low one-story adobe buildings] where all can hear and see, and I will speak to them." A ladder was brought and the functionaries went upon the roof.

Mr. Alcalde and people of New Mexico [saluted the General]:

I have come amongst you by orders of My Government, to take possession of your country, and extend over it the laws of the United States. We consider it, and have done so for some time, a part of the territory of the United States. We come amongst you as friends—not as enemies; as protectors—not as conquerors. We come among you for your benefit—not for your injury.

Henceforth I absolve you from all allegiance to the Mexican Government, and from all obedience to General Armijo. He is no longer your Governor; [great sensation]. I am your Governor. I shall not expect you to take up arms and follow me to fight your own people who may oppose me; but I will now tell you, that those who remain peaceably at home, attending to their crops and their herds, shall be protected by me in their property, their persons, and their religion; and not a pepper, nor an onion, shall be disturbed . . . .[8]

Before General Kearny had delivered his warning to the Las Vegans, Colonel Ruff had been inspired with the Kearny urge to speak. Therefore, before moving the troops through Las Vegas, he adjured them: "You are the only mounted company under my command today and the one designated for a charge of the regiment. The enemy is near at hand; your position is in front. Show them that you can ride them down."[9]

Then, in the words of Lieutenant W. H. Emory, who had ascended to the rooftop with the General, "We descended the ricketty ladder by which we had climbed to the tops of the houses, mounted our horses, and rode briskly forward to encounter our 600 Mexicans in the gorge of the mountain, two miles distant."[10] The army "charged through the pass," but there were no Mexicans there. Then meekly the soldiers continued their march. They arrived at Tecolote about noon, where they were "willingly received." Here Kearny made another speech.

---

[8] Emory, *Notes of a Military Reconnoissance;* Connelley, *Doniphan's Expedition,* 191.

[9] Edwards Journal in Bieber, *Marching with the Army of the West,* 154.

[10] A gap near what is now known as Romeroville where the Santa Fe Railway and Highway 85 parallel to leave Gallinas Valley.

Captain Cooke came into camp, accompanied by Dr. Henry Connelly. Cooke had little to tell other than that James Magoffin with his drunken companion, Señor Gonzales, had elected to stay in Santa Fe. Connelly explained his presence by saying that he was "commissioner of General Armijo to negotiate with General Kearny." Just what he was to negotiate he did not state, but he did disclose that James Magoffin had called on him in Santa Fe, since the two "could talk freely." The real purpose of Magoffin's call was to discover if Armijo would, in fact, resist. The information Dr. Connelly had was that "he was not determined to resist," but Colonel Diego Archuleta was "decidedly in favor of making a defense." And if Archuleta could have his way, "a strong stand will be made a few miles from the city." The Governor had called a public meeting, at which he had told his countrymen that he "was willing and ready to sacrifice his life and all his interests in defense of his country." However, when money for defense was asked for, the assembly gave not money, but authority to float a loan for one thousand dollars. Further, Cañoncita (Apache Canyon) was occupied by an unknown number of regular and volunteer troops. Dr. Connelly could not say that he knew what Magoffin's mission was with the Governor, but he had the impression that the mission had been accomplished, for Magoffin had told Connelly that at first "there was fight in Armijo," but after a private conversation, "I quieted him."[11]

[11] In Benton's *Thirty Years' View* there is a disclosure which could have come from no one except James Magoffin (II, 683): "Armijo promised not to make a stand at the defile, after which the invaders would have no difficulty. But his second in command, Col. Archuletti, was determined to fight, and to defend that pass; and if he did, Armijo would have to do the same. It became indispensable to quiet Archuletti. He was of different mould from the governor, and only accessible to a different class of considerations—those which addressed themselves to ambition. Magoffin knew the side on which to approach him. It so happened that General Kearney had set out to take the left bank of the Upper Del Norte—the eastern half of New Mexico—as part of Texas, leaving the western part untouched. Magoffin explained this to Archuletti, pointed to the western half of New Mexico as a derelict, not seized by the United States, and too far off to be protected by the central government: and recommended him to make a *pronunciamiento,* and take that half to himself. The idea suited the temper of Archuletti. He agreed not to fight, and General Kearney was informed there would be no resistance at the defile."

The march of the seventeenth of August brought the army into camp at the "castle of the Pagos, a very ancient ruin on the Puerco or Pecos." Soldier Hughes "dared to ascend the Altar & stood in the very spot where the Vestal fire had blazed for ages & wrote my name upon the white-washed wall near & in rear of the sacred altar." Next day good news came. It came first in the custody "of quite a youth ... dressed in the fashion of the Americans." His small mount seemed to vie with the rider, contending against the flapping of arms and legs. The youth was a messenger bearing tidings from the City of the Holy Faith. He was not a messenger of defeat, only a messenger of retreat. Armijo had fled; so had the army stationed in the canyon. Armijo was only making his "military retreat until he should receive orders from his government." He had withdrawn down the river, taking with him all the regular dragoons as a bodyguard. This seemed to be necessary, for a part of the caravan consisted of all the money, plate, and supplies he had been able to pack upon the animals. The governorship was being assumed, because of "the flight of General Manuel Armijo, the desertion of the soldiers ... and the fear of the military forces of the United States," by Lieutenant Governor Juan Bautista Vigil y Alarid. The messenger disclosed that the American merchants, residents of Santa Fe, well-wishers of the Kearny army, had come out of their barricades—where they had assembled for mutual protection against the *Nuevo Mejicanos,* who had been muttering, *"Tejanos!"* and "North American Invaders!"—and were now on the road between the canyon and Santa Fe to greet the oncoming army. The new governor would welcome Kearny and his army into Santa Fe.

John T. Hughes, diarist, made the daily entry (August 17, 1846), some facts, some deductions from flying rumors:

> The Spaniards have fled in every direction. Governor Armijo has left with 200 to 400 regulars for El Paso. Part of the citizens of Santa Fe have left and fled into the mountains—Some Dragoons sent at 1 A.M. to reconnoiter the pass ... hedged in on either hand by a very high range of mountains & at the Canyon or breach through the rocks. Here it was that Gen. Salasar & Armijo prepared to oppose our march—the

position was well selected; but they had neither the harmony nor the bravery to defend it—the camp exhibited the appearance of about 2,500 men . . . it was agreed that they would not fight the Americans before they left Santa Fe.

At three o'clock on August 18, Cooke brought the advance guard through the abandoned canyon fortification. He was in sight of the army's goal—Santa Fe—adobe houses, "earthy tabernacles." General Kearny now came up from the rear just as the sun broke through its enveloping clouds. Superseding Captain Cooke, he took the position of honor, "in advance & entered the town with ten companies, in fine array & banners streaming in the breeze . . . while the batteries fired a salute of near 20 guns." Marcellus Ball Edwards, on entering the city, "found the whole of the illiterate portion of the population . . . expecting to be branded on the cheek with the letters 'U.S.,' such as are worn on the soldiers' sabre belts. Women could be seen . . . with their hands covering their faces or sobbing aloud." After the batteries had ceased firing, "the American flag was erected in the public square so as to wave over the Palace Royal, or Gov. Armijo's Residence," after which the troops camped on a "perfectly bare spot in the sand, after a travel of 29 miles, not having halted to eat a bite." Mess call did not sound that night, for the General, in his eagerness to reach the capital, had neglected to order up the supply wagons. "Neither man nor horse had anything to eat; nor did they get anything until the next morning"—that is, those who obeyed the orders against fraternizing with the enemy went to bed hungry, but "some few got a piece of bread or cheese from the Spaniards"—always from women, a universal kindness.

Governor Vigil and some thirty citizens who had constituted themselves the committee of welcome met the triumphant Kearny while the American guns pounded out notice of his approach. Governor Vigil bowed himself out of his short-lived office. Kearny then entered the Palace of the Governors. At the solicitation of former Governor Vigil, they partook with gustative satisfaction of Vigil's El Paso wine. Soon the General was noticed to be "in fine spirits," whereupon he fitted himself into quarters "suitable to a governor of New Mexico." The animals were not so fortunate. For "want of forage" they had "become feeble and incapable of further exertion. Without a blade of grass or other foods they stood tethered to their iron pickets or sank to the earth in exhaustion. Thus the city of Santa Fe was bloodlessly possessed by the American forces."

It was nine o'clock the next morning before General Kearny made another speech. In preparation for it, not having an audience, he "called together the Governor adinterim, the Secretary of State, the Alcalde, & other civil officers." John Hughes, who had been out the greater part of the previous night looking in on *fandangos,* accepted an invitation "to go down in town to hear Gen. K.'s speech to the Spaniards & to see them take the oath of allegiance to the Gov't. of the U.S." There, "under the eye of Gen. Kearny," was I. Herkins of the Saline Company. He was not only hungry but suffering from the after-effects of a too liberal consumption of Taos Lightning. Having drunk, he now wanted to eat and consequently quarreled with another soldier over an ear of green corn. John Hughes was sketching the public square when he was ordered to arrest the fighters. Since he was a better artist than Samaritan, his efforts were futile, whereupon the General recruited Captain Turner, Major Swords, "and others" to the peace squad. The drunken Herkins, seeing himself outnumbered, drew his sword and began putting it to effective use, wounding the pacificators while giving an exhibition of swordsmanship theretofore not seen on the plaza, Captain Turner only excepted. While Herkins fought with his back to a fence, Captain Turner came boldly upon his antagonist, who was not, in his drunken and hungry state, equal to the assault, and "wrenched his sabre from him with his own." By force, then, Herkins was removed from the plaza to the camp, where he was tied spider-web fashion to a wagon wheel. This manner of subjugation, in the opinion of an onlooker, was "not comportable to the dignity of a Missouri volunteer." Herkins' resort, however, considering his restraint at the moment, was limited to utterances of choice abuse. He was then gagged, whereupon he "became very sick." His sickness brought release, after which he was placed in the custody of the guard to await the inevitable court-martial.[12]

At the conclusion of the Battle of the Swords (Major Swords, challenged, declining), General Kearny, speaking through an interpreter, few auditors understanding English, told the assemblage:

> We have come amongst you to take possession of New Mexico. . . . We have come with peaceable intentions and kind feelings toward you all. We come as friends . . . to make you a part of the Republic of the United States. We mean not to murder you, or rob you of your property. Your families shall be free from molestation; your women secure from violence. . . . we do not mean to take away your religion. . . . I do hereby proclaim that, being in possession of Santa Fé, I am therefore virtually in possession of all New Mexico. Armijo is no longer your governor. . . . You are no longer Mexican subjects: you are now become American citizens. . . . I do hereby proclaim my intentions to establish . . . a civil government . . . similar to those of our own States. . . . I am your governor,—henceforward look to me for protection."

Then, "In the name of the Father, and of the Son, and of the Holy Spirit," he administered the oath of allegiance to the governor-ad-interim, the secretary of state, the *prefecto,* and the *alcalde;* and seeing that the Stars and Stripes floated from only a slight elevation, he ordered a flagstaff one hundred feet high to be erected in the plaza amid shouts for the new governor, the third one within three days. Kearny

---

[12] The court-martial convened in due time for the trial of Herkins. In the opinion of his fellow soldiers he was a "turbulent, broilsome fellow," but none wanted to see him shot; however, all wanted "to get rid of him." The court-martial officers were co-operative, sentencing him to "six months' hard labor with ball and chain, after which he was to be put in solitary confinement and fed on bread and water ten days, [and] then dishonorably discharged from the service with a reduction of his pay." Kearny approved, but "on account of the impractibility of carrying it into effect," revised the verdict, remitting all except dishonorable discharge. When "the drumming or whistling out of camp took place," the regiment was paraded. Herkins was "marched from the guard tent . . . by six of the guard with bayonets at his back, and a fifer playing the 'Rogue's March' . . . . [He was] soon as free as an un-caged bird." But Herkins had the last word: "He says his discharge is as honorable as any he wishes."

then came forward to shake the hands of those "well pleased . . . at the idea of becoming citizens of the U.S.," after which he strode into the Palace of the Governors to compose a letter to General Wool, introduced with the bombast that he had taken possession of New Mexico "without firing a gun or spilling a drop of blood." Then he issued another proclamation containing a singular and revealing declaration:

> . . . as the undersigned, at the head of his troops, on the 18th instant, took possession of Santa Fe, the capital of the department of New Mexico, he now announces his intention to hold the department with its original boundaries (on both sides of the Del Norte) as a part of the United States, and under the name of the Territory of New Mexico.[13]

The soldiers, now rested from their trek halfway across the continent, "rambled through town." Some entered private houses, where they found the "women not handsome [but] rather more intelligent than the men"; they attended "phandangoes almost every night." Marcellus Ball Edwards explored "the public plaza, or square, on which is situated the state house, the dismal *calabozo,* and most of the trading houses." He saw the *calaboza* cleaned out " and a string of human ears found in it. These were the ears of the Texan prisoners shot by order of Salazar, and cut off and presented to his excellency, Governor Armijo, as evidence that they had not escaped." On Sunday many attended one of the Roman Catholic churches. Santa Fe, they learned, had six. A "great many women—all kneel down—no seats." There were no public schools. "the business of education being intrusted to ecclesiastics." The streets were "crooked and narrow." the whole presenting "very much the appearance of an extensive brickyard." The *Nuevo Mejicanos* were "generally under the medium size . . . of a swarthy, copper complexion . . . from the fair Castillian to the darkest hue of the aborigines . . . hospitable, but ignorant and treacherous."

Soon after settling himself in the Palace of the Governors, General Kearny had two visitors, a priest from Taos and a "sensible young

[13] Connelley, *Doniphan's Expedition,* 208.

Purbleau [Pueblo] chief." Father Martínez was the priest; he came "to hold a parley with General K[earny] ... acknowledge the authority of the conqueror, receive his commands, and ask protection for the churches and church property." After being assured by General Kearny that "their religion in the amplest manner [would be] preserved to them ... [he] returned home peaceably and favorably disposed towards the Americans, more subdued by kindness than by force of arms." As he left, he saw the young chief "waiting to see the general." The chief came, so he told Kearny, because he "had heard of him & came to see him & know what his intentions were." He merely wanted to know "if he intended protection or not." The priests had told him that the Americans would "kill & plunder, take their women & brand then on the cheek with the American brand, rob them of their daughters, & drive the men into the fastnesses of the mountains." He came to say "he would not suffer this," and if such was the truth, he would go back to his people and fight the Americans; "that it was better to die honorably, in defence of his people and country, than to suffer these outrages," and now he wanted "the truth of these things before they would go to war." He, too, went back to Taos pleased with the presents he was given "by way of compliment."

Finally, on the twenty-eighth of August, the General set out to give the people a civil government. With Private Willard P. Hall and Colonel A. W. Doniphan, who were lawyers, in charge, a set of laws was put together, which has since been known as the "Kearny Code," although it was entitled "The Organic Laws and Constitution." It was printed on the small press previously in the possession of Father Martínez when he issued his *La Verdad*.

After considerable show of force in the territory, on September 16 the General dispatched an account of his accomplishments and future plans of the War Department. "There can no longer be apprehended any organized resistance in this Tery. to our troops, & the commander of them, *whoever he may be will hereafter have nothing to attend to, but to secure the Inhabitants from further depredations of the Navajoe & Eutaw Indians.* [Italics mine.]

On September 22, 1846, he announced the appointment of the civil officers:

> Being duly authorized by the Presdt. of the United States of America, I hereby make the following appointments for the Govt. of New Mexico a Territory of the U. States—The officers thus appointed will be obeyed & respected accordingly—

> Charles Bent, to be Governor. Donaisio Vigil . . . Secy of Tery. Richard Dallan . . . Marshal. Francis P. Blair . . . U.S. Dist. Atty. . . . Charles Blummer . . . Treasurer. Eugene Leitrendorfer [*sic*] . . . Auditor of Pub. Accounts. Joel [Joab] Houghton—Antonio José Otero—Charles Beaubian . . . judges of the Superior Court.[14]

On September 24, he gave notice to the Adjutant General of his contemplated departure: "Having finished all my public business in this place, having organized a civil government for the Tery. by appointing the officers & causing a set of laws to be prepared and published for it, & having made the necessary Military arrangements for maintaining the perfect order, peace & quiet, now so happily existing, I intend in compliance with the instructions from the War Dept to leave here to-morrow with Major Sumner & his 300 Dragoons for Upper California." On September 25, General Kearny marched toward the west, leaving Colonel Doniphan behind to await the arrival of Colonel Sterling Price, who would thereafter take command as Doniphan moved toward Chihuahua.

Before going away, however, the General would, in one final gesture, "show all Mexicans . . . the injustice and absurdity of all the imputations . . . that are . . . systematically propagating through the country, and have found believers where ignorance is so great." He had been directed by the War Department "to leave no lasting animosities to prejudice the future friendship and commerce of the two countries." Therefore he would be the diplomat as in Shakespeare: *Like a fashionable host that slightly shakes his parting guest by the hand.* He would give a grand *baile* as his final gesture. But there was a perplexing problem; the chief commissary had no war chest.

[14] *Ibid.*

It so happened that *La Tules* was yet in the city. Despite a favored relationship with former Governor Armijo, she had been left behind at the time of his retreat southward to safety, an oversight which had miffed the queen of a certain stratus of Santa Fe society. And *La Tules,* as commonly known, but Doña Gertrudes Barcelo in fact, remained to magnify her notoriety and her monte room located on the

La Tules, as depicted in *Harper's Magazine,* April, 1854.

east side of the plaza.[15] Being "in funds," Doña Gertrudes indicated both her ability and her willingness to supplement the inadequate exchequer—if only she would be admitted to the grand function upon the arm of a beribboned and imposing United States officer, a gesture to restore her community status.

The time for the *baile* came. Many of the invited guests remained conspicuously absent "owing to the death of an old gentleman a few days since, the relation of half the city," but Susan Magoffin, the only woman who had come along with the Army of the West, was there.[16]

[15] W. G. Ritch Papers, No. 93: "Profligacy and Prostitution—Adulterous Character of the Old Priesthood," 1 Mo. 64, 4 Mo. 287; "Immortality—general," 4 Mo. 24 (index). La Tules was "a Mexican woman . . . a noted prostitute and keeper of a gambling house on the east side of the plaza [Santa Fe] in the location where, in 1876, George Caster had a barber-shop. She was a monte-dealer against whom her fandango-house operator sister, Dolores, consistently gambled, Tula doing the dealing. Dolores was 'kept' by a Mexican artillery officer, prior to the invasion of the Kearny forces. Tula 'lived' with Augustin Disnovly, who had, among his other avocations, that of monte-dealer for his irregular *esposa,* and a clerkship in the Santa Fe court." At her death—according to Ritch—she was buried in front of the altar in the church commonly known as the Cathedral of San Francisco. "Barcelo[na] arranged with the Bishop [Lamy] for the burial and Ch. Services before she died paid the Bishop $1 000 to secure the service & *sepulchr.* The funeral was very large and was attended by everybody Am & Mexicans generally. Said to have been the largest funeral ever held in the city. A woman of no education but great natural ability."

[16] Susan Shelby Magoffin, *Down the Santa Fe Trail,* 145.

So was *La Tules*. As seen by Susan, she was "the old woman with the false hair and teeth," who smoked a *cigarrittos,* and rocked the *cuna* to the thumping of a guitar and the whine of a violin. The reporter for *The Republican* was also impressed; there had been nothing like it, nor was there to be again: ". . . we have never heard of nor anticipated the same general turnout or display."[17]

[17] "The Ball," December 18, 1847.

CHAPTER THREE

"A DEEP-ROOTED PREJUDICE AND HATRED AGAINST AMERICANS"

THREE DAYS after General Kearny moved toward California, Colonel Sterling Price arrived "in quite a feeble state of health." Then for four successive days the troops of the Second Regiment "dropped in." They had been fifty-three days on the trail. Their horses were only "moderate." Three men had been lost en route, two from sickness, one in an accident. By September 9 the "town [was] full of Americans." News came from the Río Abajo that the Navahos had killed five Spaniards and driven off ten thousand head of sheep and cattle, as did an order from Kearny for Doniphan to delay for a time his march toward Chihuahua and divert his military might against the Navahos, who had promised to come and make peace, but had failed to do so and had continued killing and raiding.

Governor Bent, showing that he understood the importance of the position he occupied, wrote two letters, one appropriately to the Honorable James Buchanan, secretary of state of the United States, and the other to Senator Thomas Hart Benton. His expressions no longer bore the brand of the mountaineer; he was the West Pointer now, writing with clarity, directness, and earnestness. He advised the Secretary of State that he had received the appointment of governor of the Territory of New Mexico "established by Brig Genl Kearney," thus raising the question of the legality of the appointment of a governor by a military commander and also of invoking law prescribed by a military commander.

Accepting his status, however, there would be points, he thought, which "will require the action of the Govt. of the United States," notably "laws for the regulation of mining . . . this being the principal and almost only source of wealth, and education," there having been "universal neglect of education among all classes." This neglect "absolutely requires the establishment by Govt. of primary schools . . . with teachers in both the English and Spanish languages." The education of New Mexicans, he warned, was most important "in view of the fact that a rude and uneducated people are about to become citizens of the U.S. and act for themselves in matters of Govt." Indeed, it was of vital importance to the peace and prosperity of the Territory." As for the Indians of the region, "most of whom are numerous and warlike, and have for many years committed all manner of outrages upon the Mexican settlement with impunity," an efficient Indian agent, "together with three sub-agents," should be appointed. There was also a necessity for maintaining a military force "for several years to come," not only "to aid the civil authorities in the administration of justice . . . [but] to hold in check the different tribes of Indians." Thus Bent spelled out the necessity for an arbiter for the three conflicting peoples.

Then, again looking askance at the legality of his appointment to a civil position created by an unconfirmed military authority to execute arbitrarily established laws, Bent introduced the subject to Senator Benton by sending him a list of Kearny-appointed civil officers, pointing out that he "would perceive that I have been appointed Governor" and soliciting, "in addition to the many kind offices already received at your hands, that you will favor me with your influence and note to obtain the confirmation by the President and Senate of the United States of this appointment." He was willing to serve, but he wished to do so within a legal framework.

Trouble multiplied in Santa Fe. It became endemic with fraternization at the saloons and fandangos, coming to the surface when soldiers steeped themselves in Turley's Taos Lightning. The Mormon Battalion came, diminishing the already inadequate food supply; and Sterling Price's men grumbled, as did Doniphan's Rovers Abroad. The Latter-Day Saints took the trail westward on September 18, with their new commander, Philip St. George Cooke. The departing Cooke had acquired impressions of the new people, first when seeing Kearny "Swearing NMs to Loyalty [at Bernal]":

"A Deep-rooted Prejudice and Hatred Against Americans"

The great boon to American citizenship thrust through an interpreter, by the mailed hand, upon eighty thousand mongrels who cannot read—who are almost heathens—the great mass reared in real slavery, called peons, but still imbued by nature with enough patriotism to resent this outrage to swear an alien allegiance, by an officer who had just passed through their frontier. This people who have been taught more respect for a corporal than a judge, must have been astonished at this first lesson in liberty.[1]

Despite the diminution of the number of soldiers in the city after the Latter-Day Saints moved out, conditions remained the same. John Hughes recorded in his diary (October 19): "Nothing new. . . . Man killed in bed with another person's wife—horribly mangled." Then three days later disease made itself felt: "Edmond Hopper, of the Polk company, died." The next repeated the ominous news: this time is was Daniel Jacobs of Benton, and by that time there were "18 new graves in the American Burial Ground." Even before the cemetery began to fill, Bent became aware of the situation, being by no means pleased with the conduct of Doniphan's troops; and Doniphan's attention was directed to the situation in terms both informative and demanding:

Santa Fe, October 9th, 1846

Col. Doniphan
   Sir:

In consequence of the numerous complaints of the insubordination and often offensive and abusive conduct of the troops of your command, my duty compels me to call on you to interpose your authority and *compel* the soldiers to respect the rights of the inhabitants.

These outrages are becoming so frequent that I apprehend serious consequences may result sooner or later if measures are not taken to prevent them.

Very respectfully,
C. B.[2]

[1] Cooke, *The Conquest of New Mexico and California.*

[2] NA, RG 98, 9 Mil. Dept. Orders, Vol. 5, p. 12; AC, "Bent Papers, 1846," Fort Union," p. 5.

47

Although the territory was quiet, according to the Governor, "except that the Navajos, Yuts, and Apache Indians continue to commit serious depredations upon its frontiers," he anticipated trouble. It could readily come from "the mongrels," so called by Cooke, the Indians—both wild and "Pueblo," the latter in the opinion of Captain Cooke being far more moral than the New Mexicans proper, "that is of mixed blood," and the insubordinate American troops. As to the conflict between the Indians and the New Mexicans, Bent anticipated no change. In conformity with Indian policy—in language which he attributed to them—"the Indians do not destroy the Mexicans, because they prefer that they should continue to raise stock for them to drive off." However, until those Indians were effectually subdued, he foresaw them blighting "the prosperity ... of this Territory" where it is "exposed to their depredations."

But he rated the Pueblo Indians differently. Although confessedly at peace with the Americans, still, "These Indians have long been in the habit of submitting themselves passively to the command of the Priest, and it is not to be doubted that they would be ready to join in any revolutionary enterprise to which they might be instigated by those whose orders they have so long been accustomed to obey with blind submission."

The Mexican inhabitants of the territory had "heretofore known no rule than that of a military Govt. To them a government of public opinion and reason operated thro' the medium of law and peaceful forms is a thing unintelligible. Added to this, they have always nursed a deep-rooted prejudice and hatred against Americans, and it is to be apprehended that their ignorance of the power of the Govt. of the United States would induce them to seize upon any moment favorable to a momentary success, to revolutionize and murder the constituted authorities of the Territory."

With the situation as he thus viewed it, Bent thought there should be, for future security, "a regiment of mounted men to take the place of the volunteer troops now stationed in the Territory," without which he felt "it will be impossible to compel the inhabitants to respect and obey the laws ... and subjugate the various tribes of hos-

Willard P. Hall, who with Colonel A. W. Doniphan drew up the
"Kearny Code" giving the people of New Mexico a civil government.

Arrott Collection

Colonel Edwin Vose Sumner (shown in his Civil War general's uniform) gave the name Fort Union to the "Headquarters on the Moro."

Arrott Collection

tiles." Governor Bent was not alone in his opinions. An unknown Santa Fean expressed the same sentiments in a letter to the *St. Louis Republican*: ". . . We look forward with gloomy anticipation to the future. There are not enough provisions in the country, including all that are now here or expected, to last the first of February. The country cannot furnish the deficiency, even were there funds to buy it. Three thousand men in a state of starvation, is a mass not easily kept in Subordination."[3]

With the prejudice and hatred of the *Nuevo Mejicanos* for the Americans, hostile Indians looking for spoils from every quarter, the shadow of starvation casting itself into the near future, and insubordination of the troops rampant, Governor Bent was presented rumors of that which he dreaded most—revolt. On October 20 he confided to Colonel Doniphan that he had "received from various parts of this territory and from various sources information" which led him to believe that "an insurrection is in contemplation by the native inhabitants in concert with some Mexican troops and the inhabitants of El Paso del Norte." Meetings of the people at the Río Abajo, Albuquerque, and other places below had been held; those meetings "were frequent . . . and they communicate by runners." Bent suggested that precautionary measures be taken by the military, which were "all important for the peace and security of the Territory . . . measures [which] cannot possibly produce evil and may do much to prevent it." But with the warnings six days old, Doniphan left toward Chihuahua on November 2, the command falling to Colonel Sterling Price, while Sumner, either ignoring the Governor or not taking him into his confidence, had left for the "States" on October 18.

Governor Bent then unburdened himself to General Kearny, long since west of the Río Grande, telling him that up to the present things were quiet in Santa Fe, "but there are a great many rumors from various parts of the territory of a rebellion." He had been informed "that Durand, Archulette, Priest y Mago [Maes?], A. I. Channuce [Leyba?], and the Armijoes of Albukerkey are the prime movers." He had his eye on them and "certainly shall give them a high berth,

[3] Issue of November 28, 1846.

49

if the facts can be proven on them. I shall keep as quiet as possible until I am in possession of sufficient proof to condemn them. One example will strike such terror into these people that I doubt another will have temerity enough to embark in such a perilous enterprise for the future."

Furthermore, said Bent, "There is a great want of discipline and subordination amongst the troops here. I am fearful that this will lead to serious consequences. They hardly respect the persons or property of the Mexicans. I shall use every means to impress upon the commander the necessity of a more rigid care with regard to the treatment of the inhabitants. We must reconcile and not exasperate." Some irresponsible correspondent to the *St. Louis Union,* however, did anything but reconcile when he wrote: "This province has been over-rated, and our Government has been grossly imposed upon and deceived. . . . Sum up the whole in a few words; the Mexicans are physically, mentallly, and morally an inferior and 'low flung' race."[4]

Colonel Price finally took cognizance of Bent's growing apprehensions and the dire consequences which might result from troop insubordination. He, consequently, disposed his troops "for the preservation of peace and subordination." He sent Hadley to the Mora and Captain Burgwin to Albuquerque, there "to maintain tranquility on the Rio Abajo," thus materially reducing the concentration of troops at the capital. Major Benjamin G. Edmonson was already on detached duty, though not yet in the Navaho country. The remaining force went under daily parade and drill. Both men and officers reacted with little co-operation and reverted to "the unrestrained, independent life to which the citizen soldier has been accustomed," thereafter being found even more frequently at Dolores Barcelo's fandango —provided she had not gone to her sister's place to play monte.

Again Governor Bent turned to Senator Benton for help. He asked permission "to consider him . . . friend" and to interest him in "all measures which I may find necessary for this Territory." He had been placed in the governor's office "to watch over the interests of

[4] The *New York Daily Tribune,* November 3, 1846, p. 1, col. 2—from Santa Fe correspondent of the *St. Louis Union,* September 13, 1846.

this new possession." He felt "a strong desire to see it prosper and grow into a valuable portion of the country." Stationing one thousand troops in the territory was "a measure absolutely necessary for the peace and quiet of New Mexico. . . . an outbreak will be attempted, (should there not be the military force stationed here I have named . . .) my knowledge of this people for many years past, renders perfectly certain." In order to meet the needs of the territory, the Governor would have Benton secure an appropriation "for the erection of public buildings at the Capital. . . . A Government house to contain a dwelling house and office for the Governor and Secretary of the Territory. . . . Another building for a legislative Hall and the necessary offices together with rooms for the Circuit and Superior Courts. Another building for a State penitentiary." And special emphasis was placed on the fact that "there is not at this time a single jail or prison in the whole Territory in which a criminal can be safely confined."

December 17, 1846, came. On that day Doña Gertrudes Barcelo, *La Tules,* "false wig and false teeth, conspicuous red hair," sought the presence of the lieutenant governor.[5] Hers was not a personal call this day; it had to do with matters of state. She was there to evidence her gratitude for acceptance at the grand *baile.* She had information of the greatest moment for Donciano, for Governor Bent, for Colonel Price. She had learned that since about December 1 there had been a plot in the making for the massacre of all Americans, the establishment of a new government, and the installation of another governor. The eventuality which Governor Bent had warned against was now a reality. The most conspicuous of the conspirators were said to be Don Tomás Ortiz, Don Diego Archuleta, Nicolás Pino, Miguel Pino, Santiago Armijo, Manuel Chávez, Domingo Baca, Pablo Domínguez, and Juan López.

Don José María Sánchez was arrested and required to testify, though ever so unwillingly, before a military tribunal. He related that the conspirators first met in Santa Fe on December 15 to mature plans already generally understood. All were to assemble four days later

[5] Report of Col. Sterling Price, February 15, 1847, in Ralph E. Twitchell, *The Leading Facts of New Mexican History,* II, n. 168.

at the parish church. At a signal from the church bell at midnight they were to seize the artillery of the Americans in the plaza, the Governor in the Palace, and the Colonel in his quarters; Don Diego Archuleta, with forces assembled on the outskirts of the town, was to complete the coup. Again Archuleta had accepted second place; Tomás Ortiz was in command. A full discussion at the December 15 meeting, however, convinced the leaders that they were not ready, and they reset the time of assault for Christmas Eve, when the troops would be "indulging in wine and feasting."

With the co-operation of the military, Bent succeeded in "securing seven of the secondary conspirators" and "placed the military and civil officers . . . both in pursuit of the prime movers," but after the lapse of several days he was "apprehensive that they will make their escape from the Territory." One of the men in custody was Manuel Chávez, who steadfastly proclaimed his innocence.

While the escaping conspirators were being tracked by the soldiers, the divulger of the conspiracy was also being sought by conspiracy sympathizers. Rumor had it that a conspirator had "told a woman." Sánchez denied that this was so, declaring, "No woman was to be privy to these things, lest they should be divulged." Another rumor identified the informant as a "mulatto girl, residing in Santa Fe, who had married one of the conspirators" and who had learned from her husband the subject of the clandestine meeting.[6] No public expression of suspicion concerned *La Tules,* and Governor Bent was discreet enough to say only, "On the 17th inst., I recd information from a Mexican friendly to the Government that a conspiracy was on foot among the native Mexicans." Then, to show that he felt that civil authority was firmly anchored in the territory, "the night before Christmas, he gave a ball at the palace—the finest entertainment that Santa Fe ever had."

Governor Bent's entertainment was merely a "whistle in the cemetery," and this the "merchants and other American residents of S. Fe" understood when they petitioned him not to weaken the city defenses. Bent, in full agreement, sent Colonel Price "additional reasons" for

[6] Connelley, *Doniphan's Expedition,* 511.

keeping the defense of the city intact, adding this warning: "There has been an attempted rebellion. The leaders of the rebellion have not as yet been secured, and though the plan seems to be broken up for the present, I have no doubt that as soon as any of the *efficient* force shall be withdrawn from the Territory, another attempt will be made to excite the people to rebellion. . . . If they find themselves able to revolt *now,* however disastrous the result may be to them, they will always have spirits among them of sufficient audacity to renew the attempt."[7]

George F. Ruxton, a traveling Englishman, "found all over New Mexico the . . . most bitter feeling and most determined hostility . . . against the Americans, who certainly in Santa Fe and elsewhere have not been very anxious to conciliate the people, but, by their bullying and overbearing demeanour towards them, have in a great measure been the cause of the hatred." This overbearing demeanor came from "the dirtiest, rowdiest crew" he had ever "seen collected together. Crowds of drunken volunteers filled the streets, brawling and boasting, but never fighting. Mexicans, wrapped in sarape, scowled upon them as they passed. . . . Under the portales were numerous montetables, surrounded by Mexicans and Americans. Every other house was a grocery, as they called a gin or whisky shop, continually disgorging reeling drunken men, and everywhere filth and dirt reigned triumphant."[8]

When news reached Governor Bent that Colonel Doniphan had defeated the Mexican Army at Brazita, he was greatly relieved; this meant that there would be no reinforcement for the revolutionists from down the Río Grande. As a result of this victory, he believed that the reasons for maintaining the defenses at Santa Fe "no longer exist." In addition, he thought that "the territory will remain in tranquility with the presence of the troops which will remain."[9] But a citizen writing to *Niles' Register* had a darker view of the situation in Santa Fe: The soldiers were "a degenerate military mob, vio-

[7] NA, RG 98, 9 Mil. Dept. Orders, Vol. 5, pp. 45–47.

[8] *Ruxton of the Rockies,* 180, 188.

[9] NA, RG 98, 9 Mil. Dept. Orders, Vol. 5, pp.47–48; AC, "Bent Papers, 1846," "Fort Union," 47.

lators of law and order, heaping daily injury and insult upon the people: one half of the captains do not know how many men are in their companies nor where they can be found. The officers themselves, are seen nightly at fandangoes, and even less respectable places of dissipation. The soldiers never drill; nothing but confusion and misrule exists. One-fifth of the entire command has died from the effects of dissipation. Price's lack of military education and his apparent inability to control either officers or men has produced among the New Mexicans the strongest feelings of distrust and hatred and a desire to rebel exists among the inhabitants."

Contrary to his theretofore more intelligent judgment, Bent began to look less apprehensively upon the signs of danger, and prepared to visit with his family in Taos. In true Mexican form he issued a *pronunciamento* before leaving the capital, cajoling the disturbed natives to peace: They were now "governed by new statutory laws"; they had "free government promised." They must not "abuse the great liberty . . . and [should] gather the abundant fruits" which awaited them. There had been those "who blindly opposed . . . and those whose vices made them notorious . . . Tomas Ortiz and the old revolutionist, Diego Archuleta . . . leaders of a revolution," but their treason was discovered and smothered at its birth. "Now they are wandering about hiding from people, but their doctrines are scattered among the people thereby causing uneasiness." The people were urged "to turn a deaf ear to such false doctrine and remain quiet [and] . . . enjoy all the prosperity which your best friend wishes you."

On January 14, 1847, attended by an escort of five—the sheriff, circuit attorney, and *prefecto* being three of the number—Governor Charles Bent left Santa Fe for Taos. The party was met there by several Pueblo Indians, who demanded release of two of their tribesmen being held by the local authorities in the none too secure prison. After the Governor heard their complaint, he told them they were now being governed by statutory laws, that they would have to await the orderly process of law. They went away sullenly.

After gleaning what local news he could, he wrote to his old friend Manuel Alvares in Santa Fe. Writing now not as the governor but in the vernacular of the mountaineer (and not dating his letter), he told Alvares:

> We have nothing heare interesting or news to communicate except Indians are stealing and Killing occasionally, they have lately Killed three Men on the Animas or beyond it, they Stole a [blurred] from the Same place, night before last they Stole from the Buffalo hunters on Ocate forty head of mules & Horses, this last was done by two Indians, some think theas depredations were committed by the Youtaws, others think thay ware committed by the Arkansas Indians.
>
> Our Priest delivered on the sunday be fore last, a verry strong anti annexation Sermon, to the wondering multitude. I have bean told that he has directed Some of the Cittizens to attack the Soldier heare and if posible to drive them of, the truth of this I do not affirm. report also sayes that he has said, that he had $3 000 for the purpos of raising recruites, for what purpose I have not heard.
>
> Had you not better prepair a communication for the U. States, touching our situation heare to be forwarded by [express?].
>
> Since my return from Santa Fe I have letters from St. Vrain on Red River   he had traded up to 31st December . . . G. Bent wrightes me 15th January . . . .
>
> Blair left for the fort on friday last he expected to reach thare in 7 or 8 days. he will return heare in the case of one month.[10]

All day long on January 19 there was recurrent disorder and carousing in the village of Taos. The Governor was advised to leave town, but he remained, evidencing no fear of personal danger. By night the village was in an uproar. Indians from the pueblo northeast of town were arriving in San Fernández de Taos in increasing numbers. The saloon and public places were crowded with drunken people. Turley's Taos Lightning was inflaming the passions of the milling multitude. Pablo Montoya, pleased to style himself the "Santa Ana of the North," and Tomasito Romero, a misguided Indian, were arousing the mob to a state of frenzy. But Governor Bent retired quietly to his house, separated from the abutting buildings on the

[10] On the bottom of the letter Manuel Alvarez wrote: "Gov B left S fe on the 14th for Taos   Killed night of 19th."

north of the plaza by a burro path, and there awaited the passing of the day. Oterbees, a whiskey peddler fresh from Turley's Lightning still, entered the plaza following behind several burros packed high with New Mexico's favorite potation. At first upon seeing and hearing the bedlam at large, he feared he had been sampling his wares with unbecoming frequency. Then he recalled that Mr. Turley had been told there was to be an insurrection. Abandoning his burro train and mounting a convenient horse, he rode pell-mell to the Río Hondo, shouting to Mr. Turley that the revolt was on, that they were murdering the Governor and all Americans in Taos.

All was quiet at the Governor's residence, however, until an early hour in the morning. Then a noisy crowd swarmed into the *placita*. The Governor, aroused by the turmoil, went to the window and attempted to quiet the disturbance. His efforts only intensified the fury. In the house, occupying another room, were Mrs. Bent, her sister, Mrs. Christopher Carson, Mrs. Boggs, the Governor's four-year-old daughter Teresina, and his son Alfred. When the mob began to shoot into the house, ten-year-old Alfred grabbed a shotgun and implored his father, "Let's fight 'em." The women broke a hole through the adobe wall and escaped into an adjacent building, but Governor Bent stood his ground until felled by arrows, one of which was shot into his eye, another penetrating his chest, and others striking his chin. With blood flowing, he fell to the floor. The maniacs then broke through the door or let themselves down through the penetrated roof, and, falling upon the prostrate man, peeled off his scalp amids shouts of glee, while he, with hand on bleeding hairless pate, tried to find protection by crawling through the hole in the wall. There he fell in his own blood, only to have his head hacked off by a fiend who carried it off, holding it aloft as he marched in a jubilant parade around the plaza.[11]

[11] Although the commonly accepted version is that Governor Bent was beheaded, yet this statement bears careful scrutiny since none of the eyewitnesses in their later years mentioned beheading.

CHAPTER FOUR

"AN ANOMALOUS
FORM OF GOVERNMENT"

THE FIRST Anglo governor of New Mexico was dead. Charles Bent had paid with his life in the attempt to lead two diverse peoples into the Anglo way. His headless body lay in his congealing blood while the fury of the mob spent itself slaying Americans, officeholders under the United States regime, and persons who had married Americans. Among those who fell were Louis Lee, sheriff, Cornelio Vigil, prefect, J. W. Leal, circuit attorney (who had just completed the ride from Santa Fe to Taos with Bent), Narciso (or Narcisse) Beaubien, son of Judge Beaubien, and Pablo Jaramillo, brother of Mrs. Charles Bent. The last two were discovered hiding in a hay stable. A fiendish woman pointed them out and admonished the butchers "to kill the young ones so that they will not have to be contended with when older." Pablo died quickly from a lance wound, thus escaping torture. Not so young Narciso Beaubien, who was lanced through the body, stripped, tortured, and scalped. This promising youth had just returned from the Cape Girardeau College to visit his father. J. W. Leal's fate was horrendous: he was captured, stripped of his clothing, then punched around the plaza ahead of a parade of lancers, shot with arrows, scalped, and left in an icy ditch, where a sow chewed at his bloody wounds.

While murder stalked mad in Taos, the dead sheriff's brother evaded the rioters and made his way to Santa Fe. There he found Colonel Sterling Price. In his wake were emissaries from the revolutionists. They carried a circular letter dated January 20, 1847. Bearing the signatures of Jesús Tafolla and Antonio María Trujillo, it urged "The Defenders of their Country" to "shake off the yoke bound on us by a foreign government . . . to raise all the forces . . . that are able to bear arms." They had "declared war with the Americans and it is now time that we shall all take our arms in our hands in defense of our abandoned country."

Lieutenant Governor Donciano Vigil, reluctantly and apprehensively, assumed the office of governor, advising his "Fellow Citizens" that "the Term of my administration is purely transitory." In an attempt to lull the potential revolutionists into quiescence, he pandered to them, stating: "Neither my qualification nor the ad interim character, according to the organic law in which I take the reins of government, encourages me to continue in so difficult and thorny post, the duties of which are intended for individuals of greater enterprise and talents." He understood his own weakness; having been confronted with the test, greatness departed from him. However, he partially arose to the emergency, decrying the revolution and pointing the finger of blame at Pablo Montoya and "his den at Taos . . . composed of others as abandoned and desperate as their rebellious chief." And as a warning against more disorder he pointed out that "discreet and respectable men are anxiously awaiting the forces of Government in order to be relieved of the anarchy in which disorder has placed them, and this relief will speedily be afforded them."

The "forces of government" being awaited had been scattered into New Mexico in small detachments, and it was difficult for Colonel Price to concentrate them. Major Edmondson's detachment was in Albuquerque, as was Burgwin's, while others were across the mountains at Mora. Edmonson and Burgwin were ordered up the river, while Céran St. Vrain, seeing the revolt for what it was, called for volunteers to help suppress it, who fell into ranks at Santa Fe with no delay. The volunteers were chiefly Governor Bent's personal friends, clerks, and mountaineers—men of experience and courage.[1] Among the volunteer privates were Manuel Chávez and Nicolás Pino, accused conspirators in the Christmas Day abortive revolt who had just been released from prison after court-martial and acquittal.[2]

[1] The volunteer company was comprised of Céran St. Vrain, captain, ten subalterns, and fifty-seven privates.

[2] At the trial Chávez had been defended by Captain W. Z. Angney, one of Colonel

With these volunteers, who had all mounted themselves, Colonel Price took the road toward Taos, the news having filtered into Santa Fe that the insurgents were converging upon La Cañada de Santa Cruz with an army of fifteen hundred *Nuevo Mejicanos* and Indians. Less than two days later a battle took place, the Price army suffering two killed and six wounded, while the insurgents retraced their march northward up the Río Grande. This gave rise to another broadside from the "Provisional Governor of the Territory to its Inhabitants" which announced the rout of the insurgents "with the loss of many killed and 44 prisoners, upon whom the judgment of the law will fall. Their hosts were composed of scoundrels and desperadoes, so that it may be said that the war was one of the rabble against honest and discreet men." And for public consumption he prophesied "that within ten days the inquietude caused by the cry of alarm raised in Taos will cease, and peace . . . will return to take her seat on the altar of concord and reciprocal influence. . . . The ring leaders of the conspiracy . . . will receive the reward due to their signal crimes, and the government, which for the present has had to act with signal energy in order to crush the head of the revolutinary hydra, which began to show itself in Taos, will afterwards adopt lenient measures, in order to consolidate the union of all the inhabitants under the aegis of law and reason."

Two more battles took place as Price pushed the rebels northward, one at Embuda, the other at Pueblo de Taos, where the insurgents made their most determined stand within the adobe walls of the old Indian houses and church. Anticipating extermination, the rebels "humbly sued for peace." Price accepted the surrender contingent

Price's officers. Prior to the trial, while Chávez was a prisoner, Price had sent Angney to him to find out if he was aware of the plotting. Chávez' reply was courteous, convincing, and probably true: "Captain, be kind enough to take my compliments to General Price and say that he has nothing to fear from me now. When Armijo disbanded his volunteer army at Cañoncito, I gave up hope of being any service to my country at this time, and my record as a man will show you that I am not at all likely to sympathize with any movement to murder people in cold blood. Tell him, also, if the time ever comes when I can be of any service to my country, General Price will find me in the front ranks."

upon the delivery of Tomasito, their leader. Tomasito surrendered himself, but soon thereafter "he had an altercation with a soldier named Fitzpatrick in the guard room at San Fernandez," and he was shot. Tafolla, previous to the surrender, had been discovered by Céran St. Vrain wearing Governor Bent's coat and shirt. In a desperate fight, he too died. Big Nigger, a Delaware Indian, who had joined in the fight and claimed to have killed Captain Burgwin as he led an assault upon the Pueblo church, escaped when he saw the end was near. He later showed up in various places in New Mexico to brag of killing three or four regulars. Pablo Montoya contracted his life to less than two days when he surrendered, for Price, withdrawing from the pueblo to San Fernández de Taos, appointed a court-martial consisting of Lieutenant Eastin (judge-advocate), Captains, Angney, Barbee, and Slack, and Lieutenants Ingalls and White. On February 6, Montoya, with record dispatch, was arraigned, tried, and convicted, along with fourteen others. Upon conviction, the self-styled Santa Ana of the North was brought out with his convicted companions, and in front of the troops formed in ranks, was hanged unceremoniously. Mrs. Thomas Boggs, stepdaughter of Governor Bent gave a colorful account of this scene:

> I well remember how severely the soldiers punished the offenders. One favorite pastime was to harness six Indians to an army ambulance, and then at a signal put them on a run from the Pueblo to Taos. They would reach us exhausted, the crack of the driver's whip heralding their approach, with blood streaming from their unprotected backs and legs— one ambulance being followed by another and another, racing as they came on. And then when the soldiers tired of this sport their unfortunate captives ending their miserable existence at the end of a rope.[3]

After the summary execution of Pablo Montoya, Price withdrew his army from Taos to Santa Fe, bringing along a large number of prisoners. Governor Vigil thereupon distributed what he represented as being a résumé of the revolution, ascribing its origin to the Armijo administration, which was "apathetic and criminal" and encouraged

[3] *Denver Post*, January 11, 1890. Mrs. Boggs' account, however, is irreconcilable with Price's official report.

"popular commotions [which] gave so much encouragement to the perpetrators of these crimes." With courage, now that the insurrection was quelled, Vigil designated the authority for issuing a circular to the people the "Supreme Government of the Territory." Thereupon Colonel Price delivered into his custody all his prisoners, and Vigil felt the onus of his "difficult and thorny post," attempting to relieve himself of "the reins of government" by resigning to the President of the United States, suggesting Céran St. Vrain as his successor, and assuring the President that St. Vrain "would meet with the unanimous approval of the people . . . a native of Missouri, though an occasional resident of the Territory for many years back." Instead of making the appointment, the President referred the matter to Colonel Price, who—sensing St. Vrain's strength in New Mexico—reappointed Vigil.

But all was not quiet in New Mexico. Captain Hendley, at Las Vegas, heard of trouble at Mora, the capture by insurgent Cortez of a trading party, most prominent of whom was Lawrence L. Waldo. But before the Captain could arrive, the *Nuevo Mejicanos* had robbed and shot their prisoners. The captain attacked the town, was killed, and his detachment was forced to retreat—but not before twenty-five rebels had been killed and seventeen prisoners taken. Captain Morin succeeded to the command of the dead Hendley, returned to Mora, and according to his report, "razed the towns [Upper and Lower Mora] to the ground, the insurgents having fled to the mountains. Several Mexicans were captured."

Thus, with all northern New Mexico except Las Vegas and Tecolote in open rebellion, Colonel Price posted his troops with orders to be vigilant in detecting and suppressing disturbances. Thereafter "the conduct of the Mexicans was watched with the utmost scrutiny." They were deprived of their guns, their ammunition was confiscated, "nor was any Mexican cavalier suffered, as had hitherto been the case, to ride with impunity about the country, and through the American camps, displaying his weapons and warlike trappings. . . . A suspicious quietude reigned throughout the territory."[4]

Francis P. Blair, Jr., Kearny's appointee as United States attorney

[4] Connelley, *Doniphan's Expedition*, 519.

for New Mexico, had obtained a letter dated January 20, 1847, which named Don Antonio María Trujillo as inspector of arms for the revolutionists. Trujillo was one of Price's forty prisoners in Santa Fe, and against him Blair prepared an indictment for treason. At the March term of court the accused was tried, Chief Justice Joab Houghton presiding. Blair presented his unique indictment:

UNITED STATES OF AMERICA
Territory of New Mexico } —ss.

In the United States District Court, at the March Term, 1847.

The Grand Jurors for the District of New Mexico, on the part of the United States of America, on their oath present that Antonio Maria Trujillo, of the County of Taos, in the Territory of New Mexico, being a citizen of the United States of America, but disregarding his allegiance to the government of the United States aforesaid, and wholly withdrawing the allegiance, duty and obedience which every true and faithful citizen of the said government and of right ought to bear toward the citizens of the United States, on the 20th day of January, in the year 1847, and on diverse other days as well before as after, with force and arms, at the county aforesaid and Territory aforesaid, together with divers other false traitors, to the jurors aforesaid unknown, and did then and there maliciously, wickedly and traitorously levy war against the United States of America and did then and there maliciously and traitorously endeavour and attempt to subvert the laws and constitution of the government to the evil example of all others in like cases offending and against the peace and dignity of the government of the United States.

The defendant had no cause to complain about delay of justice, for he was immediately convicted, and the Honorable Judge Joab Houghton seemed to have been at his best when sentencing him. This he did in trenchant terms from his improvised bench where the defendant stood meekly before him.

Antonio Maria Trujillo! . . . Antonio Maria Trujillo! A jury of twelve citizens, after a patient and careful investigation, pending which all the safeguards of the law, managed by able and indefatigable counsel, have been offered you, have found you guilty of the high crime of treason. What have you to say why the sentence of death should not be pronounced against you?

Your age and gray hairs have excited the sympathy of both the court and the jury. Yet, while each and all were not only willing but anxious that you should have every advantage placed at your disposal that their highly responsible duty under the laws to their country would permit, you have been found guilty of the crime alleged to your charge. It would appear that old age has not brought you wisdom, nor purity, nor honesty of heart. While holding out the hand of friendship to those whom circumstances have brought to rule over you, you have nourished bitterness and hatred in your heart. You have been found seconding the acts of the most traitorous murders that ever blackened with the recital of their deeds the annals of history. Not content with the peace and security in which you have lived under the present government, secure in all your personal rights as a citizen, in property, in person, and in your religion, you gave your name and influence to measures intended to effect universal murder and pillage, and overthrow the government and one widespread scene of bloodshed in the land. For such foul crimes an enlightened and liberal jury has been compelled, from the evidence brought before them, and by a sense of their stern but unmistakable duty, to find you guilty of treason against the government under which you are a citizen. And there only now remains to the court the painful duty of passing upon you the sentence of the Law, which is that you be taken from hence to prison, there to remain until Friday, the 16th of April, next, and that, at 2 o'clock in the afternoon of that day, you be taken thence to the place of execution, and there be hanged by the neck until you are *dead! dead! dead! muerto! muerto! muerto!* And may the Almighty God have mercy on your soul!"

The last three words, obligingly translated by Judge Houghton into Spanish, were likely the only words the convicted Trujillo understood. But *"muerto, muerto, muerto"* did not come on the sixteenth of April; neither was the prisoner taken "from hence to the place of execution," for the voluble trial judge and the aspiring United States attorney both had doubts about the legality of executing a man for treason against a government to which he owed no allegiance. Consequently, with the connivance of both officials, Governor Vigil addressed himself to the Secretary of State asking the intervention of the President of the United States to grant a pardon "on the grounds of his age and infirmity." The President of the United States declined to act, suggesting that "clemency should be determined by Governor Vigil." Quietly Trujillo was pardoned and released from custody. The Secretary of War detected "the error of proceedings" against the rioters and on June 26 admonished Colonel Price to "prevent its recurrence."

Detection of the error of proceedings, however, came too late for the relief of "upward of forty prisoners confined in the northern district." The court after adjournment at Santa Fe had promptly gone to Taos. There the civil authorities were placed under the protection of Lieutenant Colonel Willock and his troops. Court opened with both Judges Houghton and Beaubien sitting at the trials. No one challenged the legality or even the propriety of such exercise of authority by one whose son had been killed by one of the prisoners at the bar. Neither did the Judge consider the impact it might have had upon the *Nuevo Mejicanos* had he left the dispensation of justice to one with less reason for revenge.

As it was, Judge Beaubien assumed the lead, calling six prisoners before the court. An onlooker saw them as "ill-favored, half-scared, sullen fellows." A jury of "Mexicans and Americans" was empaneled, "one Chadwick" gleefully accepting prominence as foreman. Blair, although again prosecuting, shared the renown with a fellow-Missourian, "one Wharton, a great blowhard." An observer left a description of the "gusty advocate from Old Mizzoo": "He was in his shirt sleeves, his hair uncombed, and, altogether . . . a rare specimen of that peculiar genus, known as a Missouri volunteer officer." The interpreter chosen was Mr. Céran St. Vrain, probably to give the affair a semblance of respectability. "When the witnesses (Mexican) touched their lips to the Bible, on taking the oath, [it was] . . . with reverential awe for the Book and fear of *los Americanos*. . . . The poor things were as much frightened as the prisoners at the bar."[5]

[5] Lewis H. Garrard, *Wah-to-yah and the Taos Trail,* 172.

Señora Bent, the late Governor's widow, and Señora Boggs, as well as Mrs. Christopher Carson, testified. "The dress and manner of the three ladies bespoke a greater degree of refinement than usual." Mrs. Bent pointed out the murderer of her husband. He was an Indian. Her identification sealed his death warrant, while he presented "a sublime spectacle of Indian fortitude."

The jury retired—an almost unnecessary formality—and was back in a few minutes. If for no other useful reason, retirement to the cloistered privacy of the jury room gave juror Baptiste, a little Frenchman "with not two ideas above eating and drinking," an opportunity to become initiated into the mystery of trial by jury and arraignment before a jury of peers. Young Lewis H. Garrard's account of the deliberations of the jury provides an insight into frontier American jurisprudence:

> On going into the consulting room, Baptiste went to Chad and asked —"Monsieur Chad*wick*! vot sall I say?" "Keep still man, until we talk awhile to the rest about it," rejoined Chad, "don't be in such a hurry."
>
> *"Oui! oui! eh bien! c'est bon; tres bien! mais Monsieur,* vot sall ve do do *avec sacré prisonniers—sacré enfants—"*
>
> "Baptiste! man, keep still; why, hang them, of course; what did you come in here for? . . . Wait until I am done with these Mexicans [part of the jury], and I will tell you what you must do."[6]

Under the tutelage of Chadwick the jury returned a verdict of guilty in the first degree. Five of the convicted men were to suffer the penalty for murder and one the penalty for treason. Announcing that the jail was overstocked with others awaiting trial and not willing to permit the prisoners to suffer the inconvenience of cramped jail-quarters, Judge Beaubien "deemed it expedient to hasten the execution," and set "next Friday" as the day—"next Friday" happening to be the following day. The hour determined upon was nine o'clock. Lieutenant Willock ordered out all the soldiers and called upon every American in Taos to come under arms; this was merely a precaution while "the reverend *padres,* on the solemn mission of administering

[6] *Ibid.,* 180–81.

the 'blessed sacrament' and spiritual consolation, in long black gowns and meek countenances, passed the sentinels."

The prison was at the edge of the town with no intervening houses between it and the fields to the north. Standing back some fifty yards from the jail was a new structure—two upright posts and a crossbeam. Someone had believed in preparedness. Long before nine o'clock the housetops in the vicinity were crowded with women and children. Eighteen soldiers fully armed marched out; then came six prisoners. With them walked the newly appointed sheriff, Metcalf. This new "arm of the law" had the distinction of being the son-in-law of the most popular saloonkeeper now that Turley, distiller of Taos Lightning, had died in the revolt.

Metcalf had been early at Estes' Tavern that morning. A crowd of restless early-morning drinkers had preceded him. He had come early to tie hempen cravats needed for the business of the morning. He, with curious volunteers, went into a conveniently accessible room adjacent to the bar. There they tried to tie the hangman's noose in one end of six ropes. The lariats were too stiff, so, with an eye to efficiency and profit, he brought forth a royal's worth of Mexican soap with which to soften all the ropes.[7] Presenting the Mexican soap to the volunteer noosemakers, "who were tugging away quite heartily," Metcalf said: "I've got something to make 'em fit—good 'intment— don't ermit very sweet parfume, but good 'nough for greasers; freeze into it, boys. This'll make 'em slip easy—a long ways too easy for them, I 'spect."

As Sheriff Metcalf went out to take his place behind the prisoners, he had on his arm six ropes laved with " 'intment." A steadily increasing number of mountaineers moved into place immediately behind the sheriff. They bristled with "Hawkins rifles" and "Green River" knives. An ominous precaution—a six-pound howitzer—was visible upon the roof of the jail, the muzzle trained at the crossbeam. A complement of soldiers stood ready, one with a lighted match in his hand. Colonel Willock moved to a position where he could view

---

[7] On Metcalf's statement of account appeared "to soft soap for greasing nooses . . . 12½¢."

the whole: 212 soldiers formed three sides of a hollow square about the crossbeam. A government wagon with team hitched stood under the gallows. The driver and sheriff assisted the six men to stand on the board lying across the bed of the wagon. Two stood in the middle, two on either side. "The ropes, by reason of size and stiffness despite the soaping given them, were adjusted with difficulty, but, through the indefatigable efforts of the sheriff and the lieutenant . . . all preliminaries were arranged. The latter, officiating as deputy sheriff for the occasion, seemed to enjoy the position—but the blue uniform looked sadly out of place on the hangman."

The stage was set. After "a few moments of intense expectation, the heart-wrung victims said a few words to their people. . . . The one sentenced for *treason* showed a spirit of martyrdom worthy of the cause for which he died . . . instead of the cringing . . . his speech was firm . . . . With a scowl, as the cap was pulled over his face . . . he uttered . . . *'Caraho, los Americanos!'* . . . at word from the sheriff the mules were started, and the wagon drawn from under the tree. No fall was given, and their feet remained on the board till the ropes drew taut. The bodies swayed back and forth . . . convulsive shudders shook their frames. . . . the hands of two came together, which they held with a firm grasp till the muscles loosened in death."[8]

The onlookers stood for some minutes; then the Colonel moved the troops away, while the ropes were slacked off. Another American had acted with forethought: he had passed the hat. Five dollars was contributed and sent ahead to Estes' Tavern, where eggnog with real American brandy was awaiting the dispersing throng. From the tavern a look back toward the north disclosed a group of widows with their dead husbands strapped across their backs slowly moving toward Pueblo de Taos.

Even before the Taos Revolt the *New York Tribune* had taken note of the domineering soldiery in Santa Fe. Its reporter, under date of December 5, 1846, had written:

> The clergy are our enemies, for reasons too obvious and too palpable to need mentioning here; the wealthy classes dislike our government.

[8] Garrard, *Wah-to-yah and the Taos Trail*, 197–98.

The patriotic must needs feel mortification and pain at seeing our people domineering in their homes; and the lower classes lived too long in a state of abject slavery, dependence and ignorance, to be at once capable of appreciating the benefits conferred upon them by the change of government. . . . Any body of men let loose without restraint in a corrupt and vicious population, like that in Santa Fe, will commit excesses, which must impair health, and such has been the case with most of the volunteers, to a frightful extent.[9]

Since "domineering" increased in intensity after the rebellion was crushed, "the disgraceful proceedings" again had the attention of newspapers in the "States." *"Affairs at Santa Fe"* was the headline of a newspaper which appeared June 12, 1847:

It is with feelings of profound sadness that we are obliged to record the disgraceful proceedings of our troops under Col. Price at Santa Fe. Their conduct has been characterized by the grossest insubordination; they plunder at their pleasure the defenseless Mexicans, and give to his complaints no answer save contumelious reproaches or disgraceful blows.

In all the abandonment of military license, the soldiers pass the day, and riots occupy the night. About one-fifth of the whole command have died from the effects of dissipation. No order prevails, no attempts at coercion is made: "the soldiers"—says one account—"are never drilled or mustered, and from the highest officer to the private soldier all is insubordination, misrule and confusion." The license they accord to the soldiers, the officers practice themselves. They keep gambling halls and groggeries—occupations to which some of them perhaps were formerly accustomed, before they assumed the still more disgraceful part of marauders, plunderers and murderers. They cheat and brow-beat the natives by day, and when night comes, "flown with insolence and wine," they resort to the fandangoes, and give full scope to their unbridled passions.

The officer in command, Col. Price, but late a Loco-Foco member of Congress, either from sympathy, indifference, or fear of losing popularity, winks at all the excesses of the soldiery. . . .

The Indians are another source of constant alarm and disaster to the

[9] Issue of March 3, 1848, p. 1., col. 5.

miserable inhabitants; against the incursion of such enemies Ge. Kearney promised them the ample security of his forces—a promise which he has never even attempted to fulfil—and one, perhaps, the performance of which the deceived and abused Mexican would not solicit—for he has more cause to fear his civilized, than his barbarous foe. . . . Who can wonder at the insurrection of the insulted, outraged, plundered inhabitants? Have they not cause for their hatred of our name and authority? Have we not justified their attempted vengeance?[10]

With such criticisms before him, Secretary of War Marcy could no longer refrain from warning Colonel Price of the dangers incident to lack of discipline. This warning he gave in an almost apologetic letter, dated June 20, 1847:

You will, I trust, excuse an allusion to another subject not officially before me: I mean the state of discipline of our troops at Santa Fe. Though I am far from giving credence to the newspaper accounts . . . they ought not to pass entirely unnoticed, and may be permitted to caution on that point. As commanding officer you cannot err in an isolated situation like yours, in enforcing the most rigid rules of discipline. The welfare of the men composing your command, as well as its safety, and the interest of your country, committed to your custody, require that the most careful attention be given to the important matter.[11]

Secretary Marcy's wrist-slapping corrective had little effect upon Price's management of his troops. He did, however, move some of them out on the Santa Fe Trail as escorts to traders continually being harassed by Indians. One of the members of such an escort was the volunteer lieutenant who helped the sheriff at Taos. This flamboyant Missouri volunteer was overtaken by Garrard upon his return to the "States." "Volunteer-like," reported Garrard, as he described the troops lack of discipline, "they were in the rear, at the side, and in advance of their commander; they disregarding military deference, he military control. For a mile and a half, others were strung along

10 The article, dated June 12, 1847, appeared in an unknown newspaper. A clipping is on file in the Museum of New Mexico library at Santa Fe, but its source is not subject to identification.

11 Marcy to Price, 31 Cong., 1 sess., *House Exec. Doc. No. 17, New Mexico and California, 1847–1850*, p. 253.

the trace, in irregular squads, riding, sauntering carelessly, some without arms, and a few with muskets, beating the sage bushes for hares. On passing the three baggage wagons, the first lieutenant—the same who helped the sheriff at the Taos execution—poked his head from under the wagon-sheet. . . . He shouted as I passed—'How are ye— would ye like to hang any more Mexicans? Now wasn't that a tall time down to Touse?' "

Exactly one month after Secretary Marcy had given Price the letter of warning, Price was elevated to brigadier general. But the state of communications between New Mexico and Washington City had not permitted him to learn of the promotion. Therefore, after the August 3 executions, "Old Pap"—as the soldiers were calling him—relieved himself of command and went east, letting Lieutenant Colonel E. W. R. Newby succeed him. It took the relief commander two months to understand the significance of the troop disorders and to take cognizance of Marcy's mild warning. On September 24, he issued Order No. 10 from his headquarters:

> It appearing that not withstanding the repeated and strenuous efforts heretofore made to the contrary a woeful want of sobriety, good order and subordination, yet prevails in and at this post, which greatly threatens, which if not entirely checked effectually, will bring fatal disease and lasting disgrace upon the army of New Mexico. It being deemed indispensably necessary in order to prevent the one as a means of avoiding the other that strong restrictions should be imposed.

The strong restrictions included forbidding the sale or furnishing of intoxicants to soldiers and prohibiting attendance at fandangoes. An impetus to the latter decision was found in what *The Republican* called "An Unexpected Disturbance at a Fandango," the result being, according to G. R. Gibson, editor, "the death of Mr. Wm. H. Holt from a pistol shot . . . done by Mr. Christian Milt, of the Artillery. Such things the commanding officer is determined to punish and suppress be they Americans or Mexicans; and although the case is among our own men, judgment and justice will be rigidly adhered to, and strictly enforced, as if a soldier had been killed by a civilian."

And to the death of this soldier, who "belonged to Captain Grove's company . . . a steady, inoffensive man," *The Republican's* News of the Week column added violence between *Nuevo Mejicanos:*

MURDER

September 24, 1847: MURDER—On Wednesday Jesus Leva was killed on the outskirts of the town and Lorenzo Tafolla has been arrested charged with murder.

In town, the military was having its troubles, too:

CAPT. DE KARPONY—This gallant officer exhibited his resolution a few days ago by arresting when no other could, an individual who drew his pistol and snapped it at him, swearing he could not, nor would not be arrested; but the Captain . . . seized upon him and felled him to the earth, holding him until the guard secured him.[12]

Thereafter the News of the Week "noted with pleasure that Captain Karpony has been appointed Col. Newby's aid, and is now discharging the duties of that station." Then Colonel Newby acted again, whereupon "Santa Fe was more orderly and quiet owing a great deal to the satisfactory manner in which Capt. Jones, Marshall [*sic*], discharges his duties." Sustained order and quietude were not to be established as within the Santa Fe tradition. There emerged from the town a complete disregard of Order No. 10, particularly in regard to "unauthorized fandangoes, balls and dances." *The Republican* joined in the clamor: "What would we do in New Mexico without a little fun and frolic of this kind? What would kill old *Time* so well?" And as if to punctuate the return to the old order (that is, disorder), Editor Gibson disclosed the holding of "a fandango on the other side of the Rio Chito, last night, given by Mr. Smith," commenting, "if joviality is any recommendation, we can with truth, say it might have been found there." And to forecast that Mr. Smith's fandango was but the beginning of the reversal, it announced, "The Santa Fe House also expects to figure some day *Seminaria proximo,* all of which the Señors and Señoras shall have timely notice of!"[13]

[12] *Santa Fe Republican,* September 24, 1847.
[13] On October 9 a fandango was advertised for the Missouri House, "got up in

Portentuous news came from Socorro while Colonel Newby evaluated the general and open revolt against Order No. 10. Mutiny had come to Lieutenant Merrit's detachment. To suppress the revolt against military authority, Newby ordered, "Troops [to be] moved south out of Santa Fe to camp near Fra Christoval." Reports soon came up the river detailing "acts of violence upon the citizens," which caused *The Republican* to join with New Mexico citizens in opposition to the usurpations of the military. On September 24, the newspaper took its stand:

> RIO ABAJO—We learn from several sources that the troops which have gone south are guilty of many unjust and uncalled for acts of violence upon the citizens of the lower part of the territory, and that there are complaints about the manner in which they passed through the country. It is no more proper for a soldier to commit acts of aggression or depredation upon the people who are told by our highest authorities that the country is annexed to the United States, and that they are required to act as citizens, than it would be for a citizen to be guilty of the same offense. . . . The people of the Rio Abajo have always remained peaceful and quiet and deserve better treatment, and if we carry on a war with them, let it be open, and not against the individuals who take part in it. The country is claimed as a part of Texas, and virtually, if not in fact, annexed, and all who are peaceful and orderly deserve the treatment of citizens, and from the beginning have been recognized and claimed as such. We feel bound to say this much from the many complaints made to us by Americans, as well as others.

The innocuousness of Colonel Newby made it good news when it was learned that Colonel Price had not only been promoted but was returning to the New Mexico command. *The Republican* simulated an announcement "with pleasure" of his appointment as brigadier general and hoped "by next month to have him with us. . . . a just return for the hardships, responsibilities and labor which he underwent . . . in the severe Taos Campaign last winter." However,

the best style and is expected to be one of the finest ever given in Santa Fe." On the eleventh, Hovey and Company "gave another of their select parties which was well attended and passed off pleasantly." Further, they announced that they "will continue to give them every night throughout the winter."

72

when news reached the territory before the arrival of Price that two regiments of volunteers, one of infantry, one of cavalry, a "full Infantry battalion, and another battalion of mixed cavalry and Artillery," were on march to New Mexico, the Santa Fe *New Mexican* reacted with mixed emotions:

> The whole territory is now shingled over with troops, the morning sun witnessing the display of glittering arms from the most northern settlements to the State of Chihuahua. Every town of any consequence has a drum or fife, or the martial notes of the bugle, to announce that the country is under military rule, and every valley sees some of the means and appliances of war which the young Republic of the North is able to bring against her enemies.[14]

But since there was yet war between Mexico and the United States, the newspaper labeled it "a grateful sight." It was a particularly grateful sight to "Americans possessing resources and much wealth."

But "shingling over" the territory with troops and promoting colonels to generals did little to change the situation in the New Mexico towns. Thomas Fitzpatrick, by no means a newcomer to Santa Fe, returned to find "conditions in New Mexico *deplorable!*" Specifically, "drunkenness was common, vice and crime was rampant." And he was "disgusted with the life of the soldiers." Even Céran St. Vrain spoke out: "A worse state of things has not existed in the country since I came here." The veteran fur trapper, mountaineer, merchant, freighter, hero of the Battle of Taos, and runner-up for governor decided to bow out of the capital and establish himself amid the tranquility of the Mora Valley. He made his decision public and invited the public "to come and examine," since his merchandise was for sale. The Honorable Judge Joab Houghton did "come and examine" and lingered long enough to purchase St. Vrain's entire stock of goods in both stores.

The Honorable Judge Joab Houghton, well known as a jurist but less so as a merchant, thereupon seized upon fortuitous incidents to place his new status before the Mexican people. Not only was Céran St. Vrain leaving Santa Fe, but St. Vrain's comrade-in-arms at the

14 The *New Mexican,* November 13, 1847.

73

Battle of Taos, W. Z. Angney, was assuming a high place in New Mexico. He had just been elected to the legislature. Judge Houghton thereupon decided it was appropriate that the citizens should assemble and pay their respects. Taking the initiative he advertised a dinner:

To THE BRAVE

The citizens of Santa Fe, wishing to give some evidence of their high regard to Capts. Angney and St. Vrain, are making arrangements to give them a dinner or a supper for their gallant conduct as soldiers and gentlemanly deportment as citizens. The subscription list is at the store of E. J. Vaughan where all who wish to participate can call and enter their names. No day has yet been fixed for the dinner, but it will come off soon, as Capt. St. Vrain has sold out his stock of goods and returns to the U.S., and the other, being a member of the legislature will soon have all his time occupied in the discharge of his duties as representative.[15]

Just what duties Representative Angney would be permitted to perform as a legislator was not clear. This the *New Mexican* pointed out, laying emphasis upon the increasing arbitrament of the military authorities:

The civil authorities seem to be so completely overpowered by the military that it would be a matter of supererogation [could the *Nuevo Mejicanos* understand the word?] to act, unless General Price, when he comes, is empowered and *disposed* to give more independence to their [the legislature's] acts. Of course, we cannot tell what will be done, but he is daily expected here.

Preparations for the St. Vrain-Angney dinner so completely absorbed the interest of Santa Feans that General Price's arrival went almost unnoticed. At the dinner, however, Judge Houghton, presiding as toastmaster, took notice of the presence of General Price in Santa Fe, reading from his prepared notes: "Gen. Price—the intrepid soldier. We hail his return with Joy." But as the General was conspicuous by his absence from the dinner, the toastmaster felt called upon to "explain in justification," saying: "The only thing that does not meet our approbation is the absence of the commanding officer of the Department, whose presence would have been agreeable to us,

[15] *Santa Fe Republican,* November 27, 1847.

and, we think, highly appropriate. But it is proper to say that, under the circumstances, he necessarily would not attend."

Despite the absence of the miffed General, "the army was well represented . . . by many who seemed to think it a proper occasion to shew a 'light fantastic toe.' " In all, "the elite of the city were out to pay their respects to our estimable fellow citizens . . . and the beauty and fashion of the city . . . made a brilliant assemblage."

Three weeks passed with the returned Brigadier General again in command, and *The Republican* eked out faint praise, being "happy to hear that there had been a stop put to so many fandangoes in the night—and particularly to those on the other side of the Rio Chicito—as they invariably break up in a 'Row,' and should they continue would no doubt terminate in the death of some person before spring."

Since General Price contemplated a march southward into Chihuahua to share in the plaudits being ladled out to Colonel Doniphan, he decided to take a page from Kearny's book, differentiate between "fandangos" and "parties" and direct attention to himself before leaving Santa Fe. Consequently, there being an anniversary to celebrate, he fastened upon February 4—the anniversary of the Battle of Taos—as the date. What must have been his chagrin when the local papers almost forgot to mention him and his "party." *The Republican* did say, however:

> 1848—Feb. 4 Gen Price & Staff gave a splendid party at the Palace in honor of the battle of Pueblo Taos Valley. Never was there a dance passed off more pleasnat [*sic*] than on this occasion. Most of the citizens were invited & many of the heroes of the battle were present.

The day following the Battle of Taos party, the General set about enforcing Newby's Order No. 10 by putting "Santa Fe and citizens under military control, prohibiting gambling, or giving intoxicants to soldiers," according to *The Republican*.[16] Being aware of the fact that the President of the United States had not changed the orders under which Kearny had taken possession of and exercised control over New Mexico, General Price now essayed similar powers for himself. First, he abolished the civil offices of territorial secretary, district

16 *Ibid.*, February 5, 1848.

attorney, and United States marshal, declaring them "unnecessary." Then, encroaching upon the legislative branch (a convention then being in session to try to form a legislature), he decreed an impost duty upon merchandise entering the region and licensed gambling, fixing the fee at two thousand dollars per annum; and when the convention demurred, threatened that honorable body, letting the legislators know that "all power" was his. For a warning he published an "Address":

> You can now secure the protection of a government which imposes no bonds upon the conscience, which will protect you in the unmolested enjoyment of your personal, political and religious rights, under the regulation of equal laws. In short, you have it in your power to secure for New Mexico all the rights and privilages of citizens under the freest government in the world. . . . And [addressing himself to the convention] I express the hope that, in view of your serious and important duties, the deliberation of the convention will be conducted with the strictest propriety and decorum; and though the right freely and properly to express opinions shall not be restricted, yet I desire all to understand that seditious and indecorous language against the constituted military or civil authorities, calculated to inflame or excite the people against the government, my desire for peace and welfare for the Territory will induce me immediately to notice. The utterers of such language will be held responsible and called to a strict account."[17]

To show in what contempt the military organization was held, when a "soldier by the name of 'Sterling,' during the firing of the National Salute at the conclusion of tattoo on that same day accidently discharged a cannon and so seriously injured himself on the left arm as to cause immediate amputation," there was no evidence of public regret. Shortly after the tragic incident contempt for the army took another and waggish turn. This time Santa Fe's "valiant young men" bowed ever so facetiously to the spirit of Price's military regimentation, now being sporadically enforced by Major Benjamin L. Beall. The Republican played up the incident under a headline:

[17] *Ibid.*, May 31, 1848; in Twitchell, *Leading Facts*, II, 267.

RATHER REDICULOUS [*sic*]

Saturday morning of this week a verbal order was issued by some of our city functionaries of a rather singular nature which shows that we are about having some laws enforced. The order was . . . that all dogs that were found running at large in the streets should be immediately put to death; Therefore, many of our valiant young men being anxious to show their military skill armed themselves with muskets, pistols, and sallied forth to meet the enemy in battle array. And our little city was nothing but confusion during the day. The distant reports of the firing was heard while the yelping of dogs and braying of burros re-echoed throughout the distant hills; and long before the sun disappeared over the western horizon the enemy was entirely put to flight. Not only were they killed on the public streets in the presence of some of our dignitaries, who laughed at the fun and cheered the heroes of the battle-field for their military valour, but it did not stop in our streets, but they even entered the houses and corrals, driving the "enemy of dogs" from their ambush, killing many a watch- or family-dog which we do say was most shameful and ridiculous, and shall leave it to the readers to say which was the *dog party*.[18]

While relations between the *Nuevo Mejicanos* and the military was at this low stage (many Anglos now siding with the native population), news came that "Ex-Governor Armijo is soon to visit the city," whereupon *The Republican* spoke guardedly: "We would be happy to see his excellency and trust that he will be treated with proper respect by the citizens and soldiers of this place."[19]

General Price, having brought, as he thought, New Mexico to heel, marched as far as Santa Cruz de Rosalia; there he forced a fight upon the Mexican army—the last of the war—despite the urging of the Mexican general to hold off as the heads of the armies were observing an armistice and that to "fight would be illegal." Price, having lost communication with his superiors, judged the Mexican avowals by previous conduct and pushed the battle to victory, thus annexing dubious laurels. After the battle, he turned his army back up the Río Grande and to his Santa Fe headquarters. Then—with the war over

[18] *Santa Fe Republican*, May 3, 1848.
[19] Twitchell, *The Military Occupation of New Mexico, 1846–1851.*

—he headed his troops eastward along the Santa Fe Trail, leaving Colonel John M. Washington to worry about keeping the peace among the three peoples.

Although he assumed command in September, 1848, Colonel Washington succeeded in doing nothing until August 22, 1849, when, after inviting volunteer *Nuevo Mejicanos* and Pueblo Indians to join with his forces, he set out with 350 men to "over awe" the Navahos. His attitude was one of bearing a rifle in one hand and an olive branch in the other. The emblem of peace might have held sway at a pow-wow at Tunicha had not a dispute come up over a horse, whereupon the Indians were fired at, their chief killed, and the tribe fled for their lives. But Colonel Washington, if anything, was a sanguine man. He followed the Indians to Cañon de Chelly, and there amid a smoke-fest the Navahos again made their marks upon a treaty of peace. Thinking he had accomplished what he intended, he took the long route back to Santa Fe, only to learn that the Navahos had preceded him, stealing horses and mules as they watched the near-by American flag wave gently on its staff in the plaza.

On October 23, 1849, Colonel John M. Washington gave up his command to John Munroe, who forthwith arrogated to himself the title of "civil and military governor" of New Mexico. Needless to say, this arrogant presumptuousness immediately intensified opposition to arbitrary military rule. Prior to Munroe's arrival two political parties had gradually formed lines of difference, their only common interest being a desire to break the military hold upon civil affairs in New Mexico. One political faction became the advocate of the formation of a state from the New Mexico Territory; the other favored continuing the government as a territory subject to Congressional supervision. Adherents of the territorial form of government wanted "the speedy organization of a territorial civil government." To them "the organic and statute laws promulgated under military orders of September 22, 1846, with some alterations, would be acceptable." The alterations consisted of the appointment by the President of the United States of the governor, secretary of state, attorney general, and United States marshal. Too, they thundered against "the dismemberment of our Territory in favor of Texas, or from any cause." They did not want "domestic slavery," which, of course, placed the "State party" within the Southern States alignment.

A memorial sent to Congress, signed by thirteen delegates who assembled in Santa Fe,[20] accomplished little, other than to induce members of Congress to consider the legal and political status of the newly acquired region. Its legal status was anomalous, like no other section of the Union; its political status was becoming increasingly important to both the North and the South, now rapidly coming to grips over the question of human slavery. Furthermore, no one knew what were the physical confines of the newly acquired land. The southern boundary between New Mexico and Mexico had yet to be fixed, and Texas was growing increasingly vocal, as well as aggressive, regarding her unorganized counties reaching to the Río Grande. Not only was Texas asserting her position on the matter of boundary, but the Treaty of Guadalupe Hidalgo signed with Mexico made it of the most importance to determine *what is New Mexico?*

[20] Twitchell, *Leading Facts*, II, 267.

CHAPTER FIVE

"A DELICATE CRISIS"

IN ORDER TO DETERMINE just what territory New Mexico encompassed, it was also necessary to determine the limits of Texas. Since 1836, when the quaking Santa Ana had signed a secret agreement following his defeat at San Jacinto, Texas had claimed all the land east of the Río Grande. Article 4 of that agreement read: "A treaty of commerce, amity, and limits, will be established between Mexico and Texas, the territory of the latter not to extend beyond the Río Bravo del Norte [Río Grande]." Since Santa Ana at the time was indubitably not a free agent, to say nothing of a free man, the legality of the instrument was dubious. And even though the Río Grande was not actually specified as the boundary, Texas nevertheless assumed the position that the Santa Ana agreement was merely a confirmation of limits always theretofore acknowledged by Mexico. The area north of El Paso and east of the Río Grande became more controversial when Governor Armijo ruthlessly wiped out the efforts of the Republic of Texas to establish jurisdiction over the controversial region through the Texan–Santa Fe Expedition. The territory remained in status quo after that—Texas claiming, Mexico holding—until the Lone Star Republic became the state of Texas, thus transferring her claims to the United States and bringing on war with Mexico.

In making the New Mexico invasion, Kearny carried a proclamation announcing the annexation of all the territory east of the Río Grande, and Captain Philip St. George Cooke, recognizing the wording, declared that he was thus "adopting the old claim of Texas." Again, at Las Vegas, as has been related, the invading commander told the people that he came to take possession of their country and extend the laws of the United States over it: "We consider it, and have done so for some time, a part of the territory of the United States."

Although Kearny's avowals, of course, were not binding upon the *Nuevo Mejicanos,* they did represent recognition by the United States of Texas' claim. And it was not until the people of New Mexico had, by peaceful acquiescence, surrendered to Kearny that the invader became the conqueror and announced his plan to take the territory to the Pacific, which in no way disavowed his earlier statements that the area to the Río Grande was considered by the United States as a part of her territory.

The boundary matter lay dormant until March 23, 1848, when Governor George T. Wood of Texas advised the President of the United States of Texas' legislative enactments on the subject:

> Sir:—The legislature of the State of Texas, at its session just closed, passed laws to organize into a county the territory of Santa Fe and establish therein a Judicial District; and as rumor has reached this State of an attempt to establish there a separate government, it is apprehended that impediments may be thrown in the way of the contemplated organization. In view of such a contingency, the Legislature of Texas made it the duty of the Executive . . . to request your Excellency to issue orders to the military authorities stationed in Santa Fe to aid the officers of Texas in organizing the county of Santa Fe and the 11th Judicial District of the State of Texas, and in enforcing the laws of this State, if it should be necessary to call upon said officers of the United States to put down any resistance to the laws of Texas . . . to the end that the State of Texas may, in no wise, be embarrassed in the exercise of her rightful jurisdiction over that territory.

The Republican, admittedly under the control of the military establishment at Santa Fe, took notice of Texas' appeal to the President of the United States, and assumed the attitude of the scoffer. Under a leaded heading it said:

TEXAS CLAIM

We are disposed to laugh at the complacency with which the Governor and the Legislative Committee of Texas, in solemn council assembled, advanced the preposterous claim, but we regret to state that the *smile* is not the only thing excited by a perusal of this strange document. *Contempt and Pity!* Contempt for the names who set up such a claim, and pity that so many fools could be found in a free and enlightened state to sanction it. . . . Upon what rights, real or fancied, does the Legislature of Texas enact the law of December 18th, A.D., 1836 . . .? Was it *conquest* or was it *purchase?* We have yet to learn that a Texian soldier ever trod the soil of New Mexico other than with his ears cut off, or as a prisoner of war; and as for purchase, the actual financial condition of Texas is a sufficient evidence that such purchase was never made. . . . but thanks to our friends—the traitors [shall] have plenty of tar and feathers!"[1]

A week later the military-controlled newspaper made a call to the *Nuevo Mejicanos,* now that there was a *casus belli* opposition to the terrible *Tejanos,* probably intended to weaken the schism between adherents of the State and Territorial parties:

CITIZENS ATTEND!

There will be a meeting of the citizens during the week for the purpose of responding to the unjust and unexpected claim of Texas in regard to our territory . . . and punctual attendance will be expected.[2]

Inasmuch as few Santa Feans knew for what purpose they were being required to attend punctually, *The Republican* deemed it to be its duty to "inform the people of New Mexico regarding the proceedings of the legislature of that state in relation to New Mexico." It therefore quoted the *New Orleans Delta* as an authority, viz:

A bill has passed both houses [of the Texas Legislature] establishing the County of Santa Fe. Two other bills have also passed, one for organizing the militia of the county of Santa Fe, and the other to establish the 11th Judicial District to be formed in that County. A Judge and District Attorney are to be forthwith appointed, and sent out to put things to rights.

Then, to set the pattern of thinking for those who would attend the mass meeting, *The Republican* editorialized, extending "information to our Texian friends that it is not necessary to send us a judge, nor

<hr>

[1] *Santa Fe Republican,* July 24, 1848.   [2] *Ibid.,* August 1, 1848.

a district attorney to settle our affairs, or put things to rights, for there is not a citizen, either American or Mexican, that will ever acknowledge themselves as citizens of Texas until it comes from higher authority. New Mexico does not belong, nor has Texas even a right to claim her as part of Texas. We would also advise Texas to send with her civil officers for this county a large force in order that they may have a sufficient bodyguard to escort them back in safety. . . . O Texans do show some little sense and drop this question and not have it publicly announced that Texas' smartest men were tarred and feathered by attempting to fill the offices assigned them."

After waiting vainly from March until mid-September, 1848, for President Polk's assurance that the army might be called on if its services should be required to establish Texas laws in New Mexico, Texas acted. On September 22, 1848, Judge Spruce McCoy Baird, recently appointed judge of the Eleventh Judicial District, wrote from Lexington, Missouri, that he would "start for Santa Fe Wednesday next." He was going in his official capacity, and could but trust "from present information we will have but little difficulty in organizing."

The delay in President Polk's decision and the furor which had been raised by the military clique dominating New Mexico (*The Republican* being spokesman), joined in by prominent Americans who saw the boundary question inseparable from the slavery question, caused Governor Wood to question Baird's trust that there would be "little difficulty in organizing." He, upon hearing that Baird was en route, with a statesman-like precision not theretofore displayed by him, cogently presented anew the full Texas–New Mexico boundary controversy, pointing to "the manifestation of the disposition on the part of some of the public men of the Union, to deprive them [i.e., Texas] of a large and valuable portion of their [her] territory . . . at the disregard of right and the violation of faith involved in this attempt." In other words, the United States, standing in a position of power, was attempting to divest Texas of land recognized to be hers when Texas became a part of the United States. And he again called upon the President to "instruct the United States officers in Santa Fe to extend every lawful aid to Judge Baird."

On the evening of November 10, 1848, Judge Baird arrived in "Santa Fe, Texas," as he notified the Texas secretary of state, "after an arduous journey across the plains," and was "about to assert the jurisdiction of Texas over this country." He found "Colonel Washington acting as Governor at present under the former organization of Gen'l Kearney, which I think is a little extraordinary in its character." His arrival was so recent, however, that he "had become acquainted with but few individuals," but he would devote some time "to that purpose" before taking "any steps toward an organization." Before the passing of the first day, he became aware "that there are some opposed to our claim and some in favor." He would "use every prudent step to accomplish the business" for which he came.

Thereafter for ten days he took "prudent steps," the first being a "rather formal letter" *to his Excellency J. M. Washington,* carefully omitting "Texas" after the Santa Fe date-line. After considering the salutation, he concluded that although "it may appear rather fulsome," he was "under the impression that he [Washington] assumed those titles," but Washington "disabused me by his reply subsequently [and] I dropped that nonsense and addressed him as 'Colonel.'" With the amenities out of the way, the Judge told the Colonel that "in obedience to his duties prescribed by law," he had come to Santa Fe and found "your excellency exercising military and civil duties over a portion of the territory which the State of Texas claims, and is unquestionably entitled to, while believing, from the information which I had on the subject, that that jurisdiction had ceased on the notification of a treaty of peace with Mexico." He told the Colonel also that "judging from the impass of the chief executive in regard to New Mexico, we [Texas] are forced to the conclusion that he [the President of the United States] recognizes the right of the State of Texas to assume civil jurisdiction over that part of New Mexico east of the Rio Grande at any time." With this notice of intention Baird disclaimed any intention of coming "in conflict with that of the temporary government [Washington]" and asked that the Colonel not "attempt any efficient measures within the limits of my duties." Then he added bluntly: "It will be appara [*sic*] to your

84

Excellency that for the future the State of Texas must regard all judicial proceeding and the exercise of all functions inconsistent with her laws and constitution null and void."

This brought the diplomatic exchanges to a collision. Ignoring the title of "judge" and addressing Baird as "esquire," the "Brevet Lieutenant Colonel, commanding," replied with military supereminence: "I shall continue the existence of the Government over the Territory of New Mexico at every peril and shall only desist when the Executive or the supreme legislative power of the United States shall so ordain." Having been presented with Judge Baird's instructions along with the Texas legislative enactments, Colonel Washington "perused them with interest." He "returned them with thanks," adding, "When they appear at the proper time and before the proper tribunal, I have no doubt they will receive all the consideration which should be extended to them in the way of establishing claims." Then, as if to forestall any effort Judge Baird might make to bring the situation before the New Mexican people, Colonel Washington apprised the benchless judge that "the press . . . belongs to the General Government, and must, of course, be under its control."

Sans a bench upon which to sit and lacking an army to enforce his mandate from Texas, "Esquire" Baird turned to an evaluation of the population. One-third, he thought, were "west of the Del Norte— and consequently out of the limits of Texas— leaving a population within the limits of Texas of some 20,000 to 25,000." Excluding the Pueblo Indians, he estimated three-fourths "were *peons,* without *education or honesty,* and many of them without shirts, shoes, or hats, and *not worthy to be trusted in any way.* . . . The remainder, to say the least of them, are Mexicans; and it is with such materials that these office-seekers, who are officious in that country, hope to form a territorial government. . . . As to the Mexicans, the world knows them to be incapable of self government either for the want of capacity or integrity . . . [and] they are able to control everything." He "did not take into consideration the American population, for . . . it is so small, compared with the Mexican population, as to amount to almost nothing—not sufficient, when the Mexicans are unarmed by military dictation, to exert even a conservative influence." Add to that, "however capable the Americans may be of self-government, it is a fact undisguised . . . that the most heartless and barefaced corruption has been, and continues to be practiced here that you can imagine." The army "gives tone to public sentiment. Some of them, while they hold onto their military commissions, are constantly on the look-out for promotion in the civil government they contemplate organizing and . . . are assiduous in manufacturing as much prejudice as possible against Texas." He attributed the efforts toward governmental guidance to "those who are trying to run ahead of fame," which "have invariably been abortion." He made one exception: "Genl. Kearneys & that was a monster."

Of the people with whom he had become acquainted, he had found one, a *Neuvo Mejicano,* "the very mention of [whose] name to Texans was *anathema marantha!* [That is, if Texans ever prayed.] He was Salazar, who had the Santa Fe *insanes* murdered and so evilly treated: he lives not far from here abhored [*sic*] by all good men . . . but thinks his life and property in danger from the Texans and will move shortly." What influence he had with the New Mexicans, Baird did not know.

He had also made the acquaintance of General Armijo, who espoused the cause of Texas "with zeal." He explained the source of the zeal: "I bought him out, lock, stock and barrel. He showed me General McClouds[3] regimentals and says no other Mexican general can exhibit such trophies." As for other *Nuevo Mejicano* acquaintances, "the material of which they wish to form a state," he thought, "Many of them, and perhaps all, are clever men: it is only their political pretensions at Santa Fe I am disposed to call in question." Some of them are "men who have grown into officials in the breath of a moment by the wildest and most misguided freak [i.e. Kearny's "Monstrosity" Code] and never dreamed of such aspirations before

[3] General Hugh McLeod of the Texan–Santa Fe Expedition is intended. Salazar was Armijo's subaltern who cut off the ears of McLeod's men and nailed them to the jail door in Santa Fe.

and now will not relinquish their stations without a struggle. Their capacity to fill those offices is not a question with them.

"As to the Americans—they with the exception of one or two are transient persons and feel no interest in the matter further than a little petty ambition. Captain Chapman lives in Mo. As the captain of a volunteer company he happened to be posted in Rio Arriba. Dr. Naugh lives in Santa Fe and is a merchant, but as there is not room for him to be elected from there he goes on a political venture and is also returned from Rio Arriba. Maj. Weightman lives in Mo. or perhaps in Washington City—was formerly paymaster but being superseded takes a temporary turn at politics as most men passing through the country do. Mr. Ashurt . . . is a California gold miner, and, from some adventitious circumstance, was induced to call at Santa Fe and dip into politics *a little*. Judge Houghton is Supreme Judge of the Territory—and I have learn [*sic*] that a short time since Major Weightman charged him in open court with partiality. The judge, without the least disparagement of his dignity, after adjournment, challenged the Maj to single combat. They took one shot & thus the matter stands—new mode of punishing a contempt in a lawyer—pretty good, too."[4]

The mass meeting called by *The Republican* when it became known that Texas was preparing to organize the Eleventh Judicial District caused "much excitement as to the manner in which it had been gotten up and conducted," and Judge Baird upon his arrival "found the convention excitement still alive." Too, he said, "without intending to disparage our worthy citizens of this remote region . . . there was real or affected ignorance of the whole matter [the boundary question]. Therefore, partly to evade the labor of reiterating the same thing over & over & over to every one who might be inquiring on the subject, and partly at the request of citizens . . . I was induced to declare publicly the grounds upon which our claim and right to the

[4] Judge Baird's letter, November 6, 1849, to the Secretary of State, in the Texan–Santa Fe Papers, Texas State Archives, Austin; also, AC, "Texan–Santa Fe Papers," No. 129.

territory rests, consequently, notices to that effect [that is, that he would make a public statement in person about the matter]."

The announcement brought him an unexpected caller, known to him only as "the hero of the Battle of Taos," "a Capt. Angney, who figured there as captain of millitia [*sic*], a lawyer by profession from Mo.—and speaker of the Territorial legislature." The visitor came, so he said, "to honor me and to call on me to know if I would approbate his making a speech also." The Judge consented to a joint appearance, "letting him do just as his vanity and ambition prompted him." For self-recommendation Angney assured the Judge that he "need not suspect him as seeking any advantage," for he was "a verry plain, open, candid, straightforward honest sort of fellow." In this fellow Baird "thought he saw a fine prospect of his ending his career like the negroes by 'jumping so high he would break his neck.' " To Baird someone confided that Angney "had just returned from a pilgrimage to that far-off and renouned city—the City of washington—for what purpose he visited, Angney did not state—but it is conjectured that he was seeking the appointment of 'Lord Horse of the Mountain' or some similar office."

The evening arrived, and the speakers were "flattered by a crowded audience." Baird delivered an explanation in which he felt "there not much force." *The Republican* said "it was not altogether correct." Captain Angney "followed . . . presenting his points with all the accuracy of a lawyer," and "his remarks were moving." So was the Captain's audience, for after Angney's first hour on the rostrum he saw the house so nearly vacated that he "moved an adjournment until another evening."

Another evening came, and Judge Baird attended "merely for the gratification of a friend." Instead of Captain Angney's appearing to finish his talk, "a Mr. Lemon appeared on the rostrum." Judge Baird, however, "happened to know him in former times figuring in the state of Kenturcy as a professor of rhetoric in Bacon College and as preacher of the gospel under the name and style of the reverend Mr. Hunter." Thereupon Judge Baird made it known that he "felt no disposition to enter into a controversy with you until I know why you changed your name." And "of course," concluded the Judge, "He passed." With the passing of the Reverend Mr. Hunter, *alias* Lemon, there was public silence—as Baird stated it—"until I left for Mo."

Before leaving for Missouri, however, Judge Baird had an opportunity to get Colonel Washington's more considered opinion. He had "no doubt of the validity of Texas' claim," but he regarded the United States as the trustee of the state of Texas; furthermore, he was charged as an army officer to maintain the status quo. In addition, his personal position was a delicate one: Were he to recognize the authority of Judge Baird and deliver jurisdiction to Texas, he would be bowing himself out of office. He therefore made Baird a commitment: He would do nothing, nor permit anything to be done prejudicial to the interests of Texas; he would co-operate with the Judge and assist in organizing whenever he thought he could do so without a violation of duty. As a military man he would act according to instructions, which meant that he would maintain his position as military governor and direct the civil affairs until ordered to do otherwise.

There was a momentary break in the situation. On the last night of President Polk's incumbency, he issued an executive directive that all lands east of the Río Grande acquired from Mexico under the terms of the Treaty of Guadalupe Hidalgo be delivered to the state of Texas "as soon as Texas shall require it."[5] The Presidential directive was not only a confirmation of the *sine qua non* of the war with Mexico but a belated confirmation of Texas' jurisdiction westward as far as the Río del Norte. The incoming President, Zachary Taylor, the hero of the Mexican War, rescinded the order before Texas had an opportunity to require delivery.

On March 18, since Judge Baird "felt an anxiety to bring matters to something like an issue, and to free our state from the imputation of sleeping on her rights," he resorted to the time-honored Spanish custom and had "a proclamation printed." But being a man "of

[5] Willie Larriett Nutt, "Texas–New Mexico Boundary Controversy, 1836–1859," M.A. thesis, University of Oklahoma, 1933.

prudent steps," he addressed a copy of his handiwork to Colonel Washington with a short explanatory note," the import of which was that "henceforward the civil and criminal Jurisdiction over said county [Santa Fe], legitimately will be assumed and exercised by the authorities of the State of Texas only, and the citizens will be required to yield obedience thereto, and all proceedings not in accordance with the laws of said State will be held absolutely null and void." This order, of course, was calculated to upset the status quo. Colonel Washington "requested" the Judge to call, and at the meeting the Colonel "remarked in substance that he was very desirous that the proclamation not issue," urging "that the country was in some confusion . . . the Indians were becoming hostile . . . that he had just called for three companies of volunteers—that the excitement that might follow the issuance of the proclamation would materially derange his plans for the defense of the country and his efforts to maintain good order."

Judge Baird, sensing that he had an advantage over Colonel Washington, intimated that he would withhold the proclamation if the Colonel would put a stop to the pratings of the "demagogues who were constantly circulating false reports among the Mexican people to the effect that Texas would hang the men for past acts of hostility, destroy their religion, enslave their women and children and confiscate their property." Washington disclaimed any power to prevent the people from circulating such reports, but he did suggest that "the paper published there by the government press had the means to some extent of giving color and circulation to these reports," and, to placate Baird, gave him his solemn promise "that he would see that it was not agitated by the government press." With this solemn declaration Judge Baird agreed not to issue the proclamation for the time being, "holding himself free to act according to future emergencies."

The stalemate in New Mexico did not please the governor of Texas. He complained bitterly to President Taylor that in New Mexico "opposition had been offered by the military government . . . to the authorities of Texas . . . certainly unlooked for . . . as it never could have been expected that the Federal Government would lay claim or assert title to that soil . . . acknowledged to be within the limits of Texas." President Taylor's reply came as a shock:

> The executive government of the United States has no power or authority to determine what was the true line of boundary between Mexico and the United States before the Treaty of Guadalupe Hidalgo, nor has it any such power now, since the question has become a question between the State of Texas and the United States. So far as this boundary is doubtful, that doubt can only be removed by some act of Congress, to which the assent of the State of Texas may be necessary, or by some appropriate mode of legal adjudication; but, in the meantime, if disturbances or collisions arise, or should be threatened, it is absolutely incumbent upon the executive government, however painful the duty, to take care that the laws be faithfully maintained; . . . and is bound to protect all the inhabitants, who were then established, and who now remain, north and east of the line of demarcation. . . . In other words, all must be regarded as New Mexico which was possessed and occupied as New Mexico, by citizens of Mexico, at the date of the treaty, until a definite line of boundary shall be established by competent authority.

With the assurance to Texas that whatever was done by "the competent authority," "the assent of Texas may be necessary," President Taylor opened the door to agreement with the observation that the federal government "would be justified in allowing an indemnity to Texas, not unreasonable or extravagant, but fair and liberal, and awarded in a just spirit of accommodation."

After Judge Baird and Governor Washington reached an impasse, the Governor expressed his satisfaction "as he was soon to be supplanted," and during the remainder of his term in office he "would not suffer the interference with the claims of Texas." Thereupon Baird disclosed that he intended "in a few days to visit Independence on matters of great importance." Baird, therefore, was off to Independence, whence he voiced his opinions effusively and with a candor which showed that he was aware that many miles separated him from the subjects of his contempt. He would speak, so he wrote, of "that country, those people, their *Territorial Movements*" as "one who is acquainted with the persons and the manner of these movements [and] cannot think of them and be grave." Although he ought to feel flattered at being appointed "to preside over that district judicially," he could "not but feel *humiliated* when I look at the people— Such a medley does not rest anywhere else upon the top of the globe. The country municipally is more comparable to a spitbox, or lumber chest, into which old broken ware is cast, than anything else. . . . I think the lamentations of the New Mexico Jeremiahs over their military government is a little out of tune . . . . Although bad, it is better than they have been used to, and I doubt seriously if they know how to appreciate anything better. There is not one of them attached to the United States & by a love of liberty, [understanding?] of her institution[s]—Dogged fear attaches them. . . . Such a people would be elevated and promoted by being placed in the position of the southern slaves; for they are distrust[ful] and false to a point. Texas well knows how to appreciate them and what confidence and consideration should be bestowed upon them."[6]

Once out of New Mexico, Judge Baird "thought of resigning"; he wished to be relieved of his appointment so that he might "go to Washington in a disinterested capacity. He envisioned himself as the proper agent to accomplish "the interest of the south, to maintain her [Texas'] boundary as claimed undivided, until the spirit of southern institutions and southern interests permanently pervade the entire territory claimed by Texas." He was, however, "well convinced that the incorporation of the people with us would be a serious injury to the State—Even if they desired unanimously to be incorporated they would be troublesome." Furthermore, he favored President Taylor's suggestion of compromise "and get rid of a troublesome and worthless set of customers."

When Southern sympathizers learned of President Taylor's pro-

[6] Report to the Committee on Federal Relations, December 12, 1844, in the Texan–Santa Fe Papers, Texas State Archives, Austin; AC, copy.

nouncement on the Texas claim, many interpreted it as an intention to drive Southerners from New Mexico. The Lone Star State reacted belligerently, authorizing the recruitment of volunteers "for the occupation of the frontier." (No limits to the frontier were indicated.) W. B. Ochiltree (yet to be lieutenant governor of the state and have a county named in his honor) wrote from Crockett, Texas, "to his Excellency P. Hansborough Bell," suggesting: "In the event your Excellency shall be empowered to raise troops for the occupation of the frontier, or of Santa Fe," he would like to take the liberty of naming "gentlemen whose experience and patriotism recommend them . . . as fit and proper persons to engage in either of those enterprises . . . one an old and tried soldier from the capture of Bexar to the storming of Monterrey . . . constant occupant of the tent . . . eager for the frontier and the adventures of the camp." He thought it unnecessary to warn the Governor, "a one time Texas Ranger himself," that "George L. Short (although favorably presented to the governor) was aforetime (as your Excellency knows) a brave and ardent spirit [and] like most old soldiers somewhat devoted to Bacchus, but it gives me pleasure to assure your Excellency that he is now a most exemplary son of temperance and has been for months past—his friends think a permanent reform has taken place as regards this his only fault." He was, in making his two recommendations, "satisfied that no two men in the East could raise a more effective corpse [*sic*] of men."

Michael K. McDermott, from Galveston, solicited a "commission of Captn. in the regiment contemplated to be raised to vindicate and enforce the rights of the state over her territory in Santa Fe." For self-recommendation, he had "been raised in Texas since the year 1833 . . . served in the armies of the Republick . . . the late Mexican War . . . stormed Monterrey." General Hugh McLeod (although not hankering for another Texan–Santa Fe Expedition) sponsored McDermott's ambitions. Benjamin O. Payn, signing himself "U.S. Army Agent," thought McDermott "has talent and will prove, if tried." Dr. John Work, from Town Bluff, Tyler County, writing "at the Solicitation of many old Rangers," could bring into "the Service of Jasper and Tyler Counties a Company of choice experienced men." There was one proviso, however—"if the governor intended to raise a Regiment to send to Santa Fe."

W. B. Coffee from Lockhart reminded the Governor that he had promised that "if anything ocured [sic] by which you could assist me, you would take great pleasure in doing so." He wrote because he had seen reports "in regard to Santa Fe that it is possible troops will be called out to enforce the jurisdiction of our State." He would like to know "when they would be likely to start." A. H. Boles, of Washington County, Texas, was more adroit in the tender of his military or surveyor's services. He had "learned that the Government desiyers raising a number of men to *Survey the boundary line* between Mexico and the United States. . . . he would be gratified to raise a company." And from over in Mississippi, Easter B. Henres laid aside any simulation of purpose to note that "after hearing of & see [sic] the insults offered to my native [Texas], and while my heart is burning within me, there is a probability of difficulties between N. Mexico or the U.S."; consequently, he was "anxious to engage in it that I may do all in my power to assist the glorious cause of the South." Conservative John James, of San Antonio, Texas, "would not object if my services can be made useful."

Kentucky was next heard from, as was Alabama, both feeling that "Texas will again be compelled to defend her territory by force of arms & that, too against the U.S. whose duty it ought to be to defend hur against any foe"; and S. S. Scott, admittedly a peripatetic Kentuckian, "would not hesitate for a moment on which side" he would cast himself. John Calhoun wanted authority to recruit in Walker, Grimes, and Montgomery counties, after which he would "march to Santa Fe to suppress rebellion and enforce the jurisdiction and laws of Texas." Sixty-four Tennesseans "learned with pleasure that Governor Bell's duty and noble sense of honor impells him at all hazards and to the last extremity to resist the gross and unjust abolition Legislatiaon of this government," and they were more than pleased that Texas had "allready mustered a portion of her Chivalrous Sons in the field, ready to defend her rights, her honor and the great principal [*sic*] of compact by wich this government is held together."

On October 23, 1848, Colonel Washington was relieved from his duties in New Mexico. Colonel John Munroe assumed the command, immediately styling himself "Civil and Military Governor of New Mexico." Three weeks passed, and the Secretary of War deemed it proper that he should know more of the situation in New Mexico than he was learning through the civil and military governor. Colonel McCall, as a consequence, was told that it was "proper to make some observations on the peculiar conditions of that [New Mexico] territory of the United States." As Colonel McCall went about making "his observations and view of the possible number of people, habits, customs and pursuits of the life of people for use of Congress when the people form a constitution and seek admission into the confederacy of the states," Governor Munroe, even more militaristically, dominated the affairs of the region.

President Zachary Taylor died, leaving the unresolved Texas boundary question to Millard Fillmore, to whom Governor Bell appealed. The new President, however, delayed "until after the appointment of those heads of Departments, and their acceptance of office, with whom it is usual on important occasions, for the President of the United States to advise." In this instance he advised with Secretary of State Daniel Webster, who on August 5 made answer for the President, he having considered Governor Bell's representation "to the late President of the United States," and he was now "directed to address you as follows":

> In that letter you say that by the authority of the Legislature of Texas, the Executive . . . dispatched a Special Commission . . . to extend the civil jurisdiction of that State over the unorganized counties . . . situated upon its northwestern limits . . . and that the military officers stationed in Santa Fe interposed adversely with the inhabitants to the fulfilment of the object . . . by employing their influence in favor of establishment of a separate state government east of the Rio Grande and within the rightful limits of Texas.

95

You also transmit a copy of the proclamation of Col. John Munroe, acting under the orders of the Government of the United States, under the designation of Civil and Military Governor of the Territory of New Mexico, and respectfully request . . . to be informed whether or not this officer has acted . . . under the orders of the government. . . .

In answer to your first interrogatory, viz: Whether Col. Munroe acted under the orders of the Government: . . . This order does not appear to authorize any exertion of military authority, or of any official, or affect in any way the primary action of the people, or even to recommend anything as fit to be adopted by the people . . . ."

Then, omitting mention of Kearny's avowal that Texas' limits extended west to the Río Grande, Daniel Webster anchored his decision upon "the Treaty of Peace which has been concluded with Mexico, by which the boundary line was established that left the territory *within the United States,* thereby confirming to the United States, by treaty, what we had before acquired by conquest; and the possession held of it, in the first place, was, of course, a military possession. The treaty added the title by cession to the already title by successful achievement of arms."

Passing on to the settlement of the "disputed boundary," Webster quoted the President as having "no hesitation in saying that he does not believe the Executive Branch of the Government, or the inhabitants of New Mexico, or both combined, have any constitutional authority to settle that question: That belongs either to the Judicial Department of the federal Government, or to the concurrent action by agreement of the legislative departments of the governments of the United States and Texas." For him it was sufficient, he said, "that this boundary is in dispute; that the territory east of the Rio del Norte seems to be claimed in good faith by both Texas and New Mexico— or rather by the United States [he corrected]. . . . It is a delicate crisis in our public affairs, not free certainly from possible danger"; but all he could do was "trust that Justice, moderation and patriotism, and the love of the Union may inspire such counsels, both in the Government of the United States and that of Texas, as shall carry the country through these dangers, and bring it safely out of them all ... with mutual respect and harmony in the great family of States."

For Texas, the situation indeed presented "a delicate crisis": A "trust in Justice, moderation and patriotism, and love of the Union" did not seem warranted with the abolitionists using the boundary dispute to weaken the slavery states; so, sensing the delicate crisis, General Winfield Scott, on August 6, 1850, laboriously alerted Colonel Munroe in Santa Fe to developments:

> About seven hundred and fifty troops are now in route via the Missouri and Lavaca [Texas], respectively, to fill up the regiments and companies under your command ... and the 7th Regiment of Infantry, with one or two troops of the 1st Dragoons will soon follow. Some two hundred men of the 7th Infantry will leave the Missouri mounted.
>
> These reinforcements are deemed necessary to enable you to protect the people of New Mexico against incursions of hostile Indians; but another and more painful contingency may be apprehended.
>
> It is known here that the Legislature of Texas has been summoned ... to meet on the 12th. instant, to adopt measures for extending her political and civil jurisdiction over that part of New Mexico, on this side of the Rio Grande, claimed as a part of Texas.
>
> It is quite possible, perhaps probable, if the disputed boundary between Texas and New Mexico, be not earlier established by Congress, that a large body of troops may be levied in all this month [by Texas] and sent to New Mexico, to effect, by force of arms, the object stated.
>
> In such an event, your position, as the immediate commander of the United States forces, in New Mexico, will be one of much delicacy and difficulty, and hence demanding adequate instructions from the highest in authority.
>
> It is held by the President of the United States to be his duty, under the constitutional obligations of the 9th Article of the Treaty of Guadalupe Hidalgo, and until the boundary between Texas and New Mexico shall be duly established, to protect to the extent of the means at his dispositions, against all violence whatever, the inhabitants of the country, known, at the date of that treaty, as New Mexico. ...
>
> Accordingly, you are hereby instructed, in the case of any military

invasion of New Mexico, from Texas, or by arms from any other state or states, for the purpose of overturning the order of civil government that may exist in New Mexico at the time, or the subjugation of New Mexico to Texas, to interpose, as far as practicable, the troops under your command against any such act of violence. . . .

. . . avoid if possible a resort to repulsive violence; but when necessary, and without losing any material advantage, by delay, . . . resist with vigor. . . . You will take all measures within your power to protect the people of New Mexico . . . and to repel force by force when clearly necessary to that end.[7]

On September 9, Congress relieved Colonel Munroe of the delicate crisis by enacting the so-called Omnibus Bill, or the Compromise of 1850, which cleared the way for settlement of the Texas boundary matter. The act fixed the boundary between Texas and New Mexico but suspended putting it into effect pending the assent of Texas. Congressional parceling out of the territorial spoils derived from Mexico cut out Utah and Nevada, as well as California, and caused Texas to retrograde her boundary stakes several hundred miles eastward from the Río del Norte, but for this concession ten million dollars was to be paid to Texas. Half of the purchase money, however, was to go into trust—"a certificate of *distrust*," as interpreted by Texas—contingent upon payment of outstanding Republic of Texas debts. Particularly arbitrary was a stipulation of acceptance as of December 1, 1850. (A take-it-or-leave-it attitude of the stronger, thought many people.) Five days before the expiration date Texas officially gave her consent. Those who knew her financial straits were aware that her impecunious position had driven her into the path of Clay and Webster.

Although relieved of preventing an invasion from Texas, Colonel Munroe was not relieved of the hatred of the hard-riding, invective-spewing self-appointed protagonist of the *Nuevo Mejicanos*—Richard H. Weightman, up to then their only vocal American friend. "By duty and by inclination," stated Weightman, he directed his attacks at Judge Joab Houghton, holding office at the sufferance of Munroe, knowing that the real blow would be felt by Munroe. He charged

[7] 2–AGO, MB, No. 30, pp. 266–68.

that "a *de facto* government obtains here of a most anomalous character, which has no parallel in our history, opposed to the spirit and genius of our institutions and laws, and unrecognized by any competent authority. This government *de facto* was established under the laws and usages of war; and upon the conclusion of peace, February 2, 1848, having been found in existence here to prevent anarchy, continues by the acquiescence of the authority—whatever it may be— to change it. Under this government, as it actually exists, the governor exercises military, executive and legislative functions."[8]

Despite Weighman's inveighing against the anomalous form of government and its executive, Governor Munroe held his office until the passage of the Omnibus Bill; however, he confided to the Secretary of War that he was having "a misunderstanding with a portion of the people of New Mexico, which was causing him some embarrassment." From that delicate position Secretary Conrad readily relieved him, at the instance of the President of the United States. On September 10, 1850, a letter went out:

> Your letter . . . I have submitted to the President. I am directed to make the following reply: The President has learned with regret that any misunderstanding should exist between a portion of the people of New Mexico and yourself in relation to the government of the country, and hastens to relieve you from this embarrassment in which that misunderstanding has placed you.
>
> I now have the pleasure to inform you that congress has at length passed a law providing for a Territorial government in New Mexico . . . [and] all controversy as to what is the proper government must be at an end, and the anomalous state of things there be determined.[9] . . . It is at all times desirable that the civil and military departments of the government should be kept entirely distinct. . . . you are directed to abstain from all further interference in civil or political affairs of that country.

The orders to Colonel Munroe went by special messenger. Included was also a notice of the passage of the Territorial Bill. Governor

---

[8] Letter from Weightman, Santa Fe, December 1, 1849, thereafter read as part of his speech of March 18, 1852.

[9] "Terminated" most likely was intended instead of "determined."

Munroe released the latter news but suppressed the instructions to desist from interference in civil and political affairs. He was reluctant to absolve himself from power; too, he must have surmised that his tenure was brief. It was; Colonel Sumner was soon to be on his way, stopping at *Los Posos,* discussing with Major Weightman the location of Fort Union.

CHAPTER SIX

"THE BIG BUG OF ALBUQUERQUE"

Upon arriving in Santa Fe, Sumner adopted Munroe's plan to make war on the Navahos. He issued orders specifying that the expedition should move from Santo Domingo on August 15, 1851. On August 14, he was in Santa Fe clearing the place of remnants of quartermaster and ordnance stores. Colonel Brooks received the residue, permitting Captain Reynolds, under command of Sumner, to proceed to the place of rendezvous. Captain W. R. Shoemaker, military storekeeper, moved eastward to take his post at Fort Union.

Sumner's delay at Santa Fe was incident to Captain Reynolds' entry into New Mexico politics, Sumner having been apprised by Weightman that Reynolds had become a candidate against him. Since Weightman had theretofore been his valued adviser—"the percussion cap of the explosion of genius at *Los Posos*"—the new commander decided to "clear the military from interfering with civil affairs in New Mexico" and so gave Reynolds ten days to settle his quartermaster accounts, retrieve the quartermaster supplies (then scattered between Santa Fe and Fort Union or on Aubrey's freight wagon on the road), and report for staff duty at Santo Domingo.[1] This Cap-

---

[1] 2–AGO, Vol. 8, pp. 414–15. On December 22, 1852, Sumner answered the inquiry of Secretary of War Conrad, to whom Reynolds had appealed, charging that Sumner had required him to leave for the Navaho country without an opportunity to account for his quartermaster property. Sumner sought to clear himself by stating: "I consider that Captain Reynolds had ample time to turn over all his property to his charge before he went to the Navajo Country. On my arrival at Santa Fe on the 19th July, 1851, I found the officer engaged in a political struggle preparing to run for delegate to Congress. I knew that no man could do the duty of quartermaster and be engaged in politics at the same time. I, therefore, determined to remove Capt. Reynolds from Santa Fe, and take him with me on the Navajo Expedition, and thus to secure his undivided attention to his military duties. He was not required

tain Reynolds did, taking out a little time for electioneering and notifying Weightman that should Weightman, under the circumstances, prevail, the election would be contested. He anticipated such a result since he was required by Colonel Sumner to give "his undivided attention to his military duties." Anticipating a contest, he authorized the law firm of Skinner, Pilans and Ashurst to represent his political interests during his absence in the Navaho country.

W. C. Skinner, of the firm, had come to Santa Fe from Missouri with Kearny in 1846, when Weightman had been his superior officer. After his release from the army, Skinner had acquired the sobriquet of "Judge." He then attached himself to Messrs. Pilans and Ashurst in a law partnership, retaining for himself the first position in the trio. Since the "Judge" had long since parted ways politically from his former commander, there was no extra strain of personal relations when the firm became Reynolds' adviser against Weightman in the contest for delegate to Congress. Pilans bore the reputation of being "an honorable, though prejudiced and impulsive gentleman," but Merrill Ashurst failed to rate that high, for, according to Weightman, he was known even to his client Reynolds—"to be a forger—a refugee from Alabama."[2]

Just prior to September 23, 1851, Skinner and Ashurst went to Albuquerque on business in connection with the recent death of one Burtinett. Ashurst remained in Albuquerque, but Skinner, "who seemed to be in quite a passion" over the loss of the election to Weightman, rode out to the *ranchos*. There he declared, "There is no justice at the ranchos." In fact, "he became rather excited." Some who saw him thought he had been in too close and recent communication with the spirit of Turley's Taos Lightning; and when he bandished a whip, shouting that he was going to horsewhip somebody, bystanders suggested that a short ride in the saddle would make the

---

to join me until about the 14th August, when the expedition moved from San Domingo, and he [left] for the states until the latter part of the month. I do not think that Captain Reynolds is entitled to any consideration for the loss of property on account of want of time to settle his affairs.

[2] Weightman's speech.

undertaking appear less laudable. Consequently, he rode away toward Juan Cristóbal Armijo's home, no one interfering.

Juan Cristóbal Armijo was a resident merchant at the Albuquerque *rancho* with his residence in one room and store connecting. Armijo was serving a customer when Skinner entered the store. Once inside the "rather excited" intruder, still "in quite a passion," drew a brace of firearms and "walked to the counter with a pistol in his hand," presenting it to the breast of Armijo. This unexpected appearance of a drunken man with a pistol did more than "rather excite" the merchant, for he recognized the pistol wielder as the red-headed lawyer whose client, Reynolds, had suffered a loss of votes to Weightman at the recent election through his persuasion.

Armijo inquired, "What is it?" The belicose Skinner was not unduly informative, merely saying, "You will see what it is!" Ambrose Martínez, who had just completed buying "some varras of brown muslin," seeing Armijo take the initiative—as well as the "man, with the light head, by the hair"—grabbed "his brown muslin and ran back of the house." He accomplished his escape just as several men came to the rescue of the hair-pulling merchant. In the ensuing mêlée someone shouted, "Give it to him! Give it to him!" A reasonable deduction is that they did, for Martínez, yet with an on-looker's curiosity, peeped into the store, and there he saw "Skinner lying dead."

The news went to Santa Fe. Coming as it did from Ashurst and timed so near to the ousting of Governor Munroe, the enemies of Calhoun began to converge upon the plaza. "Squads of men [wrote Editor Kephart] might be seen collecting and mingling like electric clouds marshaling for a thunder-shock. There were curses, not loud but deep, and the oft-repeated exclamation of 'Poor Skinner'!! mingled with the deep-breathed and fearful vows of vengeance, told how fearful were the elements that were warring in their bosoms."

Preston Beck, hothead, merchant, and army sutler, assumed the chairmanship of the impromptu meeting. Two days had passed since Skinner's death, and "only the history of the whole affair as derived from Mr. Ashurst" had come from the Río Abajo; consequently, "the mass meeting was held under circumstances of great excitement—of frequent excitement." A resolutions committee was appointed to report on "the murder of Mr. Skinner." The resulting resolution spoke of "the inhuman murder and brutal butchery—murder most foul." It had its origin "in the policy of the governor." No reference was made to Sumner.

After hearing that Skinner's death had its origin "in the policy of the governor," a mob hastened off to the Palace of the Governors. There the Governor was found engaged in a game of whist. Excited partisans, drunken men, misguided men, pushed into the Governor's privacy. He was accused of neglecting to "protect the citizens of Bernalillo—they believed it a fact—and so stated it—that the murder had been done because the murdered man was a political opponent of his Excellency." He was likened unto "Nero, fiddling over the burning of Rome." They demanded that the militia be called out. "It was proposed by some to raise a company immediately, march to Bernalillo, and execute the most summary vengeance." They proposed that the Governor designate the assembled mob as a posse *comitatus*. The Governor refused, assuring all that the "course of the law will be taken."

Governor Calhoun's refusal to be swayed by seekers-after vengeance was the signal for the *Gazette* to double-lead its column, and former minister, now editor, Kephart did his editorial best:

ANOTHER HORRID ASSASSINATION IN BERNALILLO COUNTY!

"Hung be the heavens with black," wrote Kephart, as he commented upon the "calmness of the public meeting." To the editor this calmness was a "triumph of the spirit of law and order over the most violent dictates of maddened passions." And while "the people's calmness speaks well of our citizens," he had "no heart to mince words in our present circumstances. There is not an American in the Territory that does not feel that his head sits lightly upon his shoulders if such a state of things is permitted to go on. We can not shut our eyes or close our mind against the conviction that, had our civil authorities taken prompt and efficient action in the murder of the unfortunate Burtinett, instead of manifesting a cold indifference, and in some instances, an ill-concealed satisfaction, the blood of poor Skinner had not this day been upon their guilty souls. Before GOD! we would not have that blood upon our soul for the wealth of a universe, and how less for the insignificant gain of a brief political triumph in the Territory of New Mexico."

Regrettable as it was to the *Gazette,* its editor believed that Governor Calhoun would do nothing "farther than to see the common, uncertain, and dilatory course of the law be taken." This he believed "from the fact that the murdered man was a political opponent of his Excellency."[3]

While the law was "taking its dilatory course," a caustic indictment went to the President of the United States. It bore the signatures of such men as Houghton, Reynolds, Collins, and others. All favored a return of the military to power. And not only did the petitioners request the removal of Territorial Governor Calhoun, but they spelled out in plain English a theory of government for New Mexico which they would approve. Specifically, they stated:

> We are fully convinced that there is no hope for the improvement of our Territory unless Americans rule it, and that the spirit of Mexican rule must be corrupt, and disgraceful in a Territory of the United States, and that we know from experience that under such rule, there can be no sufficient guarantee for the secure enjoyment of property, and even life.

Government was to be entrusted "not to the 61 547 souls" (the population of New Mexico), but to "the 538 persons born in the United States," the total number of Anglo-Americans then living in New Mexico unconnected with the army. Weightman, seeing in this the hand of Editor Kephart, the last-ditch effort of the militarists, commented: "If I were to undertake to correct all Padre Kephart's lies I would have all my time taken up."

Colonel Sumner, after getting two days behind schedule in blocking Captain Reynolds' efforts to defeat Weightman, got off to his her-

[3] Governor Calhoun sent two members of the Supreme Court, the Attorney General, and a private prosecutor hired by the Odd Fellows to the place of Skinner's death. Testimony was recorded, and Armijo was held for the grand jury, which refused to return an indictment.

alded expedition against the Navahos. He took with him from Santo Domingo "four companies of horse, 1 of Artillery, and two of Infantry." He halted at the Pueblos of Laguna and Zuñi "and there confirmed those Indians in their friendly disposition toward us." Thereafter he saw no Indians until after he passed Cañon Bonito.

At the cañon an Indian came into Sumner's camp proposing to take a message for the Colonel to "two Navajo chiefs who were in the vicinity." Sumner told the messenger that if the chiefs would come to him, he would talk with them. This the Navahos refused to do, whereupon Sumner issued the order: "All Navajos to be fired upon whenever they are seen hovering about." Proudly he reported the results: "We killed and wounded a number of them." He could not say how many, but all in all he was quite disgusted with the Navahos: "They never faced us, or gave us an opportunity to inflict upon them any signal chastisement."

Since the Navahos "would not come out and fight," Sumner abandoned the expedition, but left Major Backus behind to establish a fort in their midst. Being in a defiant mood, he named the post Fort Defiance. He then set off on a sight-seeing trip, "proceeded around Cañon Chelle with the Cavalry and two mountain howitzers." He penetrated the gorge eleven miles, but found no Indians; however, he thought the Cañon de Chelley was "a phenomenon of nature with sheer walls . . . to six hundred feet high." Thereafter the Indians discovered the troops. The Indians were on top of the rocks, and from that vantage point "fired upon the troops with their muskets and arrows." Then they gratified their glee "by rolling down stones." Sumner found it difficult to go farther into the cañon as the road "became worse, and there was no adequate object in continuing to explore the Cañon, at the risk of losing men, who were entirely defenseless as our arms would not reach the Indians on top of the precipices." He "thought it proper and prudent to leave the Cañon." After this prudent move, when they had settled down outside the mouth of Cañon de Chelley "to rest the horses before retracing the path to Fort Defiance, a party of Indians stole in between my picket guard and threw a few shots upon Camp." This made Colonel Sumner consider this expedition not "as decisive as I could wish [and] it was hardly possible to close an Indian war of many years standing with one expedition." But he had hopes that "the large post at Cañon Bonito will, in a short time, effectually restrain those Indians."

His confidence in the effectiveness of the kind of troops he commanded had been shattered by the expedition. He found it "impossible to make long marches with Cavalry, on grass alone, loaded down as they are with arms, accoutrements and clothing." His horses, too, were unequal "to the Indian horses in speed or bottom" "consequently, our Cavalry cannot act offensively in the saddle." Further, "broken down horses are a great embarrassment, requiring a large part of the command to protect them which could otherwise be used offensively on foot."

By October 8, rumor had succeeded in carrying the news of the expedition to Fort Union faster than the command had traveled: Sumner had lost many horses to the Indians and to the harshness of the West; he was disgusted with his cavalry; he would recommend to the Adjutant General that he be permitted to "withdraw from this Territory 4 C of Dragoons"; he preferred a dismounted rifle regiment to take the place of the dragoons—"even Infantrymen would do." If he could substitute such a force, he would "feel more confident in his ability to carry out the orders he had received." He would not— could not—admit failure, but "the expedition was not as desisively [*sic*] as I could wish."

On the first of October, Captain Bowen was advised that his winter quarters would be finished by the last of the month. Ten days later he "awoke this morning and found the ground covered with snow and the storm was raging with considerable violence." He thoughtfully observed, "If this is the commencement of winter we will often wish ourselves back in Houlton before its close." An inspection of the house-building showed that "quarters are slowly progressing toward completion," but there was no likelihood that he would be able to occupy them before the first of November. Kittie "had been quite unwell, having had a troublesome cold, chills and fever." Then he "was compelled to turn in for one day, being threatened by inflammation of the bowels," but being "poulticed and cupped," he got "quite well again."

During the poulticing and cupping, Colonel Sumner arrived at the post. Sumner was not effusive over his campaign. Captain Bowen listened attentively for military evaluation, "but there was little said since the return of the expedition," and Bowen "fancied that the Colonel did not meet with the success he anticipated. It was not, however, exactly like the expedition of the celebrated King of France, who, with twice ten thousand, marched up a hill and then marched down again, for *Col S. fixed upon a point, left five companies to garrison it, and called it Fort Defiance.*"[4]

When Captain and Mrs. Bowen had first arrived at the tent city, Mrs. Bowen was "really glad that we are to be settled in the country instead of a town." Mrs. Sibley was talkative. Disclosing that she was a bride, she took Kittie into her tent, where "everything looked so cool and home like." She admitted her temptation at the pretty shops she found "on her unnecessary journey to Santa Fe," made so that Sumner could "decide where to locate," and "exposed her husband's pockets to rather heavy drafts." In fact, the shopkeepers had inveigled her "into the extravagance of buying nice furniture." This Kittie thought unnecessary, since she would be "equally as comfortable with my home-made lounges and benches." Isaac had been provident, having "had frames of two easy chairs made at Leavenworth," and she would now "take some of my extra pillows and cover them with turkey red and find them charming." Although enthusiastic about the sociable Mrs. Sibley, her impression of the Major was less favorable. Further, she could not "think such a girl would marry a man who had two wives; one is bad enough." And soon, Kittie found out that the Major was not a man "to assist a woman, at all, and would poke about his office all day instead of being at home to relieve her." She began to feel sorry for Mrs. Sibley: "She came out with the idea that brides could live on air and be furnished from the same source, consequently she had to buy a little of everything." To Kittie it "was too provoking to see one's money go for nothing." She was "rather

[4] Isaac Bowen to "Dear Father," October 11, 1851, AC, Bowen Letters.

astonished at the Maj's want of foresight, after having so many wives, and keeping houses, that he should not bring groceries, at least."

As to her own "good man": "All I can say is that I am fortunate in having a husband who never waits for me to think or act, but keeps me supplied before I have time to wish. He knows even to the laces and edgings what I need, and made out my fancy-list when he was lying on his back sick in bed; everything useful and plenty."

From the information that Kittie had been able to glean, Fort Union had been located "particularly with a view to extensive farming operations." The "point is well supplied with a delicious spring, and we have its water brought twice a day. For the stock and for irrigation there are several ponds and one lake. The river runs six miles below us, and there the mail comes on its way to Santa Fe. There is a fort owned by a Mr. Barcly [*sic*], and the post office is at the fort on the Moro." Since there was no "distributing office short of Santa Fe," the mail was most inconvenient, "for all letters directed there must go." She hoped there would be a change so that "our letters will come directly here, for five days seems too long to wait after the mail has passed."[5]

Of course, no land had been tilled during the year, but "the head farmer is cutting hay for winter use but has not more than thirty tons as yet and there are 900 head of cattle, besides several hundred horses and mules to winter."

Sumner's experimental farm project ran afoul of Manuel Alvares, the owner of the land on the Ocate where it was decided to turn soldiers into agronomists. To Sergeant Pollock fell the distinction of being "head-farmer-soldier"; and he was "dispatched to the scene of action." The scene of action was likewise the scene of the Alvares grant. And Manuel Alvares, yet a *jefe político* in New Mexico and no particular friend of the military regime, checkmated Colonel Sumner's intended pre-emption by hiring H. H. Green to oust the United States Army from its trespass.

Green—soon to acquire the nickname of *The Optic's* "Old Fogy" —nursing a discharged soldier's natural aversion to army decrees,

5 AC, Bowen Letters.

as well as undue physical exertion as he recalled later—"declared war at once on the government." Not unlike the Navahos when Sumner would "inflict a signal punishment," the presumptuous Green "was simply laughed at for my officiousness." He succeeded, however, in keeping away Thomas Pollock's plows, biding the time Colonel Sumner should return from his war, after which an accord was reached with Alvares and the farm was opened.[6]

Kittie Bowen, with a desire to show her own efficiency, commandeered an Ocate cow, which she milked. Result: she had "a pint of cream, and stirred up nearly a pound of butter in a tin cup just to say 'I had made butter before Mrs. Sibley,' who had been *fixed* a month and *lived without butter* and the milk of two cows—and I have but one at the present, but will have more as soon as I want them."

Following the making of butter in a tin cup, "Handy Ike" erected bowers, "which were pleasantly protective against the bright sun until a rain came." The rain disrupted a plan "to have Maj and Mrs. Sibley, and a few others in to tea," and they had to wait "to have our bowers dry a little more." Thereafter Kittie and Ike "got quite straightened out, and began to live after the old sort." Trouble always developed, however, when she attempted to get her washing done. She had a "stove that sits out of doors and won't draw quite well enough to keep a hot fire." In fact, the draft of the stove was so poor that she "usually cooked by a fire built on the ground." She "fancied that everything tasted uncommonly well, but it might have been that my appetite is too good to see the defect." Anyway, she was "as well off as my neighbors, and I have no ambition to shine in New Mexico."

During Major Sibley's temporary absence from the post, his quartermaster duties fell to Captain Bowen. Kittie, immediately sensing an advantage in the situation, "teasing him [her husband] until some workmen were set at the stove," and thereafter she "was independent, for it works like a charm." While Sibley was absent, "rumor trickled through military channels that Maj. Sibley will be stationed at Santa Fe as soon as some one comes from the states to relieve him." The removal of Major Sibley did not particularly disturb Kittie,

[6] *Las Vegas Daily Optic,* July 17, 1891.

although it would mean she would "lose my nearest neighbors, but despite the fact that Mrs. S. is very agreeable, she is nobody to pine after."

The weather turned unpleasant on the last day of August, and three days of rain followed. They abandoned the airy mansions outside and took refuge again in the tents. There was no cause for anxiety, however, as "the houses for winter are growing slowly, just putting windows and door frames. . . . Good luck has provided for us; we have plenty of clothing and bedding, and will not suffer if snow catches us in tents." Too, she now had a servant who "was geting things settled in the kitchen." She could trust her "enough to keep us from starving, while I make up winter drawers and night-shirts for my good man." She made as much of their clothing as she could, as "the St. Louis prices are ruinous; in fact, buying in New Mexico is rather tough, for what we pay for the commonest things here would buy us luxuries in the States, and since Sumner's orders about buying at the commissary, many have reported him to the President." That was not all: "The sutler's prices exceed anything I ever heard of. . . . Those who use the native flour say it is sweeter than American flour and makes as good griddle cakes as buckwheat." American flour was $11.78 per hundred pounds, while the Mexican was $7.78.

On September 13, "Major Carleton and his command arrived from the Arkansas where he had been ordered to keep the road open for merchants and government trains." Kittie was prepared for his appearance. Only that day she had cooked "a big shank for soup." Before putting in the seasoning, she took out the meat and marrow, "had it nicely chopped and spiced . . . and baked four mince pies . . . really tasted like home and did not cost a cent hardly." The Major had orders awaiting him to "make one more trip to Fort Mackay and back before winter." Obeying would require him to leave immediately, but he took advantage of Sumner's original order to rest his troops for a week and accepted Captain Bowen's invitation to eat mince pies.

Stern old Major Carleton, after his shank soup and mince pies, excused himself and "went to Barclay's Fort, five miles distant, where his wife is staying." Mrs. Carleton had been left at Barclay's Fort when the troops headed for Fort Union, "that nearest prominently inhabited point of habitation," since Sumner in his wasteful haste had neglected to provide facilities for the families of officers and men.

The evening after Major Carleton left for Barclay's Fort the neighbors were sitting in the Bowen tent discussing the dragoons return trip when Major Carleton's lieutenant said, "I wish we could have a dance before I go." That wish brought action: "No sooner said than it was agreed to come off the following evening. The young men were to pitch a hospital tent 20×30 and furnish music and the ladies were to send in whatever could be got up at so short notice. Although there were seven other ladies besides, it all fell to Mrs. Alexander, Mrs. Sibley and Myself. Mrs. E. and Mrs. S. made different varieties of cake. I boiled a ham, made butter biscuit and hot coffee. Our table looked very pretty, and coffee and cold water were the only beverages. As good fortune would have it a load of peaches and grapes came in that morning from El Paso, and the young men furnished abundantly of these rarities."

Mrs. Bowen "worked pretty hard that day" and attended the dance "only to see the others enjoy themselves and play matron in the way of presiding at the supper table, pour coffee, etc.," but it "went off well, and everybody seemed delighted . . . in fact, quite a charming dancing party we got up"—the first dance held at Fort Union.

Three days of "chilly rainy weather, which was rather gloomy" followed. The soldiers built large fires in front of the tents and "managed to keep warm—yet it was forlorn enough." In the "midst of all," reported Mrs. Bowen, "Maj Carleton's command, accompanied by the families of two officers, left for the states." Although Kittie wanted to get away from the discomfort of the tents, still she expressed a preference to staying "and run[ning] the risk of a winter here than start out at this late season."

Captain Bowen was not as efficient in acquiring soldier gossip (or probably not as free in relaying it) as was his wife. Soon after Colonel Sumner's reappearance at Fort Union from the Navaho expedition, Kittie was aware of the fact that he was "not in very good standing among his officers in this country, and *speaking as citizens,* they call him hard names, sometime not giving him credit for bravery."

During the first days of November, 1851, another snowstorm came to make life rigorous at the new headquarters. The snow was followed by "one or two days of high wind, which nearly buried us in dust." However, by this time, good luck had come to the Bowens. They had been "fortunate enough to get into quarters," and although they had "but one room and a kitchen finished," still they found it vastly more comfortable than out in the tents. "We escape the constant dust, if nothing more, for in this territory nearly all the time we have high winds and the soil becomes so dry and powdered that the air is filled with the most disagreeable kind of dust." Mrs. Bowen still professed to "like this climate it is so dry—despite the winds, but the winds are horrible sometimes. They generally commence in the north and blow a hurricane for two or three days, carrying dust, stones, straw and everything out of doors. Then we will have a week as mild as summer. At the end of a week a south wind springs up and carries all the dust back again, drifting in some places like snow and penetrating every unprotected crevice." In one of these dust storms her "bedroom carpet was so covered that the colors could not be distinguished," but they would *"shovel* out occasionally" and then find their house as "pleasant and comfortable" as any they had ever lived in. In their new quarters they had "rooms very tidy and comfortable," plus "large stone fireplaces that gave genial warmth and cheerfulness." The Bowen house—like that of the Sibleys—fronted the south, and she had "bright sunshine all the day," but she was "vain enough to think that our rooms are pleasanter than the other ladies." Isaac contributed his share to the comfort. He had "a Dragoon tailor make up their carpets" and experienced "little trouble in moving" out of the tents.

On October 12, Colonel Sumner put 71 wagons and 473 mules on the road toward Fort Leavenworth. He had been back at Fort Union but four days when he decided upon this great economy measure: wintering his mule herd out of the department, where the expense would be less, and returning them again in the spring. Captain Bowen, of course, was aware of the Colonel's preparations, and he wrote nostalgically to his father-in-law: "Col. Sumner has returned from the Navajo expedition and the train that accompanied his command will leave for Leavenworth tomorrow. . . . I wish we were to accompany the train to the states, for, if there ever was a country which our creator had deserted, that country must be New Mexico. However, we anticipated but little pleasure, enjoyment or comfort during our residence here, but that little may be less than we anticipated."

Kittie Bowen, hampered by fewer inhibitions than her husband, added to Isaac's letter to her father. Of Colonel Sumner she wrote: "I will not say anything." Then she proceeded to say it. Her father and mother would "hear enough of Colonel Sumner's doings through the paper." If she "could get hold of a few numbers of the Santa Fe papers," they might "read in full the contempt the inhabitants have for him. . . . He is very unpopular in his command and throughout the country, and his excessive economy with regard to troops and animals has just the same effect as meanness in a household, viz: a failure in all arrangements. A good cook must have good material to work with, so with a good army, or anything else! . . . At some of the northern posts recently established, troops are on half rations because the cattle for the trains of supplies are so poorly fed that they die on the way, and we hear that the last train sent to Navajo was unable to reach its destination, and the troops were going out to meet it and draw it in themselves. Economy won't work in such a poor country as this."[7]

Now that the officers at Fort Union were in "their primitive . . . log houses, white-washed logs overhead, chinked, and covered with earth to shed snow and rain, "Sumner decided upon another economy. He would send two companies of dragoons to Galisteo. There the soldiers would protect against Indians raiding from the southeast toward Santa Fe and reduce the cost of providing forage at the new

[7] Kittie Bowen must have been endowed with prescience or a superabundance of common sense, for poor economy it turned out to be. The mule herd started across the plains so late in the season that after they had traveled as far as Cottonwood Creek, a blizzard struck and nearly three hundred mules died, as did one soldier, and many troopers were severely frostbitten before rescue reached them from the east.

headquarters. There was a lack of full accord concerning this anticipated movement on the part of some of the officers, but Kittie Bowen voiced a practicable sentiment, saying: "We do not need much protection in this out-of-the-way place. We never think of Indians and have not heard that any were near." About the only people she ever saw at the post were "Mexicans who come in with donkey loads of vegetables and fruit for sale; and we are so quiet that no sentinels are posted except over the provision and clothing tents." Her chief reliance was her "big dog which takes care that no cattle come about the house, and they are the only nuisance we are likely to dread."

Besides moving some of the dragoons to Galisteo, Colonel Sumner decided to make an inspection of the lower Río Grande posts. After ordering Captain Bowen and Major Sibley to accompany him, he changed his mind, and upon "reflection thought he would leave them until spring as they both have considerable sums of public money in vaults [i.e.,] their respective bed-rooms." Being left with public money under her bed did not please Mrs. Bowen, who "feared she might spend it for onions." The order could not have been carried out, anyway, for "while chasing some wild cattle, the Captain's horse fell, throwing him, and rolling over him." Another annoying incident occurred, further delaying Sumner's departure. Major Thompson, having been apprised that he was to accompany Colonel Sumner, with "no means to shelter his wife, [had] left her at Barclay's Fort, where she was to remain until the major returned." On the first of November, he moved his troops over to Barclay's Fort, "en route to Galisteo . . . where he made camp, intending to take advantage of the journey to visit his wife." Instead, however, as had been frequently his habit, he got ingloriously drunk. It was a common statement among his officer acquaintances that "the man with the poker was after him." He fancied, while in his cups, that some of the men were going to kill him. Thus, while one of the men "was cooking by the fire, the Maj. called him and presented a pistol to his head, but immediately lowered it and told him to go about his work. When he was stooping over the fire, the Maj. deliberately shot him in the back, the ball passing through the body under and into one arm." A doctor was summoned from Fort Union, whose report the following morning was, "He is still alive but little hopes of recovery."

The major was put under arrest and turned over to the civil authorities," but as the wounded man did recover, the civil authorities "let the Maj off with paying $600 on condition that he would join the temperance society, so the Maj. did, but in Santa Fe broke the pledge so soon that the society expelled him."

Prior to leaving Fort Union on the anticipated inspection trip of posts and a conference with Governor Calhoun as he passed through the capital, Sumner had simulated humility by retracting the position he had previously taken that he would not furnish the Governor or the Indian agents with escorts while they were performing their duties. He would now, he conceded, "with pleasure furnish the necessary escort" so that the Governor might "put into effect immediately the treaty stipulations with the Utahs." That service would be useful to the Colonel, too, for "he wished the Indian Department to apprise that people that it was his intention to place a post in that country next spring." Furthermore, he wanted the Utahs to know that he expected "to continue on the most friendly terms." But as for the Navahos: "They have set at naught so many treaties that it seems useless to treat with them." Instead, by employing Fort Defiance, he wished them "to feel that we have a grasp upon them that they can not shake off . . . and if they do not put a stop to their depredations, nothing will do but their entire extermination."

At the personal conference with Sumner, Governor Calhoun insisted that the military should furnish the requested escort for the Indian Department, and in addition 250 well-mounted men (militiamen) "for the preservation of the quiet of the Utahs during the winter, goaded as they are by our own people and, at the moment, by the Kiowas and other Indians." And since the Indians presented problems both to the civil government and to the army, he importuned the Colonel that "We ought, if possible, to act in concert."[8] In support of his position, he handed the Colonel a "petition just received at this moment":

[8] Calhoun to Sumner, October 31, 1851, AC, "Fort Union, 1851," File 2, p. 55.

SANTA FE, November 9th, 1851.

SIR:

A volunteer company, composed of the American citizens of this place have organized, for the purpose of protecting, or aiding to protect the inhabitants from the frequent incursions and depredations of the Wild Indians who surround us, and as you are aware, are continually coming into our settlements. The difficulty we labor under, for our complete and effectual organization is the want of suitable arms and acoutrements. And we respectfully pray Your Excellency to furnish us with them, and in case you may not have them at your command to request Col: Sumner the Mil commander of this Dept. to supply us with the necessary arms, from the surplus arms in his possession.

Very Respy,
Your Obt Servants

PRESTON BECK, JR. CAPT.
J. E. SABINE *1st Lt.*
ELIAS BREVOURT *2nd do*
D. V. WHITING *3rd Lt. & Adjt.*

H. E. J. S. Calhoun
Govr. of the Territory
New Mexico.[9]

Upon reading the petition, Sumner, with ill-concealed hauteur, withdrew from the conference, requesting that any further communications be made in writing; then he lingered in Santa Fe until November 12, carrying on a spirited correspondence with the governor. Finally he concluded to "accede cheerfully" to the appeal of the American volunteers "for the loan of arms," but he made it plain that military control would remain with him. The cheerful accession was found to have "two conditions to the loan, viz: That these arms will be immediately returned whenever demanded by the Commanding Officer of the 9th Dept.—and secondly: That they are never to be used in making hostile incursions into the Indian Country unless this volunteer company is acting in conjunction with the regular troops." From the captain of the volunteer company came the rejection: "We decline accepting arms upon the conditions im-

[9] Calhoun to Sumner, November 10, 1851, Calhoun *Official Correspondence,* 445–46.

posed by Colonel Sumner: First, because we would not be an independent company, but liable to have our arms taken away from us
at a moment's notice, and 2d.: Because we do not wish to be restricted
in our incursion by the commander of the 9th Department." So, turning aside from the hope of aid from Sumner, Captain Beck asked
that the proper application be made to the Secretary of War.

Versed in the ramifications of making application to the Secretary of war and not wishing to subject the people of New Mexico
to more hazards of Indian molestations, the Governor again placed
the responsibility upon the Ninth Department with the force of truth,
writing:

> The numerous murders and depredations recently committed by
> Navajo, and perhaps other Indians, in this Territory, call for an effec-
> tual interposition. . . . For more than twelve months past the people
> have continued to ask for permission to protect themselves, and have
> not obtained it. Justice and humanity forbid that I should interfere
> further in their wishes to protect themselves. . . . As the Governor of
> the Territory, the solemn duty is imposed upon me, to assist them . . .
> and that duty I shall proceed, to enter upon, unless I perceive the dis-
> tribution of your troops have secured the end desired . . . . Hence it
> may be absolutely necessary to allow the people to defend themselves
> . . . and it is my well considered opinion that your positions are
> utterly untenable.[10]

Rejecting as untenable Sumner's threat of using United States troops
to prevent New Mexico citizens from going into Navaho territory
to punish the Indians for raids, the Governor likened such action to
having the very arms pointed at them which had been given the
army for the defense and protection of United States citizens. It was
only "right and lawful to allow the people . . . to protect themselves
. . . when . . . the military arm of the government" was inadequate.
He would never consent "to fold my arms, and quietly look on such
scenes of desolation as we have recently witnessed in this Territory,
without making an effort to remedy it."[11]

[10] Calhoun to Sumner, November 10, 1851, *ibid.,* 447–48.
[11] *Ibid.,* 448–49.

Sumner then backed down, telling the Governor: "After mature reflection, I have determined that I shall *not* use the regular troops to expel from the Indian Country the marauding parties that your Excellency may think proper to commission, as it will not be their fault." With this declaration, Sumner took the trail downriver, closing the Battle of the Billets at Algadonis, New Mexico, with a sarcastic refusal to write any more: "I have received your official communication of the 11th Inst, after I left Santa Fe, and I have given it all the consideration that I think it is entitled to."

From Fort Conrad, Colonel Sumner, in an effort to justify his disagreement with the Governor, stooped to fan the fires of sectionalism by holding before the War Department the visage of the *Nuevo Mejicano* as a "slaver," a "sneaking predatory warrior," who sought profit from human slavery. This time it was not the black man but the Indian who was to be enslaved. To the Adjutant General he wrote:

> I regret to trouble the Genl. in-chief with a voluminous correspondence with Governor Calhoun. I have endeavoured to avoid these difficulties . . . but . . . it was so important to prevent any Mexican marauding parties from traversing the indian country . . . . This predatory war has been carried on for two hundred years, between the Mexicans & Indians . . . . *They steal women and children, and cattle, from each other, and in fact carry on the war* . . . like two indian nations.
>
> This system of warfare will interfere very much with my measures, and indeed do away with all the advantages . . . from the establishment of Fort Defiance. This large post is in the very midst of the Indians and cannot fail to cramp them in their movements, and it will harrass [*sic*] them so much, that they will gladly make peace, and keep quiet.[12]

Then, while moving all the way down the river to Magoffinsville, he gave instruction to the officers: "If any Indians come within striking distance—you are to take no men prisoners." To strengthen the enforcement of penalties for "crime against the Indians, henceforth all persons arrested of crimes against the Indians" were to be taken to military posts "and held until they are required for trial."[13]

[12] *Ibid.*, 445.
[13] Order No. 46, December 19, 1851, NA, RG 98, 9 Mil. Dept. Orders, Vol. 5, p. 105.

Christmas Day, 1851, came with Colonel Sumner still away from Fort Union. Captain Bowen, wishing to celebrate, "gave a dinner to everybody at the post."[14] The weather was "mild, no snow and plenty of sunshine." Everybody "had a nice time and an excellent dinner, a roast of pig, a saddle of venison a month old that would have brought ten dollars in New York, a fillet of veal, cold roast fowls with jellies, and all the *fixins* . . . and there was a form of calfs-foot jelly which the mess sent." Mrs. Carleton contributed "a corn-starch blanc-mange," while Kittie "made a gallon of farina." They had no wine for the occasion, "but a strong cup of coffee" put everybody in good spirits, after which the guests devoured two pound loaves of fruit cake of Kittie's baking which *"tasted almost as good as Mother's."* Seated were sixteen guests at the Captain's and Kittie's table, "the first Christmas Dinner celebrated at Fort Union." Besides the seated guests at dinner, there were so "many in the kitchen" that Kittie "could not count them—for the butcher must have a taste of the pig and the frowzy frenchman, who had care of the little fellow, must have a taste, and half the waiters in garrison were on hand to do anything I had to do."

At the dinner table there was much about which to talk. Captain John Pope was just in from his scout with Lucien Maxwell. He had come upon Colonel Sumner's wagon train which had been ordered back to Fort Leavenworth for economy's sake, and he had a disquieting story to tell. Those who had gone toward the States had encountered a storm three days east of Fort Union. The mail teams had frozen to death, and "those who were going in to the States . . . had to walk most of the way, not daring to build fires to keep warm for fear of the Indians." Two come upon by Captain Pope were Captain A. W. Reynolds—sent out of the department by Sumner at the behest of R. H. Weightman—and Mrs. Pilans, wife of Attorney Pilans, member of the one-time law firm of Skinner, Pilans and Ashurst. Mrs. Pilans was "going south for her health . . . with two children." When Captain Pope found them near Fort Mackay, their distress

14 Kittie Bowen to "My Dear Father," January 1, 1852, AC, Bowen Letters.

had transformed them into "the very hardest looking characters I saw on the road."

Colonel Sumner got back to Fort Union during the night of December 31. The first thing in the morning of the new year "the companies had a review. This was followed by an acceptable invitation "to the gentlemen . . . to lunch at Colonel Alexanders." After partaking of the post commander's hospitality, "everybody turned out to observe protocol, paying a call-of-respects to the Department Commander." This punctilio over, "they called upon the ladies." Mrs. Bowen had anticipated her guests "with a tureen full of eggnog and some nice cake." Then good fortune arrived: "Just as the company came in, a box of fresh apples from the States came to Isaac, and we had the gratification of sharing with our neighbors."

The Colonel commanding employed his New Year's Day in making a record of his accomplishments since he had arrived in New Mexico. This he sent to Adjutant General Jones.[15] Upon inspection he found Forts Fillmore and Conrad "well advanced, and the troops were now in quarters built by themselves"; the labor done by the troops had "improved the health and efficiency of my command." At "El Passo [*sic*]" he had been able to "effect an economy" by "breaking up entirely the establishment, which was very expensive and useless." To check the Indians in "the Apache Country," he had put a post at the Copper Mines; this he thought—as he thought of Fort Defiance—"will effectually curb that tribe." The "squadron of horse stationed at Galisteo and a company of Infantry at Taos" were scheduled to be sent into the Utah country. That plan, however, would remain in contemplation "until spring opens." He had disagreed again with Governor Calhoun, about the bestowal of gifts upon the Navahos. It was a "mistake so important that I wish to make known to the department my decided dissent and disapprobation to this measure."

Reluctantly he came to discuss Fort Union: "I find it indispensably necessary to remove my headquarters from this post to Albu-

[15] Sumner to Jones, NA, RG 98, 9 Mil. Dept. Orders, Vol. 5, pp. 118-20.

querque, on the Rio Grande, in order to be nearer the new posts in the Indian Country. Circumstances might arise which would make it important that I should be within striking distance of these posts." He set the date of "transfer to Albuquerque" as "the 1st proximo." Obviously he had concluded that the Fort Union region was no longer "Indian country." The only Indians known to have been in the vicinity came during the Christmas holidays, while Colonel Sumner lingered at Jemez complaining to Governor Calhoun about bestowal of gifts. The Indians evidenced no hostility, and Kittie Bowen was amused as she watched them "hunt over these mountains without giving any trouble . . . seeming friendly enough in this part of the country."[16]

After finishing his report, Colonel Sumner walked over to Captain Bowen's home, coming, he said, "to pay his official respects" and distribute "among the ladies a crate of quinces from the lower country." Acquisitive Kittie "took seven pounds of them and had good luck in doing them up." And then before Colonel Sumner had put the finishing touches to Fort Union as headquarters of the Ninth Military Department, Kittie Bowen registered another first. She gave birth to "an eight and three-fourths pound, blue-eyed baby boy with hair almost black." Isaac named his son "Cary" for his father-in-law. "Doct McDougal, an old and experienced surgeon was in attendance." The new mother had the "almost constant attention of the wife of the mechanic, who came out of kindness, a very nice woman, who understood her part well." Since she would not accept compensation, "not a dime," she was "paid in more ways than one, in milk, butter, and little presents of all sorts acceptable at this place."

Before moving down to Weightman's Albuquerque, Sumner let it be known that, for the time being, "only his adjutant and one surgeon" would go with him; and he wound up affairs in Fort Union by writing again to headquarters.[17] He saw "with great satisfaction

[16] Kittie Bowen, January 1, 1852, AC, Bowen Letters.

[17] Sumner to Jones, NA, RG 98, 9 Mil. Dept. Orders, Vol. 5, pp. 192–93. This letter is erroneously dated, as is obvious from the photographic copy in the Arrott Collection. This error is important as it gives the date of location of Fort Union one year later than it actually occurred.

... [that] the posts I have established in this territory are already exercising a favorable influence in our Indian relations.... The Utahs and the Jicarilla Apaches have been perfectly quiet." The reason: "The tribes are influenced by this post [Fort Union]." Too, "The Gila Apaches have paused," a response to a policy of "rods of iron over their heads." He "had heard of no depredations . . . since the establishment of Fort Webster."

It was true that he had heard of no depredations, but only lack of speed in communications had prevented him from receiving a letter written two days before by Major Howe at Fort Conrad containing news to the contrary. By way of background, during the fall of 1851, at the little town of San Antonio, New Mexico, a *Nuevo Mejicano* had engaged three Gila Apaches in "a friendly game of chance." They conformed to Lord Byron's philosophical observation:

> *For few men*
> *(till by losing rendered sager)*
> *Will back their own opinions*
> *by a wager.*

And when the Mexican's pair of Jacks failed to crown a pair of Queens, one Apache grew sager—with a pistol ball through his body —while his two companions lay dead at the gaming table.

The wounded Apache carried the story of their misfortune to his tribesmen, who came to San Antonio the following day and demanded "in conformance with the Whiteman's law" that the "Mexican be confined for trial." In a gesture of compliance the *alcalde* had the slayer placed in jail, and the "Indians left satisfied; but as soon as they were gone, the murderer was permitted to go at large again, and when the Indians heard of it they became furious." Colonel Sumner took notice of this "remissness of the civil authorities," and during the December conference with the Governor "brought it to his notice and expressed the opinion that villain should be arrested and tried." But "the common, uncertain course of the law was dilatory"—especially in dispensing justice between *Nuevo Mejicanos* and Gila Apaches, the law of the Medes and Persians being unknown; so the Gilas rode straight to Sumner's life-line, the dread *Jornada*. If they could not have justice, they would seek vengeance.

Howe's dispatch of January 25 from Conrad confirmed Sumner in his decision that his removal of headquarters immediately was justified. Major Howe had sent out "an escort of one non-com officer and ten privates to escort the members of the Court on the 'Jornada.' . . . owing to the barking of dogs during the night he supposed that Indians were near . . . and started at sunrise prepared for the Indians [but] they received a volley from both sides of the road without seeing anyone. . . . the saddle mule to the wagon and three men were killed . . . [and later] one other was killed and one wounded. . . . soon some forty [Gilas] appeared mounted and followed the six men some three miles. The Corporal reported two Indians killed and one wounded. . . . The corporal is sure there were white men among the number as they had large whiskers and curly hair that he was so well satisfied that he cursed them in english."

With a Gila Apache war in the making, Sumner turned his thoughts to the kinsmen of the Gilas—the Mescalero Apaches, whose range was east of the Río Grande north of El Paso and up the Río Pecos. They had been quiet for so long that Sumner was alarmed. He therefore decided to put Major Carleton on the move again. Rumor at Fort Union had it that "Major Carleton goes tomorrow with his company of dragoons on a scouting expedition *somewhere* . . . cannot tell the exact direction, but to scare up the Apaches, if there are any." The location of the Mescaleros was as indefinite to Carleton as to Sumner, but he got orders to go down the Pecos in search of them. He was to proceed in the direction of the Bosque Redondo, to make a reconnaissance in that section of the country, "open a communication with the Muscalero Apaches, and should he meet them, it was important to "impress upon them the necessity of their abstaining from all depredations upon the whites." He was to say to them "plainly, that we wish to be at peace, but that we are always prepared for war and that the President of the United States has said that whenever an Indian tribe commits any depredations that a military post shall be established immediately in the heart of their country to compel them to remain at peace." For the subsistence of his command, he might buy fodder "at reasonable prices," but failing to buy economically, "you will have to trust to grazing."

Carleton's reconnaissance toward the Bosque Redondo terminated February 24, 1852. He had "found a fine country down there" but no Indians. Sumner regretted that Carleton "did not see any Indians," but "the fine country down there" inspired him to say, "If I had troops to spare, I should establish a post there immediately."

The party came into Las Vegas on February 23. When the troops dismounted for the day, the weather was "cold and windy"; the men were tired; the horses needed shelter and food. The town could "furnish fodder at reasonable prices, and Major Carleton decided to stay there for the night." He sought out Judge Grolman, whose home faced the plaza near the hotel. Upon being invited, as he hoped he would be, he became the Judge's guest for the night. The men, dismissed from duty, "seemed to behave themselves very well until a late hour in the night," that is, until after "the Major had visited the guard," but there was a fandango in town, which the men attended. The next morning at reveille five or six troops were absent, but during stable duties most of them returned to Judge Grolman's stables, and although "appearing to be generally sober, they looked as if they had been drinking freely." Privates McCleave and Freely failed to report for duty. Major Carleton left the sergeant in charge to worry about absentees and went off to the Judge's house to take breakfast with his host. When he returned to his troop, the quartermaster sergeant could not be found and a teamster was now so drunk that he could not hitch his mules. A check at the stables disclosed evidence that many of the men were drinking and "that a great many arms, equipment, and horse equipage were scattered around . . . as if no one owned them." Freely now having made his appearance, made, also, "some impertinent reply accompanied by an insolent look when ordered to obey 'boots and saddles.' " McCleave, having returned, from "his gestures and actions seemed determined openly to resist." He had a saber in his hand. His rifle stood behind him. Carleton grabbed the rifle, "at first determined to knock him down with it!" Happily, at that moment a sergeant appeared with half a dozen men, and Carleton, with an abundance of discretion, ordered the men to seize McCleave "with main force and tie him to a wagon." This restraint was effective but a short time; he untied himself.

"During this time ... the corporal of the guard was running around after Freely." Meantime, the drunken teamster came to tell the commander that he was sick, and when upbraided by Carleton, the sick teamster "expostulated with the Major most insolently," broke away, "and did not show up at Fort Union until two days afterwards." All of this caused Major Carleton "to think, then on the spot, that there was a determination on the part of many of the men ... to throw every obstacle in the way of ... leaving Las Vegas that morning." Such a conclusion could be deduced from the fact that "it was the most boisterous, and dusty day I ever saw in my life; so much so that all the landmarks which were to serve as guides to my new route across the country, were entirely concealed from my view."

Finally the troop moved out, accompanied by two wagons, in one of which Major Carleton intended a sick man should ride, but he was chagrined when a "citizen [of Las Vegas] reported ... that a Mexican and a boy had been placed in this heavily laden wagon." The Las Vegan objected to their being taken along with the troops as "they belonged to him, and he wished to have them put out." Carleton refused as "I did not want to be mortified by having citizens see them get out of a public wagon, and besides ... was determined to bring them out some distance that I might, by causing them to walk back, punish them for their impertinance in allowing themselves to be put into it."

As the perturbed commander "mounted his horse ... [and] opened the ranks of his company ... just as when the comany is on a campaign" preparatory to moving out, he saw "McCleave lying on his back in the plaza ... Freely on his back half-way across the plaza ... while McNally, the drunken teamster was not with the guard," all of which Carleton interpreted as "feigning in order to be placed in the wagon out of the storm." So he ordered the men tied to the wagon, "and if they would not walk, they should be made to walk."

Private Patrick O'Brien then contributed to Major Carleton's discomfort by riding up, bending forward in the saddle, and sliding to the ground "as if by design . . . lying on his back as if perfectly dead drunk." This got him another position "tied to the wagon"—and when Carleton appeared oblivious to their discomfort, Freely, although he had no gun, "cursed" the commander "and offered" to shoot him. Of course, this was most displeasing to the militaristic Carleton, who produced "a gag"—"it was a piece of rope"—and this he "directed to be used," putting it into Freely's mouth "and tying it back of his head." Thus gagged and trussed, the prisoners were made to come along behind the wagon. Soon they came to Gallinas Creek. Not being able by this time to walk, Patrick O'Brien was dragged across the creek. On the farther side Major Carleton overtook the wagons dragging the men, and thought "they acted as if drunker than when they left the plaza." He had water brought from the stream "to be dashed on them until they could walk," but "he concluded not to throw the water on them as the day was cold and inclement." (A few buckets of water additional probably would have been inconsequential after being dragged through the creek.) They were put on their feet, but they fell down again, "still resting their hands on the feed-trough and dragging their toes in the dust."

While the men were dragging behind the wagon, the Major went ahead to give orders "to hurry up" as he wished to get to Fort Union before dark. As the wagon speeded up, "the horses trotting down hill . . . coming down the descending ground toward the Sapillo," O'Brien swung at the end of his tether, and the wagon sergeant stopped and put him aboard. He then rode off to the Major to report that O'Brien was dead. Carleton was "surprised and shocked," wondering aloud, "Is it possible."

At Fort Union the body of the dead trooper was delivered to the post surgeon, and Carleton reported the incident to Colonel Sumner, now in his new Albuquerque headquarters. Sumner "hardly thought it necessary, but perhaps it was, in this case to have such cases investigated, and thus shut the mouths of ill-disposed persons," so, "on your application," he permitted a court-martial to convene, the president of the court, on March 26, filing its findings: "The Court of Inquiry, after mature deliberation . . . are of the opinion that the death of the late Patrick O'Brien . . . was caused alone by the poisonous effects of alcohol."

Again Colonel Sumner was late, lingering at Fort Union until February 4 before making the change of headquarters to Albuquerque. Captain Isaac Bowen was directed to go with him to inspect supplies as far south as El Paso. "Nobody sees the necessity of this . . . but Col S likes to see everybody on the move and as uncomfortable as possible" was the unsolicited distaff opinion. Captain Bowen maneuvered so as not to travel with Sumner, taking along with him an extra supply of clothing, including "a blouse or sort of frock made by Kittie out of a blue blanket to wear on the tramp of more than a thousand miles," she determining "to make my good man as comfortable as I can make him." Before the Bowen's departure, Kittie had an invitation from Mrs. Carleton to live with her during the absence of the husbands. Kittie declined the invitation since she would "rather take her chances alone than enter into *partnership* with anyone except my husband; furthermore Mrs. Carleton has a child and an *ugly slave and I will not allow our girl to associate with the black*." As Captain Bowen rode off, he left his wife sitting "rocking the cradle with one foot and employing her left hand to furnish her mouth with candy," thinking of "Mrs. Carleton, Mrs. Shoemaker and Mrs. Sibley [who] are to *add to our society* in a little while. Surely, this is a growing country."

On April 1, Captain Bowen returned from the long ride. "He was so stiff that he could barely stand when he got off his horse." He had left his baggage behind to come later. He tantalized his wife all day trying to get her to guess what he had in his trunk for her. She responded by presenting "my man with a wedding present, a *ruffled shirt*," which she had made during his absence. He put it on "with a white vest, black coat and hat and he truly looks like a bride-groom today." Unexpectedly that evening the trunk came. In it were "six pieces of solid silver ware, and mugs holding nearly a quart, and plates, which make very pretty waiters for glasses, 1 salt cellar lined with gold and 1 tureen with a spoon which can either be used for a gravy boat or sugar dish or cream bowl . . . the whole pure as it came from the mines, and is hammered into the oddest shapes. . . . The whole weighs nearly six pounds, and although very roughly made, have the *stuff* in them." He had "bought them from Gen Armijo who has been governor of New Mexico and a general in the Mexican army, a rich old fellow who entertains his friends in princely style."[18] Isaac told how he "selected these pieces out of a huge chest full of pitchers, platters, cups and everything that can be used on a table." He gave "$1.25 an ounce" and thereafter was offered a handsome profit on this bargain.

After the purchase of the silver, Armijo became the *arbiter elegantiae,* sending "a box of pear marmalade" which Kittie found "as delicate as anything I ever tasted"—his compliments to the wife of the Captain! To the Captain himself went "a dry cheese and a quart of brandy." Ingenious Kittie immediately "found the most sensible way of using liquor." She poured the brandy in a jar and "packed in the cheese—hard," thinking "in a month's time it will be a finer flavor than it was at first."

Before Sumner's Albuquerque headquarters was a month old, Governor Calhoun had become convinced that, even from his position nearer the Indians, the department commander was not going to stop the depredations. Therefore, on February 29, 1852, he wrote Secretary of State, Daniel Webster: "I deem it my duty to enclose to you the accompanying petition from . . . Socorro, and a correspondence . . . with Col. Sumner. . . . The troops of the United States are at present totally useless, on account of the inability of the mounted men to perform their duty, the feeble and half starved condition of their horses will not allow them to travel, and Infantry is of no use whatever in checking Indians who are well mounted and whose animals are in the best order."

With this direct and blunt attack on the efficiency of himself and

[18] Kittie Bowen to "My Dear Mother," April 2, 1852, AC, Bowen Letters. At the time of General Armijo's flight from Santa Fe rumor had it that he had taken the silver from the Palace of the Governors upon "heavily laden mules"; this purchase bears all the earmarks of substantiating that rumor.

his army, Sumner took notice of both the situation in the Gila country and Governor Calhoun's determination. He therefore reported:
"Everything is very uncertain at the south," and it just might be that
"I will have to make a campaign against the Apaches." He was, however, "being very much pressed for transportation" and regretted "it
will not be in Maj. Sibleys power to give another team." Contemplating the needs of the uncertain south, he directed the First Dragoons "to move from Albuquerque to LaJoya—that is, provided he
should be able to find good Quarters for the men, and sufficient forage for the animals, at reasonable prices."

He discounted Calhoun's fears of the Navahos, assuring army
headquarters that "these Indians, I think, will give no more trouble
if we can keep the Mexicans from marauding upon them." As to the
Gila Apaches, they "are the only Indians that are now troublesome
in this department," but it was "too much . . . to expect an entire stop
can be put to all Indian depredations. They are educated to believe
that the stealing of horses is an act of prowess, and a few young men
may occasionally band together for this purpose, but this propensity
will soon wear out."

In reply to the petitioners from Socorro who no longer had confidence in Sumner's army and who had lost confidence in the "well
armed and well fed Troops upon whom we have hitherto relied as a
broken reed," he thought these "people of the town require less protection than the people of the country; indeed it is not too much to
say that if these Mexicans, when banded together in large numbers,
have not the manliness to defend themselves from small parties of
roving Indians they deserve to suffer. It is not their fear as much as
their cupidity that makes them desire to have troops stationed among
them; they want the government money." To relieve himself of the
goading, however, he complimented Major Morris on his zeal to quiet
the Gilas, advised him that although "under the circumstances he
could not spare troops to make another scout" and "did not think it
advisable to employ volunteers," he would permit Morris "with the
means he had to make any movement that you think prudent and

beneficial." That matter he would leave entirely to Morris' judgment. Thinking it over for three days caused him again to change his mind. He therefore issued orders[19] to Lieutenant I. S. Maxwell, Third Artillery, D Company, to march to Albuquerque without delay prepared for field service against the Apaches. As a consequence of this troop movement, command at Fort Union would devolve upon Major Sibley, "but in his absence Captain I. Bowen will assume command." With the prospect of Captain Bowen in command at Fort Union while Colonel Sumner attempted to pacify the Governor and New Mexico citizens, rumors came to Fort Union of a more portentous character: The *Nuevo Mejicanos* were plotting another revolt. Bowen evaluated it for what it was:

> There is some talk of revolution among the Mexicans in Santa Fe, but I recken [*sic*] that it is all humbug, for we are quiet here. Col Sumner must keep his troops moving continually if for no other purpose than to render them uncomfortable, so, if you hear of troops changing post, rest assured that my version is correct.

There was, however, much talk of revolution, again, at Santa Fe, and the alarmist, Indian agent John Greiner, fanned the excitement in a letter to one of his friends:

> Here I am in the Palace of Santa Fe sitting along side of Governor Calhoun, writing letters to my old friends in the "States," far, far away. If I succeed in getting safely back again among my friends under Providence I shall consider myself a highly favored man. Between the savage Indians, the treacherous Mexicans and the outlawed Americans a man has to run the gauntlet in this country. Three governors within twelve years have lost their heads (Perez, Gonzales and Bent) and there are men here at present who talk so flippantly of taking Governor Calhoun's head as though it were of no consequence at all. Everybody and everything in this country appears at cross purposes. In the first place the civil and military authorities are at war. . . . The American residents are at war with the Governor, while the Mexican population side with him. . . . the Eutahs and Apaches, who get drunk whenever they get a

[19] Order No. 26, AC, "Fort Union, 1852," File 1, p. 46.

131

chance . . . boast of how many whites they have killed, and talk very glibly of how many scalps they intend to take. There is a great and deep gulf between the Americans and Mexicans yet, and the love they bear each other has by no means waxed warm. There is hardly an American here that stirs abroad without being armed to the teeth.[20]

While John Greiner, unable to understand the Dryden philosophy that "rashness is a better fault than fear," spread the apprehension that the taking of Calhoun's head was of no consequence at all, Calhoun wrote to Sumner bluntly questioning his proposed line of action, particularly condemning a campaign against the Gilas and otherwise tendering unacceptable advice, advice which was wholly without his purview as governor. He would have the commander know that

> By selecting a Central position, where your animals could be recruited and be ready to move at a moments notice, and where facts could be obtained more readily . . . and where you could be put in direct communication with the principal Pueblos—you would in my humble opinion do more to protect the lives and property of our people at this time than by heading an expedition to the Apache Country.

After giving Colonel Sumner this unsolicited and unappreciated advice, the Governor felt called up on to explain the underlying cause of his anxiety: he was in great physical distress. Sumner, he wrote, was "perhaps advised of my weak, feeble, and almost hopeless condition—and I feel that I am speaking almost as a dying man—yet I feel desirous of doing all in my power to promote the public weal." He would have visited the commander instead of writing but for his utter inability to mount his horse. For the last four weeks he had been unable to stand without assistance and he had been confined to his bed. He professed an appreciation of Sumner's position—"the absolute & unqualified necessity of making a demonstration against the Apaches," but was at the same time under the impression that it was "more important at present to look to the well being, and safety of the Citizens." Then apologetically he admitted that it was not the governor's place "to speak to you of the defenses of this Territory . . .

[20] Twitchell, *Leading Facts,* II, 284, n. 206, citing *Journal of American History,* Vol. III, p. 546. Letter dated October 1, 1851.

[it is] your duty alone," and asked pardon "for this gratuitous communication."[21]

Colonel Sumner responded like a courteous gentleman. He regretted "very much to hear of [the Governor's] extreme illness," admonishing him to "dismiss all care about these public matters until you are better." In the meantime Calhoun might rest assured that "I will take such measures, that whoever expects to find me unprepared, will find himself mistaken." Furthermore, in deference to the Governor's opinion, he would "postpone my contemplated movement against the Apaches" and "quietly, but promptly, make such arrangements, that I can rapidly concentrate a sufficient force for any *emergency* . . . and leave myself sufficient troops for any exigency."[22]

A few days after receiving notice of the Governor's illness and after completing "some arrangements I am engaged in," Sumner rode from Albuquerque to Santa Fe. En route he "saw no appearance of disaffection as I passed through the country." He concluded that "if there is anything in these rumors [of pending revolt], it is confined to the lower classes, instigated, perhaps, by a few desperate unprincipled, gamblers and speculators, who have everything to gain and nothing to lose by fomenting commotions." He knew that in Santa Fe "there are several desperadoes . . . who were conspicuous in the revolution of 1847," and "these men will be closely watched." When he arrived in the capital, however, he was "surprised to find it in a state of anarchy. All prisoners had been released for want of means to subsist them, and all law seems to be set at naught.—At the same time there was a constant dread of revolution, which kept up a feverish excitement, that was likely, every moment, to lead to some collision with the Mexicans," and he "saw it was indispensably necessary to take measures immediately, to suppress all this disorder."[23]

He called upon the Governor, who had written him on April 12 that it "has pleased Divine Providence to bring me through the crisis

21 Calhoun to Sumner, April 7, 1852, in Calhoun, *Official Correspondence,* 518-19.
22 Sumner to Calhoun, April 8, 1852, *ibid.,* 521.
23 Sumner to General R. Jones, April 22, 1852, NA, RG 93, Letters, 9 Mil. Dept. and Dept. of N. M., 1851-61, Vol. 9 (pages not numbered); also, AC, "Fort Union, 1852," File 1, p. 60.

of my disease" and place him in "what according to my own opinion and that of my physicians is a state of rapid recovery." In an effort, to reach an accord with Sumner, Calhoun had asked that an additional artillery force be brought to Santa Fe "if it can be made to harmonize with your policy." To that Sumner would not agree, but a company of infantry being transferred from Fort Union to Albuquerque was ordered to Santa Fe; this reduction brought the total number of troops remaining at Fort Union to 150.[24] Then, despite his knowledge that Colonel Munroe had been relieved of command for usurpation of civil authority, Colonel Sumner made a bold move in that same direction. Laying aside his feud with the Governor, he said that if the Governor "thought proper to ask for military aid, that I would give it at once."[25]

Enfeebled by illness, apprehensive of the Indians and *Nuevo Meji-canos,* with a bankrupt treasury, with unco-operative civil officers, several of whom had gone to the states (including the treasurer, taking the money with him), and with a judge who "steams it high" sitting with associates "who are sober, steady, moral men—but nothing else," and being unwilling to risk further chaos in the capital city, the Governor succumbed to putting his name to a letter which virtually bowed him out of office:

EXECUTIVE DEPARTMENT
SANTA FE N.M. April 18, 1852

Col. E. V. Sumner
Commanding 9" Mil. Dep. U.S.A.
SIR

I feel it my duty on behalf of the *people of this city,* to make appli-cation to you to furnish such aid, as may be necessary to assist the civil authorities in maintaining peace & good order, which they are utterly unable to do, at this time, in consequence of a want of sufficient power to enforce the police regulations, and without which a more wretched state of things must ensue *in this City.*

The feeble attempts made to administer the laws, and the turning

[24] Post Returns, Fort Union, April, 1852, AC, "Fort Union, 1852," File 1, p. 68.
[25] Sumner to Jones, April 22, 1852, NA, RG 93, Letters, 9 Mil. Dept. and Dept. of N. M., 1851-61, Vol. 9 (pages not numbered).

loose of the criminals who cannot be kept in confinement, owing to the want of means to furnish them with the necessary food—has brought about the present alarming state of affairs.

Very Respectfully,

Your Obdt Servt

J. S. CALHOUN[26]

Having usurped the functions of the governor in the face of positive orders previously given Colonel Munroe, the department commander then sought to justify his action. Instead of accepting Governor Calhoun's explanation of the denouement, Sumner declared, "The Extreme illness of the governor and the absence of the secretary of the Territory have had some influence in producing this unsettled state of things." Immediately he took measures "to suppress all this disorder." He established a "military police to act in support of the civil authorities." He mounted "a strong guard at the Governors house on the Plaza," he added to the Fort Marcy garrison "a large company of Infantry," and this done, he had accomplished "the quiet of the town."[27]

With "the quiet of the town" accomplished, Governor Calhoun announced his intention of returning to the States, but he would like to know, in the event that the governorship were left vacant, to whom it would go. Sumner assured him that he would support either of the two highest civil officers, Judge Mower or Judge Watts—that is, provided they could agree between themselves which should take precedence—but in the event they could not agree, then [said he], "I will protect the interregnum: In other words, I will protect all the civil officers in the performance of their several duties, they being responsible to the authority from which they derive their power. The office of Governor to remain vacant until orders are received from the general government." Then, to make certain that the governor was divesting himself of his authority to Sumner, the department commander caused Calhoun to give notice:

[26] Calhoun to Sumner, April 18, 1852, in Calhoun, *Official Correspondence,* 527.

[27] Adding "a large company of Infantry" was pure bombast for the ears of the Adjutant General. No record substantiates the statement that he ordered other than the "detachment of Recruits"—seventy-seven men—to Santa Fe.

To the Public

It is hereby announced that no interregnum will take place in the office of the Governor of this Territory. If Governor Calhoun should be obliged to leave for the States before the arrival of the Hon. Secretary of the Territory, the Military authority of this Department will so far take charge of the Executive Office as to make the preservation of law and order, absolutely certain.[28]

As a kindly gesture toward the departing Governor, whom he trusted would reach his home in safety, Sumner suggested that he should "go to Fort Union and rest there a few days." He tendered his comfortable house, "and it is entirely at your service." For a security escort, "under existing circumstances in this territory, instead of sending Major Carleton's whole company to the Arkansas," he would send a platoon only, but he would direct "this Officer [Lieutenant Johnson] to regulate his marches" to suit the convenience of the sick man.

On May 5, Sumner found Calhoun "very ill" but determined to undertake the journey. Calhoun's son-in-law, Santa Fe's postmaster Love, had provided for any eventualities, including a coffin "in which to inter the governor should he die." The gubernatorial party left Santa Fe on May 6. Sumner amended his orders, directing Major Carleton at Fort Union to send twenty-five men to the Arkansas instead of twenty, "for the Governor is very ill." Calhoun arrived at Fort Union on May 11 "in a feeble state of health." Carleton was "doubtful if he would be able to proceed further." However, the rest at Fort Union helped him "now to begin to take nourishment." He was not to take nourishment from any subsistence from Sumner, however, for on his application, Sumner refused any such assistance. He regretted that he could not furnish him with the subsistence stores: "Owing to the great abuses here and elsewhere very stringent orders have been issued on this subject." He suggested that Calhoun might be able to make some arrangements with the Agent of the flour contractor." He could, however, furnish for use en route, to be "turned over to Major Ogden at Fort Leavenworth" "two wall tents, two water tanks, and second hand harness for 8 mules."

[28] Calhoun, *Official Correspondence*, 528.

Kittie Bowen went down to the corral to see "Governor Calhoun [as he] left Tuesday for the states, hoping to reach home to die . . . a fine old gentleman. . . . Last fall he got the scurvy and the yellow jaundice took hold of him reducing him so much that in traveling he has a bed in his ambulance and has to be lifted in and out like an infant. The postmaster at Santa fe is his son-in-law but his daughter is in the states and his utmost endeavor is now to reach home—his only hope, to reach home; all the family he has. Mr. Love went with him and Col. Sumner sent a dragoon company to escort him. Doct. McParlin, our agreeable young doctor, was sent to take care of him, altho we expect the next mail to bring word of his death. Mr. Love . . . provided everything in case he should die on the plains, but we all hope to hear of his reaching Georgia."[29]

The enfeebled Calhoun did not reach Georgia. He died somewhere on the plains, the place of burial being questionable, but probably in Independence, Missouri. "The melancholy intelligence of the death of Governor Calhoun" came to Colonel Sumner on July 31. The Governor was dead; the military was completely in power again.

Sumner's first official act after re-establishing military headquarters in Santa Fe—"that sink of vice and extravagance"—was to "extend the reserve at Fort Union to eight miles square." The fort was to be "the central point," and "all citizens living within the limits will be removed from the reserve without destroying their property." Isaac Bowen was charged with the duty of marking the limits, but he demurred, "as he had no instruments," asking that "Captain Pope be sent to perform this duty." Alexander Barclay, hearing of the Colonel's intention, served notice that there would be no surveying: these men were encroaching upon his lands. The Fort Union environs belonged to him; he would defend his property.[30]

On April 22, Major E. B. Alexander, commanding at Fort Union, was relieved by Major James H. Carleton. It took only four days to determine that previous orders to close "the dram selling establish-

[29] Kittie Bowen to "My Dear Mother," May 28, 1852, AC, Bowen Letters.

[30] Alexander Barclay from Fort Barclay to Colonel Sumner, May 25, 1852, AC, "Fort Union, 1852," File 1, p. 87.

ments in the vicinity of Fort Union" had not been carried out. Acting as Colonel Sumner's legal adviser—*sans* the license—Carleton pointed out that "the intercourse law passed by Congress applies to this case" and the "situation warrants the immediate seizure of all stores of the vender." Then, as an afterthought, the would-be lawyer concluded it might be a safer procedure to anchor seizures upon an allegation of seizing government property. He therefore told the commander, "These places, without a doubt are the receptacles of the property and many of the stores stolen from the depot, and are places where the thieves congregate to lay schemes on further depredations." As a result, Marshal Stevens went to Fort Union and Carleton ordered him, "with the assistance of troops," to arrest ten men "under Act of Congress, approved March 3, 1847, to preserve the peace on the frontier. Result: "Six houses were burned down by the raiders, ten men were sent off for trial at Santa Fe, while the contents of the houses were turned over to the A.A.Q.M. at this Post."[31] Two of those caught in the dragnet were Messrs. Barclay and Doyle, merchants and owners of Barclay's Fort, Barclay being the claimant to the land included in Sumner's expansion order. These prisoners immediately filed suit for thirty thousand dollars' damages, for trespass and "for the destruction of a quantity of whiskey." Carleton complained that the action of Barclay and Doyle was quite unfair, "for he had sent to them a copy of Orders No. 30 establishing the military reserve." He had also sent them word that if they brought more liquor to "sell to the troops on the Reserve it would be destroyed." So designing were "these men, Barclay and Doyle, that they would send their liquor via a wagon so that they could move it off or on the reserve at their convenience." He brushed aside their claim of ownership of the land, being "willing to speculate that the contention was groundless as the Mexican government never ratified it [the grant]; and if this point be vigorously contested, and the venue changed from Taos County to Santa Fe (as it can be done), then the case will come up before Judge Baker."

The postponed orders to Assistant Quartermaster E. S. Sibley to tour

[31] Carleton to Sumner, May 13, 1852, AC, "Fort Union, 1852," File 1, p. 82.

the New Mexican posts and inspect the stores came. Since Fort Union afforded no vault or safe in which to secure the army money, Sibley, not being able to take it along with him, shifted the care of the money to Captain Bowen, who remained at the post temporarily functioning as commander. This disposition of the government funds displeased the Captain's wife, who protested: "Maj. Sibley is taking his tour of inspection, and Isaac had to take all his funds. One corner of our bed room is piled several feet square with boxes of silver." To offset the inconvenience of stored silver, however, was the Captain's status plus his foresight. They "had butter and eggs and all substantials." In fact, "we are the only ones in garrison who have had butter all winter, and the only reason is that Isaac takes care of everything himself. . . . The corn and hay that he draws for his horse is divided between horse, mules, cows, pigs and chickens, and all have enough to grow fat upon." They had "forty-seven chickens, three little porkers, and a calf, besides the large stock. We were never living more comfortable." One complaint, however, was general: "No one in the garrison, *except Maj. Sibley,* has anything but a mud roof, and a heavy shower would give our carpets and 'fixins' a beautiful color." There seemed to be no remedy: "The old worn out mills break down two or three times a day and there is no telling when the rest of us will get boards for our houses."[32]

Isaac Bowen's tenure as Fort Union commander soon came to an end. Sumner had had the paymaster to "bring every dime" of the army funds from Santa Fe to Fort Union. That caused Major Sibley "to pile up his funds, $110,000, in our bed rooms . . . four feet square and the same in height"—as Kittie Bowen measured it. Then Sumner changed his mind, and "it is traveling back again; at least $40,000 of it was, it going back with a small escort." At Santa Fe Captain Bowen was to "take charge of a waggon load of silver."

Taking advantage of Barclay's challenge to Sumner's right to preempt land in the vicinity of Fort Union, several other men moved into the region, chiefly "selling liquor to soldiers of this command," complained the post commander. Also they "purchase Soldier's cloth-

[32] Kittie Bowen to "My Dear Father," May 1, 1852, AC, Bowen Letters.

ing, harbor deserters, purchase property stolen from individuals &
the U. States. . . . It was a matter of such import to the troops" that
he wanted to be instructed if "I can prevent a Staff Officer of this
Depot from purchasing from *such degraded characters.*"[33]

Colonel Sumner did not limit his aversion to "degraded characters."
In his view, "The Mexican people are thoroughly debased and totally
incapable of self government" and there was "no latent quality about
them that can make them respectable citizens." He did exclude "some
educated gentlemen with respectable families—about enough for
magistrates and other official persons," although he doubted "if there
is a tribe of Indians on the continent who are more abandoned in
their commerce between the sexes than the great majority of this people."[34] This condition prevailed despite a paean of morality the New
Mexico Legislature had enacted into law proscribing pimps. Of the
law Captain George Sykes proclaimed: "A Clergyman of the Country who has lived for more than half a century in New Mexo framed
that Law—the Legislature passed it, the Governor approved it, and
all respectable people endorse it."[35]

Sections seven and eight of the quadrivial document read:

> *Pimps* are those persons, male or female, whose business is to procure
> women for the purpose of lascivious connection with men, the fact be-
> ing public or made so, by the nature of same . . . shall, upon conviction
> be publicly whipped receiving thirty lashes, and furthermore shall be
> carried upon a Jack Ass, through the streets among the people, upon
> some feast day, in which passage until its conclusion they shall be fol-
> lowed by the town crier, who shall cry out not less than five times the
> cause of their punishment.

> If the person exercising this Office should be women, the number of
> strikes shall be inflicted . . . upon the buttocks and not upon the shoul-
> ders, in consideration of the weakness of the sex . . . the punishment may

[33] McCrae to Nichols, October 6, 1853, AC, "Fort Union, 1852," File 1, p. 59.

[34] Report of the Secretary of War, 1852, 32 Cong., 2 sess. *Sen. Exec. Doc. No. 1,*
Part I, pp. 25-26.

[35] Court-Martial Proceedings, Captain George Sykes, 1852, AC (copy): Captain
George Sykes to members of the court-martial.

be commuted to three months service in a house to which they may be assigned with a shackle on their feet.[36]

Although it was Sumner's avowal that he had taken the troops away from Santa Fe to avoid "that sink of vice and extravagance," still many of the sisters-of-sin of the old abode moved eastward with the army to ensconce themselves among the rocks and caves overlooking Sumner's new Fort Union. Notable among the denizens of the caves were María Alvina Chaireses, sometimes known as "Jesusitta," or to the soldiers as "Black Sus," and María Dolores Trujigue y Rivale. Caverns, although providing shelter, lacked the everyday rudiments of living for even those whose wants were few, so, through a comity of womanhood (aided by her expendable wares) and annointable sentinels, a system of subsistence removal was devised which soon brought furrows to the brow of the dependable and meticulous Captain Isaac Bowen. His six months' report for the first half of 1852—Return of Provisions—showed "Dropped from Subsistence Stores" as "Wastage or Stolen":

9,379 pounds of bacon	1,313 Star candles
3,400 " " flour	37 bushels of salt
4,303 " " coffee	1,191 pounds of ham
870 pounds of crushed sugar	2 $2\%_{32}$ bushels of beans
207 pounds of soap	5,254 pounds of clear sugar
70 gallons of pickle	20 bushels of dried peaches

This immense loss caused Captain Bowen to file with Colonel Sumner a plea for relief in which he said: ". . . this affiant believes the greater portion of the above articles were stolen by the enlisted men of the command stationed at Fort Union and sold to the grog shops and bawdy houses in the neighborhood." This was sufficient for Colonel Sumner to have raids made upon the camp tag-tails; and, as has been seen, spearheaded by Major Carleton and his supporting deputy marshal, the raid netted not only a thirty-thousand-dollar damage suit by Messrs. Barclay and Doyle and much destruction of property

[36] W. G. Ritch Papers, No. 93: "Profligacy and Prostitution—Adulterous Character of the Old Priesthood," 1 Mo. 64, 4 Mo. 287; also Josiah Gregg, *Commerce of the Prairies,* I, 239.

but "twenty women, supposed to be prostitutes," found in the houses of "those whiskey sellers and in the rocks in the vicinity of Fort Union." Major Carleton personally assisted "in making some arrests of these whiskey sellers and men supposed to be inculpated in government property" stealing, and he "saw ten or fifteen women in one of the houses." Being told "that some caves in the bluffs which overhang Fort Union were infested with these women," he ordered the sergeant of the guard to take them "off the military reservation." All were not taken off, however, since some of the articles found in their possession were government property, including government saddles, axes, bridles, guns, and sugar candles. The guns and saddles were in their houses while the axes and candles were in the caves. The captured men were shackled and ushered off to Santa Fe for trial by the civil authorities, but no such fortune fell to the women.

Prior to the raid on the caves, Major Carleton admitted that he had found "the Command exceedingly intemperate ... more so than any command of the same size that I have ever seen in the Services, intoxication and crime to an alarming extent among the troops." On the day of the raid, "the groggeries were occupied by one or two men [who] had been whipped and drummed out of the service for desertion; one was a ruffian well known in this country by the name of Header, a discharged soldier who has since been shot; and judging from the appearance of the others, I suppose a more abandonned [sic] set of wretches could not have been found in the Territory. .... The demoralizing influence they exercised over the troops was notorious among all the officers and others at the post." To this Dr. John Byrne, of Fort Union's Medical Department, added: "The prostitutes ... at Fort Union resulted in sixty cases of venereal disease being treated at the hospital." Private Alexander Lavery admitted "the habit of visiting these women in the rocks day and night [carrying] rations to them," in return for which "one of the women gave me the disease"; equally as generous "were Jesusitta and Dolores, the former commonly known as black [sic] Sus," to Corporal John Einsiedel. To Corporal James Cowan, Jesusitta was an "acquaintance of upwards of three years ... a common prostitute upon the streets of Santa

Fe, where she acted badly, but worse at Fort Union," where she "lived in the rocks, the men of the command being in the habit of visiting day and night." The raid upon the denizens of the rocks reached the ears, if not the eyes, of Kittie Bowen, who described the shambles:

> All the shanties and groggeries around this post occupied by miserable Americans have, by order of the chief of Santa Fe, been burned down and the keepers put in irons and sent to that town for trial. . . . A great deal of quartermaster property was found in the search, and some gentlemen who were out on horseback when the places were set on fire said that the Mexican women scattered like sheep from all the places and hid in the rocks on the mountain. The Mexicans are very bitter toward Major Carleton for informing the sheriff and requesting him to destroy those places.

After the arrests and at the change of guard Captain George Sykes relieved Major Carleton. Sykes and Dr. Byrne had previously served together on a court-martial during which they discussed ridding Fort Union of its "vampires." The doctor got advice from counsel that it was doubtful whether it could be done by the civil authorities, and he would not recommend doing it with military force. Then, when Sykes and the doctor saw Black Sus and Dolores in Fort Union's guardhouse, the two discussed giving them a few light blows before discharging them so that they would be "frightened and not return." Sykes demurred—not because of the "Law of the Territory" which authorized "laying on of hands . . . upon their buttocks," but because "he did not like to whip women." Whipping women, contended the doctor, could be accomplished "in a manner so as not to hurt them, and only frighten them;" and thus readily persuaded, Captain Sykes "ordered out the depraved women" and paraded them at ten o'clock in the morning with "many persons present." Private Alexander Lavery was commanded to whip them; this he refused to do, "as he did not like it." Despite the refusal, however, he was ordered again: "Go on and try your hand at it," which he did "until ordered to stop." He rated the whipping as "trifling, slightly laid on . . . over their shoulders and clothing. . . . one had a shirt on, the other had her chimese . . . the rebosos were only taken off." After restoring their rebosos, "the

143

hair was cut off their heads with scissors . . . shivered through, some of the hair not being cut." "And with a blare of martial music, drums beating, Jesusitta and Dolores—lacking jackasses to ride and unfettered, "scattered like sheep" to take protection at Barclay's Fort.

Captain Sykes's method of disposing of the "cave dwellers" immediately was classified at Fort Union as top secret, and might have remained so had not Black Sus and Dolores told their tale of woe to C. H. Merritt, who wrote the *Santa Fe Gazette*, February 5, 1853, calling attention to the "outrage which has recently been committed at Fort Union by individuals wearing the uniform of the United States."

Correspondent Merritt had formerly been a soldier under Kearny. He had lost his full loyalty to the army, however, at a later day in an effort to suppress a revolt against his authority at Camp near Cristoval (within the vicinity of Socorro), when his own "privates drew up a set of resolutions requesting him" to resign.[37] Still fretting under the humiliation of the incident, Merritt used the Santa Fe newspaper as a medium of exposure, and Colonel Sumner came into possession of his disclosure:

> Major Carleton and one Captain Sykes have been in the habit of whipping citizens, both Americans and Mexicans, when found near the fort, for the offenses, as they say, of selling liquor to the soldiers. This summary punishment is inflicted without trial; thus incurring the risk of punishing the innocent as well as the guilty. These same worthy individuals a short time since caused Mr. Joseph Doyle, one of the proprietors of Barclay's Fort, and a gentleman of high respectability to be driven from the fort; an outrage that in no case should be submitted to, but *E*specially as the Fort stands upon Mr. Barclay's own land. But, Mr. Editor, I have not yet reached the extent of these outrages. About the same time two unfortunate women were found in a cañon about a mile from the Fort, whereupon the brave Captain Sykes, with a guard of some ten men, proceeded to arrest these women, took them to the Fort, placed them in the guardhouse where they remained during the night in company with about twenty other prisoners of the opposite sex. The next morning these women were taken from the prison &

[37] *Santa Fe Republican*, October 26, 1847: "Troops Move South out of Santa Fe."

Brevet Major William T. H. Brooks, commander of Fort Union
from August 3 until December 18, 1852.

Arrott Collection

Fort Union in 1859, from a pencil sketch by Joseph Heger.

Arizona Pioneers Historical Society

flogged . . . then subjected to the further indignity of having their hair Cut Close to the head and drummed around the barrack and off the military ground.[38]

Sumner sent Major Morris, at the moment in command, notice that, "as he was the Comd. Officer at Fort Union," it was expected that he would prefer charges against Captain Sykes. This Morris peremptorily refused, saying: "I consider the charge false and infamous. I will not affix my name to anything I look upon as untrue." Thus rebuffed, Sumner required his own assistant adjutant general, S. D. Sturgis, to make the charge, and a court of ten officers was convened at Albuquerque. During twenty-eight days testimony was taken, to the "no common mortification" of Captain Sykes, who, in a fervid oral defense of himself, established the fact—to the satisfaction of the court—that he was not guilty of conduct unbecoming a gentlemen. To the findings of the court, Colonel Sumner demurred. He could not "agree with the court in attaching no criminality to . . . the charge." But since the Captain was held guiltless, Sumner could only in generalities blame the officers at Fort Union for their "relaxation of discipline," thus permitting the "depredations upon the public property at Fort Union," such, in the future, to be "controlled by the increased vigilance on the part of the officers and by coercive measures upon the troops, and not by unnatural punishment upon the helpless."

During Governor Calhoun's severe illness, prior to vacating his office, he assigned to John Greiner the duties of acting superintendent of Indian affairs in New Mexico. Soon Greiner discovered that Sumner claimed that title by virtue of having become in fact acting governor of New Mexico, and Greiner was given to understand that Sumner "had the power to assume the responsibility and would assume it." Greiner, "supposing that the public service would not be much benefitted with a controversy between the Col. and myself," submitted to his authority. Whereupon Sumner justified the complete military take-over by stating to the War Department that "No civil government, emanating from the government of the United States, can be maintained here without the aid of a military force; in fact,

[38] *Santa Fe Gazette,* February 5, 1853.

without its being virtually a military government." He believed "all intelligent men in the Territory [were] fully sensible to this truth." His reasons for these deductions were: "All branches of this civil government have equally failed—the executive, for want of power; the judiciary, from the total incapacity and want of principle in the juries; and the legislative, for want of knowledge—a want of identity for our institutions."

News of the death of Governor Calhoun reached Washington in due course, as did Sumner's letter of May 27, 1852, outlining his low opinion of all things New Mexican and his assumption of military dictation. Both the President and the War Department acted promptly. President Fillmore appointed Dr. William Carr Lane to be territorial governor. The Secretary of War directed Colonel McCall to inspect the Ninth Military Department "before General Garland shall reach the command."

Dr. Lane was conveniently in Washington at the time of the appointment. He hurried back to St. Louis, reaching there July 24, 1852, where he found "his best friends, as well as his family, dissatisfied with the appointment, mainly on account of his age and the prospective difficulties of the task which he had assumed. But a week later he bought a stage ticket for Santa Fe, "paying two hundred and twenty-five dollars for a seat," and was on his way to New Mexico on July 31. Before Colonel McCall could start west to the Ninth Military Department, he was superseded by Colonel Joseph K. F. Mansfield, and Mansfield was delayed so long in leaving that he actually traveled with General Garland's relieving contingent, getting to the Arkansas River only ten days before Colonel Sumner decided to avail himself of a leave of absence, June 30, 1853.[39]

On August 3, 1852, after being relieved of the command at Fort Union by Major William Brooks, Carleton left for Fort Atkinson on the Arkansas River, there to meet Governor Lane's stage. Sumner had provided a military escort commanded by Carleton and composed otherwise of Lieutenant Johnson and a company of dragoons, a brass cannon, two baggage wagons, and one ambulance. As a stage

[39] Mansfield Report, AC, "Fort Union, 1853," File 1, p. 1ff.

passenger Dr. Lane had "found no Indians on the route." The trip from Fort Atkinson went well "without having met any trouble" until near the Point of Rocks, some thirty miles east of Fort Union. Here Dr. Lane told the escort commander that he could no longer travel except in an ambulance, diagnosing his own condition as "renal calculus" and making "up his mind to encounter the torments of the damned." Not being quite willing to suffer the pangs of his ailment, however, he turned doctor again and began to "dose himself with opiates, then resorting to chloroform and ether." Since his own ministrations brought "temporary relief only, he sought to avail himself of the skill of Dr. McDougall, who "with old Mr. Sheets" was of a party going eastward. Dr. McDougall declined to prescribe, "except to forbid any ether under the apprehension I was injuring myself dreadfully." Thereafter he was "forced to beg for that indispensible drug" as if for his "very existence."

Dr. McDougall and old Mr. Sheets continued eastward while Dr. Lane's condition "became even more acute." At midnight, August 24, Major Carleton sent a "flying squad" from Point of Rocks to Fort Union for Surgeon Byrne, who arrived on the evening of the twenty-sixth. While traveling to meet Surgeon Byrne en route, Lane "saw nothing and knew nothing"; and his anticipations of relief were vain. Surgeon Byrne did not go out to meet his patient; he was "indisposed." At Fort Union, however, he did attend, "and did it skillfully, when he was able to call, which was seldom." After two days at Fort Union "the paroxysms passed," and Dr. Lane reported himself "steadily regaining my health and strength." The restoration to health he attributed "to some degree to the kindly entertainment by Major Carleton and his lady at quarters." None of it, however, could be accredited to a welcome from Sumner. News of the new Governor's arrival at Fort Union was relayed to Santa Fe. John Greiner sent an express asking when the party would reach the Rock Corral, an intimation that a reception committee would be there, but nothing arrived from Sumner. Major Carleton, on September 3, reported that Dr. Lane was at the fort. And Dr. Lane took advantage of Carleton's express bearer to confirm his presence to the department commander.

After Dr. Lane celebrated the return of his health by an inspection of the post, he accepted Isaac and Kittie Bowen's invitation for the evening of September 4, and "there they supped." Kittie saw him as "a hale old man of sixty, I should think, who had left an extensive practice of medicine, a family and wealth to be governor of this undesirable republic and republicans. The honors accruing from the position have yet to be made public. No person has discovered them." Kittie was not her usual calm self that evening with the new Governor —not that a dignitary of state would disconcert her, but on the previous night just before she went to bed she "saw a small bug on the pillow." The presence of the unwelcome creeper so exasperated her that "during the day she had the bed overhauled, but fortunately found but two and no signs of any more." This search "kept her busy all day about home . . . annointing the joints well," hoping there would be no untoward consequence at the dinner that evening with the Governor. The only way she could explain the presence of her night-time creepers was "They must have come from a borrowed book that I sometimes put under my pillow after I am through reading."

On September 6, still lacking instructions from Sumner, Major Carleton assumed the responsibility of continuing with a token escort for the Governor. On nearing San Miguel, the Governor visited a ranch close by, and after it became known that he was the *gobernador,* his status improved immensely: "A sort of divan, with half a dozen cushions, was spread for me alone, upon which I was urged to lie down. The whole *house* was offered for my use; and it was particularly urged that I should remain for a repast." After the repast the party continued its journey, only to be overtaken by the sheriff, who reported that he had two prisoners in his jail who had broken jail at Santa Fe and who were charged with being connected with a gang of robbers. "The *alguacil mayor* was very anxious to be relieved of their custody: he had no food with which to subsist them, and he feared that they might escape from his custody." Major Carleton, acting on behalf of the army, agreed to "guard them to Santa Fe" provided the sheriff would keep them in his charge until morning.

Since the two could not agree on this point, the Governor intervened and ordered the sheriff to keep them all night. He acquiesced unwillingly, saying, "They will break away from my guard," whereupon Governor Lane ordered that in that case, "Your guard will fire upon them." After the order, the Governor commented: "Thus it happens that my first official act in the execution of the law has been one of terrible harshness."

At the Old Pecos ruins the Governor took notice of his prisoners and his line of march. It was set in no stage of glamour or dignity of state: "The poor wretches of prisoners rode, both of them, on *one* little mule: behind them rode 2 dragoons; the other 4 dragoons, the baggage wagons and two carriages being sometimes in sight, sometimes out of sight, so it seemed to me that the prisoners might make their escape through the thicket and ravines if they should choose to do so."

That night the Governor's party settled down as best they could amid the Old Pecos ruins, making themselves anything but comfortable in a heavy rain; and on the morning of September 9 they made an early start for Santa Fe. Inspecting the prisoners before the start, the Governor found the wrist-irons cutting mercilessly into the flesh of one of them. Extracting a promise that he would not "take to the thicket and ravines," he unfettered the felon, who was "put on executive parol" as well as upon the donkey again, and joyously the "outriders" led the way to the Stone Corral, arriving in grand style.

Garrulous John Greiner with "an escort of citizens, Chiefly Mexican," awaited the Governor. After "an introduction to each," the line formed again, and they were off toward the capital. On the route they came upon "many citizens, in carriages and mounted, who joined the escort with spirit." They entered the city and drove to the Palace on the Plaza amid a thundering salute from Colonel Brooks's artillery. At the *Palacio,* Dr. Lane was received by Colonel Sumner, styling himself "the Military Governor ad interim and Commander of the Military Department." The reception, however, was swallowed up by the presence of a "large concourse of people." This suggested to the secretary that other things should be swallowed; hence they adjourned to secretarial quarters, where "they partook of a collation." If Colonel Sumner was present, no journal-keeper recorded the fact; neither was his absence noted until the following morning when he ordered the flag hauled down from its staff in the Plaza, where it had flown since being hoisted by Kearny in 1846. After bundling up the only visible emblem of United States authority, he "left the city for Albuquerque," though not until he had made it known to Colonel Brooks "that he wished it to be distinctly understood that the civil government in New Mexico was not to depend in any way upon the military authority, and he wished him to consider his forces only as a guard for United States military stores." Further, the inaugural ceremony was to proceed without the presence of an unfurled American flag, for, according to this last Sumner-ism, he "was not authorized by the government to furnish him [the Governor] with government stores."

Sumner skulked in his quarters at Albuquerque until September 24 before he informed the Adjutant General of the United States Army that: "Governor Lane arrived at Santa Fe on the 9th instant, and on the following day I relinquished all charge of civil affairs and returned to this place." He was, so he said, "pleased that things continue quiet in the department: the only hostile Indians in the Territory are a small band of Apaches, headed by the chief with whom Major Richardson had the difficulty last spring." That chief, Delgarito, "continued sour and suspicious." Much emphasis was placed on the establishment of "the new posts [which] have had the happiest effect." Particularly was he pleased with Fort Union, and for evidence of what had been done, he relayed to the Adjutant General the report of Assistant Quartermaster E. S. Sibley, in charge of construction, showing the buildings which had been erected there.[40] Those

---

[40] Report of the Secretary of War, 1852, 32 Cong. 2 sess., *Sen. Exec. Doc. No. 1,* Part I, 74–75. Assistant Quartermaster E. S. Sibley's report showed: "Nine sets of officer's [*sic*] quarters; each set—with one exception—which is composed of three rooms and a kitchen—18 feet long and 15 feet wide. These quarters have earthen roofs, and five of them in addition have board roofs. The other sets of quarters will also be covered with board roofs as soon as lumber for the purpose can be sawed, and it can be conveniently done.

buildings were "in most instances made of logs, at a slight cost to the United States . . . quite comfortable, and will answer well the purposes for which they are required." There was one instance in which he had not had the "success I expected"; that was "the farming operations." However, he could assure the War Department that "all difficulties will vanish when it is known and felt that no officer will be continued in command of a post who does not exert himself to carry out the orders of the government in relation to this matter," and he was still convinced that "the scheme [is] unquestionably practicable and advantageous to the troops as well as the government." For proof of his assertion he cited what had been done by one major "on a small place of thirty acres, he having produced with the company's labor, 28²⁹⁄₃₂ bushels of barley, 113⁵⁄₃₂ bushels of wheat, 163¹⁸⁄₃₂ bushels of corn, 11 487 pounds of straw, 11 470 pounds of fodder, at a saving to the War Department of $353.60"—to say nothing of "a fair crop of vegetables."

One day during mid-January, 1853, Fort Union had unexpected and unwelcome visitors. Without any warning whatever, suddenly "the garrison was full of Apaches." Much to the relief of all, they

"Two barracks—each 100 feet long and 18 feet wide, with two wings 50 feet long and 16 feet wide: board roofs.

"Hospital—48 feet long and 18 feet wide, with a wing 46 feet long and 16 feet wide, board roofs.

"Storehouse—100 feet long and 22 feet wide, with a wing 45 feet long and 22 feet wide: board roofs.

"Commanding officer's office and courtmartial room—48 feet long and 18 feet wide: earthen roof.

"Offices for assistant quartermaster and commissary of subsistence—38 feet long and 18 feet wide: earthen roofs.

"Smokehouse—100 feet long and 33 feet wide; board roof.

"Guardhouse and prison—42 feet long and 18 feet wide; earthen roof.

"Blacksmith's and wheelwright's shop—30 feet long and 18 feet wide: board roof.

"Bakehouse—31 feet long and 17 feet wide: earthen roof.

"Icehouse—22 feet long and 30 feet wide; earthen roof, covered by a board roof.

"Quarters for laundresses—114 feet long and 18 feet wide, 6 rooms: earthen roof.

"In Addition—yards to 5 sets of officer's quarters have been enclosed, and two corrals have been made, each 100 feet square.

"The lumber used in the construction of these buildings, with the exception of 14872 feet, has been sawed at the post."

came "begging." Some came to Captain Bowen's quarters, Kittie seeing them as "the most frightful beings that the sun ever shone upon. Some of their red faces seem to be a foot through the cheeks." Others peered into Major Carleton's quarters when "his little four year old daughter was standing on a chair looking out of the window . . . when they came up to the window to peep in. She was so scared that she fell backwards from the chair and went into a fit." Willie Bowen, however, took them in his stride, thinking them "a great curiosity," but his mother thought "they look savage enough for canibals [sic]." Since they were not cannibals, Mrs. Bowen served her "guests fine wild turkey, ham, tongue and salad, with ice cream, cakes, jelly and preserves," and "they all enjoyed it very much."

On June 1, 1853, Colonel Sumner decided to leave the Territory, and, availing himself of an approved leave of absence, appointed Lieutenant Colonel D. S. Miles to command "during my temporary absence."[41] But after a two-day absence, he returned to his Albuquerque headquarters, the reason being "unexpected difficulties [that have] arisen with the Navajo Indians," and forthwith resumed command, relegating Colonel Miles "temporarily to command the post of Albuquerque." It soon became obvious that Sumner's return to the command was meant, in fact, to be temporary, just long enough for him to place the entire Ninth Military Department in readiness for war. Circumstances were affording him a long-sought opportunity and excuse for putting a military force "into the heart of the Indian Country." That excuse came when "a Mexican had been wantonly murdered, and without the least provocation, murdered by a party of Navajoes." Therefore, he posted Order No. 23, "to go into immediate effect . . . with Colonel Miles . . . ready to march on the 11th proximo . . . direct to Fort Defiance . . . Brooks with Artillery . . . Sykes with Infantry . . . Carleton with dragoons . . . leaving Fort Union on the 8th . . . while Ewell would be responsible for the defense of the Rio Grande frontier." Moving from Fort Union "would be 50 good beef cattle and no salt meat." The troops were not to commence hostilities until "they arrive at Fort Defiance, unless they

[41] Order No. 20, June 1, 1853, NA, RG 98, 9 Mil. Dept. Orders, Vol. 36, p. 171.

meet Indians who show a hostile spirit." Having thus given orders, he again availed himself of his leave, on July 1, 1853, requiring Colonel Miles to post Order No. 27, affirming "all orders and regulations now in force." When he departed, the Santa Fe newspapers recorded no regret at the loss of "The Big Bug of Albuquerque." Theretofore *The Santa Fe Weekly Gazette* had made public its evaluation of him: "Certainly it is, he has held himself impossible and aloof, as a superior being, from his fellow creatures . . . . True, it has been possible to see him; so also, it is possible to see the President of the United States; and—by the Bible—The Almighty has been seen by man, face to face. But toleration is not friendship, nor does politeness imply confidence."[42]

[42] "The Big Bug of Albuquerque," *Santa Fe Weekly Gazette,* February 19, 1853, p. 3, col. 3.

CHAPTER SEVEN

A GARLAND FOR PEACE

TRANSFER OF COMMAND of the department to Colonel Miles was accomplished July 1, 1853. Sumner, in his hurry to get away, left Santa Fe June 30 traveling with Major Hadner, Major and Mrs. Morris, "and 20 or 30 discharged soldiers," headed for Fort Union.[1] When he passed through Fort Union, the Colonel's leaving was noted merely by the observation that he "moved into the parched and yellow country . . . they will have a warm time, but will have home at the end of the journey to reward them." General Garland was much delayed in his westward movement, crossing the Arkansas River on July 20. Although, by Sumner's orders, Colonel Miles had been in command of the department since July 1, General Garland, upon entering the Ninth Military Department, likewise assumed command. No clash of instructions resulted however, for the General had opportunity to command only his traveling contingent: Major E. Backus, commanding some troops, Lieutenant William D. Smith, in charge of a large number of horses, Captain L. C. Easton, in charge of fifty-one baggage and commissary wagons, an assistant surgeon, and David C. DeLeon, bringing some recruits. In addition, there was Captain McPai, accompanied by "a pleasant family—his wife and two daughters who are very agreeable and accomplished, and, what was to excite the garrison of Fort Union the most—*they brought a piano.*"[2]

General Garland and his party arrived at Fort Union on August 2, further congesting the living quarters there. The Bowens invited Major Backus and his family, "including a young lady," to share their quarters, and they occupied "every inch of room—floors and

[1] Kittie Bowen to "My dear Mother," July 3, 1853, AC, Bowen Letters.
[2] *Ibid.*, August 15, 1853.

all." Besides these visitors, the Bowens "took in as many more at meals as can squeese [*sic*] around the table . . . filling the house to overflowing" and creating so much commotion that none could "find silence enough to catch a nap." To add to the turmoil, "the young lady took it into her wise head to get sick . . . and there was rather more nursing to do than was agreeable. . . . The worst of it all was that—she being a snappish old maid—nobody could do anything to

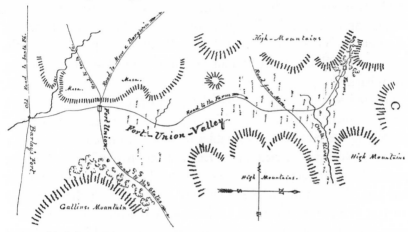

Mansfield's sketch showing the location of Fort Union (1853)

please her." She did, however, get well after two weeks and, having had her fling with the West, "started back to the States," Kittie bidding her farewell with, "She is welcome to her fits, if she don't come back again."

Colonel J. K. F. Mansfield, who had orders to inspect the Ninth Military Department before Colonel Sumner left but did not arrive until the "Old Martinet" was well out of the department, took the first six days of August, 1853, to inspect Fort Union. He found the post to be "the general depot of supplies . . . Lieutenant Colonel Horace Brooks" commanding. The artillery present was reduced to "79 in the aggregate," with "not a subaltern officer present." Of the artillerymen, one was in the guardhouse and six in the hospital; infantry, 56, with nine in the hospital and Captain George Sykes "the only officer." Dragoons—42 present, of which 2 were sick—"37 horses and 5 ponies." "Thus the line of the army present consisted in the aggregate of 3 officers and 144 rank and file for duty." Dr. Byrne, of the hospital, was absent, his place being supplied by Dr. O. W. Blanchard, "a citizen of respectable standing in his profession. . . . the hospital comfortable." Mansfield condemned eight horses and five ponies, for "the Mexican Pony is wholly unfit for the dragoon service." At the inspection Major Carleton was absent, he being north of Ocate in search of "a party of Indians who had committed depredations on his horses."[3] The quartermaster thought Carleton's search was not worth the effort, saying, "The animals are so poor and worthless that I will shoot any Indian or white man who dares to bring them back."[4]

Colonel Mansfield found that the troops had been cultivating "a garden which is irrigated by raising water by mule and hand power," supplying the post with "vegetables in part." A more extensive agricultural effort was carried on at Ocate, twenty-five miles north of the post, where fifty acres of corn were planted and seventy-five tons of hay cut, this venture into soldier husbandry putting the "farming interest in New Mexico about 14,000 dollars in debt." Mansfield, however, suggested "keeping up of this farm as it is well irrigated" and could be used "more as a convenient locality to recruit horses and fat[ten] cattle for beef, and gather hay, than profit to be divided among the soldiers."[5]

Colonel Mansfield was not pleased with the lack of care of enlistments in the Ordnance Department. He observed "one ignorant German who could not understand English when spoken to; such men are not fit for this service."

As to the Chaplain, he wrote: "This is a chaplain post, but the council of administration have not succeeded in getting a Chaplain to conform to their peculiar views."[6]

---

[3] Mansfield Report. See *Mansfield on the Condition of the Western Forts* (ed. by Robert W. Frazer), 33–34.

[4] Kittie Bowen to "My dear Mother," October 1, 1853, AC, Bowen Letters.

[5] *Mansfield on . . . Forts,* 34–35.

[6] *Ibid.,* 38.

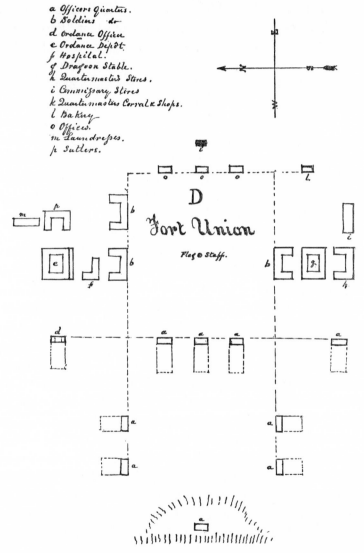

a Officers Quarters.
b Soldiers do—
d Ordance Officer
e Ordance Depot
f Hospital.
g Dragoon Stable.
h Quartermasters Stores.
i Commissary Stores
k Quartermasters Corral & Shops.
l Bakery
o Offices.
m Laundresses.
p Sutlers.

D
Fort Union
Flag o Staff.

Mansfield's plan of Fort Union (1853)

Barclay and others who had sued the United States for trespass, claiming that Sumner had erected Fort Union on their property, won their action against the government, and General Garland became aware of the fact that "the owner may at any time claim damages or eject us." This made him reach the conclusion that "Fort Union is entirely out of position for a depot" and decide "to withdraw the supplies to a more convenient point, Albuquerque." Henceforth, supplies destined for Fort Defiance and the posts south of it were to be "intercepted and placed in the Depot at Head Quarters for storage without rehandling at Fort Union." Not knowing what might be the fate of Fort Union as it then stood, General Garland had orders posted that "there would be no more building at Fort Union." Should there be need, however, for additional storage, he suggested "the buildings erected for the smokehouse . . . be fitted for temporary use . . . the present garrison to be left there for the winter."[7]

With the completion of Colonel Mansfield's inspection and the probability that Fort Union would be abandoned, Major Sibley's services were dispensed with, and he availed himself of relief orders, scheduling his departure from New Mexico "for the plains on the 25 [August] with a large party." This disruption of quietude in the Sibley home caused the children to become "cross and a great deal of trouble," making Mrs. Sibley wish that her husband "were a little *younger* to help her in taking care of his own production." Upon the departure of the Sibleys, Captain Isaac Bowen was "the last remaining officer of the original trio at Fort Union who established *Aristocrat's Row*." He had intimations, however, that his transfer was imminent. If he could "not get a post east of St. Louis, he preferred to remain here [Fort Union] rather than go south." The Bowens were in accord: neither wanted a transfer to New Orleans; dire rumors were reaching Fort Union that yellow fever was raging there. Mrs. Bowen "would rather stay in a health[y] country forever than to go to a climate like New Orleans—how dreadful the scourge has been!"[8]

---

[7] Order No. 399, September 8, 1853, NA, RG 98, 9 Mil. Dept. Orders, Vol. 9, p. 41.

[8] Captain Isaac Bowen and his family ultimately were transferred to New Orleans, Louisiana. All except one child died of the "scourge" in 1857. The Bowen letters

While marking time for General Garland to determine the fate of Fort Union, "nearly every family at the post joined in a party to Moro —a small town 29 miles away." Word was sent "several days ahead so that all was prepared" for the Fort Union visitors. ". . . a real fandango was given in the house we stopped at—to show us what Mexican parties are. The women dressed very prettily . . . mostly after American fashions . . . but the men of all classes came in from their work with patched breeches and dirty shirts as well as faces and hands and arranged themselves on the mud floor. Each one makes a motion to whatever female he wants to dance and she hops up to join him. The most awful music is produced from a violin, a guitar and clarionette, and sometimes the men sing." Kittie Bowen's "Little Willie" "could not sleep for the noise, but Margaret thought it fine." After "staying all night, sleeping on the floor and eating Mexican cooking," the Fort Union folk "thought it worth while to hasten to comfortable home" and to "praise providence that they were not born Mexicans."

The Bowens were house guests of "a Spaniard, born in old Spain, who bragged about his 'tastes and refinements unknown among the Mexicans of this latitude.' " He was rich, "and his wife's father was an American." His house "was hung with valuable pictures and there were 14 large mirrors in the room that we ladies occupied. Cushions were piled all around the immense room—high enough to sit upon and at night these same cushions are spread on the floor for beds." There were but two chairs in the house, the "mistress sitting all day on a rug by the fire wrapped in her rebosa smoking." She "was young and pretty, and covered with jewelry." Some of the more interested men at Moro wanted to know if all the ladies were married, "and if not, would it be possible for them to get a white wife." For recommendation, they "had plenty of money."

Colonel Philip St. George Cooke, having returned to New Mexico as "the second officer in rank in this Department," was assigned to

finally came into the possession of Miss Gladys Bowen, Bennington, Vermont, who graciously provided copies to James W. Arrott for inclusion and use in his Fort Union Collection.

the command of Fort Union.[9] A less pleasing duty than making Cooke's assignment confronted General Garland when he arrived at Albuquerque. He must evaluate the activities of his predecessor. Distasteful as it was, he wrote candidly and without animus:

> It is never considered in good taste to attack one's predecessor, but I am forced to do it, else the odium of bad management, extravagant expenditures &c &c will fall upon me. . . . I am constrained, in some degree from the fact that my predecessor is an *old friend* and acknowledged throughout the army to be one of the most efficient and gallant officers in the *field;* he is also a man of untiring industry, but his energies have been misapplied, and he has left the department in an impoverished and crippled condition. . . . His sole aim appears to have been to win reputation from an economical administration . . . in this he will have been found to have signally failed . . . his economy run [*sic*] into parsimony, the result of which was the loss of a vast number of horses and mules.

Besides exposing Colonel Sumner's niggardliness in his effort to make a reputation at the expense of the defense of the territory, General Garland reported "with as much regret as sorrow that Colonel Sumner embarrassed me not a little by placing an order on the books of the Department for a campaign against the Navajoes"; but through the judicious policy of Colonel Miles, "it did not become necessary."

Governor William Carr Lane's administration was short lived. He inaugurated a policy of rationing the Indians, spending some twenty thousand dollars, and made treaties of peace to consummate his plans; then Congress let him down by failing to make appropriations to carry out his arrangements. The result was that the Indians returned to their old habits of thievery and murder, and the Governor ran for delegate to Congress, only to be counted out by José Manuel Gallegos. This so incensed him that he resigned and left the territory, imposing his duties upon the territorial secretary, W. S. Messervy. Secretary Messervy served until the arrival in August, 1853, of another appointee, David Meriwether.

[9] AC, "Fort Union, 1853," File 1, p. 61; Order No. 39, October 23, 1853, NA, RG 98, 9 Mil. Dept. Orders, Vol. 9, p. 63.

The incoming governor could not be classed as a complete stranger to affairs in New Mexico. In 1819, while an employee of the American Fur Company, he, with a party of Pawnees, had entered New Mexico to trade with the Indians. They were attacked by Spanish troops, many were killed, and Meriwether and a Negro boy were imprisoned in Santa Fe's *carcel,* the doors of which later were to be adorned with the ears of members of the ill-fated, ill-advised Texan–Santa Fe Expedition. Now, in August, 1853, as governor of New Mexico, Meriwether was again on the Santa Fe Trail, and by chance overtook General Garland west of the Arkansas River.

While the Governor and the new commander traveled together, an incident took place which resulted in a cordiality beneficial to each in their administrations. Two Mexican girls held captive by the Kiowa Indians escaped and joined Meriwether's wagon train, the wagonmaster holding off some forty Indians who attempted to recapture them. In the defensive action, wagonmaster McCarthy, in true Irish style, whacked an Indian woman on the head with the butt of his ox-whip, knocking her from the wagon in which the girls had been secreted, and left her to her own resources on the prairie. The rescued girls told of an incident of Kiowa cruelty which they had witnessed which involved an American woman and her child. The woman was "obliged to submit to the most brutal and inhuman punishment . . . while the Indian seized the child and threw it up in the air and caught it upon the point of his lance as it came down. The rest of the band amused themselves in the same manner, and thus they passed the child among them upon their lance-heads until the dead body was pierced like a sieve."[10]

On August 8, two days after Colonel Mansfield had completed his inspection of Fort Union, David Meriwether—the one-time prisoner in Santa Fe—stood in the plaza, near the old *carcel,* and took the oath of office as governor of the territory. And then—stranger things may have happened—"the roof of the cell where he had been shackled fell in."[11]

[10] W. H. H. Davis, *El Gringo;* also Calvin Horn in *New Mexico Magazine,* April, 1958, p. 26.
[11] *Ibid.*

Twenty days after "the roof fell in," Governor Meriwether had need for his friend Garland in controlling the Utes.[12] Indian Agent Graves, citing a number of depredations, was proclaiming, ". . . they are unfriendly and there is danger of a serious outbreak." Peter Joseph, a merchant of Taos, had sent his man Pedro Barello "some distance beyond the mountains with provisions to the party who had his stock in charge." Four Utes "took his horse, saddle & bridle—and everything he had—and spared his life that he might go back and tell the Americans that they were going to meet . . . to agree upon a plan to make war on the Americans." Further, "a party of Mexicans from the vicinity of Las Vegas, engaged in hunting . . . and while grazing their horses . . . were attacked by a band of thirty or forty Utes, who succeeded in taking five or six of their horses and killing as many more." They had saved themselves "by flight."

But this was not enough for General Garland, so he told Meriwether, "to make him come to the conclusion that the Ute Indians meditate any hostile movement." To appease the Governor, he apprised him of the fact that he "intended to have a peaceful settlement of all difficulties with the Utahs as soon as practicable." Before he could do so, and only eleven days later, the same prowlers struck boldly and contemptuously at the army. Macrae reported from Fort Union, "The thieves took 22 of the best of the Govt animals and left 34 of no value." Six days later Macrae referred to the general situation on the routes to the Arkansas River: he thought it necessary to send a force "to enquire in to the conduct & intensions of a very large number of Indians on that route." Before the force was sent, however, news came from Rayado that "Comanche Chief, Bald Head & Kiowa Chief, Little Mountain, with about 500 warriors" had left for the south, thus relieving Fort Union.

The movement of five hundred Comanches and Kiowas toward the White Mountains, plus a letter from Major Backus disclosing "the bad conduct of the Apaches of the White Mountains," caused General Garland to take "decided steps," ordering out "a strong force to chastise these lawless rascals." Garland, however, thought "that

[12] Order No. 388, NA, RG 98, 9 Mil. Dept. Orders, Vol. 9, pp. 34-35.

nothing could have been more inopportune than this occurrence, for, in the first place, I am not fully prepared for a hostile movement, and, secondly, two influential Mexicans, Senors Jose Luna and Don Juan Chavis, propose to establish a colony of two hundred families near these mountains in November." The two gentlemen were leaving "today for Santa Fe to confer" with the Governor upon the subject.[13]

Command of the expedition fell to Major Carleton. Explanations given to army headquarters indicated purely military exigencies:

> Two companies [under Major Carleton], dragoons, will examine the country about *Gran Quivira,* going as far south as . . . the White Mountains. It is one of the ranges of the Apaches, and it is desirable to open a communication with them at this time. It is also desirable to collect Topographical and Geographical knowledge of this part of New Mexico, as yet believed to be unexplored by any American citizens.

Garland added three more companies to the expedition, these to go under Brevet Lieutenant Colonel Chandler. Chandler would give "special reference to the difficulties with the Muscalero Apaches. . . . The marauding propensities of these half starved vagabonds will have to be checked by the strong arm of the military." Should the "vagabonds" be found with "animals in their possession, stolen from the inhabitants of New Mexico," Carleton and Chandler were to "take measures for their restitution, or a fair equivalent." Specifically, Major Carleton, "with the efficient men of the dragoon companies," was to make a thorough reconnaissance of the country around the Gran Quivira, "taking notes and making observations."

Major Carleton got his orders at Fort Union. He left on December 5, but became involved in a situation which was interpreted by the General commanding as an effort on the part of some *Nuevo Mejicanos* and conniving military officers to traffic in human slaves with the Apaches. A Mexican woman had been rescued from the Comanches and delivered to Fort Union by a civilian teamster em-

[13] Order No. 408, Garland to Meriwether, September 14, 1853, NA, RG 98, Mil. Dept. Orders, Vol. 9, p. 45.

ployed by the Quartermaster Department, and, according to the report which went to Governor Meriwether and thence to General Garland, she was being held there in slavery. General Garland intemperately directed post commander Philip St. George Cooke "to take measures to have this woman sent forth to Santa Fe and delivered to His Excellency Gov. Meriwether—Superintendent of Indian Affairs." If the man restraining the woman "is a soldier, he will be confined, and charges preferred . . . if a citizen in the employ of the government . . . discharged—and turned over to the civil government."

Cooke, complying with orders slowly, learned that the "the offender —if such there is—" was a teamster named Northrup. Questioning another teamster, he found that the woman had been taken to Fort Union, but that a Mr. Kahn "had engaged with Northrup in taking the woman to his house and both were actuated only by charitable and praiseworthy motives." Colonel Cooke sought out the recent captive, "and from this poor woman's unhappy story it will appear that her husband had been killed by Indians, and the driver of the Wagon, in which she was returning to Texas, was brutally murdered by five Comanches—she was made captive—with two boys— and atrociously abused—she escaped & fell in with these Mexicans when free but famished." While she was in the custody of the Mexicans, Major Carleton and teamster Northrup came upon her "at a house at Pecos, nearly naked, and in every way an object of great commiseration . . . far gone in pregnancy." Kahn and Northrup, "if erring at all," with humane and charitable motives "clothed her and offered to send her to the States in the way she might choose," but she chose to remain at Pecos.

Upon learning of General Garland's displeasure, Major Carleton, disregarding previous orders, left "to undertake to carry & deliver her to Governor Meriwether." Colonel Cook deduced that the incident showed "that New Mexicans were long used to traffic with the Apaches, for the spoil of their fellow citizens . . . & suggests a suspicion of such friendly intercourse with these aggressive savages & that it might better, for a time, be a military one."[14]

14 Later in his career Carleton was accused of holding Indians as slaves and con-

Major Carleton's orders were awaiting him when he reached Albuquerque,[15] "as was Mr. Chaves, who chose to go along." Although Carleton found the weather "singularly unpropitious for an expedition," nevertheless it got under way from Old Vigilance,[16] at 11:00 A.M., December 14, 1853. The road was muddy and rain was falling. They traveled seven miles, reaching the residence of Spruce M. Baird, no longer aspiring to be the Texan judge of Santa Fe County, Texas but content to act as Indian agent when not practicing law. The weather became even less propitious, the rain turning into snow; but they plodded along during the next two days, finally arriving at Casa Colorado.

Learning that "the sudden arrival . . . of so many armed men" was "a matter of great astonishment" to the people and that they planned to give "a ball in honor of our coming," Carleton decided to expand his "observations as regards the general appearance of the inhabitants of the country." This he did—as he wrote—"in a few words." Being much pleased with his "few words," he filed them later with the Smithsonian Institution, having—like Shakespeare—"immortal longings in me."[17] Among his "few words" Carleton noted:

> The dirty little villages through which we have passed, as well as those we have seen in the distance, have generally turned out their inhabitants en masse to get a sight of us. This gave us a sight of them. Had we been painters, it doubtless would have been an interesting one; for men, women and children—mostly assemblages—exhibited themselves in groups picturesque, as well as grotesque. Some blanketed with sombreros and cigarritos; some with whitewashed and some with scarlet-dyed faces, some with rebosos, some nearly naked, some on housetops shading their eyes with their hands, and some peering through chinks

niving with his own officers to do likewise. See the *Santa Fe New Mexican*, December 9, 1864 and February 23, 1867.

[15] Order No. 508, Albuquerque, December 3, 1853, NA, RG 98, 9 Mil. Dept. Orders, Vol. 9, p. 95.

[16] Camp Vigilance, so called by Sumner.

[17] Carleton's Diary was sent from the Smithsonian Institution to the U.S. Senate, where it was copied, and later came to life through the *New Mexican*, July 27, 1867, p. 2, col. 1.

and crannies in the walls of their dwellings; but all curious as to whence we came and whither we were going. The natural expression of *Quien Sabe* appeared deeply written on every countenance. In no rancho or village have we seen a single solitary indication of industry, thrift or cleanliness since we left Albuquerque; (and it may be remarked parenthetically that we have yet to see in that town the first evidence of those cardinal virtues). Indolence, squalid poverty, filth, and utter ignorance of everything beyond their cornfields and acequies, seem to particularly characterize the inhabitants who are settled along the east bank of the river. We have seen nothing denoting energy on the part of anyone, *save by that shown by old man Chaves* and his two sons-in-law. On the contrary, we could but observe among them what seemed to be a universal proclivity for rags, dirt and filthiness in all things; with sheer laziness and listlessness marking their movements and all that they do.

For good measure Carleton included in his observations a description of the ancient Indian establishments, Abo and Gran Quivira (probably his most valuable contribution to his immortality), quoting a tradition as given to him by old man Cháves, regretting, in conclusion, since he came there "to note realities," that "our business is not that which will permit us to clothe with imaginary grandeur these vestiges of a people whose names has [*sic*] been erased from the books of nations, nor that which will allow us to indulge in abstruse speculations as to their race or their language. These things belong to the past and the philosopher. With all these pleasant reveries and romantic fancies which these desert ruins are so wonderfully calculated, we can have nothing to do!"[18]

Inspector General Mansfield's report on the Ocate–Fort Union farming operation was sent to army headquarters with Garland's observation that "it [farming] has failed entirely, and created a debt of $14,000 or thereabouts." That was sufficient to cause the project thereafter to sear like an Indian corn-patch before a Kansas sirocco. First, Captain Macrae, responsible for the farm as well as having Fort Union duties, demurred when he discovered that "the soldier doing duty at the *Govt farm* has been paid *Extra pay*. Also two Mexi-

[18] 23 Cong., 2 sess., *House Misc. Doc. No. 37*, Vol. I (Ser. 807), pp. 296–316.

cans were hired at a compensation of nine dollars per month & some ration each day." To clear himself of any charge for such extravagance, he pointed out that he had "been informed this is by order of Col Sumner, when Comdy Officer of this Department." Then Cooke, succeeding Macrae, sought to hasten the harvest by sending two additional men, "expecting that much better progress will be made in gathering the corn." But the "experienced farmer, Mr. M. R. Sumner" and his extra-pay soldiers, plus the two additional men, made haste slowly, so slowly in fact in gathering sixty acres of corn that Colonel Cooke declared that they had had "ample time to get in the corn" and notified them that "the Govt will have no further occasion for your services." With this action General Garland concurred, declaring that "the attempt to cultivate farms at the several military posts in New Mexico, has, with one inconsiderable exception, proved a failure." He, therefore, asked authority to stop "all further farming operations," and to bolster his recommendation sent along Colonel Cooke's report:

> Without considering a multitude of incidental expenses, a soldier in the Dept. costs the government $217.– per annum; the farmer's wages were $750.– a Mexicans wages and rations amount to $181.– so that, with ten of these soldiers, the produce of the farm this year has cost in the *single item* of labour $3,131—deducting $176.– for hay produced— it will leave for the cost of corn $5.14 per bushel, about $12.85¢ per fanega, which then has to be transported twenty miles. . . . Corn can be bought in the territory, delivered, on the average for about $3.00 the fanega.

Whereupon, in the language of Old Fogy, "the novel idea that took possession of the noodle of the secretary of war, by which the army of the extreme west was to be made self-supporting, turning the soldier into a farmer and his sabre and musket into hoes and rakes," came to an end.

The low opinions of the *Nuevo Mejicanos* held by such men as Sumner and Carleton did nothing to promote the confidence of the people in the military establishment. The breach was anything but repaired when Acting Governor Messervy encouraged the *Nuevo*

Mejicanos to return to their hit-and-run marauding of the Indians. He even went so far as to authorize the assembling of the New Mexico militia, ostensibly for the purpose of community defense but actually to hunt upon Indian territory and (of great significance to the *Nuevo Mejicanos*) resume trade with the Indians despite the fact that it had been outlawed. That General Garland was conscious of the problem is disclosed in his complaint to the Governor:

> While on the subject of Indian depredations I call your attention to the fact, generally known in New Mexico, that large armed parties of New Mexicans are in the habit of going into the Indian Country, or perhaps more properly speaking, their hunting grounds, where they will kill off the very game on which the Indians depend for subsistence. This will have the effect, of course, of forcing upon the Indians the necessity of either breaking up their hunting parties, or of depredating upon the settlements, or, worse than either, of starving to death. I have adverted to this subject with the hope that your Excellency will devise some means by which this evil may be corrected.

The *Nuevo Mejicanos'* disregard for the laws of the United States which denied them the privilege of trading with the Indians attached even to the ensign of that power, as was evidenced during mid-February, 1853. The Governor had had a large flag made as an emblem of his authority. During February one of Santa Fe's citizens "gave a very fine and select ball," according to the *Weekly Gazette's* account. "For the purpose of adorning the dancing saloon . . . the large flag was applied for and obtained. During the evening some malicious persons cut and mutilated the flag to such an extent as to render it, perhaps, unfit for further use. . . .

"As the act was one every way disgraceful to the perpetrators, a judicial investigation was had," but "terminated without throwing any light upon the subject." The investigators expressed themselves "surprised at the fact that an act . . . so ungentlemanly and dishonorable could have been committed in a place so public and yet the offenders be entirely screened from public knowledge." Obviously the judicial investigators were not versed in *Quien Sabe* philosophy when *Nuevo Mejicanos* were *particeps criminis*. Failing to disclose the guilty persons, the *Gazette* took it upon itself "as a duty to present the subject" to its readers "in the proper light," branding "such a man as he who cut the flag . . . not capable of insulting the American government." Then it threatened, "All who place themselves in its [the government's] way and against it are doomed to be overrun, trodden down and utterly annihilated."

The *Gazette's* Editor Kephart could not forego challenging the Secretary of War and his views on the government of New Mexico. In doing so, Kephart became the keenest reviler of constituted authority. His tirade could not but have repercussions among the *Nuevo Mejicanos,* who were already daringly slashing the American flag; now they interpreted the *Gazette's* stand as license to flaunt their contempt.[19]

Beginning during the last quarter of 1853, Fort Union was repeatedly called on to protect persons or property. Following the trouble in Taos and difficulties at Las Vegas, Captain Macrae got a report which he was unable to fathom. A messenger left Fort Union for Albuquerque accompanied "by a party." They were never heard from again. Macrae concluded that "the Indians, Utahs or Apaches, have committed the act." Then there were Indian thieves in the vicinity of Rayado; Lieutenant Adams "was on their trail." Mr. Mitchell of Rayado rode down to the fort to ease the tension of the army and say that the thieves who stole the government mules at Ocate were "three young Utahs," but the *"principal* men among the Utahs were anxious to preserve the peace." The Utahs, Jicarillas, and Mescalero Apaches (at least those in the upper Pecos) remained comparatively quiet until early January, 1854; then there was a report to the Governor that there had been an assault on a party from San Miguel near Red River. Flight had saved the teamsters' lives, but they had lost their equipage and needed help from Fort Union to recover their wagons.

---

[19] Secretary Conrad, under the influence of such traducers as Sumner and Carleton, recommended to Congress that all efforts to bring New Mexico under the United States form of government be abandoned, and the *Nuevo Mejicanos* allowed to revert to the Old Mexico style of government, or another form to suit themselves, reimbursing Anglos for their property should they leave the country. See the *Santa Fe Weekly Gazette,* February 15, 1853.

Then two men were killed near Las Vegas. Again Fort Union got a call, this time "to collect all the information you can with respect to the two men killed in that vicinity." If opportunity presented, Colonel Cooke was to "chastise these thieves and murderers." Furthermore, it was to be done "effectually." The duty fell to Joseph B. Maxwell. The information he collected caused him to believe that the *Nuevo Mejicanos* who wanted their wagons back were probably intruders on Indian lands, that the murderers of the white men were *Nuevo Mejicanos*. In fact, he arrested one and charged him with the murders. This posed a difficult situation for the Las Vegas local authorities; but any semblance of embarrassment vanished when the local judiciary "let him off on some trifling testimony of his relative."[20]

Lieutenant Maxwell's first impression of the Red River affair was confirmed by J. M. Giddings, "a very respectable citizen living not far from San Miguel." The truth was: "Many buffalo hunters with wagons were out in the Indian Country: Some of them had been warned off by the Indians, who told them that as long as they brought only a few pack animals they did not care so much," but "buffalo hunters with many wagons" were forbidden. Despite the warning one Pedro and his companion, Salazar, established a camp, "which several Indians repeatedly visited." Then, "during the absence of Pedro Gonzales, young Salazar & several others, killed two and wounded the third of these Indians, who escaped." Other Indians made good their escape on horses belonging to the hunters, but "discovering that they were being chased, these they brought back & surrendered." The extent of the property loss to the *Nuevo Mejicanos* was "a very few animals of an abandoned herd . . . eaten by Indians, probably half-starved." On finding out the truth, Colonel Cooke concluded wisely, "It would seem that white men and Indians are, at the present, most in need of protection."[21]

On February 13, 1854, Lieutenant David Bell, Second Dragoons, found it necessary to go from Fort Union to the aid of Mr. Waters on Red River. A union of Jicarillas and Apaches had resulted in Waters'

[20] Cooke to Nichols, January 29, 1854, AC, "Fort Union, 1854," File 1, p. 10.
[21] *Ibid.*

being "robbed . . . of cattle and maltreatment of his herdsman." Lieutenant Bell was to "have them severely whipped and take a pony for Mr. Walters, and in case of insolence, or of their being overtaken flying from pursuit," attack. Failing to find the robbers, Bell returned to Fort Union. On March 2 he was ordered out again "with the efficiently mounted members of C-H 2d Drags" scouting down the Canadian. He was to bear in mind that the "general object of his scout was to protect the frontier" and specifically "to get in his power some important party of these Jicarillas or Utahs & compel them to surrender the depredators in Water's case & have them whipped & also require the delivery or an equivalent in ponies." He might "employ a person suitable as guide and trailer," but his detachment "would have to get along without additional mounts, for there are no American Horses to be had—and the horses of the country will not answer for Dragoon Service."

Five days after Lieutenant Bell had marched out of Fort Union to the northeast, he was back with quite a story to tell. He had, this time, come upon Jicarillas seventy miles from Fort Union, "beyond the Canadian." He identified them as some of those who, in October, 1849, had attacked the caravan of Dr. J. M. White, killing several of the party and taking captive Mrs. White, her daughter, and a Negress slave. That wholesale slaughter on the Santa Fe Trail, near the Point of Rocks, had become a *cause célèbre,* not only because of the wantonness of the act but because of the failure of Major Grier, commanding the party of pursuit, to act upon Kit Carson's advice, with the result that Mrs. White was murdered within yards of her rescuers. That night, after Major Grier's tragic blunder, the dragoons bivouacked on the spot from whence the Jicarillas had fled. One of the dragoons, not yet hardened to the crassness of retributive Indian fighting, recorded in his diary the vengeful act of one of the United States troops:

> After dark a noise was heard near our camp. At first we supposed it to be an animal of some kind: 3 or 4 of us made examination through the willow bushes and found an Indian child, which I suppose was about 8 months old. It was strapped to a board as all Indian babies are. I found

it. An old gruff soldier stepped up and said: "Let me have the brat."
I handed it to him. He picked up a heavy stone, tied it to the board,
dashed the baby and all into the water, and in a moment no trace of
it was left. The soldier's only comment was: "You're a little feller now,
but will make a big Injun bye and bye. I only wish I had more to treat
the same way."[22]

Lieutenant Bell brought a prisoner back to the fort—an Indian
woman captured in the running fight. She was imprisoned, remaining at Fort Union until May; then the "treatment" was reversed.
Taking advantage of an opportunity for vengeance, she "killed the
sentinel with a butcher knife and escaped."

Bell's account of the battle was not wholly consistent with his orders. He tried to explain that he had "had an interview with them
[the Indians]," but as the interview was "not to their liking," he "was
forced to attack them." The attack, as a consequence, was "unavoid-
able." This unavoidableness netted him two dragoons killed and four
wounded. The Jicarillas, on the other hand, "succeeded in escaping
to impracticable ground, which was near, taking with them a number wounded, leaving five killed." While the Indians held their position on impracticable ground, Lieutenant Bell took a position with
his force "to protect a large herd of depot cattle which were thought
to be in Canon Largo on the Canon," but the Jicarillas, instead of
remaining secure, "made an attack on it [Cañon Largo], as their
first revenge." But as the attack began, something well-nigh unbe-
lievable happened. The Utahs, under Chico, understanding what was
happening to the army, gave partial protection to the American herd
against the Jicarillas. A gesture of good will toward the white men!

Of the numerous tales related when Bell's men got back to Fort
Union, diarist Dragoon Bennett recorded this one: "They have had
a hard fight with the Indians and have killed a number of them.
Among those killed was the Chief of the Jicarilla Apaches, Old Lobo,
who has boasted that he has had intercourse with Mrs. White. Although Old Lobo was pierced by seven bullets, he drew his bow and

[22] James A. Bennett, Clinton E. Brooks, and Frank D. Reeve (eds.), *Forts and
Forays*, 25.

killed a young man named Arnold. They both fell and died grappling in each other's arms."

This turn of affairs was most disquieting to Colonel Cooke, who warned General Garland: ". . . there can be little doubt that Apaches and Utahs, numbering by estimate 300 warriors, are now, or speedily will be, in open war with us. . . . I can mount & efficiently arm but 36 men of my only company of Dragoons: 13 of these I expect to send on the 14th inst. to meet the mail 100 miles from here—a defensive measure, and the merchants at this season send their trains to Missouri for goods. . . . It is for the general to decide how I am to meet it."

The seriousness of the Indian threat was not fully comprehended by General Garland. To placate Colonel Cooke, however, he authorized the assistant quartermaster "to purchase as soon as possible ten or fifteen American horses fit for Cavalry service and turn them over to Co. H. 2d Drags." The quartermaster was unable to find the kind of horses needed, so the deficiency was supplied by preparing "a command of 20 dragoons with the use of eight condemned ponies."[23] Thereafter, however, "six very fine horses were purchased and three rejected, as the price was too great."

Some Mexican hunters came into Fort Union to report that they had met two Apaches beyond the mountains toward Mora and had seen a wide trail leading into the mountains. This information was interpreted by Colonel Cooke to mean that the Indians were leaving the plains, taking to the mountains north of Fort Union. The *alcalde* of Mora left the impression that the Indians seen at Mora were not hostile; they consisted of "45 lodges of Apaches—including probably only ten men—gone there in great alarm." This impression was not borne out by Mr. Bransford, also of Mora, "who recognized one or two who had been in the fight with Lieutenant Bell." Then General Garland turned militant. He instructed Fort Union "not only to keep open the road by which the mails are carried but to press these Jicarilla marauders to the last extremity." It was not even advisable "to patch up a hasty peace with them: *talking,* in the present state of affairs, will be of no use." If Cooke needed "additional force," he was in a position

[23] Cooke to Nichols, March 14, 1854, AC, "Fort Union, 1854," File 1, pp. 25–26.

to send it.[24] The commander had issued orders for forty or fifty men to go to Mora, and should those Indians not have dispersed, Major Blake, in charge of the expedition, was to "attack the males, if not quite submissive & make prisoners of women." Cooke was deluded enough to believe that "the Apaches may have *left*, frightened perhaps by the arrival of the troops from below." And, in the mind of Colonel Cooke, this "concluded the Indian campaign—that is—so far as Fort Union is concerned."

But such was not to be. Cooke having drawn into Fort Union his entire force—307 soldiers—a messenger came from Major Blake at Taos: "Apaches & Utahs, numbering 250 warriors, attacked Lieutenant Davidson's Company, 60 strong, at Sienquilla, and very near overwhelmed it." Leaving Captain N. C. Macrae in command, Colonel Cooke immediately moved out with all available force, registering out: "Destination not known."

[24] Nichols to Cooke, March 12, 1854, NA, RG 98, Dept. of N. M. Orders, Vol. 9, pp. 137-38.

CHAPTER EIGHT

NUEVO MEJICANOS TO THE RESCUE

GENERAL GARLAND, upon learning of the annihilation of Davidson's command, ordered Cooke "to proceed forthwith to Don Fernandez de Taos with such force as can be spared from Fort Union . . . [and] take charge of operations." Garland at the same time would go to Santa Fe "to be near and receive any reports."[1] The information received by both Colonel Cooke and General Garland was meager: that combined Jicarillas and Utes—250 warriors—had ambushed Davidson's sixty men, overwhelming them, so that only "about seventeen men, most of them wounded, return from the battlefield." Since Colonel Cooke's maximum strength would not exceed "two hundred Dragoons and a company of Artillery armed with rifles," it did not appear that the Colonel could "prevent further disaster," so, humbly, he called "upon the governor for two or three companies of volunteers." To make the situation definitely worse, two days later Garland was informed that one hundred Mescaleros were by-passing Albuquerque, marching north in the general direction of Anton Chico, Las Vegas, and Fort Union. This squeeze movement definitely posed a threat to the safety of the Fort. To offset the threat, Major Backus was put on their trail, moving out of Fort Fillmore, "to cripple them as much as possible." The situation at Fort Union was not entirely hopeless, however. "By relieving most of the Extra & daily duty men," Macrae thought he could "have a force of 25 or 30 enlisted men for scout duty."

Colonel Cooke moved to Cantonment Burgwin, established headquarters there, then broke it up almost immediately to move on to Taos, arriving there April 3. His first move was to communicate with

[1] NA, RG 98, Dept. of N. M. Orders, Vol. 9, p. 152.

James H. Quinn and Kit Carson. With Quinn he made a contract to accept him as a volunteer with the rank of captain, Quinn to furnish thirty Taos Pueblo Indians and *Nuevo Mejicanos* as spies or scouts. Kit Carson was entirely out of sympathy with the proposed campaign, but reluctantly joined since the safety of the Anglo-Americans was involved. Carson hastily delegated his own duties to John W. Dunn, "my Interpreter," and awaited the time when he could make his position clear.

During mid-afternoon on April 7, after twenty-five miles of travel "up and down high mountains . . . over bad country," having found "Remnannts of Lieutenant Davidson's equipment . . . floundering through snow from two to three feet deep," the contingent suddenly saw the Indians not over three hundred yards away. "Up to that time," stated Quinn, "Carson had always been ahead with the Spy Company"; but sensing that the Spy Company must have support, "he had gone back to bring up the troops." Quinn charged hard with the Mexicans and Pueblos, "it being no time to swap knives." Learning from Carson that there was a battle in progress, Colonel Cooke came up "most beautifully" and pursued the Indians about two miles, the movement costing the Colonel "one regular soldier killed and one wounded in the pursuit."

The Indians, although "they returned our fire with spirit," retreated sustaining losses, falling into a stream which could not be forded by horses, while Colonel Cooke returned to their camp, "built a large fire and some hundreds of dollars of Robes, Elk Skins, and other Indian plunder, was burnt." The result: "No dead Indians, but a number of wounded, because they discovered us first and were prepared to fight until their families got away." Later, however, it was discovered that "the Apaches lost seventeen women and children, who, losing themselves in the flight, perished by exposure to snow and hunger."[2]

---

[2] Journal of a Spy Company. Notes of a spy company under Colonel Cooke, furnished by Quinn at the request of William H. Davis, April–May 2, 1854, and taken from photostats of the "Journal of a Spy Company" in the Henry E. Huntington Library and Art Gallery, San Marino, California.

Mechanics Corral, Fort Union, September, 1866.

Arrott Collection

Brevet Brigadier General William Grier, commander of Fort Union,
July 12, 1868, until June 1, 1870.

Arrott Collection

The Indians moved on toward Abiquiu, leading through "very high mountains" covered with "about four feet of snow and sometimes more." At Abiquiu, Kit Carson made his disapproval of the campaign known, and, withdrawing from the Spy Company, "camped above the Pueblo." Here the army was joined by forty more *Nuevo Mejicanos* under the command of José María Chávez. Carson wrote the Governor:

> Having become acquainted with the commencement of the War on the Apaches about Taos, & accompanied Col. Cooke in his present expedition, I have to report to you, first, that, in my opinion, they were driven into the war, by the action of the officers & troops in that quarter:—that since they have been attacked, with loss of lives, property, suspicions; vigorously pursued through the worst mountains I ever tracked through, covered with snow:—that their suffering & privations are now very great,—but that thinking there will be no quarter or mercy shown them, they will resort to all desperate expedients to escape any sort of pursuit & they have scattered now in all directions.
>
> Under the circumstances, I will wait at Albiquiu [*sic*] for your consideration of the matter, & decision:—My opinion is that it would be best for them to be sent for, and a fair & just treaty made with them. I have no doubt they will be glad to surrender all the government property which they got possession of from Lt. Davidson's men.

Colonel Cooke kept the army in camp until April 18, "reorganizing." That day they moved again, toward the west, over "dreadful hills . . . the hardest day yet." On April 19, Cooke complained of being ill and remained in camp. The Spy Company found that the hard-pressed Indians "were now eating their dead horses, the skeletons being left along the trail with the meat of[f]." Then the campaign wound up at El Rito, the troops "all with the chills. Cooke very sick," so sick, in fact, that although "he tried to come into camp with a few spies, he had to stop and lay down with a fire." Carson's attempt to bring peace was of no avail with General Garland. He would "listen to no proposition of peace until these marauding Apaches have been well whipped." There must be "neither rest nor quarter until they are humbled to the dust." He wanted to hear "above all things that . . . the devils that murdered the White family . . . have been hung."

Then Garland, realizing the efficiency of the *Nuevo Mejicanos* and Pueblo Indians who had gone out of Taos with Cooke, offered to supply Colonel Cooke with "60 Inftry, accompanied by some 40 Pueblos & Mexicans (likewise on foot), whom Capt Valdez of Moro could soon select, raise and command." Cooke received General Garland's offer of assistance coldly, intimating that he had "a plan of co-operation from Taos" and thinking that "Col B[rooks] could at least defend himself with one hundred men." This made the General suspect that Colonel Cooke intended to terminate the campaign; and when Chico Valdez came into camp with four of his band proclaiming that "the Utahs are all peaceably and friendly disposed toward Americans" and had joined only because it was "either fight or die," Cooke warned the Utes to stay away from the Jicarillas, intimating that the Utes would not be attacked if they did so, informing them, "I am going again after them & if they run away into the mountains & I cannot catch them, I can get a thousand New Mexicans, who can run like them on foot in the mountains & hunt them down."

After warning the Utes to stay away from the Jicarillas, he filed a report on his reorganized army with General Garland. He had sent twenty-five men back to Taos; he retained twenty-five to do train-escort duty. He had sent "about 20 to Fort Union"; thirty broken-down horses went with them. He had organized "a company of *demounted* dragoons, about 40 strong"; he had retained "perhaps as many as 25 additional irregulars"; he had "about 190 regulars . . . with provisions for 2 days."

Those provisions he was not going to need. Seeing that Cooke's intention was to bring the campaign to a close, Garland ordered: "In consideration of the present state of your command, you take post either at San Fernandez de Taos or Fort Union, as you may elect, and after supplying your command . . . resume offensive operations against the Jicarilla Apaches. . . . In the meantime . . . Major Brooks . . . will keep the field." Thus tactfully divested of the command of the fighting forces, Colonel Cooke moved back to Fort Union to supersede Macrae, but holding to a semblance of his authority by designating his position as "Headquarters, Forces in the Field, Fort Union."

In order to account for the expense incident to employing the *Nuevo Mejicano* and Pueblo Indian spies and trailers, General Garland explained the situation to army headquarters:

> It is due to his Excellency [Acting Governor Messervy] to say that during the military operations the Jicarrilla Apaches (and the not unfounded fear of confederates from other tribes), he has aided me with his influence and authority. . . . I have been induced to authorize the employment of some Pueblo Indians and New Mexicans for the double purpose of trailing the Apaches through the difficult passes of the Rocky Mountains and of getting them so far committed to us to insure their fidelity. . . . The Pueblos can be relied upon—not so with a part of the Mexican population—which are not only not reliable but quite equal to the Indians in thieving and duplicity."[3]

The expense to the War Department was $6,325. Since Quinn's scouts were being retained in the service, there would be other expense, estimated at forty-six dollars a day. He was discharging Captain Valdez' forty men, as "they were never to be compared with Quinn's men." All agreed that Captain Quinn displayed "sagacity and indomitable courage—the same remark will equally apply to Kit Carson—sub-Agent of Indian Affairs."[4]

Colonel Cooke, following his return to his "headquarters, forces in the field, Fort Union," believed "that there is something serious south." There was, indeed: Ennis J. Vaughn had been vilely and diabolically murdered. Since Vaughn, Esquire, was a "peaceful and upright citizen," a proclamation was published by the executive. Murders had been "repeatedly committed"; now a call was made to all "Good Citizens, friends of order and public safety, to use all diligence to arrest and bring to justice the perpetrators of this foul deed."

[3] Garland to Thomas, June 5, 1854, NA, RG 98, Dept of N. M. Orders, Vol. 9, pp. 191, 200-201.

[4] Garland to Thomas, New York, June 30, 1854, AC, "Fort Union, 1854," File 2, pp. 35-36.

It was not even hinted that Vaughn had been murdered by Indians, but when fourteen other New Mexicans were also killed, Cooke declared the Jicarillas guilty. Acting Governor Messervy thought otherwise, believing the murderers to be Kiowas, Cheyennes, and, probably, Arapahos. Messervy therefore implored against "adding more enemies to the field," and counseled against hasty action. General Garland agreed with neither Cooke nor Messervy. He declared: "The recent foray in which 14 Mexicans were murdered in San Miguel County is attributable to a dastardly act by three men from that county . . . who without any other motive than plunder shot three Cheyennes or Arapahoes and stole their horses. [And] these Indians, as is their custom, took their revenge."

In counseling Colonel Cooke against fostering open war in San Miguel County, the Governor was aware that Fort Union had but 211 soldiers available for duty, insufficient to cope with another enemy; further, the impressment of citizens into the militia, authorized by the civil government, was meeting with little success. In order to recruit even the semblance of militia companies it had become expedient to limit each man's service to three months, discharging one-third of each company each month. To satisfy the objectors, Acting Governor Messervy admonished "great prudence that the service shall be equal upon all." Furthermore, Messervy wanted to delay any definite action since Governor Meriwether was "daily expected" to return to the territory.

Brigadier General José Gallegos and his adjutant, Miguel Sena y Romero, not wishing to shoulder the responsibility of failing to protect their settlements, complained that "the militia of the county are entirely unarmed, and hence it is dangerous and unnecessary for them to make an expedition." They would like a supply of arms "that we may be able to defend our lives." In fact, two days before they wrote, they had "attempted to raise a party to pursue . . . but in consequence of a want of arms we could not get 15 men to go out, excluding ourselves." Acting Governor Messervy could only suggest "that you do the best you can under the circumstance until the arrival of his Excellency." Cooke also had his opinion: "I shall consider the militia, which has been turned out, as a quite satisfactory protection against any attacks now apprehended upon settlement to my south."[5]

Finding that Santa Fe was a more convenient location for army headquarters, General Garland moved back to the capital, so that he could communicate more readily with the Governor, declaring at the same time that "Albuquerque is the dirtiest hole in New Mexico and is only occupied from necessity." Closer communication with the Governor resulted in a message to the legislature. "Gentlemen," said the Governor, now back from the States,

> In the discharge of my official duty, it again become proper for me to lay before the Legislative Assembly the condition of the Territory. . . . I regret extremely to inform you that since the last adjournment of the Legislative Assembly our citizens have suffered much from the depredations committed by the Indians, Many valuable lives have been sacrificed, several of our people borne off into captivity, and a large amount of property lost. Many valuable United States troops united with the militia to prevent such occurrences. These depredations became so frequent and the prospects for the future so alarming as to induce the Honorable Wm. S. Messervy, then the Acting Governor of the Territory, to call out a portion of the militia of the Counties of San Miguel and Arriba to assist in protecting the frontier. But I am sorry to inform you that, for the want of arms, ammunition, and other equipment, the militia had but little opportunity of rendering much valuable service, and I am equally as sorry to state that the officers in command have reported to the Executive that, in some instances, portions of the militia ordered out refused to obey the call and assist in protecting the lives and property of the community.

Then, pretending that the disobedience had stemmed from "individual inconvenience and great sacrifice," he proposed that the legislature enact a "volunteer system," thus encouraging citizens "to enter the service of their country willingly, cheerfully, and of their own accord, for they will be more likely to render good service than those who may be forced to fight by compulsion." Attention then was directed to the fact that "individuals have engaged in trade with the Indians, in some instances selling them powder and lead, whilst oc-

[5] Cooke to Nichols, June 6, 1854, AC, "Fort Union, 1854," File 2, pp. 23–24.

cupying a hostile attitude toward us." Such trafficking with the enemy was well-nigh incredible, but nevertheless a fact: "Without strong evidence of the fact, it would be difficult to bring the mind to believe that whilst the community generally was engaged in hostilities, and a portion in a deadly struggle to protect their lives and property from the relentless savages, individuals could be capable of supplying the savage foe with the means of prosecuting hostilities." These words were sufficient for the release of a spirit of rebellion on the part of the *Nuevo Mejicanos,* who, on March 25, 1855, hanged Governor David Meriwether in effigy from the flagstaff in the main plaza at Santa Fe, before the Palace of the Governors. Before this occurred, there had been a significant change at Fort Union. On September 17, 1854, Colonel Thomas F. Fauntleroy arrived at the fort. The next day, he assumed command of the post, and Cooke renamed the fort "Fort Union military headquarters," there being only eighty-three soldiers present for duty.[6]

The man power at Fort Union was so low when Fauntleroy took charge that "even the extra-duty men and citizens ... employed were not able to cut sufficient grass for the regulation allowances to the public animals," although he had a superabundance of "privates of the band and several musicians." Being thus handicapped, he issued orders to detachments in the field "not to go into the Raton Mountains: You might probably meet Chacon."

Misfortune of another character overtook the army just at this moment. Heavy rains fell throughout New Mexico. General Garland's headquarters building at Santa Fe caved in. The General was absent, but the mishap left the adjutant "sloshing around in a mud-pile." And from Fort Union came a distress call, "The roofs of the quarters occupied by the troops, at this Post, are in such a bad state as not to afford protection from the weather." To meet the emergency, Fauntleroy moved everybody out into "tents condemned by the Board of Survey."

The troops occupied their tents but briefly. On the tenth of November word came that Indians had struck again "twenty-five miles south-

[6] Post Returns, September, 1854, AC, "Fort Union, 1854," File 2, p. 82.

east of this post." They numbered between "four and five hundred," and "they were driving off a herd of cattle." Fauntleroy had but "forty-seven Dragoons—all told, but out they went, leaving at headquarters only four non-Commissioned Officers and fifteen privates of the Infantry for duty besides the sick and prisoners." To complicate the situation further, he had positive standing orders "to furnish an escort for the mail twice a month of from twenty to twenty-five men each." He therefore called for immediate reinforcements, "a full company of Infantry, at least, and one additional Dragoon Company."[7]

In due time, too, he was promised facilities so that the tents could be abandoned. Santa Fe headquarters would send "a man capable of running the saw mill & have lumber sawed out as soon as practicable." Furthermore, General Garland intended to order Captain Ewell to march up from Los Lunas and "drive the marauders from the Pecos and the Red." But Fort Union's few men brought their own relief. They took the trail of the Indians and recovered 140 cattle, "besides counting forty more dead on the line of retreat." They brought back other news, too. Before the detachment arrived at the Beck ranch, the Indians had killed "three shepherd boys, a fourth not having been heard from, and is thought a prisoner." Then, substituting for the four shepherd boys, they "drove back eight hundred sheep," although four hundred others went along with the Indians.

On January 11, 1855, a distressing report came from north of the Raton Mountains. Mr. Atwood rode into Santa Fe to see the General. He related that on Christmas Day a body of Utes and Jicarillas, one hundred or more, attacked Pueblo (now Colorado). Fourteen men were killed; two were wounded; one woman and two children had been carried away. "They were all mexicans [*sic*]." In addition, the Indians took two hundred head of stock. Mr. Atwood had been at the scene "a few minutes after the Massacre and assisted in burying the dead . . . saw the Indians driving off the stock." General Garland decided to keep the matter secret, and no mention of it was made to Fauntleroy. Major Blake, who had the same news from Mr. Atwood, however, was notified "that he should come to headquarters as soon

[7] Nichols to Miles, NA, RG 98, Dept. of N. M. Orders, Vol. 9, p. 257.

as practicable." The General "wanted to arrange with him personally to make a campaign, but it was most desirable that the matter should be kept secret until the troops were in the field." Colonel Brooks at Fort Massachusetts was taken into the secret. Major Carleton was given even more information: he was "to lose no time in equipping his company . . . for active field service of at least two months duration." The expedition was "to consist of at least two hundred and fifty men . . . half dragoons . . . and the other half either of volunteers or hired guides and spies." Carleton was told that the incident was so important that "all duty must be made subordinate to this movement."

But at nine o'clock that same night, Garland was forced to change his orders. A hurried order went to Los Lunas to Carleton: "Start immediately in receipt of this." The cause: That very afternoon, at four o'clock, Galisteo—literally in the front yard of the capitol—had been attacked; seventy horses and mules had been driven away; some people had been wounded; some captives had been taken. Not certain where the Indians were headed, Fauntleroy was importuned "to cut them off" if they retreated toward the Red River.[8] Responding promptly, Fauntleroy sent out "all the Dragoons which I could send, with due regard to the condition of the post & the regular duties required twice a month in escorting the mail." Four days later, Fauntleroy's troops were back in garrison. They had examined the country generally in the vicinity of their route and had found nothing "but some old signs . . . and the carcass of an ox that had been butchered by [the Indians]."[9]

Other troops moving from Fort Marcy were "on the ground at daybreak" and had better luck. They chased the Indians for "two days and three hours . . . left three dead where we met them . . . wounded four others." They were apologetic for not being more successful, but "the morning of the encounter was so cold that after the first shot the men could not reload their guns so they used their sabres, having three of their own men wounded, one so badly that he died." A check

[8] Nichols to Fauntleroy, January 11, 1855, NA, RG 98, Dept. of N. M. Orders, Vol. 9, p. 265.

[9] Fauntleroy to Nichols, January 22, 1855, AC, "Fort Union, 1855," File 1, p. 12.

at Galisteo showed "one man killed, wounding another, stripping a dozen women, and a loss of seventy mules."

Before the Galisteo attack had become history, General Garland had other troubles to divert his attention from the secret expedition. On January 18, 1855, several soldiers were discharged from the army at Santa Fe. They bought a wagon and announced that they were going to Tecolote. Paymaster Cunningham, for lack of a safety vault, had been keeping the army's money at his home, as was the custom. "That night three men—*not mexicans* [*sic*] badly beat and robbed the Major at his home of $40,000." Just before daylight, according to the adjutant general's information, "three men, not mexicans, engaged a mexican for which they paid him four dollars, to show them the mountain road to Tecalote." Both the sheriff and the army officers thought there was a strong probability of collusion between the discharged soldiers and Major Cunningham. Consequently Garland urged Fauntleroy to "spring these men and give them a thorough overhauling."[10] No men appeared at Fort Union, and there was no "overhauling." Major Cunningham demanded a court-martial in order to clear his name. As to that, Garland would only state that he "would forbear to make any remarks other than to specify the sum lost was $35,985, and that Major Cunningham has omitted to state in whose hands the remainder of the funds are deposited."[11]

After so many false starts to put a secret expedition in pursuit of the murderers of the fifteen citizens on the upper Arkansas, General Garland recognized his weakness and called on Governor Meriwether for assistance. He wanted "a force of Mounted Volunteers to assist, not only the defense of the frontier settlements but to follow up and chastise these murderers who are every day becoming more bold and more hostile toward our people." Necessary for the existing emergency was "one Lt. Col. one Asst Surgeon, five Captains, five

[10] Nichols to Fauntleroy, January 19, 1855, NA, RG 98, Dept. of N. M. Orders, Vol. 9, p. 273; AC, "Fort Union, 1855," File 1, p. 11.

[11] Whittlesey to Major F. A. Cunningham, May 20, 1855, AC, "Fort Union, 1855," File 2, p. 63. Paymaster Cunningham cleared himself before the court-martial of collusion, but continued dilatory in his duties, many officers complaining of his repeated failure to pay the troops.

first and five second Lieutenants, twenty Sergeants, twenty corporals, and four hundred privates." Their service was to be limited to six months, "unless sooner discharged by proper authority." The Governor acquiesced. One week later authority went to Taos "to engage a company of thirty spies and guides." Their compensation, "when mounted," was not to exceed two dollars a day. It took the Governor just one week to assemble two companies of volunteers which he had recruited at Taos, offering them to Major Blake at Cantonment Burgwin, along with their captains, Charles Williams and Francisco Gonzáles. Major Blake accepted the offer, but finding no arms with which to equip the troops, marched them down the mountain to Fort Union.

On January 29, 1855, Governor Meriwether again responded to Garland's call for volunteers, announcing that he had "now in this place and ready to be mustered into the service of the United States a company of volunteers under Captain J. H. Mink." Garland could not accept Mink. He had been informed that a criminal charge had been lodged against him, "which, if true, will be an effectual bar to his being mustered into the service." The General would, however, want the volunteers, with Mink eliminated, as well as another company, "whenever they present themselves properly organized and equipped," a requisite being that "Each man must have his horse and horse-equipment, and must be the owner thereof."

Now that troops were being enlisted, General Garland disclosed his secret to Colonel Fauntleroy at Fort Union, doing so by relieving the Colonel from command and replacing him with Captain N. C. Macrae. This was made expedient by the return to the service of "the Old Reliable,—renowned for his service with Colonel Price in the Taos Rebellion—Ceran St. Vrain." He was coming to the army again, this time with the rank of lieutenant colonel, commander of the New Mexico Volunteers. His superior officer was to be Colonel Fauntleroy. This completed General Garland's plans, which could no longer be considered secret.[12]

[12] NA, RG 98, Dept. of N. M. Orders, Vol. 9, p. 290; also S.O. No. 12, February 5, 1855.

Before Garland disclosed his plans, Blanco, a Utah chief, and Huero, a Jicarilla Apache, the son-in-law of Chacon, head chief of the belligerent Apaches, with a party of 180 warriors, returned to the scene of their Christmas Day crime. They "killed four citizens" and, to make the crime more reprehensible, "three of them Americans." Then they took off again with another hundred animals.[13]

Colonel Fauntleroy's orders now became specific: He was to "hunt up and punish a party of Utah and Apache Indians, who on the 25th Dec. last murdered fifteen men at a place called Pueblo, taking two boys and a woman into captivity . . . and on the 19th of January, killing four citizens, three of them Americans." He was to follow the offenders "wherever they go, and not to hesitate to attack any Indians who may think proper to shield them. . . . Do not recognize the principle urged by peace establishment men that we can wage war upon one part and not the whole of the nation." He was to go to Taos at once, "there to make arrangements for the field." Again came a disruption of plan. At two o'clock on the morning of February 9, "several Mexicans aroused him [Fauntleroy] from his slumber to tell him that twenty miles from this place on the waters of the Ocate" they had been attacked by eight Indians. One of the party had been killed; they had lost five or six of their horses. Disregarding Order No. 63 directing him to "repair at once to Taos," within two hours Fauntleroy had "12 Dragoons in the saddle & on pursuit." The pursuit, however, was to be both limited and cautious. They were to "confine their operations principally to the collection of information," and only in the event that they came upon a small party were they to fight. There was no fight. Before the day was over, they came riding back, with the mail escort, confirming the attack: they had "found the dead body of a Mexican" as well as hearing that fifty lodges of Jicarillas were within fifty miles of Fort Union.

The volunteers who had gathered at Fort Union under Captain S. Cunningham got off to a bad start. In fact, they would not start at all when ordered on a scout by Captain Deus, but remained at Fort Union, incurring the wrath of the post adjutant.

[13] The second attack on Pueblo (Colorado), January 19, 1855.

There was more confusion at Taos. General Garland interfered with Fauntleroy's plans by detaining Major Blake at Cantonment Burgwin until the arrival of Lieutenant Trevitt, who, "although sent for in all haste" had not reported for duty. The Colonel was also deprived of the services and presence of Faustin Baca. Through the graciousness of Captain Chávez, "this volunteer had been permitted to go to the house of his Father in San Miguel, there to remain for three months." When Garland was told of this, "in great disgust" he classed it "a swindle upon the Government," issuing orders that no furlough should be given during the campaign "unless in extreme cases and for short periods." Furthermore, this must be "mentioned to Colo. St. Vrain."

South of Fort Union, Captain Ewell, trying to prevent the Mescaleros from moving northward to a junction with the Jicarillas and Utes, had a misfortune. Captain Henry W. Stanton and two of his men were killed "due to the impatience of one of his officers smarting under disappointment in the Mexican War." But Ewell left "fifteen dead, among them . . . their great war chief, Santa Anna and one of his sons," and thinking that the fight was over, Ewell moved back near Albuquerque, leaving four men at a grazing camp with his horses. Ewell had failed to discover that the Mescaleros were following him, and when night came, February 23, fifteen Mescaleros circled the tent, "threw it down upon the soldiers, thus entangling them and wounding all, none of whom had fewer than four wounds." While the soldiers were thus sealed beneath the canvas, the Mescaleros shouted their defiance, proclaiming that they did not want their horses—"they just wanted to kill the soldiers."

This incident once more disrupted the concentration at Taos. Major Carleton was sent after the Mescaleros, and by March 14 Garland had a full-fledged war with the Mescaleros in progress with D. S. Miles in command, supported by Carleton and his dragoons and a number of volunteers and spies.[14] The General's March report to army headquarters contained nothing definite about Fauntleroy. All that was

[14] Order No. 3, Sturgis, March 14, 1855, NA, RG 98, Dept. of N. M. Orders, Vol. 36, p. 329.

known at Santa Fe was that the Colonel and St. Vrain had left Taos with separate columns, the Colonel's force numbering "over five hundred Regulars and Volunteers." Since the weather continued bad, the General feared "they will suffer much from the cold," and it would "not be surprising if he heard that many of the horses had perished in the deep snows of the Rocky Mountains." Six days after the General had written of his apprehensions, a tale-bearer found his way into his presence. He carried bad news: Fauntleroy had "abandoned hot pursuit." To the General this "had the appearance of an abandonment of further active participation in the campaign." His first reaction was "to transfer the command . . . to Lt. Col. St. Vrain," but upon second thought he ordered that Fauntleroy "resume immediately operations agreeable to original instructions." Furthermore, Colonel St. Vrain was not to be placed under the command of any other officer "except yourself." Should Fauntleroy not be able to take the field, transfer must be made to St. Vrain, who would thereafter report direct to headquarters. Finally, should the animals of Fauntleroy's command be broken down, then "the General expects the Campaign to be made on foot."

Such straight talk galvanized Fauntleroy into action. He chased his quarry four days, killing eight and causing the Utes to separate from the Jicarillas. Moving back to Fort Massachusetts to refit, Lieutenant Magruder spoke "well of the troops, volunteers included," after which he stalked the Utahs twenty-eight days more, finally ambushing the Utahs around a campfire, Fauntleroy describing the slaughter as "most beautiful to behold! . . . the enemy being swept like chaff before the wind." Fauntleroy congratulated himself: "None [of his men] had been killed in the action; however one died some hours later, having had his leg amputated from a wound." Counted Indian dead, forty. The battleground was Ponca Pass. Then the Colonel decided to return to Taos in order to reunite his command.

At Taos trouble was waiting. Company F, First Dragoons, had preceded him; and before the Colonel arrived, all members had vigorously attacked an ever present and abundant supply of Taos Lightning, with the result that the company rioted, and by force of arms found themselves languishing in durance vile awaiting court-martial. Diplomatically, Fauntleroy handled the situation by "transferring temporarily" a detachment to Fort Union, where there was great need of fighting men, Commander Whittlesey having but 106. Others were indiscriminately assigned throughout the territory—all but two privates, who were "sent out of New Mexico in irons . . . to be put to labor with ball and chain at Fort Leavenworth." The recalcitrants, however, were to travel in style. Captain Ewell was to command an escort of one noncommissioned officer and twelve men accompanying Governor Meriwether, who had tired of New Mexico. Besides the comforts "for the distinguished party," there was added "a wagon for the prisoners with such transportation as may be necessary for the prisoners."

On July 9, 1855, the Colonel commanding the Army of Northern New Mexico joined his forces with those at Fort Union. Eleven days later he surrendered his command, reassuming the duties at Fort Union. In explanation, General Garland told Army headquarters: "The campaign is now drawing to a close, by reason of the volunteers, who, I am gratified to say, have maintained good discipline, and vie with the regular troops in the prompt and efficient discharge of their duty." He was happy that his refusal to recognize peace establishment men's principles had ended in "The Utah Indians (against a part of whom we have been engaged) . . . making an appeal for peace."

To bring the campaign to an official end, on January 18, 1856, joined by Acting Governor W. W. H. Davis, the legislature "sent its compliments in a high degree to the officers and men of the United States Army serving in the Department." Garland acknowledged "these kind and complimentary expressions . . . so unexpectedly conferred," promising that "the same gallantry and energy . . . will in no degree be abated in the future." As a compliment to Lieutenant Colonel St. Vrain and his officers, whose services terminated with those of the volunteers, he published Order No. 19,[15] declaring that the department commander could not under a proper sense of his obligation

[15] August 6, 1855, NA, RG 98, Dept. of N. M. Orders, Vol. 36, pp. 338–39.

withhold the expression of his warmest approbations to the manner in which Lieutenant Colonel Céran St. Vrain and his officers had discharged their duty while in the service of the United States. "The whole period of their service had been spent in active campaign, and whether in the mountains covered with eternal snows, or in the arid plains, they vied successfully with the old troops . . . in following up the enemy, never failing in a single instance to inflict upon them the punishment which their many acts of atrocity had rendered so necessary. And amid all the privations and trials . . . not a murmur of discontent reached the general's ears."

CHAPTER NINE

"INSTRUCTIONS IN THE ARTS OF CIVILIZATION"

FROM JULY 9 until July 20, 1855, Colonel Fauntleroy made Fort Union the headquarters of the Army of Northern New Mexico, and on the latter date he dissolved that status to become post commander. Immediately he was aware "that all the quarters of this Post want extensive repairs, many entirely rebuilding." In fact, "a whole set of Company quarters were in a state of rapid dilapidation & the stables for one Company have to be rebuilt entire." Occupying these dilapidated quarters and stables were 238 men and the dragoons' horses. The units consisted of three companies and one company of artillery, the last only "temporary at post."

Fauntleroy was quite displeased to find that two of the companies of dragoons were detailed to provide the annual supply of hay. Making hay-mowers of dragoons he branded as "doubtful policy." Captain Sykes took umbrage at Fauntleroy's attitude (although it was "but a mere four hundred tons to be cut . . . the necessary quantity)," accusing the new commander "of an effort to shirk the detail." To this, of course, Fauntleroy took exception, branding Captain Sykes's letter as "containing a statement which is not true." Furthermore, the Captain "evinces a degree of impropriety in the view of the comdgn officer." But after thinking the matter over, Fauntleroy gave General Garland the assurance that it was his "intention, regardless of Captain Sykes, fully to carry out the mode of getting the hay by the troops so far as indicated by the decision at the Hd Qrs Dept. of New Mexico." To do so, he would have to "relieve the four men now cutting logs," thus deferring repairs on the post.

About mid-August, 1855, Major Isaac B. Richardson came into the vicinity of Fort Union with the recruits sent by the War Department from the East to take the places of the New Mexican Volunteers discharged.[1] Although the recruits came to "the vicinity" of Fort Union, Richardson would not conduct them into the environs of the fort proper, keeping them designedly out of the jurisdiction of the commander.

Having thus retained jurisdiction over his command, Richardson condescended to go into Fort Union to make "the usual call of respects to the commanding officer," at which meeting he stated verbally the purport of his orders. Miffed at this aloofness, Fauntleroy asked "if the purport of his orders was his *exact orders.*" Richardson replied that he gave them "verbally and from recollection." Fauntleroy countered, "That is not sufficient," that his orders "were required." Faced with a positive demand, the Major left, promising to comply. But he did not return, and thereafter "positively refused to show Fauntleroy the rolls of the Dragoon recruits." Fauntleroy's first reaction was to place the Major under arrest for this impudence— which had taken place in the presence of General Garland, who was there to see the distribution of the troops. But he considered "the nature of the Command, and his having in his possession a very large amount of public money . . . and it would have subjected the command to a delay that might have proved injurious," so he awaited the departure of Major Richardson and filed with the General "charges and specifications" and requested that a court-martial be assembled.

Before giving orders for assignment to companies, General Garland looked over the recruits. He was displeased "with their quality and condition." He rated "the Infantry arm about the poorest set of recruits I have ever seen. They were in a bad plight, having lost most of their clothing by fire on the plains. Quite a number were afflicted with scurvy." The sick the General sent to the hospital; the others to fill "F Company, whose rioters were yet in jail."[2]

---

[1] Fauntleroy's letter of August 17, 1855, to Easton fixed the arrival as August 17 "or prior thereto" (AC, "Fort Union, 1855," File 2, p. 99), while Garland's letter of August 31 gives the arrival as "about the 20th inst."

[2] NA, RG 98, Dept. of N. M. Orders, Vol. 9, pp. 390–91.

While Colonel Fauntleroy was nursing his grievance, both at Major Richardson for impudence and at General Garland who chose not to receive the "charges and specifications" against the Major, A. W. Stephens Brice rode over to Fort Union from Las Vegas to report that the Comanches, hard pressed from the east by the Texans, were "250 strong at Mr. Hatchs [sic] Rancho and were doing him great injury." Fauntleroy promptly sent Lieutenant Johnston with thirty men—"all I can spare under existing circumstances"—with orders to give what protection he could, but "by no means to bring on hostilities—*unless* you should be fully able to sustain your command." This would "give Privates of F and H Company, First Dragoons" their first experience since the mutiny of F Company at Taos. General Garland heard about the Comanches and gave diametrically opposed orders: "Should there be evidence of hostility on the part of the Comanche Indians . . . the troops will at once give battle and drive them from that part of the frontier." But, true to Comanche style, before the troops arrived, the "250 strong" left the country, and "Mr. Hatch came to Vegas with Lt. Johnston & expected to return the next day alone." The troops went back to Fort Union; they had not seen an Indian.[3]

As the Comanches dispersed, Mr. Bransford of Mora arrived at the fort "to make a verbal statement that on the road to this Post on the day before yesterday he met a party of Mexicans with the dead body of a Mexican boy, who they represented as being killed near the crossing of the Red River by some Apache Indians." Fauntleroy was suspicious of this incident; he therefore investigated without sending out a scouting party. He learned that the Mexicans "had returned by Fort Union in the night & did not make any report, not wishing it known that they were trading with the Comanches!!"[4]

In September, 1855, there was a break-through in the attitude of the *Nuevo Mejicanos* toward the United States regular army.[5] Some

[3] Fauntleroy to Nichols, September 26, 1855, AC, "Fort Union, 1855," File 2, p. 217.

[4] Fauntleroy to Nichols, September 26, 1855, AC, "Fort Union, 1855," File 2, p. 116.

[5] The first application of a *Nuevo Mejicano* to enlist in the U.S. Regular Army was received at Fort Thorn, New Mexico.

194

Nuevo Mejicanos applied to Lieutenant Colonel J. H. Eaton of the infantry for permission to join the infantry. Surprised at the change of attitude, although they had been commended for their loyalty and zeal while serving in New Mexico volunteer regiments, and still dubious of their acceptance of North American institutions, he sent their applications to General Garland. "The department command," so Garland replied, "can see no objection to their enlistment, to the extent of four or five to a company, but their inclusion in the regular army," he hedged, "should be for special duties." Thus he enlisted the first *Nuevo Mejicanos* into the regular army of the United States, a dubious compliment to their loyalty after ten years' inclusion in the United States of America.

Chief among the obstacles encountered by the army during its first decade in New Mexico were the roads, bad and indifferent. There were no good ones. Traces-of-passage, misnamed roads, fanned out in four directions from Santa Fe when Kearny arrived in the New Mexico capital. One so-called road followed the Río Grande southward only to encounter an insurmountable obstacle at the *Jornada del Muerto*. North of Santa Fe high mountains hedged traffic close to the Río Grande, making it necessary for wheeled traffic to detour for one hundred miles, although the over-the-mountain trace was only thirty-five miles. The route from Taos to Ocate, thence to Fort Union, was so bad that only empty wagons could pass. "The roads on the other side of the mountain east of Santa Fe [according to the Secretary of War], those leading to Las Vegas, El Moro, and El Rayado, were mere bridle-trails along the beds of mountain torrents." By the end of 1853, as the Secretary of War advised Congress, twenty-two companies of soldiers were scattered widely over the territory, occupying ten forts. (Garland added another, Fort Stanton.)

Even New Mexicans commented on the condition of the roads, and from the time of the establishment of Fort Union to the beginning of the Civil War the New Mexico Legislature appealed to Congress eleven times to improve roads.[6] Congress responded, appropriating thirty-two thousand dollars, but allocated it to the Taos–Santa Fe

---

[6] *Laws of the Territory of New Mexico, 1851–1861.*

and Doña Ana roads. The same amount was provided by Congress on March 3, 1855, to be spent from Fort Union via Santa Fe to Albuquerque, and on a road westward to Abiquiu. This supplemental appropriation, sponsored by Jefferson Davis, then secretary of war, was intended to make it possible for General Garland to get work done on the road from Fort Union to Santa Fe. John J. Abert, under whose general supervision as topographical engineer road work was to be performed, selected and sent to New Mexico Captain Eliakin P. Scammon; and Captain and Brevet Major Sprague, of the Eighth Infantry, was also assigned to duty with Captain Pope of the Engineers. But Pope was giving his attention "to experimenting for water east of the Pecos River, while Captain Sprague had been ordered to construct and repair certain roads."[7] Upon learning of this assignment, Garland dishentenedly stated that he expected "but little at his hands; his habits are not at all satisfactory." And although the General expected but little from Sprague, he got less from Scammon. From the time of his arrival, Captain Scammon "evidenced an affinity for Taos." This affinity consisted of such cordial and daily relationship with the successors of the distillers of Turley's Taos Lightning that his bookkeeping became such a "complexity" that even he could not decipher it. He "seemed to be some seven thousand dollars out of balance." Scammon undoubtedly was not surprised when he received this note from the General:

> The Department Commander deems it expedient to suspend all the operations connected with the construction, and repair of road . . . under your direction, and directs that you immediately pay off and discharge all the employees under your command. The general . . . wishes, at once, a statement of the appropriation for the above purpose.[8]

Three weeks later General Garland clarified his action for the headquarters of the army:

[7] Garland to Thomas, August 31, 1855, NA, RG 98, Dept. of N. M. Orders, Vol. 9, pp. 390–91.

[8] Order No. 301, Nichols to Scammon, October 4, 1855, NA, RG 98, Dept. of N. M. Orders, Vol. 9, p. 412.

. . . I have directed Capt Scammon to suspend all the operations connected with the construction and repair of roads . . . under his direction. . . . This was necessary on an account of an entire inefficiency on the part of Capt. Scammon arising from drunkenness.[9]

Captain J. N. Macomb succeeded to Scammon's duties; and on June 12, 1857, General Garland ordered the new superintendent "to take the necessary measures to possess himself of the funds, instruments, books, maps, and other property belonging to the Topographical Department . . . and proceed to examine the road from Fort Union to Santa Fe . . . with a view to . . . improvement." Not only did Macomb examine the road, but his first report showed that on the Fort Union–Santa Fe road 1,122 days' work had been performed, in addition to 139 days' use of teams and wagons. Most of this, in conformity with Jefferson Davis' wish, had been done by contract to "local citizens who live along the line of construction; and they had converted that section of the Santa Fe Trail from a single wagon track thirty-three feet."

Taking advantage of the lull in Indian scares, General Garland gave thought to the physical condition of Fort Union, then quartering only 116 soldiers.[10] Ignoring Colonel Fauntleroy, post commander, Special Order No. 27, dated April 1, 1856, was published, naming a board of officers to consist of Brevet Major W. A. Thornton and Captain L. C. Easton to "proceed to the junction of the Moro and Sapello Rivers, the Wagon Mound, and their vicinities, and examine the country with reference to the selection of a site for a military post, embracing all the facilities required . . . a site of such extent as will embrace within its limits sufficient grounds for an arsenal." Such an area must be "subject to lease, with the privilege of purchase within three years at a price fixed upon when the site is designated."

Before making any decision for removal to new grounds, however, he found it necessary to consult with the surveyor general of the ter-

[9] Order No. 327, Garland to Thomas, November 1, 1855, NA, RG 98, Dept. of N. M. Orders, Vol. 9, pp. 433–34; Jack L. Cross, "Federal Wagon Road Construction in New Mexico Territory, 1846–1860," MS, University of Chicago; 34 Cong., 3 sess., *Sen Exec. Doc. No. 3*, 252.

[10] Post Returns, Fort Union, March 1856, AC, "Fort Union, 1856," File 1, p. 115.

ritory. That precaution, he observed, had not been taken by General Sumner when he selected the Holes in the Prairie for Fort Union. As a consequence, the recent decision which gave ownership of the Fort Union environs to Messrs. Doyle and Barclay made it necessary for General Garland to lease Fort Union "at an extravagant rate or submit to the process of ejectment, carrying with it an immense loss of Public Property." To minimize the loss if the War Department should not approve his lease of the Fort Union grounds, Garland informed army headquarters that he was already "preparing suitable storehouses at Albuquerque for the reception and safekeeping of the property"—all this while the committee sought a site for a new Fort Union in the same general area. As to Albuquerque (he must have forgotten that he had called it the dirtiest hole in New Mexico), it was "a more central and accessible position, taking the year 'round: it is a place of greater security than Fort Union . . . with its insufficient storehouses . . . in a state of decay." So, he continued, "This seems to be a proper occasion to refer to the embarrassments in the way of either rebuilding or repairing Fort Union."

On June 1, 1856, the strength of Fort Union dropped to eighty-seven men. On June 27, General Garland granted its commander, the querulous Fauntleroy, a leave of absence "with permission to apply for an extension of four months," and upon receipt of the Special Order, the Colonel was "to consider himself relieved from duty at the Post of Fort Union." Furthermore, he must "immediately relinquish the command of it to the officer next in line of the army on duty there." With Fauntleroy's mind inflamed against all about him, he was bowed out, Brevet Major William N. Grier succeeding. As June came to an end, with Fauntleroy leaving, sixty-seven dragoons took up station at the post, making the garrison 154 strong. With these troops came Assistant Surgeon Jonathan Letterman "on transfer by request."[11] On Major Grier's desk was a "report of the condition, capacity &c of the buildings of this post." Grier found it "so correct and complete in itself" that he had little to add, except to

---

[11] AC, "Fort Union, 1856," File 1, p. 145. The signature of this distinguished doctor in the records shows the spelling both "Letherman" and "Letterman."

say that "even with such repairs as can be made to the Quarters, they will be barely tenable, but not really comfortable or very safe for another year." He suggested that "if another post is to be built at or near this site, during the summer of 1857, much time would be gained by getting out the lumber during the coming winter," and that could be done by fifteen or twenty men.

General Garland's mid-year report to headquarters was written under discouraging conditions.[12] His relations with the Navahos were "the engrossing subject." The conference held at Laguna Negra brought "unsatisfactory results . . . despite the great pains taken by both Major Kendrick and Agent Dodge to encourage and instruct these people in the arts of civilization," and they then assumed "an almost threatening attitude." Trouble with them "would be difficult to avoid." There was such a shortage of food for the army that if troops were sent to the Navaho country, they would be forced "to use the fields and flocks of these misguided people for the subsistence of our own men and animals," which would make the Indians again "a marauding people." There were other minor matters, also; for instance, "some thefts . . . by other bands of Indians . . . by lawless men, who cannot be controlled by their chiefs," who were seemingly obligingly out of the reach of the army. "But there was no evidence, however, of hostility . . . other than that of the Navajos." Seven "unarmed Mexicans" had been slaughtered near Mora. All except Garland believed that the murderers were Jicarillas. He thought that this outrage "could be traced to the Indians of the Arkansas River,"[13] who were Cheyennes and Arapahos.

Added to the discouraging conditions at the beginning of the second half of the year was another disturbing factor. On July 26, the First Regiment of Dragoons was ordered to leave for Tucson and California. It was anticipated that they would be replaced by a regiment

[12] Garland to Headquarters of the Army, June 30, 1856, NA, RG 98, Dept. of N. M. Orders, Vol. 9, pp. 495–96.

[13] Garland to Thomas, July 31, 1856, NA, RG 98, Dept. of N. M. Orders, Vol. 9, pp. 507–508. He was correct; the Arkansas tribe was paying a revenge call for Fauntleroy's and St. Vrain's expedition.

of mounted riflemen, who were supposed to be at Fort Bliss not later than August 5. In view of this fact, Garland decided "to temporize with the Navajoes," instructing Kendrick "to arrange matters in such a way that the necessity may not be forced upon us to take up arms at once."

Now that the fighting force in the Ninth Military Department had reached its lowest strength, Colonel Chandler stirred up the Gila Apaches, causing their agent, Steck, and the Governor to berate him for firing into "non-belligerent Gilas." Garland took umbrage at Agent Steck's position, defending Chandler on the grounds that "it was an error—a justifiable error—and as soon as Chandler discovered that they were friendly Indians, he ceased firing and indemnified them to their satisfaction." In defense of the army, he would have the Adjutant General know that "the homily of Agent Steck might just as well have been omitted . . . for the officers of the Army have too much intelligence and humanity of feeling to make a ruthless attack upon ever a savage foe."[14]

On August 27, General Garland sent an urgent message to Colonel W. W. Loring at Camp Holmes, near El Paso. His presence was "imperatively required at Fort Union"; he was "not to wait for transportation." A similar order went to Colonel B. L. E. Bonneville, with the Third Infantry at Fort Fillmore. He informed Bonneville that he was leaving the department and that Bonneville would command. The transfer of the dragoons to the Pacific had left but fifty-three men at Fort Union with First Lieutenant H. B. Critz in command. Colonel Loring arrived at Fort Union on September 27, with eighty-one inexperienced mounted riflemen, plus his "non-commissioned Staff and Band." His riflemen were "entirely out of ammunition, both of revolver and rifle." This detachment, however, brought the garrison to "150 strong."[15] On October 11, Garland placed Bonneville in command of the Ninth Military Department, slept the night at Fort

14 Order No. 150, Garland to Cooper, July 31, 1856, NA, RG 98, Dept. of N. M. Orders, Vol. 9, pp. 506–507.

15 NA, RG 98, Dept. of N. M. Letters, Vol. 10, pp. 19–20; Post Returns, Fort Union, September, 1856, AC, "Fort Union, 1856," File 1, p. 170.

Union, and left the following day. Six days later he was met "on the plains on the way to Fort Leavenworth, getting on well."[16]

Major Simonson arrived at Fort Union and annexed his detachment "awaiting orders." The garrison strength was thus increased to 305 men, 156 having been added since the first of October. The additional men caused Loring's attention to be directed "to the dilapidated condition of the now disintegrating fort." As was customary, he called for an inspection report, the duty this time falling to Assistant Surgeon Jonathan Letterman, who saw the establishment "from a medical point of view." The doctor had no high opinion of the fort to which he had requested assignment. He found it "shut in on the east by the Gallina [sic] mountain, seven miles distant, and on the west by a precipitous mass of sandstone, about 150 feet in height." A portion of the post was in immediate proximity to those rocks and upon sharply descending ground, and, as a consequence, water drained from the higher portion of the post across the lower area, "not infrequently running into and through some of the buildings." There was no timber near the post, "all that is required for building and for firewood being brought from a distance of six or eight miles." No stream of water was sufficiently near to be of service. "Quite palatable water," however, could be hauled from a spring near by, "but it occasionally gives rise to diarrhea." The garrison was spread "over a space of about eighty or more acres . . . to present the appearance more of a village . . . than a military post."

About the regular troops, he had little to say, other than from a medical standpoint. Of the irregular garrison, Dr. Letterman had much to say. In its early days the fort had provided an oasis on the long trek from Independence to Santa Fe. New arrivals at Fort Union were welcomed with unconcealed pleasure. Now, after five years, visitors and regular troops alike were enduring annoyances which they were eager to exchange for the tribulations of the road, the rigors of the march, or the dangers of battle. "The unseasoned, unhewn, and

[16] Order No. 238, Bonneville to Thomas, October 31, 1856, NA, RG 98, Dept. of N. M. Orders, Vol. 36, p. 373; NA, RG 98, Dept. of N. M. Letters, Vol. 10, pp. 33–34; Post Returns, Fort Union, October, 1853, AC, "Fort Union, 1856."

unbarked pine logs, placed upright in some, and horizontal in other houses" were rapidly decaying. Indeed, the house which the doctor occupied had rotted so much that "an ordinary nail will not hold." The deterioration of all quarters was so complete that "one set of barracks have lately been torn down to prevent any untoward accidents that were liable at any moment to happen from the falling of the building." The consequences of such accidents, however, "were less awesome than the consequence from using the quarters which stood," for "the unbarked logs afford excellent hiding places for that annoying and disgusting insect, the *cimex lectularius* [bedbug], so common in this country, which is by no means backward in taking advantage of, to the evident discomfort of those who occupy the buildings." Weather permitting, post personnel almost always slept in the open air.

Despite rotting timbers, infestations of bedbugs, and dirt roofs ("not a room even being left dry in the hospital—tents being used for the sick, and canvas to protect the hospital equipment"), Dr. Letterman "found the buildings were undergoing repairs." In fact, originally "the fort was badly laid out and badly built," so that it was "now essential that the post be rebuilt and buildings erected with some regard to the welfare of those who are destined to occupy them, and not on the principal of shortsighted and extravagant economy."[17]

In November, word of a matter of serious portent came to Fort Union's commander, Colonel Loring. There was trouble at Bent's Fort over the Raton Mountains, and William Bent had called on St. Vrain for assistance. St. Vrain, of course, relayed the call to Fort Union.[18] The Kiowas had attacked Bent's Fort, and only through the intervention of the Cheyennes, William Bent's friends, was the fort saved from their ravages. After the attack the Kiowas withdrew to winter quarters. That they might renew their hostility was obvious, so William Bent needed help.

On November 22, Colonel Bonneville directed Loring to send a

[17] 36 Cong., 1 sess., *Sen. Exec. Doc.*

[18] Nichols to Loring, November 22, 1856, NA, RG 98, Dept. of N. M. Letters, Vol. 10, pp. 38–39.

party of twenty men and two officers to the old fort, "ostensibly to look into the Commissary stores at that place, ascertain the amount and condition, and report the same. The principal object, however, is to ascertain the state of affairs at that point in regard to Indian matters." The strictest secrecy must prevail, so that "in the event of a campaign against the Kiowas, they may be taken by surprise." To maintain Fort Union's strength during the absence of the troops traveling to Bent's Old Fort, troops from Cantonment Burgwin were "to report for temporary service at Fort Union or elsewhere as circumstances may arise."[19]

Loring was greatly handicapped in complying with the order by the physical condition of both the troops and their mounts. "They had suffered much on their march to the Department, particularly the backs of their horses; arising, most probably, from badly fashioned saddles." Too, the troops were separated from their ammunition and clothing, which were "yet coming on in the rear." Loring fitted them out "in an issue of dragoon's clothing—they are now comfortable." The matter of ammunition was different: "Not anticipating the arrival of the Regiment, little preparation was made in this kind of ammunition, and unless theirs be brought up in good condition, there must be a great deficit." What little ammunition there was, however, could be "used with great economy."

Then, while Loring's detachment went north to Bent's Fort "to look into the commissary stores," good news came from the Mescaleros. Cadeta delivered eight horses which his tribesmen had stolen. His action, however, was offset by "the painful intelligence of the capture of Captain Dodge, Indian Agent for the Navajos, by the Mogollon Apaches . . . the same people" fired into by Colonel Chandler "by error."[20] Thinking this a favorable pretext for making war on the Gilas, Bonneville immediately began to "repair the credit of the subsistence department," which had gone in debt $207,952.30; of that sum $57,750 had been approved by the new department

---

[19] *Ibid.,* also pp. 45–47.

[20] Bonneville to Thomas, November 29, 1856, NA, RG 98, Dept. of N. M. Letters, pp. 43–44.

commander in his brief tenure. Now he called imperatively on the headquarters of the army "to take early measures . . . to supply Colonel Grayson, Commissary of Subsistence, with sufficient funds to meet the demands against him."

While Bonneville was arranging his financial affairs in anticipation of a war with the Gilas, a disturbing incident occurred on the route to Fort Defiance which indicated that there might also be Navaho trouble just when not wanted. The cattle being driven to the fort vanished. Their disappearance was interpreted as a breach of the peace by the Navahos. "Indefatigable exertions of Major Kendrick, however, solved the problem; the drivers themselves had made way with twenty-one of the missing beeves."[21]

While Bonneville hankered after a campaign against the Gilas, Loring pined for one "against the northern Indians." And before Bonneville would encourage preparations to "surprise the Kiowas," he told Loring that he wanted "to see the report of the Officer who has been sent to Bent's Fort, with your views endorsed thereon." On January 8, 1857, Lieutenant Alexander Macrae returned from Bent's Fort "without accident," to report that he had found the camp of the Kiowas two hundred miles from Fort Union. They were well mounted and formidable in number, and a successful attack would require not less than four or five hundred men with "100 Utahs as guides, trailers and spies," plus fifty wagons "for the transporation of the Commissary Supplies and garrison equipment, Ammunition &C."[22] This report was discouraging to Loring; Fort Union had "only eight complete teams for post purposes and twelve for the depot." The report, however, suited Bonneville's purpose perfectly: "It was complete, full of information and to the point." Furthermore, there seemed to be "no necessity for an expedition against the Kiowas;" there would be no scouting "in the vicinity of the Kiowa camps." The latter prohibition was particularly advisable since he

[21] Bonneville to Thomas, November 30, 1856, NA, RG 98, Dept. of N. M. Letters, Vol. 10, pp. 45–47.

[22] Loring to A.A.G., January 9, 1857, AC, "Fort Union, 1857," File 1, p. 4.

had concluded that "the service of the troops will be required elsewhere."

The probability of using the troops elsewhere was contingent in Bonneville's plans upon the fate of Indian Agent Dodge. Since it was generally believed that Dodge was merely being held for ransom, Captain Thomas Clairborne, without higher authority, offered a reward of one thousand dollars for the safe return of the agent "to be paid by the Government." Bonneville countered immediately, "... this amount of money cannot be paid by the Government from Military appropriations"; such was "... entirely within the Indian Department, and being such, all rewards are due from that department." He would do his utmost for Indian Agent Dodge, but that utmost would be "confined to operations with the troops."[23] The discussion soon turned out to be academic, for information came "that Captain Dodge was killed at or near the place of his capture."[24] And to Bonneville the depredations of the Mogollons were "of too outrageous a character to be passed over—they must be punished. . . . There will be a perfect deluge of this country by our troops." The Mogollons were "to be [so] thoroughly chastised, and their bands so broken up, that they will not be heard from again as a distinct people."[25]

Preparations were thereafter intensified as Bonneville's War began to be a reality. A supply depot was established. Two mountain howitzers went along to defend it. Twenty-five men were hired "as packers, trailers, guides, spies &c &c," including Blas Lucero. He was to be engaged "permanently at the rate of Forty dollars per month." On campaign he would be paid "three dollars per day plus one ration." Colonel Loring was to be withdrawn from Fort Union along with four officers and 120 mounted men, thus reducing the force at the fort to fifty-eight.

[23] Nichols to Clairborne, January 16, 1857, NA, RG 98, Dept. of N. M. Letters, Vol. 10, p. 65.

[24] Nichols to Kendrick, January 30, 1857, NA, RG 98, Dept. of N. M. Letters, Vol. 10, pp. 71–72.

[25] Bonneville to Thomas, January 31, 1857, NA, RG 98, Dept. of N. M. Letters, Vol. 10, pp. 72–73; also, Nichols to Steen, February 17, 1857, *ibid., pp. 80–81.*

Before withdrawing toward the Gila country, Loring made an unpleasant discovery concerning two Americans. On February 27, 1857, the merchant train of J. B. Doyle (of Barclay's Fort renown) and Uncle Dick Wootton left Fort Union eastward over the Santa Fe Trail, carrying the potential for renewal of the war by the Plains Indians. To offset such a catastrophe, Colonel Loring sent a warning:

Mr. J. B. Doyle &c

Sirs—I have been informed that your train, which has started for the States, has in it ten kegs of powder—how much more is not known. The impropriety of so small a party passing through the Indian Country with so large a quantity of powder is too obvious to bear a comment, the natural inference is that it is destined for trade with the Indians. Considering the relations it can be but criminal, and none has done more to impress their hostilities than Mr. Wooton, the man in charge. You will be held responsible for such a disposition, and if I do not send for it, I shall at least report your conduct to the proper Authorities, both here and in the States.[26]

The expedition to Bent's Fort, besides calming Loring's ardor for a war, brought other results. Lieutenant Ransom had taken his orders seriously and while at Bent's fort had actually inspected the government property in storage. His findings were: "19 barrels of pork—Rusty, Musty—and Rotten: 9 sacks Flour—damaged by water . . . totally unfit for use: *Deficient*—1,139 pounds of hard bread; 800 pounds of flour; 24 quarts of beans; 106 pounds of rice; 109 pounds of coffee; 694 pounds of sugar; 35 gallons of vinegar; 66 pounds of soap; 247 pounds of died apples." The deficiency, explained the Lieutenant "was the difference between the amount shipped to Bent's Fort . . . and the amount actually there." The reason for the deficiency he did not venture to say "since the stores had been there a long time."

During the concentration of troops destined for the Apache country, all did not go well. One of the units scheduled to travel by way of Santa Fe gave Bonneville concern. On March 11, a soldier of Company E, Third Infantry, went into a drugstore in Santa Fe, "and a druggist of the city shot him down." Several of his companions, be-

[26] Loring to Doyle, February 23, 1857, AC "Fort Union, 1857," File 1, p. 38.

coming "irritated at the outrage, repaired to the jail to punish the offender who had been confined there." There was "a melee; one of the city prisoners was killed, and three wounded." In the midst of the excitement an officer appeared at the jail, and Bonneville "found it gratifying that the moment the voice of the officer was heard . . . they gave his orders prompt and ready obedience." The next morning the company was paraded without arms. Participants were identified, confined, and offered to the civil authorities. The offer "was declined," and the prisoners were remanded to the military "for safe keeping." Bonneville thought the safest place for them for the time was "at far-away Cantonment Burgwin," so over the mountain they went, only to be back in Santa Fe before the end of April. There they "were tried and duly acquitted," whereupon the Honorable J. J. Davenport, chief justice, commented: ". . . however unfortunate the Military may have been in the conduct of their men, the officers have exhibited a high regard for the laws and a prompt determination to support them."[27]

When Colonel Loring left Fort Union for the Mogollon campaign, he left behind the culls of the garrison. In the opinion of Loring's successor, Captain L. Jones, they were "by no stretch of the military imagination the 'Whitest honey in fairest gardens called!' " There were thirty-seven of them, not including Private Thomas Howard of Company I, Mounted Rifles, in "confinement with ball and chain &c" and in the guardhouse since four days prior to Loring's departure. With this command Jones struggled three weeks, then unburdened himself to his superior:

Hqs. Fort Union
May 6, 1857.

Major

I would very respectfully state for the information of the Department Commander that the command left here for duty is so small and of such worthless material (after the very critical selection for the Gila Expedition)—that I am anxious to get the Services of every available man, for the necessary Main and Stable guards and herding parties and

[27] Nichols to Thomas, April 28, 1857, NA, RG 98, Dept. of N. M. Letters, Vol. 10, p. 108.

for the labor so essential for putting the quarters in repair before the rainy Season—

I have now detailable for all those purposes only 4 non-commissioned officers, 1 Bugler, and 32 privates, and in regard to most of the latter, they would be more appropriately in their vocation *under* than *on* guard.

I have a double motive in making this statement, first, to bring directly to the department commander, the true condition of my command, and Secondly in this connection, to recommend very respectfully to his favorable consideration, the case of Private Thomas Howard of Company I, R.M.R., Sentenced—see Dept. Orders Special No. 53, dated April 14, 1857—with a hope that so much of his sentence may be remitted as refers to his "confined with ball and chain &c"—

Howard a good and efficient soldier when sober, makes me very solemn pledges to abstain entirely thereafter from drinking, and I feel confident that the public interests would be subserved, by taking him from the baneful associations of this guardhouse, and restoring him to duty under those pledges.

While Colonel Bonneville prosecuted his war against the Apaches, General Garland made his way around the circle and came into El Paso, arriving there May 11, 1857. Awaiting him was a letter from Bonnevillle, who advised his intention "to conduct the campaign in person." Whereupon Garland took little time to make his decision: The following morning he resumed command of the department. Then, he went to Santa Fe, arriving May 27. With adroit inoffensiveness he set about evaluating Bonneville's administration of the department during his absence, at the same time foiling Bonneville's aggressiveness and keeping Bonneville from spreading his war to the Mescaleros.

On May 7, Captain Jones took two days' leave from his rag-tag command at Fort Union; when he returned, he discovered that Private Frayne had likewise taken leave, escaping from the guard. The private, however, was apprehended and brought back the same day of his desertion. Commander Jones, not having completed his detached-service duties, left again on May 15; so did Private Frayne. Again he was apprehended, being re-jailed on the sixteenth. The army was required to pay thirty dollars for his arrest, and the same amount for Private John M. Forrest, who likewise was tiring of his Fort Union duties.[28]

On June 2, Colonel Bonneville communicated with General Garland at Santa Fe. Nothing he said indicated he was having "important and favorable results." He was chiefly concerned over the difficulty he anticipated should he extend the campaign, for he was "out of bacon." Garland solved the dilemma immediately, sending back a messenger with the answer, "If the campaign depends upon an additional supply of bacon, it will have to be abandoned." On July 14, Bonneville rendered an accounting of his war: He had captured nine Mogollon women; attempted a surprise attack and was discovered; had a battle, killing twenty-four Indians, four women accidentally "and including one afterwards"; made twenty-seven prisoners; destroyed many fields of corn; rescued a Mexican boy from captivity; had nine United States soldiers and two officers wounded. Then twelve days later General Garland wrote finis to Bonneville's War by posting Special Order No. 75: "The campaign against the Gila Apaches . . . is therefore considered at an end, with results creditable to the officers and troops engaged."[29]

Colonel W. W. Loring returned to Fort Union from his Bonneville campaign on September 27, 1857.[30] Knowing that more troops were needed in the department, Garland had previously called for 700 recruits, besides many horses, but Loring found his Fort Union command numbering only 224 soldiers.[31] On October 1 an incident occurred which suggested the need of an additional force. An unexpected guest arrived without "provisions and clothing." Introducing himself as Frank DeLisle, he said that he was in search of Colonel Albert Sidney Johnston, who was en route to Utah to suppress the Mormons. He had met two parties of Cheyennes and Kiowas, "one 60 and the other 40," who had divested him of all his belongings,

[28] Lane to C.O., A. Rifles, AC, "Fort Union, 1857," File 1, p. 83.

[29] S.O. No. 75, June 26, 1857, NA, RG 98, Dept. of N. M. Orders, Vol. 28–A (no p. no.).

[30] Post Returns, September, 1857, AC, "Fort Union, 1857," File 2, p. 38.

[31] Garland to Thomas, August 1, 1857, NA, RG 98, Dept. of N. M. Letters, Vol. 10, p. 132.

"and now he was afraid to . . . hunt further."[32] After talking with DeLisle, Loring thought "the express may be important"; consequently, to aid the messenger, he immediately detailed an escort from the Mounted Rifles "to go along with the mail" and sent DeLisle along with this protection, since it was hoped Colonel Johnston would be found "somewhere on the Red River."

As the Fort Union garrison continued to be reduced, the recruits ordered August 1 were "daily expected at Union." They were to be "stopped there or vicinity." On October 30, they were "encamped at Ocate and would be into Fort Union, October 31." Most encouraging was the fact that funds for the Quartermaster and Pay departments were with this contingent, as well as the much needed horses. Otherwise, General Garland found nothing in the department to encourage him. He did, however, have a rumor that a new governor was en route; he welcomed the advent of a new governor "as most propitious, for all the leading officials of the United States had departed." Governor Meriwether had taken leave in May. Less than a month previously Loring had furnished transportation for Acting Governor Davis and the Chief Justice. The Palace of the Governors was presided over by "only a private secretary of the former Governor." The revenue of the territory was unequal to its expenses, and any governor willing to assume the civil burdens was welcome. Indeed, such an official did arrive, on November 12, in the person of Governor Abraham Rencher, just as Major Carleton took a sixty-day leave "with permission to apply for an extension of four months." (Private James Mahon, of Loring's Mounted Rifles, indicated his willingness to do likewise, but before he could make his escape, Loring locked him in Fort Union's none too secure bastile to await charges of desertion.)

[32] Loring to Frank DeLisle; Loring to Nichols, October 2, 1857, AC, "Fort Union, 1857," File 2, p. 42. After DeLisle came to Fort Union, Lieutenant Du Bois received a newspaper from the East which disclosed that President Buchanan, despite General Winfield Scott's advice to the contrary, had held that the Mormons in Utah were in rebellion against the United States and was sending Colonel Albert Sidney Johnston with an army to suppress the rebellion. Johnston got snowed in near Fort Bridger, and army headquarters did not know of his plight; hence the message carried by DeLisle.

In the early days of January, 1858, a Utah Indian came into Fort Defiance carrying as identification "a certificate of baptism and membership in the Church of the Latter Day Saints." He had been charged with bringing about peace between the Utes and the Navahos. He had been "sent by Indians who were only ten days from the Great Salt Lake" to inform the Navahos that the "Mormons were instigating the different tribes to bury their animosities with a view of arraying themselves against the United States government." Upon receipt of this information, General Garland acted immediately: a messenger went both to Washington and to Albert Sidney Johnston. To Johnston he offered aid, at the same time suggesting a diversion from an attack upon Salt Lake City. He would have Johnston "throw a column of men . . . not less than 800, into the country of the Utah Indians," who were "becoming impatient . . . tampered with by the Mormons."

Two weeks later the General's dignity was insulted: he learned that Captain Marcy, with a detachment of sixty men, seeking aid for Colonel Johnston, had come into his jurisdiction, and was even then in Taos, without reporting "in person on his arrival . . . in accordance with the requirements of the Regulations." Garland pointed out Marcy's lese majesty, deeming "it proper—and such is the custom —that you should report your arrival accompanied by an exact return of the troops." Captain Marcy was in no hurry to repair the General's frangible dignity. He was no ordinary transient. With his "escort of forty soldiers and twenty-four citizens as guides, packers and herders," he had been away from Johnston's army since November 24, tramping through snow-covered mountains in "a perfect state of banishment from all the comforts of civilized life and society."

At last, on December 27, when they had nothing to eat but the carcasses of their dead mules, Marcy had hopefully sent "two Mexicans and three of our best remaining animals with a letter" to Fort Massachusetts. The snow-bound men followed slowly. "The snow now was from four to five feet deep, and the leading men were obliged in many places to crawl upon their hands and knees to prevent sinking to their necks." But their messengers had gone through, and returned. "They brought a handful of coffee . . . a large plug of tobacco." Following, however, were three wagons—messengers from Fort Massachusetts. With Captain Bowman's compliments came "a demi-john of brandy," and when the coffee, tobacco, and demijohn was passed around, the men "devoured them most voraciously." Then, with rescue near at Taos, Sergeant William Morton died the following night—"made sick from overeating." At Fort Massachusetts, Bowman placed all the resources of the garrison at their disposal. And on the evening of January 21, Marcy was in Taos. He had been marching seventy-seven days.

Thinking of his men and the mission on which he had come, Marcy first saw the "escort comfortably quartered at Cantonment Burgwin [then] set about purchasing the animals required." Back in Taos four days later, he "was so busy that [he] hardly had time to write, or do anything else except eat since [he] lived on mule meat." He established himself comfortably, "staying with a merchant here who gives me a nice carpeted room with sofa and other civilized furniture, a most welcome change after sleeping and living out doors for six months, generally with a bed of 3 or 4 feet of snow." Too, he was "beyond the necessity of eating any more mules and horses."

On March 6, General Garland made official acknowledgment to Colonel Johnston that Marcy had complied with "the requirements of the regulations," and declared that the Ninth Military Department would give Colonel Johnston "every facility in its power." In the meantime, Captain Marcy went off to Fort Union, and since there was no direct communication by the department commander with Johnston's emissary, Garland could only report that he presumed "Captain Marcy has fully accomplished the object of his visit . . . and has, no doubt, left Fort Union on his return to Utah." Garland's presumption was premature. On March 8, Marcy was yet in Mora, occupying all his time in purchasing horses and mules. He "had about 1,200," and thought he "would set off for Utah about the tenth of the month." He was going to "take wagons . . . and a very fine carriage which a gentleman has presented," and he "thought he would be comfortable." In his pocket he had an order from the now appeased department commander to take along "an additional officer and twenty-five riflemen."[33] At Fort Union, Captain Marcy found a lieutenant who was yet "fuming over the inefficiency of Old Bonny Clabber,[34] thought by Lieutenant John Van Deusen DuBois to be not only inefficient but lacking in soldierly bravery"; and when approached, DuBois "was very anxious to go," thinking from "the very modest narrative" of Captain Marcy that the Mormon expedition with him would be "very like romance."

On March 9, Marcy and his command moved out, first to Rayado, there to receive 960 mules and 160 horses previously purchased for the expedition. Lieutenant DuBois was two days late in getting ready, "and just as he was bidding goodbye to all a Mexican reported that three of the men detailed to go with him had, the previous evening, killed a woman." This called a temporary halt while DuBois confined the men and Loring sent in their places "three as worthless scoundrels as I ever saw." DuBois "knew them all" but "had no choice." On March 12, they were as far along as Maxwell's, where "Mr. Maxwell was his usual genial self, giving a *baile* on the 17th where women were plenty & quite pretty," and they had a "gay enough time to repeat it the succeeding night: this time it was another & a gayer *baile,* ending with a supper of ox-ribs & tortillas at 3 A.M." By nine the following morning they were in the saddle en route to Salt Lake City, "thirty wagons and sixteen hundred animals in the caravan."

After the departure of Captain Marcy, another messenger came to New Mexico from Johnston. He had "learned that the Mormons meditate an attack on Captain Marcy's party for the purpose of capturing or dispersing the government animals." He would, as a consequence, have to have from New Mexico "an additional force to thwart the designs of the Mormons." This was "indispensable," and

[33] *Campaigns in the West: The Journal and Letters of Col. John van Deusen DuBois* (ed. by G. P. Hammond).

[34] The nickname of contempt used by the soldiers for Colonel Bonneville.

he would "ask that the general will order an additional force" and "give Captain Marcy every desirable facility."[35] Special Order No. 30 was immediately posted by General Garland: Marcy was to be reinforced by two infantry companies from Albuquerque "and one company of horse from Fort Union." Loring was to make the company from Fort Union "sixty strong"; also Colonel Loring was to go along and remain "until the public animals are safely turned over to the Commanding Officer of the Army of Utah." Upon joining his detachment with that of Captain Marcy, he "would assume command of the entire escort."[36] On April 7, Colonel Loring marched out of Fort Union, having ordered Captain Marcy to await him at the "Bon-qui-Bouille on the north side of the Arkansas,"[37] about forty miles from Bent's Fort. Finally on June 23, Loring and the Fort Union reinforcements, after joining with Johnston's army, "camped on the other side of Jordan," quietly going into quarters, having made a journey wholly ill advised and uncalled for. And DuBois wrote in his journal: "I have seen the Saints!"

Camp Floyd, Utah, was established, and the one-time Fort Union soldiers "found it a pleasant place to rest." For amusement, "faro occupied every favored nook, and wine flowed like water" until July 18, when orders came: "All is fixed, and tomorrow we start for Fort Union." General Garland sought to hasten Loring's command by sending a messenger with the intelligence, "We are on the verge of a war with the Navajo Indians." Bowman was to detach himself from

[35] A. S. Johnston to A.A.G., Dept. of N.M., January 10, 1858, Report of the Secretary of War, 1858, Dept. of Utah, p. 412; also, Porter to Randolph B. Marcy, January 11, 1858, *ibid.,* pp. 42–43.

[36] S.O. No. 30, March 22, 1858, NA, RG 98, Dept. of N. M. Orders, Vol. 39, p. 131; also, Nichols to Loring, March 22, 1858, NA, RG 98, Dept. of N. M. Letters, Vol. 10, p. 202.

[37] This Loring failed to do, having missed the rendezvous by some twelve miles; however, he assumed command by messenger. In the meantime disaster visited the camps in the form of fires and violent winter storms. ("A terrible windstorm . . . it blew our fires in such long flames that on one side our hair was burned & on the other we froze"—Marcy.) After the storm they moved on, and Du Bois wrote "history" in his diary: "Cherry Creek—May 9 . . . We are encamped on Cherry Creek. Gold was found by one of the men today."

Loring's command while the remainder of the force was to "hasten to Fort Union." On September 10, Loring came within sight of Taos. He held the troops out of town that night, fearing to trust them. The next day he was at Black Lake. Taking Lieutenant DuBois with him, he rode ahead as far as Guadalupia "& slept that night in a house— the first since leaving Fort Union." At mid-day, September 13, the two officers rode into Fort Union; they had ridden 861 miles.

During Colonel Loring's absence from Fort Union, General Garland, with the connivance of Colonel Brooks, had let Navaho relations deteriorate to the point of war. The point of no return was reached when an Indian killed Colonel Brooks's slave boy, Jim. Both Brooks and General Garland, however, recognized the danger of open hostilities "until Colonel Loring returns." Then Garland promised "two fresh companies from Fort Union, and a company of Infantry from Cantonment Burgwin," and, in preparation, posted Special Order No. 64, requiring the Mounted Rifles to get ready for active service in the field.[38] Bonneville, who was slated to command, "would hold the project in the greatest secrecy." Brooks was to make "no hostile demonstration . . . until your reenforcements and supplies shall have arrived."

On September 2, General Garland, having arranged the details of the campaign, decided to leave the department, letting the command, again, go to Bonneville. Then two days before he intended to depart, "with surprise and regret" he learned "that an ill-timed attack" on the Navahos had already been made.

One of Bonneville's first acts as commander was to send to Mora for Colonel Céran St. Vrain and for Valdez, the "best guide for the Navajo country." Loring was much surprised when he received Order No. 2 directing him to report to the commanding officer with a noncommissioned officer and five mounted men for escort duty across the plains. That duty finished, he was to relieve Captain R. M. Morris from September 20 to October 5 on "official business," so that Morris might become a member of the Navaho expedition. Sensing that he

[38] S.O. No. 64, August 6, 1858, NA, RG 98, Dept. of N. M. Orders, Vol. 39, pp. 154–55.

was being purposely passed over, Loring, on September 24, made official application to be included in the expedition, knowing that Bonneville was now punishing him for failing to detach himself from the Gila campaign as readily as Bonneville thought he should have. Bonneville failed to confront the issue, laying the blame on General Garland.[39] But rumor was already widely accepted as a fact that the new Bonneville War was being foisted upon the Navahos for the purpose of affording certain officers opportunity to gather laurels. To meet the accusation of favoritism, Colonel Bonneville felt it necessary to state to headquarters:

> . . . to supersede Colonel Miles now, would imply disapprobation, and would be unjust to an old and faithful soldier. . . . I learned that General Garland stated, that I have had my turn on the Gila, Colonel Loring his on the Utah or Mormon expedition; and that it was just to allow Miles his with the Navajos.[40]

DuBois, back at Fort Union, taking note of the passing of events and persons, wrote in his diary: "We gave them [some passing recruits] a ball in the quartermaster's storehouse & did all we could to make them comfortable. That is all that September has done for us. General Garland and his staff & Dr. Leatherman [*sic*] went to the States a few days ago leaving the gallant and experienced Indian fighter(?) —Col. Bonneville—in command."

While the seekers after laurels carried on their war with the Navahos, their festoonery withering with each encounter, the opponents of such niggling found a spokesman, who, although he preferred anonymity and described himself only as "Civis," laid the bloody cadaver boldly upon the very doorstep of the Capitol. He chose as expositor *The National Intelligence,* Washington, D.C. In careful but blistering phrases he denounced the Bonneville War. He denounced its instigators: They had *"blundered* into what may be the greatest Indian difficulty we have had out of Florida. . . . If ever a Territory

[39] Wilkins to Loring, September 21, 1858, NA, RG 98, Dept. of N. M. Letters, Vol. 10, pp. 265–66.

[40] Bonneville to Thomas, October 19, 1858, NA, RG 98, Dept. of N. M. Letters, Vol. 10, p. 277.

needed a man of large experience and tried ability New Mexico now has that need. If the need may be *considered* supplied in the present commander, this makes it not the less proper to point out the fact of its existence. . . . Some instant step ought to be taken to ascertain if the war ought to be carried on at all! . . . If the war itself meets with general disapproval, the mode in which it is conducted is far from giving general satisfaction."[41]

In a classical bit of sarcasm, the legislature of New Mexico passed "An Act to Organize the Militia," assigning as the cause therefor the expediency of the management of the Navaho War with "the utmost available skill," this skill to "be assembled without charge to the United States, the forage and subsistence to be furnished by the militia, and the militia to serve without pay." At the end of the third week in November, Superintendent of Indian Affairs Collins joined the advocates of peace, and called upon Bonneville "to discuss the subject of the Navajo War."[42] The commander and superintendent agreed to make peace with the Navahos provided "the Indians evince a sincere desire for peace and agree to commit no more depredations on the settlements, [to] receive and follow with earnestness such advice as may be given them by the authorized officers and agents of the government." And as the Navahos "promised," Bonneville announced his "hope to make a happy termination of the difficulties." This hope was followed by posting on Christmas Day, 1858, General Order No. 11 bringing "the war with the Navajos to a close." So back to Fort Union went the troops, making the garrison 255 men.[43]

[41] *The* (Washington, D.C.) *National Intelligencer,* October 20, 1858, "Civis."

[42] Bonneville to Miles, November 21, 1858, NA, RG 98, Dept. of N. M. Letters, Vol. 10, p. 290.

[43] Fort Defiance, December 25, 1858, AC, "Fort Union, 1858," File 4, p. 110; Post Returns, Fort Union, December, 1858, AC.

CHAPTER TEN

"QUIETING THE UNEASY FEELING ON THE FRONTIER"

Now THAT the Navaho war was over, Bonneville announced to Governor Rencher that he had left a strong garrison at Fort Defiance under Major Backus "for the support of that judicious officer in case it should be necessary." He neglected, however, to mention that he was holding at Fort Union "twenty-one Navajoes, prisoners taken during the war, as hostages." He hoped "the disposition of the troops [would] serve to quiet the uneasy feeling and excitement on the frontier consequent upon the late military operations in the vicinity." Furthermore, in Bonneville's opinion, the campaign had been conducted in such a manner as to avoid "the necessity of relying upon, or falling into the hands of speculators."[1] To indicate his desire to economize, he forthwith ordered Colonel Loring to inaugurate "efficiency and strict economy" at Fort Union and to discharge immediately all spies and guides.[2] Furthermore, he let it be known that "for the best interests of the army," hereafter, "all officers should avoid any clashes with other Indians, if possible."

Even as he counseled avoiding clashes, the Superintendent of Indians Affairs directed his attention to "a party of Utah Indians in the vicinity of Wolf Creek, between Barclay's Fort and Wagon Mound ... in the vicinity of a large herd of Cattle." So, to support his policy, Bonneville ordered Loring "to send an Officer and detachment to their camp to ascertain their disposition" and "direct that they return to their own country." Loring's reply was prompt. He already knew of the presence of the Utahs; he also was aware of the presence of

[1] Bonneville to Thomas, January 8, 1859, NA, RG 98, Dept. of N. M. Letters, Vol. 10, pp. 300–301.

[2] Wilkins to Loring, January 16, 1859, NA, RG 98, Dept. of N. M. Letters, Vol. 10, p. 382.

"large bodies of Comanches," who were committing depredations and making threats. The department commander, he pointed out, had "placed him in command of several hundred miles of frontier with less than a company of horse to protect it"; furthermore, in conformity to the Colonel's economy order, he had discharged "five days previously" all the needed guides and spies. Now the Comanches were "encamped within a Short distance of the Cimarron and nearer this Post than any other settlement in New Mexico."[3] Then, in compliance with orders, Loring sent "Lieutenant DuBois & six men with Lieutenant Claflin," who found the Utes "about twelve miles from the fort and in a most beautiful spot," their camp consisting of "sixty lodges or 180 fighting men." BuBois told them "to go home," but "doubted their obedience."

On January 28, while Lieutenant DuBois was "quietly sitting by the fire ... reading a letter from home," he was "stampeded by an order directing the entire command to turn out under arms." Whitlock from near-by Sapello, was calling for aid against the Utes. "It was the same band which I had ordered to go to their own country." After much "talk" the Indians agreed to spend the night at Fort Union, then go on to Mora, where they were met by Kit Carson, their agent, with whom they went off quietly to their own country. DuBois went back to Fort Union to write in his diary: "Thus ended the glorious campaign of 1859 against the Mowatche band of Utahs."

Just as the "glorious campaign of 1859" came to an end, rumor sifted over from Mora "that eight men had been killed on the Arkansas by the Comanches & 1,000 sheep stolen." Loring let DuBois evaluate the rumor; he thought little credence could be placed in it, for "this news came from Bent, who wrote to Hatcher, who wrote to Playe. Bent and Hatcher are notorious liars, so there is no certainty even in this story."[4]

Disgusted with the situation at Fort Union, Loring, on February 4, 1859, requested a leave of absence.[5] Bonneville rejected his request,

---

[3] Loring to A.A.G., January 10, 1859, AC, "Fort Union, 1859," File 1, p. 15.
[4] Du Bois Diary, February 12, 1859.
[5] Wilkins to Loring, NA, RG 98, Dept. of N. M. Letters, Vol. 10, p. 318.

believing that the army would be required to "occupy Chihuahua" and that Loring would be needed in "the movements consequent thereon." However, after the adjournment of Congress, he would "take pleasure in sending the leave asked for."

While Loring awaited the adjournment of Congress, disease ravaged the horses and government herd of beef cattle at Fort Union. Three hundred and fifty-seven beef cattle were condemned and killed, the herd presenting "a mass of corruption." Food, as a consequence, was in short quantity and poor quality at the post. The condition of the fort became worse. Army fashion, another inspection was ordered. This time the board was to examine the "plans and estimates for rebuilding."

After Congress adjourned, Loring claimed his leave of absence, "everything having been quiet at Fort Union." For those going away on leave, April 19 was set as the day of departure. "First came Colonel Miles, promoted to the command of the 2d Infantry. Then, 2d, Lieutenant Backus—sick—Captain Levitt—Capt. Gibson, M.S. going to get married: Lt. Averell, walking on two sticks—and Lts. Whipple and Craig—All the party gradually collected until Col. Miles only was wanting; he arrived on the 2d of May & today they bade us goodbye. . . . Poor Owen Chapman, while at Albuquerque on his way to the states to die, became so weak that he scarcely expected to live to see another sun. While in this situation he sent for the quartermaster—an old friend—& asked him to make him a sign—

" 'Certainly, Owen! What do you want it for?'

" 'Well, Rucker, paint on it: *"Dying done here" by O. Chapman.'*

"And then he added:

" 'Many die and leave no sign.' "

Upon learning that Colonel Miles, who had connived with Colonel Bonneville to keep Loring out of the Navaho campaign, was a member of the States-bound party, Loring, on April 23, availed himself of an east-bound Mexican train. Turning the command at Fort Union over to Captain John Walker, he was next heard from "at the upper Spring on the Cimarron," putting distance between himself and Colonel Bonneville. Bonneville learned of his departure only on May 6, when Walker was relieved, J. S. Simonson being ordered up from Fort Craig to assume command of his regiment and the post."[6]

Major Simonson, however, failed to report at Fort Union, and was merely "heard of as on his way" and a week later "had not yet arrived." Thereupon, Lieutenant DuBois, availing himself of some "ostensible business at Head Quarters," rode over to Santa Fe. DuBois' diary tells the story: "I visited all my old inamoratas, and being detained two days to get the old man sober, I returned home. On the way Major S told me I would go with the command this summer."

Bonneville's orders for the summer were devious. However, Simonson finally gave DuBois a command: "38 men from E—the entire command was to comprise seven officers and two hundred men." They were just "to make a show of force" and "make explorations." They were also to retrieve property stolen by the Navaho *ladrones*. To accomplish that, of course, "some Indians will be killed." DuBois noted, "His order says: 'Kill four or five at least, of this tribe, as a punishment for their depredations.' "

On June 14, Major Simonson and Lieutenant DuBois left Fort Union, Simonson taking the lead. Going "through cedar timber to the Ojo Caliente [they] bathed in the warm springs." With one day of rest, they went on to Abiquiu. There they went to a *"baile* at Pheifers [*sic*] the Indian Agent." The non-commissioned officers gave a concert, "not a success in itself—but certainly a move in the right direction," but there was no real fun "until about eleven." About this time, "Lamouche, the Utah war chief, after drinking all our healths, became drunk—attempted to kill—he was finally tied hand and foot & when I went to sleep was singing his war song."

Thereafter they marched about the Navaho country annoying the Indians. In one instance, on July 28, Captain Walker, despite the none too firm admonition of Bonneville that theirs was to be a "kind and gentle course, . . . decided upon seizing several of the principal Chiefs in camp, both to prevent their efforts being used to keep us from our exploration and as hostages for the good conduct of the so-called *friendly* Indians." The hostages, however, left in the darkness.

[6] NA, RG 98, Dept. of N. M. Orders, Vol. 38–B (no p. no.).

The explorations took the first column as far west as the five Moqui villages. They found them "built on mesas ... the sides are twelve hundred feet high ... all speak the Navajo." More bizarre than laddered mesas, however, was the appearance of the women: "The married women wear their hair smooth, but the virgins take the hornes of the goat & winding their hair on these on either side, then fasten the hair so wound up to the side of the head. Not only is the head-dress graceful, but it is an honest sign of being in the market. They seem to have no idea of God. Their women are virtuous, but can be bought, provided secrecy can be secured for what seems to them a fortune."

The military explorers found the Moquis "peaceful, cowardly, generous (perhaps through fear), hardworking and dirty (except some of the young girls)." They had "no horses, no fire-arms—live on corn-cakes, allowed the Navajos to do what they pleased in their villages; had many customs which Moses gave to the Israelites, especially with regard to men, and all together were the *strangest people in the world*."[7]

One of the scouting parties, after trailing around seeking unknown murderers but acting under orders "not to attack the tribe," wound up again in Ojo Caliente on September 26. Being surfeited with the annoyance of the troops, the "Indians came into camp with their bows strung and arrows between their fingers." Captain Schroeder, in charge of the detachment, interpreted the movement for what it was: either fight or cease annoyance. Schroeder realized that "they seemed only waiting a good chance to attack us." He therefore made a quick and literal interpretation of his orders: "He did not think that his orders justified the clash & in fact, they positively forbade his doing anything. . . . The band was before us, and we could do nothing!" Bonneville's order had read: "This is not to be a general war . . . but simply a merited chastisement for . . . robbery."[8]

There was more scouting, however, after the challenge. On the way back to Fort Defiance, DuBois' column "succeeded in killing

[7] Du Bois Diary, July 29, 1859.

[8] Order No. 64, Wilkins to Shepherd, Report of the Secretary of War, 1860, II, 340-41.

Indians." Afterwards they arranged an ambush, "secreting Lieutenant Hildt with 25 men in a deep canon." Before the detachment was
a mile away from camp, "five Indians rode in. Two of them were immediately dismounted by the fire of the hidden soldiers—one was
killed—the other carried away by his companions." For this, Lieutenant DuBois and his riflemen "were shot at for about three miles every
step we took." And then, in Fort Defiance on November 12, they were
greeted with the cry: "Lieutenant, we're going home. . . . Upon . . .
taking a toddy, the news was confirmed." The next day, they headed
for Fort Union, only to learn that as they left Fort Defiance, "the
Indians came in & drove off 85 head of sheep."

With Colonel Loring out of the department and no longer exercising influence over the Fort Union personnel, sycophants suggested
to Colonel Bonneville the authorship of the "Civis" article criticizing
the incompetence displayed in the Navaho war of 1858. The finger
was pointed at none other than the resident chaplain at Fort Union,
the Reverend Mr. Stoddert. Colonel Bonneville confronted Mr. Stoddert with the rumor and received an evasive answer. Bonneville an-
grily countered that the reply did "not assert in positive terms that
you are not the author of that article signed *'Civis,'* and I hear from
so many sources that you are, and I demand to know *positive:* Are
you the author of that article or not?" But the Colonel might as well
have left the words unspoken, for the Reverend Mr. Stoddert refused
to answer. However, when he was informed that Colonel Bonneville
was being replaced, he went to Major Simonson and tendered his own
resignation, thus writing "Finis" to "Civis."[9] That he was, after conniving with Colonel Loring, sacrificing himself for the Colonel is
indisputable.

During the interim of Bonneville's discontent over the "Civis" affair, the Comanches "gave prospects of difficulties," and post commander Morris was told "to hold in readiness to march at a moment's
warning . . . every man that can be spared at Fort Union (N.C. &
Band excepted.)." Simonson replied: "If the post is to remain occupied and soldiers on extra-duty to be employed, there is not a man

---

[9] Simonson to Wilkins, December 8, 1859, AC, "Fort Union, 1859," File 2, p. 9.

to be *spared*. If on the contrary all men for duty, and extra duty, are those to be considered as required, this post can furnish forty-five privates, three sergeants, and two corporals, equipped for the field, *with* the following deficiencies: Twenty-six horses, 300 lbs lariat rope and twenty mules, the latter of which can only be procured by breaking up the post teams."[10]

Although there was a minimum of troops at the post, there was a maximum of discomfort. Mrs. LeRoy was in "Very Critical Condition." Since she was a "laundress of Company G, Mtd Rifles," her quarters were rated, "if they are procurable."[11] Too, "the window's in the adjutant's office needed repairing," the quarters of K and G Rifles were not habitable, now, or for the approaching winter: G Company's quarters were so dilapidated that the commander had ordered them "partially taken down" and that company would be compelled to live in tents. There was a great "necessity of a Medicine Officer being ordered to duty." He then had "two dangerous cases in Hospital, and had lost two from want of proper Medical attention." Lieutenant Holt's health was such as to "unfit him for active field service." To "substantiate the necessity of immediate action upon this momentous subject," Morris enclosed a "list of those who had died since the departure of the Surgeon."

The department commander referred the report to the medical director, who found it "impossible to furnish a Medical Officer"; furthermore, he did not know of a "Citizen Physician who would give up his business to go to Fort Union." In the meantime, Captain Morris could not wait; he sent to Sapello for Dr. Whitlock to attend Captain Wainwright, "critically ill with the billious fever," but since the doctor could not get there until the next day, Morris did the best he knew how, ordering "Captain van Bokkelen, A.Q.M. to make a frame for a Mosquito bar for the sick man in the Hospital."[12] Just at that time a man was brought in "who has broken his leg."

[10] Morris to Wilkins, July 13, 1859, AC, "Fort Union, 1859," File 2, p. 114.

[11] Morris to van Bokkelen, July 9, 1859, AC, "Fort Union, 1859," File 2, p. 108.

[12] Morris to Dr. Whitlock; Morris to van Bokkelen, August 11, 1859, AC, "Fort Union, 1859," File 2, p. 7.

On October 21, Captain Morris personally conducted the mail eastward with an escort, under Bonneville's orders, of "two officers and seventy-five men, as well as twelve wagons, the teamsters of which were armed." They made a camp at Cottonwood Springs. There a surprise was in store for them, in the person of Colonel Thomas T. Fauntleroy, who presented himself and "forthwith assumed command of the department," facetiously remarking that Captain Morris' orders needed modification.

General Order No. 5 was issued by Fauntleroy on November 2. It completely revamped Bonneville's headquarter staff. Four days later by Special Order No. 132, Fauntleroy ordered all troops, excepting the garrison at Fort Defiance, "temporarily withdrawn from the Navajo Country." So as not to appear to disapprove of Bonneville's War, he assigned as the cause for the withdrawal "the advanced state of the season and extreme cold of that climate." Bonneville was instructed to remain in Santa Fe to "await orders."

For a month there was an ominous tranquility in the department; then the Kiowas attacked the mail escort at Cold Springs. There was also an alarmists' meeting at Las Vegas, which asserted that no protection could be expected from the department commander and asked for the "chastisement" of the Plains Indians "before we have any security." Governor Rencher seemed to agree, and on January 30, 1860, informed Fauntleroy that he was assuming the responsibility of defending the territory with volunteers. It was the general belief that the Kiowas and Comanches from the eastern plains were the sources of greatest danger. Major Simonson, commanding at Fort Union for the moment, fell under this apprehension, and on February 13 brought the excitement to its highest pitch. He issued Order No. 7 —an emergency order. The guard was increased—a picket was stationed "beyond the Creek east of the post." It would "oppose any force advancing toward the Garrison. Companies G and H of the Rifles will repair to the General Parade and await further orders . . . arms will be kept loaded (the Rifles uncapped) . . . Quartermaster employees will be properly armed . . . for such information has been received as renders it necessary for this garrison to be in readiness to repel a sudden attack."[13]

For three days Fort Union "stood at the ready." Finally the truth was revealed: A large body of Comanches and Kiowas were quietly encamped on the Red River in the vicinity of the settlements. To counter the situation, Fauntleroy asked army headquarters to send "one regiment of Infantry, and a Light Battery."[14] He had no immediate use for the battery, but "in case of a movement in the direction of Chihuahua the Battery would be indispensable."

Headquarters took a different view of the situation. There would be no battery for a movement in the direction of Chihuahua, neither would it further countenance the buildup of another campaign against the Navahos. And to bring Fauntleroy's renewed efforts along this line to a close, he was ordered "to direct all preparations for a general campaign against the Navajos to cease." Thereafter he was "to act on the defensive—protecting the settlements as far as possible until the arrival of more troops in the Department." And, too—he ominously pointed out—". . . a considerable portion of the mounted Troops will be required for other service."[15] So far as New Mexico was concerned, there was to be a new fort "established on the Gallinas, at or near where the Fort Smith road crosses that stream, or preferably, if a suitable location can be found east of that point, on or near the Canadian." It was to be "the depot for the Department, have a garrison of four mounted and two Infantry companies, and be called *Fort Butler.*" Forts Garland, Bliss and Stanton would continue to be garrisoned, but "all other posts, now occupied in the Department of New Mexico, will be abandoned."[16]

[13] Unsigned letter to Thomas, Headquarters of the Army, NA, RG 98, Dept. of N. M. Letters, Vol. 10, p. 411.

[14] Unsigned letter to Thomas, Headquarters, Army, NA, RG 98, Dept. of N. M. Letters, Vol. 10, p. 411.

[15] Fauntleroy to Cooper, Washington, D.C., March 25, 1860, NA, RG 98, Dept. of N. M. Letters, Vol. 10, p. 412. This is a direct reference to the possibility of war between the states.

[16] Repeated efforts to find a suitable location were made—some in earnest, some obstructively, such as Captain Wainwright's. See NA, RG 98, Dept. of N. M. Letters, Vol. 10, p. 418, in which Fauntleroy set aside Township 13 N., Range 30 E., Sec.

The month of September, 1860, closed at Fort Union with only 171 men attached to the garrison. On October 1, it was further reduced by eighteen men taken from the Mounted Rifles when Second Lieutenant Joseph Wheeler accepted orders "to go to the Ocate and pursue a party of Indians who were reported depredating in that vicinity." He was rationed for six days, but two days later he was back in the fort not even having "pursued the party." Thereupon he was transferred to the service of the Comanche-Kiowa expedition yet stalking around on New Mexico's eastern plains, chiefly trying to keep alive their horses, which were suffering desperately from "black mouth" communicated from the Fort Union herd of cattle to the horses.

Another officer ordered to scout the plains for marauding Indians was Lieutenant DuBois. Before leaving Fort Union, he had received newspapers from the East. They were "all filled with secession." Now it was coming—"frothing over from the States—nothing but secession talked of at the post." Morosely the Lieutenant reacted to the secession talk: "Our glorious union will at last prove a failure because man must needs have a brother for a slave. So much for Republicanism!" And when time came to start the scout, he was ill: "Lying sick in an isolated army post with Colonel Crittenden and Roberts pushing back the mail-attackers—threats of secession frothing over from the 'states.' " So, he "must get home soon. If there is trouble I would be where I may not be condemned for inactivity." Of all the officers at Fort Union "only Lt. McCrae of North Carolina, Capt. Shoemaker M S & myself are thoroughly loyal. The 'northern men' are equally affected—right that they should be, for there is no doubt in my mind that the Constitution protects slavery . . . with the minority I have always believed—[but] if the politicians force us into war, as I think they will, I go in for the government—whether right or wrong—& most certainly so if slavery is to be increased & a big slave power established."[17]

21–28, inc. plus 33–36; inc. also Township 13 N., Secs. 19, 20, 29, 30, 31, and 32 for Fort Butler. When secession seemed imminent, the project was abandoned.

[17] Du Bois Diary, January 5–February 12, 1861.

Crittenden returned to Fort Union from the Comanche expedition "too weak to attack their camp alone," and requested "the co-operation of Major Sibley, 1st Dragoons, from Taos, with as many men as you can mount." Sibley, however, found obstacles in the way "both as to facilities and soldier-participation." He was "weak at Fort Union, as regards transportation." Too, First Lieutenant John Pegram and Second Lieutenant B. Sloan "had determined to disassociate themselves from the United States Army." They had on January 16, 1861, "filed their intentions to resign their commissions and had asked for leaves of absence to proceed to their homes "to await the decisions of the President." Previously, Canby's second in command in the Navaho country, Captain Lafayette McLaws, had set the example. Canby had concurred, as he "could do so without detriment to the service."

Kit Carson, hearing what was taking place, tendered his services "and those of the Utes" to bolster the disintegrating commands. Fauntleroy directed Sibley to accept the offer, directing that "for transportation, mules from trains, moving on the Santa Fe Trail, be pre-empted, except those hauling a supply of bacon."[18] As scouts against the Comanches relaxed, the *Nuevo Mejicanos* began to move more freely back into the eastern plains, causing Crittenden to observe "that traffic is awful" and to order that "the Mexicans with packs [who] passed yesterday on the way ... bound for the Comanche Camp on Red River, should have their packs examined and their ammunition seized."[19] At the same time Fauntleroy thought it not objectionable "to furnish . . . arms and ammunition to the *Settlers* for purposes of defense," but officers must "carefully avoid calling out or organizing any organized bodies of *'Volunteers'* for any purpose whatever." On this point he had "positive instructions from the war office."[20]

[18] Willcox to Sibley, January 19, 1861, NA, RG 98, Dept. of N. M. Letters, Vol. 10, p. 536.

[19] Crittenden to Roberts, February 21, 1861, AC, "Fort Union, 1861," File 1, p. 38.

[20] Maury to Stevenson, C. O., Fort Stanton, February 22, 1861, NA, RG 98, Dept. of N. M. Letters, Vol. 10, pp. 550–51.

While commissioned officers were tendering resignations and *Nuevo Mejicanos* returning to their lucrative trade with the Comanches and coming under such suspicion of disloyalty that arms for their protection were being withheld from them, Fort Union became the center of a scheme to discharge men who had been enlisted owing allegiance to foreign countries. Of Private Christian Bartholomus [*sic*], when discharged by order of the War Department under the scheme of deception, Major Simonson had this to say:

I have this day discharged Christian Bartholomus, a private of the Band, Regiment of Mounted Rifles, in obedience to the Secretary of War. . . . final statements directed to the care of the Consul Saxe Weimar, St. Louis. . . . I beg to add that Christian Bartholomas [*sic*] is one of the men heretofore reported as being in the conspiracy to procure discharges through Foreign Consuls, Agents, and Ministers; that he enlisted about one year ago, at which time he was promised a furlough, which furlough was given to him on the 6th of May, 1860. . . . After he left on furlough, it was ascertained that he seduced the wife of Private Henry Ebert, a brother soldier, companion in the Band, and devoted friend and Countryman, from Saxe Weimar. A week or ten days after Bartholamas [*sic*] started for the States, Mrs. Ebert robbed her husband of valuable papers, &c took the Stage and followed her Seducer, leaving two young children, one a Suckling babe. . . . It is believed that the representations Bartholomas made the Consul of Saxe Weimer, or whoever interceded in his behalf, were utterly false—that he has no just claim for his discharge, and that instead of meriting the Aid and Sympathy of his Countrymen, he deserves Condemnation for betraying a friend, seducing a wife and mother and encouraging her to rob her husband. I am informed that Bartholomas's case is similar to the others —that the Commencement was an advertisement in some of the German papers in the United States or in Europe, in the nature of a Notice to himself to attend at a certain time and place for the transaction of family business, important to his interests or to secure a legacy,—or that his distressed mother or family are in great want and affliction, and need his presence. These notices are signed by a fictitious or real name. The papers containing the advertisement is sent to the individual advertised for; he cuts out the notice or sends it to the Consul, Agent, or Minister from his native Country, accompanied by a pathetic letter, sometimes asserting among other things that the writer was inveigled into the Service of the United States, or was compelled by poverty to Enlist, or Enlisted in a state of Intoxication, and that it is important that he should return to his Country and Allegiance, to prevent loss to himself and family and imploring the interference of the Consul, &c in his behalf. Not one in ten of these men intend to return to their Country: None have been inveigled—the whole proceeding is false and a Swindle!

While *Nuevo Mejicanos,* Saxe Weimars, Southerners, and Black Republicans worried over their allegiances, if any, loyalty to the army came into the open at Fort Union on March 10. DuBois, having already made his decision, "became involved in several bitter political discussions." Propositions were made him "to go in the southern army & high positions were offered" him. He declined, admitting "it is hard to fight as a 2d Lieut" when he "might have a much higher rank." He knew "Republicans are ungrateful," but "so be it! . . . Do my duty *now:* is the watchword for a soldier." Then, when there was an intimation of threat, DuBois took his position: "If an effort is made to seduce my regiment, I will assume command myself & fight it out."

DuBois felt that "most of the officers going south themselves & all the west pointers, *except Longstreet,"* were urging their soldiers to remain loyal.

The day that he made his decision he was granted leave to be absent from the department for six months. Others to go East were "Captain Holloway—sick; Lieutenant Kelly—to await the action of the President; Mr. Webb—Fort Union sutler—destination unknown; Some furloughed soldiers—to go under the supervision of the ailing captain —using government transportation: the others to go on the stage, leaving Fort Union, March 17."

March 17 came. DuBois found it "very hard to bid McRae goodbye. Thank God! he is true to his country." And then they rolled away in the stage for home. Their first stop was at Maxwell's; then off again "to the sumit [*sic*] of Raton Mountain." There they found the "long overdue flour train . . . a very large train belonging to the contractor Russell, who was mixed up in some way with Floyd in the Indian bond swindle." The Lieutenant found that the train had already been "seized by several parties—one Yankee—smarter than the rest—had stolen off thirty wagons & sent them by the Sangre de Christo Pass to get them to market." Passing beyond the stolen train, "the stage reached the crossing of the Arkansas in a terrible snow storm." There they met the mail. "Col. Loring was on it—on his way to take command of the Department of New Mexico." DuBois "doubted his loyalty [*sic*]," and questioned him." He says he is *sound.*"

On March 22, 1861, Colonel William W. Loring arrived in Santa Fe. He carried with him Special Order No. 17, dated January 22, 1861, from the War Department. In accordance with that authority, he issued General Order No. 9, thereunder assuming command of the Department of New Mexico. And Fauntleroy was out.[21]

Upon assuming command, Loring "felt it his first duty" to call to the attention of army headquarters "the condition of affairs which he found existing throughout the Territory." He had little praise for what had happened in the past, and the future was not a subject for comment. The expedition against the Comanches and Navahos had caused the loss of a very large portion of the means of transportation; Major Isaac Lynde, commanding at Fort McLane, was authority for his statement that "the public ox-train of fifteen wagons had been attacked by Indians," then, ten days later had fallen prey "to a party of desperate men of the mines, at the instance of Mr. Kirk, the wagon-master," who ran them into Mexico. Too, these same inhabitants of the mines, "whose object is plunder, formed a plan" to attack Fort McLane, "capture the public property, and take all the arms from us." Loring, however, asserted his confidence in Major Lynde, "who thought they would be mistaken," for he proposed "to defend the post unless overpowered by numbers." Also, "there was a condition of

[21] G.O. No. 9, March 22, 1861, NA, RG 98, Dept. of N. M. Orders, Vol. 38–A (no p. no.).

231

affairs" at Albuquerque, where "a plan was laid by the people . . . to possess themselves of the Government stores at that depot." Furthermore, the people of that vicinity were beginning to "refuse to credit the Government," and "the troops are becoming uneasy and restless about their pay." He therefore felt it his duty to warn headquarters of the army that "unless they can be assured at a very early date that they will be paid off, very serious consequences may result."

As to the Indians, "the great scarcity of means of transportation, and the difficulty in hiring it, must necessarily cramp the fields operations." He thereupon took it upon himself to "suspend until further orders" the use of the Mounted Rifles against the Mescaleros. Upon recalling the Rifles, he had mounted companies unoccupied; therefore, he posted a "Circular" telling the people of New Mexico that "an escort will be organized at Fort Union for the protection of the families of officers, and other persons, desiring to go to Fort Leavenworth." The east-bound party would "set out about the 25th of April." He then ordered in to Fort Union the "Public property now at Hatch's Ranche," and as soon as the property was removed the troops would withdraw from there also. Then he ordered Brevet Major H. H. Sibley from Taos, but before the movement could be made, he changed his mind, directing Sibley to "send an officer and thirty men in the direction of Abiquiu and Jemez in order to inform the proper authorities of those places, and their vicinity, of the nature of the agreement entered into by Col. Canby and the Navajoes."

At the end of the first month of Loring's command of the department the strength of Fort Union had dwindled to 141 men. Among those at the post was Joseph Wheeler, who tendered his resignation, asking permission to go on leave to his home in Georgia, there to await the action of the President.[22] Loring again changed his mind, and instead of bringing in Lieutenant Ira Chaflin from Hatch's Ranch

[22] NA, RG 98, Dept. of N. M. Orders, Vol. 38–C (no. p. no.). Joseph Wheeler, born in Georgia, resigned April 22, 1861; later lieutenant general, C.S.A. After the war he re-entered the United States Army and in 1898 served in the Spanish-American War in Cuba.

to Fort Union, he, with a detachment went to the prairies southeast of Fort Union, ostensibly to give protection to the settlements from the Comanches but in reality to make peace with these Indians as he had "heard that the Texans (then allied with the Confederacy) were treating with them." With the future in mind, he concluded that "any agreement I shall make with these savages, I shall stipulate for the exemption of Texas from their incursions."[23] A generous gesture of an enemy on behalf of his enemy, unsolicited! To make the stipulations, Loring selected Captain R. A. Wainwright, who went with Loring's regrets to the chiefs because of his "inability to confer with them in person." The whole Comanche nation, thereafter, must not "depredate upon the property and lives of the people of the United States, of this Territory, of Kansas, of Texas."

While Captain Wainwright was off to a "talk" with the Comanches, taking with him a Fort Union detachment, Captain Duncan was admonished "to exercise more than usual vigilance in protecting the Ordnance & other Stores at Fort Union from molestation by any evil disposed person." This vigilance should be "in a quiet manner and without attracting attention or arousing excitement."

Then, without attracting attention or arousing excitement, Lieutenant B. M. Thomas quitted the Fifth Infantry, leaving behind his resignation, while he repaired to his home to await the decision of the President.[24] There was more concern, however, when it was rumored that Major James Longstreet, paymaster, was "going South." The troops were generally unpaid; but Longstreet turned in his cash, admitting that there were those "who might brand him 'traitor,' although none could call him 'thief.' "[25] Then Loring's adjutant, Dabney Herndon Maury, issued his own order relieving himself, so that

[23] Loring to Townsend, April 22, 1861, *W. O. R.*, Series 1, Vol. I, p. 602.

[24] NA, RG 98, Dept. of N. M. Orders, Vol. 38–C (no p. no.). Bryan Morel Thomas, born in Georgia, resigned April 6, 1861; later brigadier general, C. S. A. See Heitman, *Register*, 1890.

[25] NA, RG 98, Dept. of N. M. Orders, Vol. 38–C (no p. no.). James Longstreet, born in South Carolina, resigned June 1, 1861; later lieutenant general, C.S.A. See Heitman, *Register*, 1890.

he, too, could go home;[26] and, after resigning, he accepted 1st Lieutenant L. L. Rich's resignation.[27]

There was an indication that the defenses of New Mexico would be further reduced. Orders came that Brevet Lieutenant Colonel Canby with the Fifth and Seventh regiments of infantry and two companies of the Tenth Infantry would "march for Leavenworth with as little delay as possible." To Loring was left the "regiment of Riflemen and four companies of Dragoons . . . the regular force," which he was to dispose "at points as in his judgment would best protect the interests of the United States." Otherwise he must "depend upon volunteers who may be mustered into service . . . under orders to be given by the War Department."[28]

At this stage of disintegration Colonel Loring reported to headquarters, "There seems no reason to apprehend any immediate disorder in this Territory." The troops were "subordinate and quiet" and his only uneasiness was "apprehension of trouble with them . . . unless they procure their payment at an early date." Furthermore, the people were "tranquil enough," despite the fact that "there are rumors of proposed political movements," but no "serious outbreak of revolution." On the same day of writing to Washington, he also wrote to Major G. R. Paul, commanding at Fort Fillmore, expressing his approbation for the course taken "to prevent violent and bloodshed among the people in that vicinity," the people having called for troops to "preserve the lives and property of citizens against lawless combinations too powerful for the civil authorities to resist." Then Loring tendered Special Order No. 68 to Colonel George Bibb Crittenden,[29] which ushered him out of the service awaiting acceptance of his resig-

[26] NA, RG 98, Dept. of N. M. Orders, Vol. 38–C (no p. no.). Dabney Herndon Maury was born in Virginia. Instead of his resignation's being accepted, he was dismissed from the service.

[27] NA, RG 98, Dept. of N. M. Orders, Vol. 38–C (no p. no.). Lucius Loomis Rich, born in Missouri, resigned May 13, 1861; later colonel, First Missouri Infantry, C.S.A. Died August 9, 1862, from wounds received at Shiloh.

[28] S.O. No. 86½, May 17, 1861, Washington, D.C., *W. O. R.,* Series 1, Vol. I p. 604.

[29] NA, RG 98, Dept. of N. M. Orders, Vol. 38–C (no p. no.). Crittenden, born in Kentucky, resigned June 10, 1861, to become major general, C.S.A. See Heitman, *Register,* 1890.

nation. Henry C. McNeill did likewise,[30] concluding to join the Texas Cavalry. Two days before Crittenden left the service, Major H. H. Sibley with Company I, Second Dragoons, was moved from Taos to Fort Union, where he took command, bringing Fort Union's strength to 449 men.[31]

There was a pause in the exodus of U. S. officers to the South until June 8, when Loring relieved Lieutenant Kearny, who did not want to go into Leavenworth as ordered.[32] Kearny's departure was followed by that of Second Lieutenant A. L. Anderson.

At this stage of the pettifoggery, Lieutenant Colonel Benjamin S. Roberts, gullible but loyal, detected the chicanery of Crittenden, but not suspecting Loring as a *particeps criminis,* rode into Santa Fe to suggest Crittenden's infidelity to Loring. For his circumspection, Roberts was directed to confine his efforts to his own duties, and was sent back to his station.[33] Then, on June 11, Loring set in motion the completion of the denouement. He placed Brevet Colonel Edward Richard Sprigg Canby "in general charge of the affairs of the department and in command of the northern district." On the same day H. H. Sibley expressed his intention of resigning but stayed on two more days at Fort Union before officially relinquishing his commission. Loring, although placing Canby in "general charge" of department affairs, did not disavow his command, merely expressing his intention "to await at Fort Fillmore the action of the President upon the tender of his resignation." Sibley thought Loring indiscreet, and

[30] NA, RG, 98, Dept. of N. M. Orders, Vol. 38–C (no p. no.). Henry C. McNeill, born in Mississippi, resigned May 12, 1861, to become lieutenant colonel, Texas Cavalry, C.S.A. See Heitman, *Register,* 1890.

[31] Major H. H. Sibley arrived at Fort Union, May 17, 1861. See AC, "Fort Union, 1861," File 1, p. 128.

[32] NA, RG 98, Dept. of N. M. Orders, Vol. 38–C (no p. no.). William Kearny, born in New York, resigned June 1, 1861, to become captain and aide-de-camp, C.S.A. See Heitman, *Register,* 1890.

[33] Horace Greeley, writing in retrospect (*The American Conflict,* II, 19), accused Secretary of War John B. Floyd of sending Loring, a North Carolinian, to command the Ninth Military Department so that the Union Army in the West might be check-mated before the war began. See also Ray C. Colton, *The Civil War in the Western Territories.* Roberts did not accuse Captains Morris and Hatch of treason.

admonished Loring that he might "by delaying your departure a week or two," effect the delivery of the government property to the Confederates in El Paso. Once in El Paso, Sibley joyously proclaimed that he was "at last under the glorious banner of the Confederate States of America." But he rebuked himself for the "sickly sentimentality" which overruled his desire to bring his whole command with him.[34]

[34] *W. O. R.*, Series I, Vol. IV, p. 55.

CHAPTER ELEVEN

REJUVENATION

As EARLY AS May 17, 1861, headquarters of the army had disclosed to Colonel Loring plans to recruit New Mexico volunteers.[1] Although Loring, in forsaking his responsibility as department commander, had placed it within Canby's power to assume the command, the cautious Canby, accustomed to soldiering-by-the-book, did so only after learning that "loyalty at Fort Fillmore was restricted to two officers." He then mustered courage enough to announce that it was necessary, in order "to protect the fort or interests of the Government," for him to assume the department command, "otherwise it might be in the highest degree disastrous." Thereafter, signing himself "Lieutenant Colonel Commanding the Department of New Mexico," he gave impetus to the enlistment of volunteers.

Thirty-nine regiments of volunteers would be raised. The commissioned officers were to be appointed by the governor. Four companies were to be recruited at Fort Union. Less than two days after Canby made his decision, Colonel Céran St. Vrain left Santa Fe for Fort Union with authority from Governor Rencher to select the volunteers for the Fort Union command. They were to be supplied with arms and camp and garrison equipment, but no clothing was to be issued. After ten days, "an allowance for clothing, $3.50 per month," was added to the inducement for volunteer service, but "each *company officer,* non-commissioned officer, private, musician and artificer of cavalry, shall furnish his own horse and horse-equipment and receive therefor 40 cents per day for their use and risk."[2] An oath of

[1] S.O. No. 86½, May 17, 1861, *W. O. R.,* Series 1, Vol. I, p. 804.
[2] G.O. No. 16, June 7, 1861, NA, RG 98, Dept. of N. M. Orders, Vol. 36, pp. 509–10.

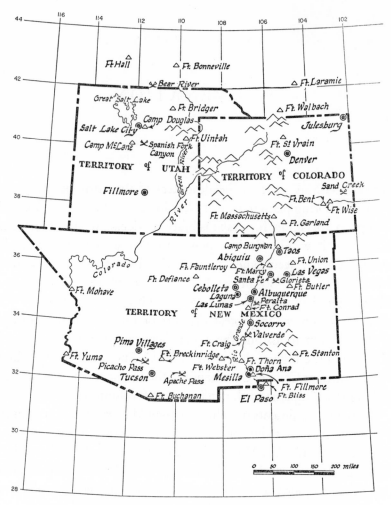

U.S. military installations in the western territories early
in the Civil War (from Colton, *The Civil War in the Western Territories*)

allegiance to the United States was an absolute condition of acceptance of volunteers.

On June 30, 1861, Canby concluded that the threats of the Confederates to trains on the Santa Fe Trail might be real. All the protection he could offer, however, was "a command of at least 100 mounted men and two companies of New Mexican volunteers as soon as the companies of volunteers could be mustered into the service."

They would go out from Fort Union "under command of Captain Duncan and return at the Crossing of the Arkansas to Fort Union." On July 3, Colonel Chapman reported one company of volunteers had been mustered on the previous day, these being recruited by Colonel St. Vrain with José María Valdez as their captain. On July 4, Captain Arthur Morris brought in another company, ninety-one men from Las Vegas. There was some delay, however, in putting Valdez' company on the Trail, for "they had to return to Mora to obtain clothing."

Less than four days had passed after the muster of St. Vrain's New Mexican Volunteers when Canby's authority clashed with the peonage system. Although in general New Mexican sentiment was against African slavery, it was the prevailing practice in New Mexico for *ricos* to subject a large population to financial serfdom, an onerous subjugation from which few ever extricated themselves. United States Army service provided a release from bondage. To the *ricos,* on the other hand, peon army service was a blow at "voluntary bondage," equally as disruptive as abolition to the Southerner. As a consequence of the flow of peons into the New Mexican Volunteers, Canby, on July 6, found it mandatory to support recruitment by issuing a circular on "Reclamation of Peons." All officers were advised that the question of reclamation of peons enrolled in the volunteer companies would no doubt be raised at their posts. "No discharge for this cause will be ordered at Department Headquarters." Those seeking the discharge of their peons would have to rely on "writ of Habeas Corpus only." The "local courts will have no jurisdiction." All petitions for such relief "would have to be filed in the United States Courts in the Territory." Territorial writs would "not be respected."[3]

For instruction and discipline, the commanding officer of Fort Union designated Captain Francisco Abreu, "the senior officer of Volunteers present," to accept all recruits at an adjacent camp—for lack of a name known as "Camp of Instruction," later named "Camp Paul,"—and there he would "constitute a Police Guard . . . [and] a picket Guard to be stationed near the Spring to prevent any im-

[3] Circular, July 6, 1861, NA, RG 98, Dept. of N. M. Orders, Vol. 38–C (no p. no.).

proper use of the water, such as washing or bathing in the spring [the source of Fort Union's drinking water] . . . and to protect the public gardens from depredations." Since the sanitary facilities of the post were inadequate for the increased number of soldiers, "a sink would be dug for the Camp, which will be surrounded by brush to screen it from view."

When Céran St. Vrain was no longer able to give his personal attention to encouraging enrollments, volunteering slowed markedly. Therefore, to complete the "organization by subsequent enrollments," Canby issued another circular authorizing payment from the day on which the volunteers were presented at the place of rendezvous, provided, of course, that they were effective and able-bodied recruits. "Having a lack of, or defect in, the left eye, or slight injury to the left hand" would not be construed as disabling. But all "foreigners and stammerers would be rejected unless they can speak readily."[4] Thus by accelerating recruitments, July came to a close. Counting detachments—Duncan, out in the direction of the Arkansas River; Macrae, en route to Fort Stanton—Fort Union strength stood at 1,003 men, an increase during the month of 426; while anomolously, Colonel W. W. Loring yet appeared on the list of officers on detached service.[5]

While Fort Union was gathering strength, disconcerting news came through an Apache—"the old guide at Fort Craig"— that he had seen "a large body of Texans at the Rio Bonita who were going up the Pecos to capture Los Posas . . . their encampment and stock covered near three miles of ground, and they had artillery with them." Captain Morris, down-river at Fort Craig, believed the "guides Statement to be truthful" and hoped his warning had come in time for Canby "to intercept them." Canby received the Apache's information on July 22, but he considered it "not reliable." He did think, however, that should Fort Union be threatened by "a superior force," it was "a justifiable precaution" for Chapman "to put in order for immediate use . . . the 24 pdr. howitzers at the depot at Fort Union

4 Circular, July 16, 1861, NA, RG 98, Dept. of N. M. Orders, Vol. 38–C (no p. no.).
5 Post Returns, July, 1861, AC, Arrott roll 3.

Entrance to the old Star Fort (Fort No. 2).

Arrott Collection

Brevet Brigadier General J. Irvin Gregg, commander of Fort Union,
June 1, 1870, to February 25, 1871,
and September 30 to October 5, 1871.

Arrott Collection

[which] have been repaired." Experienced gunners were not necessary. "The dismounted men of the Rifles and Dragoons will probably furnish sufficient for the management of any guns that may be needed for the defense of the post." Looking to the future, Canby thought it "important also to have some of the volunteers instructed in the use of artillery."

Volunteering, after the initial surge to serve under Céran St. Vrain and Kit Carson and following the relaxation of standards, dwindled to a minimum. Headquarters at Santa Fe found it necessary to "send out an influential Mexican to stimulate the population between this and Fort Union" for volunteers to fill up Fort Union's companies to their maximum.[6] B. S. Roberts, having been elevated to the command of the Southern New Mexico District, availed himself of a more efficient method of "voluntary" enlistment. He made it easy for Colonel Stapleton to bring in the needed men:

> Head Quarters, S^n Mil Dist
> Dept N M
> Fort Craig 3d July 1861

Colonel R. H. Stapleton
Sir

If any of the Officers or Soldiers of the Militia, called into service under your orders from your immediate commanding General, refuses to obey your call, I am instructed to Send you Military force to compel their obediance, but it is hoped there are no New Mexicans So ignoble in their natures as to refuse to respond to this call of duty to defend their Territory and their homes.

> I am Very Respectfully,
> Yr obt. Servt,
> B. S. Roberts, Col. Vols. Comdg.[7]

Upon Roberts' authority, "voluntary" recruitment was vigorously stimulated. Francisco Aragon entered the service on July 23 as *Tiente Segundo* [second lieutenant] in *Voluntanos Montados;* and by hiring "Expressmen," the *Tiente Segundo* soon had the constables at

[6] Anderson to Chapman, August 6, 1861, AC, "Fort Union, 1861," File 2, p. 60.
[7] Original in Archives of New Mexico, Santa Fe; copy in AC, misc.

Corrales, San Antonio, Las Padillas, Parajita, and Albuquerque informed of his dearth of volunteers; whereupon these *alguacils* readily presented him with seventy-four "volunteers." Upon delivering recruits, however, neither messengers, constables, nor justices of the peace neglected to tender accounts for services rendered, typical of which was the following:

THE UNITED STATES To O. P. HOVEY . . . . DR.			
1861 November 13	—For Amount paid for Collecting recruits from the 3d Division for Captain Francisco Aragon's C° as per . . . vouchers herewith viz:		
	For Amount paid Expressmen, constable,	68	75
	Francisco Aragon Capitan, N.M. Militia.		

At the end of July, 1861, with Fort Union's strength at its peak, 1,003, and the regulars prepared to march to Fort Leavenworth, after much delay a messenger came from Major Lynde reporting "an engagement with the Texans near Fort Fillmore." The messenger stated that the Union forces had sustained "a loss of three privates killed, two officers (Lts. Brooks and McNelly) and four privates wounded." Furthermore, according to the messenger, the commander had abandoned the fort and "was moving toward Fort Stanton." Again the rumor was discredited by the cautious Canby, who thought, however, that Fort Union should send "one of the rifle companies to Albuquerque for temporary duty."[8] On the same day, Kit Carson arrived in Fort Union. He, too, had a report through Indian traders that "a large force of white men was coming up the Canadian or Pecos River. The

[8] Anderson to Chapman, August 2, 1861, AC, "Fort Union, 1861," File 2, p. 46.

force was about three miles long." Although not convinced of the authenticity of the trader's statements, he was not willing to brush aside these repeated rumors. He proposed that if the Texans were coming, he should collect in a few days a sufficient number of Mexicans and Ute Indians to steal all their animals before they reached Fort Union. Colonel Chapman agreed, thinking "it advisable . . . if time will permit."

Time would not permit. At "2½ P.M." that same day, a letter from Canby, written at Santa Fe, reached Fort Union telling of the surrender of Major Lynde and his whole command to three hundred Texas Confederates. Chapman, frightened, went into action. He would "endeavor to enroll and arm all the reliable citizens of the Fort Union neighborhood." He regretfully reported, however, that he had "taken no steps toward fortifying the post." There was a reason for this apparent neglect: He could not "spare a sufficient force to defend any work he might erect . . . for its defense that would not be commanded by higher ground in the rear and on both flanks." "After examining the ground," he now saw that the enemy, "once in possession of the bluffs in rear, would render this post untenable," and "in attempting to defend it," he would "lose all the ordnance stores." As a consequence, he had decided to remove the post "out of range of field-pieces & small arms . . . construct an entrenched camp with bomb-proof Magazine and store houses sufficient to contain all the stores." By retiring from under the bluffs, of course, it would "be necessary, in case of an attack by a superior force, to burn this post lest the enemy should get possession of it." In the meantime, Chapman pledged himself "to defend the old post of Fort Union at all hazards and as long as I have a man to pull a trigger."

Chapman designated Captain Grover as superintendent of the construction of the new fort. To expedite the digging, he sent Lieutenant Enos to Las Vegas for additional shovels. As for the workmen, he placed little confidence in "these Mexican Volunteers." They were "more afraid of the Texans than they are of death, and in case of an attack of the latter, I cannot rely upon them." He would therefore

"use them in the construction of proper defenses and stationed behind entrenchments they may give good service."[9]

On August 4, the Confederates were nearer to Fort Union than
Chapman thought them to be. On the morning of August 5, one of
Captain Deus's men, who had had to encamp within four miles of
Fort Union the previous night, came into the fort to talk with Colonel
Carson. He had seen "two white men yesterday afternoon mounted
on American horses, which appeared to have been ridden hard, about
one and one-half or two miles northeast of the post, with spy-glasses
examining the post and grounds in this vicinity. They remained
about an hour and a half, then galloped off." They had questioned
Deus's man "as to the No. of Companies &c at this post." When Carson reported this information, Captain Vigil and Lieutenant Pike
accompanied the man to the "point where the white men stood, discovered their tracks and picked up several pieces of dried buffalo
meat [subsequently crossed out and 'beef' substituted]." The Lieutenant followed their trail for seven miles.

With this information Canby recalled Colonel Carson's suggestion
that he steal their horses, so "to that duty Carson was assigned at
once," authorized "to organize as large a party of Mexicans and Ute
Indians as he may consider necessary."[10]

The seriousness of the surrender of Major Lynde's down-river
force finally registered on Canby. Admonition, consequently, was
rushed to Chapman: "Your post . . . must be held at all hazards." If
attack before entrenchments and storehouses were completed, trains
"should not be unloaded, as the wagons will not only serve for storage, but may be of service for you for defense purposes." Carson was
to send out his spies "and annoy and cripple the Texans by driving

---

[9] The second Fort Union, called the Fort Union Star Fort because of its shape, was
dug approximately one mile east of the original wood structure. After it was finished,
it was determined by experiment that the cannon in use by the Union Army would
fire over and beyond the new entrenchment. Similar artillery was in the possession
of the Confederates, thus making the Star Fort an unobstructed target from the
western cliffs.

[10] Anderson to Chapman, August 5, 1861, AC, "Fort Union, 1861," File 2, p. 54;
also, Chapman to Carson, NA, RG 93, Fort Union Orders, Vol. 46–A (no p. no.).

off their animals." Canby thought, also, that the "mounted volunteers may be usefully employed for this purpose."

At the new "Star Fort," by August 7, Chapman had two hundred men working "every four hours day and night," Captain Grover and Lieutenant Nicodemus alternating in directing the work, and they thought "in a day or two it will be sufficiently advanced for defense."[11]

On August 8, 1861, Canby issued another circular,[12] a notice that he had suspended the writ of habeas corpus. As justification for his bold step, he said he feared "the treasonable designs of persons disloyal to the Government of the U.S., particularly agents & spies, persons engaged in furnishing information to, or in other treasonable correspondence with the enemy, or in inciting insurrection or rebellion." All commanders were "cautioned against any abuse of this power by unauthorized arrests or by annoyance to peaceable and well disposed citizens."

Not knowing the extent of the damage done by Lynde's debacle, all communications being in the hands of the Confederates, Canby began to consider seriously the probability of Fort Union's being assaulted. He directed Chapman to remove all women and children from the fort, sending them to Las Vegas and Mora, "the quartermaster to provide quarters and subsistence."[13]

The Confederates soon found that they held so many prisoners surrendered by Lynde that they were unable to feed them, so, on their pledge not to fight again (not that they had), all were sent to Canby's supervision, but Lynde was "to consider himself in a state of arrest, with the town of Albuquerque as the limits of that arrest." From Albuquerque the prisoners were forthwith ordered to Fort Union, Major Lynde, Captain Phillips, and Lieutenants McNally and McKee reaching there August 24 and the "command" on the following day.

Major Chapman had orders to "provide them with a suitable place to encamp about a mile above the post." Such equipment as they had

[11] Chapman to Anderson, August 7, 1861, AC, "Fort Union, 1861," File 2, p. 62.

[12] Circular, August 8, 1861, NA, RG 98, Dept. of N. M. Orders, Vol. 38–C (no p. no.).

[13] Anderson to Chapman, August 11, 1861, AC, "Fort Union, 1861," File 2, p. 72.

would be turned over to the Ordnance Depot. Captain J. H. Potter, yet growling that "That damned old scoundrel traitorously surrendered us," too, had orders "to point out a suitable place to encamp." He selected a site above the first location but "on the same water." When morning came, however, "the water had ceased to run." Investigation disclosed that Captain Shoemaker, M.S., had diverted the spring water to irrigate his cabbage patch. Chapman, when appealed to, pretended to the waterless parolees that the area was "not within Fort Union environs—not government property," and he would not interfere. But Captain Potter was made of sterner stuff; he posted a guard of parolees with orders to see that the water was not diverted from its usual course. Shoemaker then appealed to Fort Union headquarters, asserting that he had been in undisturbed possession of his garden and the water with which to irrigate it for ten years. While the water flowed alternately to the cabbage patch and to the parolees, Chapman "regretted exceedingly that Potter's remnant was having a dearth of water," and referred the controversy to Santa Fe. On September 13, Canby ruled, of course, that Fort Union was the center of an eight-mile-square reservation, that the water was government property and subject to troop use.[14] After reorganization, the ill-provisioned parolees began their trek across the plains, only to suffer insupportable hunger and thirst; some of the men became so thirsty, in fact, they became mentally deranged; others, to allay their pain, opened their veins and drank their own blood.[15]

On August 3, 1861, Canby began another effort to recruit *Nuevo Mejicanos,* this time to replace the regulars lost to the service through Lynde's surrender. General Order No. 26 directed that the independent companies, both infantry and cavalry, "be raised at once to the maximum": four additional companies of mounted volunteers would be mustered, two of them to rendezvous at Fort Union. Only "Pueblo Indian Spies and Guides were to scout in the direction of the Canadian Fork," and "an influential Mexican" must go "to stimulate the pop-

[14] Potter to Chapman, September 14, 1861; Chapman to Potter, September 15, 1861, AC, "Fort Union, 1861," File 3, p. 29.

[15] Ray C. Colton, *The Civil War in the Western Territories,* 17.

ulation between Santa Fe and Fort Union, and send in volunteers." There would be no tents for shelter, but this lack might be compensated "from the remains of the old fort." Again, there was an apathetic attitude among the *Nuevo Mejicanos*. Colonel Roberts, having abandoned Fort Stanton to take refuge at Albuquerque, in an effort to reinforce, found that they were "disposed to defend their own homes, but seemed indisposed to leave their homes to join in the defense of the United States military posts. They did not see the necessity of organization: Too, it was the busy season, when Mexicans are mainly securing their crops; but after the crops were secured, they would fill up the ranks."[16]

Colonel Chapman was not convinced that the Confederates would abandon an assault on Fort Union; he therefore applied his best energies during mid-August to the completion of the Star Fort, employing "the whole force of the Command on the defenses." Erection of storehouses was suspended while all dug at the new Star Fort location. And, as a guard against surprise, Chapman ordered Pfeiffer's Utes into the region toward Anton Chico, "the road much traveled of late by trains coming to Fort Union." Before noon of the same day, however, the commander saw "a party of Indians moving up the valley from the Volunteer Camps. This movement of Indians was in the wrong direction, and he hastened to call on Colonel Carson to inquire: 'For what purpose?' Kit told him: 'The Utes have all gone home. Nothing will induce them to stay. Sickness in the Chief's family, the cause.' "[17]

Finally, on August 26, Star Fort (Fort Union) was completed and ready for occupation. All it needed was some "dressing off." Now Chapman congratulated himself: he had accomplished more than he expected. "With a Garrison of 600 good and reliable troops it can be defended against any force likely to be brought against it."[18] He had the force—1,304 men.

[16] Roberts to Canby and Chapman, August 20, 1861, AC, "Fort Union, 1861," File 2, p. 94.

[17] Chapman to Anderson (postscript), AC, "Fort Union, 1861," File 2, p. 98.

[18] Chapman to Canby, August 26, 1861, AC, "Fort Union, 1861," File 2, p. 103.

Again Chapman was told that Confederate spies were near the fort. He, consequently, sent a detachment to Loma Parda, where P. A. Valley and B. F. Hartley were arrested on suspicion of being spies. Upon examination, they convinced the Colonel that they were not spies. They had a more lucrative occupation: they had come to gamble with the men. They were released after having taken "an oath not to aid or abet the enemies . . . and immediately leave the vicinity of Fort Union."[19]

During the height of the Confederate spy scare Governor Rencher arrived at Fort Union with orders that he be provided with "transportation and the Necessary Camp Equipage . . . and any other arrangements that may be necessary for the Safety and Comfort of the party." He was crossing the plains with his family and leaving the governorship to Henry Connelly, a resident of Santa Fe since 1848.[20] This unanticipated drain on Fort Union's escort facilities was followed by another of a similar nature, when Assistant Surgeon B.J.D. Irwin required an escort of "one non-commissioned officer and eight men to protect him on his journey to Fort Leavenworth."[21] The doctor's requirements were more than Fort Union could provide: "There were no more Kettles on hand." Furthermore, even Captain Sanches' newly recruited company was limited to "mess pans and one iron pot," and still "another Company (31 aggregate) just arrived . . . from Mora" could only be furnished "mess pans and axes." But on September 20, regardless of the shortage of "Kettles," the doctor with twelve mounted volunteers took the trail eastward. Learning at Fort Wise that the Santa Fe Trail was "entirely clear of rebels," the doctor thought it imprudent to continue with the escort as "they are very destitute of the proper outfit," and they were instructed to return to Fort Union.[22] At Red River, Captain Martínez met his returning detachment and, indignant at their condition, wrote to his colonel:

[19] Chapman to Anderson, August 28, 1861, AC, "Fort Union, 1861," File 2, p. 108.

[20] Circular, August 29, 1861, AC, "Fort Union, August, 1861," File 2, p. 109.

[21] Anderson to Chapman, September 8, 1861, AC, "Fort Union, September, 1861," File 3, p. 18.

[22] Irwin to Ritter, October 1, 1861, AC, "Fort Union, October, 1861," File 4, p. 1.

Red River, October 10, 1861.

Colonel 1st Regiment of Mounted New Mexicans,

Mr. Jose G. Gallegos,

My Superior in this place:

I meet Six men of my Company, who by order of old Chapman were dispached [*sic*] to the U.S. [with] a certain Doctor, a man of consideration, to whom my men were delivered by the accoused [*sic*] old man, seeing that they were not in any manner recommended by him, to suply [*sic*] them with what was necessary to live upon nor on account of their pay. I determined to return them back to my Company. These miserable and unfortunate men with difficulty arrived here with their horses with their provisions behind him, and all this by the fault of the old commander, I have *refered* [*sic*] to. I suppose he does so believing that we greasers, as they treat us, do not know to distinguish the bad faith with which they conduct themselves in their duty.

My Colonel, I pray you, will have the kindness to cause your interpreter to explain to the commander Chapman what I say in this letter. I have met with no accident and will proceed on my march, God willing, with all the regularity posible [*sic*] to defend and protect the property of the federal government which has been confided under my orders....

I am affectionately, your Servant Who desires to see you.

CAPTAIN S. MARTINAS[23]

On September 17, Fort Union and the Department of New Mexico sustained a loss which neither could well afford. Colonel Céran St. Vrain quit the army, on "account of a multiplicity of private business," which made him unable "to do justice to myself or be efficient in the service."[24] Lieutenant Colonel Christopher Carson was promoted to the vacancy.

Because of the difficulty of transporting money into the territory after the Civil War began, soldiers went without pay for long periods at a time. Canby attempted to alleviate one condition arising from the lack of funds through a circular which read: "Until the regular

[23] Martínez to Gallegos, October 10, 1861, AC, "Fort Union, October, 1861," File 4, p. 21.

[24] St. Vrain to Chapman, September 17, 1861, AC, "Fort Union, September, 1861," File 3, p. 83.

troops of this Department are paid, the Commissaries of Subsistence are authorized to issue half-rations of beef, flour, coffee and sugar to the children of the authorized laundresses when living at stations where there are public supplies." Feeding the laundresses' children, however, failed to quell the tide of resentment toward the army. Therefore, on November 18, Canby called for help from the Paymaster General, pointing out the great embarrassment to the military operations caused by lack of funds. "Many regular troops have not been paid for more than twelve months and the volunteers not at all."[25] The Paymaster General was equally embarrassed, for Sterling Price, now with the Confederates, captured the funds intended for New Mexico, and, in the language of Canby, "almost entirely paralyzed the military operations in New Mexico."

In the hope of warding off the growing crisis, Canby borrowed money "on the official and private credit of the quartermaster, his commissary and himself" through inducing "some of the leading capitalists [to] advance or loan the funds necessary to relieve the Government." When the advances or loans from the capitalists, who entered into the agreement with "alacrity," proved insufficient for the Colonel's requirements, he introduced a system of assessments against persons suspected of sympathy for the Confederacy. (The degree of "alacrity" displayed by those "assessed" was not measured.) The rumors persisted, however, that the United States was bankrupt since it could not pay its soldiers. Canby railed that such rumors "secretly but industriously kept alive all the elements of discontent [among the volunteers] and fanned them into flames." He feared that, as a result, "the volunteer forces, already organized, will melt away by desertion." Perhaps such rumors would even stimulate "active opposition to the government."

Then Lieutenant Colonel J. Francisco Cháves added substance to the complaints of the volunteers by filing, on November 26, a protest against discrimination, avowing that the *Nuevo Mejicanos* at Fort Union were "slighted in nearly every respect." "That accused old

---

[25] Colton, *The Civil War in the Western Territories,* 21–22. The situation is here amplified creditably.

man," Chapman, immediately summoned Cháves into his presence and told him that, not only had "they not been slighted in any respect whatever," but he would "venture to say that the volunteer soldiers of your command have never been so well fed, clothed and quartered as at present, and never will be again after they have left the Service of the U. States."[26] Canby himself took notice of Colonel Cháves' complaint, reminding him that if officers "enter the service with the expectation of carrying with them the luxuries, or even the comforts of the home, it is an idea of which they cannot too soon divest themselves."

On December 9, Canby assigned Colonel C. R. Paul to the command of Fort Union, relieving Chapman,[27] the assignment including "the command of the Eastern District of New Mexico, and Superintendent of the organization, instruction and discipline of the Volunteer troop[s] now at, or to be assembled at Fort Union."

Colonel Paul was at his station on December 13, 1861. Less than a month later, Colonel Paul realized that his right to command might be jeopardized by the presence of volunteer officers who outranked him and applied for a promotion.[28] Canby, two days later, rejected the application, although the situation did present "some difficulty." He assigned as his reason for denying the request; "the prejudice of the Mexican population towards the Americans." That prejudice, so he said, "is so great that if the field officers are taken all together from the latter class, it is to be apprehended that it will delay, if it does not defeat, the organization of these regiments." He admitted that it was "not a good military reason, but it is a necessity from the character of the people we have to deal with." Then unabashedly he announced his intention to give preference to *Nuevo Mejicanos* and "to recommend for commissions as field officers . . . particularly Colonel Gallegos and Lieutenant Colonel Valdez."

While Canby refused promotion to Colonel Paul, he reiterated his fear of revolt, telling the War Department, "The Mexican people

[26] NA, RG 98, Dept. of N. M. Orders, Vol. 38–C (no p. no.).
[27] S.O. No. 210, NA, RG 98, Dept. of N. M. Orders, Vol. 38–C (no p. no.).
[28] On January 12, 1862. Paul's authority was ignored later and at a crucial moment.

have no affection for the institutions of the United States; they have strong but hitherto restrained hatred for the Americans as a race, but they are not wanting persons, who, from the commencement of these troubles, have secretly and industriously endeavored to keep alive all the elements of discontent and fan them into flames. The long deferred payment of the volunteers has given much plausibility and coloring to their representations as to have produced a marked and pernicious influence upon these ignorant and impulsive people."[29]

Four days after he had voiced his apprehension, the department commander took notice of a revolt in Colonel Pino's company at Camp Connelly. It was followed by another mutiny, at Fort Union. Word went to New Mexico headquarters that "there had been a serious revolt in two companies" caused by the men's "not having been paid and clothed as they were promised." William J. L. Nicodemus, assistant acting adjutant general, acting in the absence of Colonel Canby, directed Colonel Paul, "without stopping to inquire into the correctness of these complaints," to suppress "by the most energetic measures, . . . all who participated in the proceeding, either directly or indirectly, and reduce them to the most absolute subordination to law and discipline." Force was to be used to the "extent that may be necessary." Until order had been restored "no concession or compromises, for a moment, were to be entertained." If additional troops were needed to carry out suppression, they would be forthcoming.[30] His orders were not needed at Fort Union, however, for Colonel Paul had acted promptly and effectively, "allaying the excitement by prudent and judicious conduct."

Not so "the second—it was not so easily managed, and about thirty of the mutineers made their escape and fled to the mountains." While the mutineers were endeavoring "to make their living by plundering the inhabitants of the Country,"[31] Special Order No. 15 was issued

[29] C.O. to A. G., January 13, 1862, NA, RG 98, Dept. of N. M. Letters Sent, Vol. 12, p. 17.

[30] W. O. R., Series 1, Vol. IV, p. 86.

[31] C.O. to Major Baca, January 20, 1862, NA, RG 98, Dept. of N. M. Letters, Vol. 12, pp. 55–56.

for the arrest of Lieutenant Colonel Manuel Chávez, Second New Mexico Volunteers, and ordering him to the headquarters of his regiment at Camp Connelly, there to wait "untill further orders." Further orders came in due time, and the Lieutenant Colonel went back to duty, absolved from the odium of the perfidy of his regiment.

The search for the mutineers was anything but rewarding. Lieutenant William McLaughlin, however, came upon a "stray" at Anton Chico, who gave his name as Carlos Gallez. McLaughlin's men, on the other hand, identified him "as a volunteer soldier at Camp Chapman," so he was taken prisoner and given rations for the trip to Fort Union, but "he would not take the trouble to take the rations with him." Then, while in camp on the night of January 28, about ten o'clock, within sight of Fort Union's prison, an "excitement" took place. It had to do with someone's attempting to stampede the cavalry horses. It provided an opportune diversion for Prisoner Carlos Gallez, for when quiet was restored, Gallez was gone and "with him one horse, one saddle, one Buffalo robe, and one blanket."[32]

Upon evaluating the mutiny, the Colonel commanding could not think "it probable that so serious a revolt could have occurred without having been excited or encouraged by the officers of the company or by persons of influence outside the military organization." To maintain discipline within Fort Union, Colonel Paul was ordered to "keep at Fort Union thereafter a sufficient number of regular troops." To suppress any activities of the "Secesh," therefore, a more vigorous ferreting out of those with Confederate leanings was to be carried on. To strengthen the hold of the army over the population near the capital, Donoldson went farther: He placed the district and city of Santa Fe under martial law, requiring all males over sixteen years of age to take the oath of allegiance to the United States, and to "do so forthwith before the Honorable Kirby Benedict, Chief Justice of the Supreme Court." The oath was required "to secure the loyal people ... from the influence ... the rebels will bring to bear upon them." The provost marshal was consequently charged with the "responsi-

[32] Martin to Colonel [Paul], AC, "Fort Union, 1862," File 1, p. 114.

253

bility for the effectiveness of the order . . . and [to] apply the *Teso-oath* to all who may be suspected of Sympathy with the invaders, and the refusal to be sworn cannot but be evidence."

 Donoldson's first attention was "to the notorious secession pro-clivities of Judge Baird and Major Welles of Albuquerque." To effect the arrest of those parties, thought Donoldson, "was not only politic, but absolutely demanded." As to S. B. Watrous, a "citizen residing near Fort Union," a more amiable approach was to be made. Colonel Paul was to "send for Mr. Watrous and explain to him the meaning of the Articles of War and General Orders," and "advise him that any future publications would be followed by his arrest." No stronger course was suggested by Colonel Canby because he supposed "him to be ignorant . . . and had no evil intentions toward the government."

Canby met opposition to his arbitrary rule from the Secretary of State, J. H. Holmes, who also functioned, much to Canby's discom-fort, as editor of *The Santa Fe Republican*. He was not in accord with the suspension of the writ of habeas corpus, the restriction upon travel without military permission, or the arbitrary arrest and trial of those who Canby "thought had treasonable designs." And he pub-licly commended former Surveyor General William Pelham for sitting out the war in Santa Fe's jail in preference to taking the *Teso-oath*. He subsequently flaunted Canby's authority, declaring that "in New Mexico military rule is more severe than in other loyal parts of the United States," and he "would experiment for the benefit of the world to show if what we publish will call down the vengeance of the department." Before experimenting, however, he deemed it important to make a trip east. Consequently he "borrowed a government horse" and disappeared. So did the United States mail, which was supposed to have been on the "borrowed horse." The circumstance of the mail failure was reported by Colonel Paul, the explanation having come from Santa Fe:

> Headquarters, Fort Union,
> January 31, 1862.
> Sir: I have the honor to state that the mail matter which ought to have reached Fort Union on the 30th inst. did not come to hand, owing to

the circumstances (as reported to me by Capt. McFerran, A.Q.M.) that *Mr. Holmes,* Secretary of State, with *permission* rode the express animals & was to have brought the mail through, but it is believed that he has carried it off with him to the States.[33]

Another man caught in the widespread net dragging in "Secesh" was none other than the hero of the Battle of Taos, R. L. Wootton, affectionately called Uncle Dick Hooten. From his tollgate high up on Raton Mountain, where he collected fees from passers to and from New Mexico and Colorado using his private road, Uncle Dick leaned perilously South-ward. He was summoned to appear before Judge Bradford to take the oath of allegiance. He promptly obeyed Marshal Sam Brown's summons, stood with other suspects, and "swallowed" the oath. When the others had taken their seats, Uncle Dick remained standing, whereupon Judge Bradford addressed him: "Uncle Dick, is there something you wish to say?"

(Wootton): "Wall, Jedge, I jest wanted to say, I've jined yer church, but by Gud, I ain't got a damned bit of yer re-leej-um."[34]

[33] Paul to Nicodemus, AC, "Fort Union, 1862," File 1, p. 118. Later that year Secretary Holmes was arrested, tried, and convicted. He was sentenced to serve three years at hard labor with a ball and chain attached to his leg; Canby suspended the sentence but deprived him of his office.

[34] *Weekly New Mexican,* July 5, 1879, p. 1, col. 6.

CHAPTER TWELVE

THE TEXANS—"A VERY ROUGH AND FIGHT-LOVING CROWD"

Doubting the loyalty of Sibley's old cavalry command and believing that the *Nuevo Mexicanos'* hatred for the Anglo-Americans was "so great" that they could not even be trusted as "field officers," Canby, on January 1, 1862, called upon the Governor of Colorado for assistance. "A large accession [he said] of the Texas force and the invasion of the Territory renders it necessary that I should again ask your Excellency to send to Fort Wise and Garland as large a force of the Colorado Volunteers as can possibly be spared."[1] The call was predicated upon "better founded reports" than those previously received. He had no doubt but that there "was a considerable force, estimated at 1,200 men, with 7 pieces of artillery . . . now on the march to this place." To prevent any civilian uprising, all the powder and lead should be taken from the merchants, although "it will be paid for by the Government if it should be used."

Although Colonel Canby had deemed it necessary to call on the Governor of Colorado for help, his plans were not disclosed. What he would do, if anything, or when he would do it, if at all, he kept from both Colonel Donoldson and the Governor. They, wishing "to be able to determine upon the most prudent course to be pursued," inquired about them, through Colonel Donoldson,[2] on the eve of the Governor's departure from the capital to visit with Canby at Belen. The Colonel's reply was vitriolic: "I wish it to be said distinctly that I will move when I get ready to move and that will be when the Country behind me is secure from a revolutionary movement."

[1] Canby to Gilpin, January 1, 1862, NA, RG 98, Dept. of N. M. Letters Sent, Vol. 12, p. 2.

[2] Colonel Commanding Dept. to Donoldson, January 25, 1862 (no signature), NA, RG 98, Dept. of N. M. Letters, Vol. 12, pp. 70–71.

After the fruitless effort to get information from Canby, Governor Connelly spent six days supervising the major general of the militia who was, at that moment and under the Governor's directions, "organizing and sending into the field all the disposable force in the Territory." The six days were employed in a campaign of "hatred for the Texans, rather than patriotism" in his efforts to persuade the natives to volunteer,[3] the idea being that the real danger would come from their old enemies, the terrible Tejanos, not from the Confederates or the Indians. Finally, on January 25, 1862, in a letter to Secretary of State W. H. Seward, the Governor set his departure date for the following day, proclaiming there was now no "fear of any armed force that Texas can send against this Territory." Later, when news came that Sibley's Texans were moving northward out of El Paso, the Governor had "no fears of the results here." He and Canby would "conquer the Texan forces; if not in the first battle, it would be done in the second, or subsequent battles." With positive assurance he told Seward: "We will overcome them. The spirit of our people is good, and I have here, and en route the elite of the yeomanry of the country to aid in defending their homes and firesides."[4]

On February 11, Governor Connelly again became reporter to Secretary Seward, stating, not from any disclosures made by Canby, but from his own deductions:

> The enemy are approaching in full force, not, I think, exceeding 3,000 men. They are within 20 miles of this post. Today, our united forces march out to meet them. The battle most likely will take place on the 13th, about ten miles below. We have no fears of the result. Enthusiasm prevails throughout our lines.
>
> About 800 militia will arrive tomorrow, there being already here and in service 500 of those led out by my late order. . . . I have great confidence they will do good service. . . . Colonel Canby has the entire confidence of the army and of the country.[5]

[3] Max L. Heyman, Jr., *The Prudent Soldier: A Biography of E. R. S. Canby,* 145, quoting William I. Waldrip, "New Mexico During the Civil War," unpublished Master's thesis, University of New Mexico, 1950.

[4] Connelly to Seward, February 6, 1862, *W. O. R.,* Series 1, Vol. IX, p. 644.

[5] Connelly to Seward, February 11, 1862, *W. O. R.,* Series 1, VIII, p. 644.

The battle did not take place "about ten miles below Fort Craig" as prognosticated by the Governor, nor did it take place on February 13, Connelly's date; nor was Canby able to move "when he got ready," for, on February 18, Sibley appeared before Fort Craig, making it necessary for Canby to concentrate his forces there. This Sibley movement, however, was merely a ruse to enable Sibley to cross his army to the east bank of the Río Grande and move up the river north of Fort Craig, thus severing Canby's line of supplies northward and forcing the Union troops to come out of the fort, cross the river, and fight upon a battleground of Sibley's selection in order to avoid being surrounded within the fort.

The battle "commenced at an early hour in the morning, February 21," and, according to Canby's evaluation, proceeded "with unvarying success" until a Confederate charge on Macrae's battery threw the Union forces into confusion and drove them from the battlefield. Captain Gurden Chapin, acting inspector general of the Union forces, an onlooker at the debacle, after hastily removing himself from the vicinity of Valverde, relayed the bad news to General Halleck:

> I write to you fully and free as . . . a member of General Canby's staff, in order that you may have a proper view of affairs here. . . . we have had a most desperate and bloody struggle with the Texans . . . and have retreated to Fort Craig. Colonel Canby did everything that man could do [to] save the day. He beseeched and begged, ordered and imperatively commanded [the] troops to save his guns, and a deaf ear met alike his supplications and commands. . . . The enemy is now above Colonel Canby on the Rio Grande, and of course has cut him off from all communications with his supplies. It is needless to say this country is in a critical condition. The militia have all run away and the New Mexican Volunteers are deserting in large numbers. No dependence whatever can be placed on the natives: they are worse than worthless: they are really aids to the enemy, who catch them, take their arms, and tell them to go home.[6]

Of course, Canby, too, made a report. He frankly called the battle

[6] Report of A.I.G. to Halleck, February 28, 1862, *W. O. R.*, Series 1, Vol. IX, p. 635.

a "disaster," reporting that it had been fought "almost entirely by the regular troops (trebled in number by the Confederates) with *no* assistance from the militia and with but little from the Volunteers, who would not obey orders or obeyed them too late to be of any service."

After the "disaster," Canby retreated to the safety of Fort Craig, where he decided to "disembarrass himself of the militia by sending them away." Too, "the number of men in the fort was more than could be usefully employed." Therefore, he availed himself of Major Donoldson's willingness to attempt to escape to Santa Fe and spread the alarm of defeat, taking with him Governor Connelly and his "yeomen—the elite of the country," who were to take advantage of the darkness and "make a detour that would place them in advance of the enemy." The Governor uncomplainingly went along, "feeling no disposition to be taken prisoner." The detour was made in good order and "effected without much difficulty and with no loss, except the dispersion of the militia." The dispersion took place in the night, few being "left in ranks after they emerged from the mountain." At this point the Governor decided that his presence would "be of no further utility," so, accompanied by a few militia officers, he sped on to Santa Fe, arriving there on February 27.[7]

At Santa Fe, Donoldson and the Governor heard that the whole force of the Texans was on the march up the river. This report brought a quick decision from Donoldson to remove all the government stores to Fort Union. The Colorado troops, who had arrived in Santa Fe by way of Fort Garland, would protect the supplies on the road to Fort Union. The governor, too, acted promptly, declaring, "I shall follow him to Union, and even to the States, should the Territory be abandoned to the enemy." One week later Donoldson was in Fort Union and Governor Connelly "in company with him." The fleeing chief executive, however, had tarried long enough to set up "the executive department at Las Vegas" as he passed, availing himself of the accommodations of the Plaza Hotel. By the time the concentration of the troops was completed at Fort Union, Connelly

[7] *W. O. R.* Series 1, Vol. IX, p. 639.

observed that "the militia had all dispersed and gone to prepare their lands for the coming harvest . . . by far the best use that can be made of them."

On March 10, Colonel Slough, answering Canby's appeal to the Governor of Colorado for help, marched into Fort Union. He had with him "950 men, who from all accounts, could be relied upon." Fort Union had three or four hundred regulars, according to the Governor's information, and, he thought that, by joining with Canby's regulars, the Colonel commanding might muster "2 000 regular troops, this is, American troops." Of course, his estimate did not take into account "the fragments of three regiments of the New Mexican Volunteers," which might number another fifteen hundred.

News of the defeat of Canby at Valverde had reached the Colorado Volunteers near what is now Trinidad, Colorado. The report had it that Canby was bottled up in Fort Craig, that Santa Fe was in the hands of the Confederates, and that Fort Union, the last stronghold of the Union in New Mexico, was in a precarious situation. With this news to stimulate him, Slough had cast aside all excess paraphernalia and urged men to hasten with all speed toward Fort Union; so, trudging through hail, snow, and a mountain storm, they had come into view of Fort Union before dark on March 10. Although almost exhausted, as they approached the environs of the fort, the First Colorado Volunteers formed "into column and marched into the Post with drums beating and colors flying." Pulling up before Colonel Paul's quarters, they halted. There they were honored (in the language of Pikes Peaker Ovando J. Hollister) "by welcoming speeches *in rather unintelligible words* both by Governor Connelly and Colonel Paul." The welcoming officials, however, said nothing about "the Battle of Valverde or the whereabouts of the enemy," and at least one soldier "thought they might as well have permitted the boys, hungry and tired, to go to their camp near the fortification as to have perpetrated this farce." After the speech-making some of the late-arriving infantrymen, through the intercession of their officers, obtained supplies from the commissary, but soldier Hollister's company, finding no arrangements for food made for them "after their long march on hard-bread, proceeded to the sutler's store, packed off some half dozen boxes of champaigne, a staving good cheese, and a box of crackers, and thereafter slept in the corral with their horses."

The next morning Sergeant Philbrook, feeling neither weak nor weary from his immediate past experience, was accosted by Lieutenant Gray, who attempted to arrest him for "drunkenness and noise," but the Sergeant objected, unloaded his five-shooter at the Lieutenant, "and hit him once. . . . The ball struck on the bridge of the nose, between the eyes, and glancing down, lodged in the lower part of the face. It did not seriously injure him." Other officers who witnessed the incident "emptied their revolvers at Philbrook," but as their aim was not as good as their intentions, the Sergeant "escaped their shots and was finally lodged in the guardhouse. This brought out B Company as the lieutenant's advocate, and, invoking the law of the frontier, called upon Judge Lynch to preside. The firmness of Captain Sanborn, officer of the day, however, cooled the excitement of the mob, and they were sent to their beds to revise their thinking: 'That the use of whiskey justifies anything; and that a free use of it is a necessary qualification of a gentleman.'" By way of rounding out the story, it must be told that Sergeant Philbrook was later court-martialed and executed.

Prior to the arrival of Colonel Slough and his Pikes Peakers, Colonel Paul was greatly disturbed by the situation. Since the Battle of Valverde things had grown worse. "All the militia and a large number of the Volunteers (natives) . . . have deserted and taken to the mountains. . . . A general system of robbery and plunder" seemed to be the "order of the day. . . . There was a general panic in the country; people were flying from their homes." Then, after the speech-making to Slough's Colorado troops and the restoration of quiet after their night out, Colonel Paul was overwhelmed with mortification: he discovered that Slough—"an officer of only six weeks service and without experience"—outranked him in the right to command Fort Union. This was particularly disturbing, for on the day before Colonel Slough's arrival Paul had advised Colonel Canby that he would "move from Fort Union with 1,200 Americans, four guns," to form a junction with the Colonel and enable the two commands to enter Fort Union ahead of the loitering Confederate forces. Before Canby received Paul's rescue proposal, he sent a message to Paul disclosing the fact that he intended to sit it out at Fort Craig awaiting reinforcements, thinking that he could "survive 60 days of seige on a 50 days supply of flour." Then, on March 20, Colonel Slough chose to assert his rank; and Colonel Paul, having no alternative, issued General Order No. 6,[8] passing the command to Colonel Slough.

But one day transpired before Canby directed, through another message which reached Fort Union:

> Fort Union must be held and our communications with the East kept open. While awaiting reenforcements, harass the enemy by partisan operations; obstruct his movements, and remove or destroy any supplies that may fall into his hands. . . . If it is necessary to abandon the post, everything will be destroyed. Do not move from Fort Union to meet me until I advise you of the route and point of junction.

One day after assuming command Colonel Slough published marching orders.[9] The prospect of a fight seemed to enliven the Pikes Peakers. That night "the boys broke into the sutler's cellar and gobbled up a lot of whiskey, wine, canned fruit, oysters, etc." When morning came and Slough received Canby's directive, he wavered, countermanded the marching order, then reissued it with the explanation that were he to comply, it would be but to permit the Texans to lord it over New Mexico. And by noon Slough's command was moving toward Santa Fe, but not before Colonel Paul had registered strenuous objections while refusing to abandon the fort. The departure was described by a participant, Hollister of the Pikes Peakers:

> About noon we succeeded in getting under way. A party started ahead to secure the plunder stolen from the sutler last night. A squad of regulars were sent after them, but they had no intention to interfere with the Volunteers, and took care to discover nothing. The boys con-

[8] G.O. No. 6, NA, RG 98, Dept. of N. M. Orders—Eastern District, Old Book 123 (no p. no.).

[9] Hollister, *Boldly They Rode;* also, AC, "Fort Union, 1862," File 2, p. 56.

cealed some, drank more, lost and sold the balance. What was drunk immediately under the eyes of the sutler was about all the good they got out of it; a doubtful good, certainly, for the command was scattered from Dan to Beersheba, burying plunder, drinking, fighting, and carousing with Mexican women at the Lome,[10] a small *Sodom* five or six miles from Union. There were dozens of us too drunk to know friends from foe, consequently most provokingly troublesome. Many came in during the night with rough usage painted on the faces in unmistakable colors.[11]

Slough, marching away with the bulk of Fort Union forces, left the fort with a garrison of only one company of cavalry, three companies of infantry, and six of New Mexican Volunteers. Slough, early on March 23, came within sight of what he mistook for "a clump of bushes or rocks," which turned out to be "Las Vegas, literally 'Those Bottoms,' which improved but slightly on closer acquaintance." It was a collection of "courts and corrals . . . sheep-pens inhabited by a race of people whose poverty of purse is equaled only by their poverty of mind . . . [who] gobbled Spanish . . . stumbling over an English word occasionally, as if desirous of entertaining their visitors."

Slough halted his command "immediately in town" and turned the men "into a corral." It failed to contain them, however, for they were soon over the fence "in search of women and plunder . . . both distressingly scarce." As for the women, Hollister found them "more sedative than stimulating." The discriminating "had no taste for their society." And their allure decreased rapidly "upon learning that the smallpox was raging in the town." The Pikes Peakers "went home" to their sheep pens carrying with them "a confirmation of life impressions of Mexican character."

While the soldiers were thus engaged, Slough was conferring with Governor Connelly, to whom he revealed that he would "leave this place in the direction of the enemy" despite the "little discord in relation to the movement now made from Fort Union." The Governor

[10] "Lome," most assuredly meaning "Loma Parda."
[11] Hollister, *Boldly They Rode.*

saw "no evil" in Slough's disobedience of orders, thinking that perhaps the "advance would curtail the movements of the enemy [even]
the expulsion of the enemy from the capital."

Leaving Las Vegas, the Pikes Peakers marched toward Santa Fe,
intending to surprise "the enemy in small force at that place."[12] What
Chivington (now in command of the advance party) did not know
was that two regiments of Confederates had reached Santa Fe on
March 16 and 17 and more troops on March 19. They were instructed
to "wait a short time, and then march on and take Fort Union." This
forward movement they initiated, moving into Apache Cañon on
March 22, where they "got word" that Union troops were "coming
down the cañon." Not knowing that reinforcements had arrived from
Colorado, the Confederates expected only *Nuevo Mejicanos* and a
few regulars—"an easy victory. . . . What a mistake!" for they met
Pikes Peakers, "regular demons, that iron and lead had no effect
upon." They began shooting down Confederates "like sheep," but
Confederate "grape and shell soon stopped them."[13] John D. Miller,
of the Colorado Cavalry, was thoroughly displeased with the way
the battle was managed. He thought the Union force had "no head;
no one to go ahead and give orders. The captains and lieutenants
stood around like stoughton bottles until it became every man for
himself"; and they fought that way until "nearly night, and there
was no water in the canyon, and they had to fall back to Pigeon's
Ranch." Apologetically, Miller "claimed the victory" but "had to
fall back for a camping place."[14]

Soldier Hollister, too, was soon making after-battle observations.
To him, "It was somewhat amusing to see the various aches, ills, etc.,
with which some of the boys were attacked. Santa Fe had lost its
charm, and any sacrifice of manhood was preferable to the chance
of another battle." But as "victory" and "retreat" are incompatible
conditions, save by adequate explanation, Chivington attempted to

[12] Report of John M. Chivington, March 26, 1862, *W. O. R.,* Series 1, Vol. IX, p. 531.

[13] Excerpts from a letter written by unidentified Texan to his wife, dated at Socorro,
New Mexico, April 30, 1862, AC, "Fort Union, 1862," File 2, p. 64.

[14] John D. Miller to his father, AC, "Fort Union, 1862," File 2, p. 68.

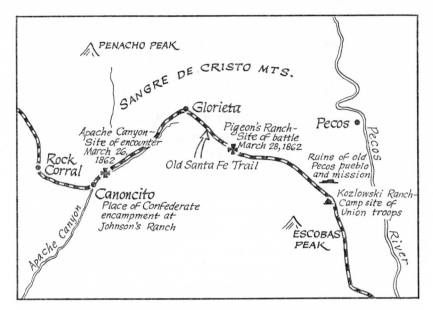

Battle area of Glorieta Pass, March 26, 28, 1862

give that explanation: It was nearing sundown; furthermore, he did not know "how near the enemy's reenforcements might be," and he "had no cannon to oppose theirs." He did not state, also, that he did not know whether or not the Confederate reinforcements had cannon. As a result, "he gathered up his dead and wounded, and several of theirs, and fell back."

Slough and Chivington, having found a camping place, postponed "the chances of another battle" until March 27. Then, having learned from "spies that the enemy, about 1,000 strong, were in Apache Canyon and at Johnson's Ranch beyond," Slough concluded to "reconnoiter in force and harass them as much as possible." Then, "to facilitate the reconnoissance" he divided his army, placing Chivington "with 430 officers and picked men" on a road leading to the left of Apache Cañon with instructions to ascend the mesa and "push forward to Johnson's Canyon." He thought that by so doing, this detachment could see to the rear of "the 1,000 strong" encampment of Confederates reported by Union spies.

After separating from Chivington, Slough entered Apache Cañon. He had "attained but a short distance [when] the enemy fired upon him." This occurred at ten o'clock, and a sharp battle continued until after four. The character of the terrain was not to the liking of the Colonel. It was only suited "to an engagement of the bushwhacking kind," and not versed in that unmilitary art, the Colonel "fell back in order to our camp, a place of retirement near San Jose."[15]

About one-thirty Chivington's detachment reached the top of Johnson's Cañon, and Chivington saw below him, one thousand feet, approximately eighty wagons and one fieldpiece, none too well guarded by some two hundred men. Quickly the Union force scrambled down the mountain. The wagons were "heavily loaded with ammunition, clothing, subsistence and forage"—all the sustaining supplies of the Confederate army then fighting Slough east of Apache Cañon. Three Confederates were killed, and the wagons were burned on the spot. "Then came heartless butchery. . . . Nearby in a corral were about five hundred horses and mules . . . the five hundred beasts were slaughtered with Union bayonets."[16]

While Chivington was gazing upon the result of his handiwork, a Confederate suddenly mounted a horse and rode, not to Santa Fe and safety, but through Apache Cañon to the fighting Confederates to bear the news of disaster in the rear to Colonel Scurry. Cavalryman Miller evaluated the situation promptly: "The Texans have possession of the field, but we have possession of their grub."[17] Since Colonel Scurry, too, understood the situation, he "retreated through Apache Canyon the same evening," bound for Santa Fe and "something to eat." The Confederates were in Santa Fe on the morning of March 30, "not having slept for three nights" and so weary that Scurry had "difficulty in writing intelligently" to Sibley, who had not been on the battlefield of Glorieta, nor nearer than Galisteo, twenty miles

[15] Colonel Slough gave the explanation of "retirement" the second time as "hearing of the success of Major Chivington." That statement was positively not true. He had no intimation of the success of Chivington's command until ten o'clock that night.

[16] William Clarke Whitford, *Colorado Volunteers in the Civil War*, 121.

[17] John D. Miller to his father, AC, "Fort Union, 1862," File 2, p. 72.

away, where a barber noticed him seemingly well supplied, "perhaps for medicinal purposes, with whiskey."

Then "unfed and blanketless unmurmuringly," the Confederates began the long retreat down the Río Grande and back into Texas, with Canby coming out of the security of Fort Craig to harry them, but never attacking. Down-river the Texans increased the speed of their departure upon hearing that Carleton and his Californians were about to reach the Río Grande and cut them off from escape. Once they were in El Paso there remained in New Mexico no Confederate military organization; and, of course, there began to be "many desertions from the southern ranks." Canby learned much about these desertions from Reuben W. Creel, who had taken upon himself the responsibility of furnishing "much information of affairs." As a reward, since he was "a most worthy gentleman," he became the consul to Chihuahua, "being, also, poor and deserving, and needing immediate and favorable consideration," and as he was a self-confessed "patriot and honest man," he could not but think of the departing Confederates as "Texans—a very rough and fight-loving crowd."[18]

18 Carleton to Creel, U.S. consul, Chihuahua, Mexico, December 8, 1863, NA, RG 98, Dept. of N. M. Letters, Vol. 14, p. 29.

CHAPTER THIRTEEN

"RESTORE THE SOVEREIGNTY OF THE UNITED STATES IN ITS ORIGINAL INTEGRITY"

BY THE TIME the effort to take Fort Union was abandoned by the Confederates, many prisoners filled the Union military jails. Since the expense incident to holding them was large, Canby took action to dispose of them. The prospect was that there would ultimately be five hundred, so each prisoner was given a number and charges were preferred "specifying fully all the facts" and giving a list of witnesses. Some were to be "discharged from custody"; others were charged with "violating parole," "enticing soldiers to desert," and "robbery," while more had "aided and abetted the enemy"; some even "lurked or acted as spies," to say nothing of those who had "given information to the enemy."

No one, however, had dared to file charges against Captain R. S. C. Lord for "hiding behind a bush" during the Battle of Valverde; but Lord's cowardice was so freely discussed among the soldiers that, wishing to offset the imputations, he demanded of the Assistant Adjutant General "a true extract [of the records] as far as relates to the mention of Captain Lord and his command." Obligingly A. A. G. Gurdin Chapin handed him the record, explaining however, that the "letter bears no signature and was never sent to its address." The unsigned letter read: "General: A Company of Cavalry escort to the Colonel, Commanded by Capt. Lord was deaf to entreaties, and ingloriously fled."

Then began the trials of various offenders, or accused, by a military commission, presided over by Captain A. F. Garrison, at Fort Union. One Ferenstein was convicted and doomed "to be confined at hard labor in charge of the Guard for a period of three months, with a ball weighing twenty-five pounds attached to his left leg by a chain five feet long." Another accused—Salsedo—was charged with "aiding the Confederate troops in the capture of Lieutenant Caxton, the bearer of important dispatches, the loss of which caused serious embarassment [*sic*] to our own operations and advantage to those of the enemy." A plea by his attorney to transfer the case to the civil courts was peremptorily rejected, despite the fact that "statute treason was ordinarily tried by the civil courts, but treasonable acts, in actual war, in so far as they endanger the safety, impede the operations, or aid the prejudice of good order and discipline in Army, are, by Statutes and by the common law of all armies cognizable by Military Courts or Military Commissions according to the nature of the offense and the status of the offender."[1]

As the Fort Union military commission neared the end of its numerous trials, Canby issued orders to the commander at Fort Marcy to "discharge such prisoners as have been pardoned and send the remainder to Fort Union." Rumor had it that "one out of nine" prisoners was to be released. But when the cells were unlocked, Canby inquired of the commander, "What has become of the missing one?" Obviously he had decided that the odds were not in his favor.[2]

Thomas J. Hill, a prisoner at Fort Union, pleaded "for the limits of the Territory as a citizen of the United States." As he saw it, his chief offense was not "having a desire to live with the Mexicans, so he went to live at Baird's."[3] A deserter, Private John McQuade, asked his captain's forgiveness, whereupon he was returned to duty without trial, "although he must make good the time lost by desertion."[4] One Jackson was not so fortunate.

Jackson was taken prisoner in Apache Cañon on March 26 and

[1] Canby, May 16, 1862, NA, RG 98, Dept. of N. M. Letters, Vol. 12, pp. 150–51.

[2] Chapin to C.O., Fort Marcy, May 23, 1862, NA, RG 98, Dept. of N. M. Letters, Vol. 12, p. 175.

[3] Hill to Chapin, May 26, 1862, AC, "Fort Union, 1862," File 3, p. 61. The reference is to Judge S. M. Baird, who at one time aspired to take Santa Fe into the Texas judicial system.

[4] S.O. No. 97, June 8, 1862, NA, RG 98, Dept. of N. M. Orders, Vol. 40, p. 116–17.

identified as the acting hospital steward, who had deserted his duty at Albuquerque to join the ranks of the Confederates, taking with him valuable hospital stores and medicines.[5]

The military commission was relieved of trying the men of the Fifth Regiment of New Mexico Volunteers charged with desertion and returning to their homes from Valverde. Canby issued Special Order No. 101 permitting them to "report themselves within a reasonable time to their commanding officers . . . with their horses, arms and equipment." Thereafter they were to be "restored to their rights as soldiers," since it appeared to him "from satisfactory evidence that many of the men of Captain Barrenti's Company . . . reported as deserters . . . acted in obedience to the orders of their officers."[6]

In early June, 1862, the vulnerability of the Star Fort Union was disclosed to Captain Plympton, then in command at the post, by actual tests made by Second Lieutenant A. W. Robb, just promoted to his commission from a clerkship.[7] Orders came immediately to "suspend the building . . . until further notice."[8] This was distressingly inconvenient, for June came to a close with 513 soldiers quartered there. Not only was the Star Fort vulnerable to gunfire, but the entrenchments, were declared to be "wholly unfit for the purposes for which they were designed" on account of excessive dampness "of the walls and flooring." Condemnation of the Star Fort and the disclosure of the hospital conditions, when New Mexico yet had many wounded men, both Union and Confederate, urgently in need of medical care, caused Canby to make a hurried trip to the fort. On July 22, he reached a decision: He did not approve of the location, but he knew of "no place in New Mexico combining the advantages of a Depot in which equal or greater objections do not obtain than at Fort Union." Furthermore, it "would be very difficult to select in any Country a position that will not be commanded to some extent

---

[5] Chapin to C.O., Fort Union, June 9, 1862, AC, "Fort Union, 1862," File 3, p. 92.

[6] S.O. No. 101, June 13, 1862, NA, RG 98, Dept. of N. M. Orders, Vol. 40, p. 120.

[7] C.O., Fort Union, to A.A.A.G., June 7, 1862, AC, "Fort Union, 1862," File 3, p. 85.

[8] Gurden to Plympton, June 12, 1862, NA, RG 98, Dept. of N. M. Letters, Vol. 12, p. 225.

by guns that are now in use." He would, therefore, complete the plans and build surface quarters adequate for the needs.[9]

With the arrival of Carleton's California Column on the lower Río Grande River, Canby abandoned the war, so far as the lower reaches of New Mexico were concerned, letting the responsibility fall upon Carleton, giving him an opportunity "to strike a blow for the old flag." Canby issued Special Order No. 128, directing: "As the forces of Brigadier General Carleton come into position, the 1st Regiment of the Colorado Volunteers will be withdrawn from the Southern Military District and proceed by detachments . . . to Fort Union." On August 24, Ovando J. Hollister, having survived the Battle of Glorieta, and being yet with his company, moved into Santa Fe from down-river, headed for Fort Union again. At Santa Fe, he found Uncle Sam's "bunting" majestically floating in the breeze while the provost marshal was "for once teaching the city some respect for authority" despite its "dirty, miserable appearance . . . traders, sports, and those connected with the Government" being the only remaining white people. However, its business was mostly "carried on by hard-fisted money-loving Jews." The next day was momentous for the veterans of the Battle of Glorieta. They reached "the classical ground of Apache Canyon" and stopped to celebrate by purchasing "Oporto wine—one quart native wine . . . Tambien, red *rot lo mismo* —mix. Net result—*patriotism*." And, "as there were never less than four talking at once, and that at the top of their voices . . . while the above mentioned preparation coursed through their veins, there was no limit to the courage and devotion to the old flag!!"

Two and one-half days later and 110 miles farther, the Coloradoans came into Fort Union again to find Commander Wallen in charge. They also found some of their old comrades-in-arms, one of whom, Lieutenant McDonold, was soon securely locked up in the *"Stone crock."* The necessity for thus restraining the Lieutenant came about as a result of Captain Lord's indulging in a general disparagement of the Colorado Volunteers, since he believed that Colonel Donoldson

[9] Brig. Gen. to A.G., July 22, 1862, NA, RG 98, Dept. of N. M. Letters, Vol. 12, pp. 330–34.

was the author of the unsigned imputation of cowardice. Captain Lord, therefore, for a want of another victim, "voided some of his venom before Mac[Donold], . . . abusing the volunteers, fierce and unstinting." McDonald thereupon "caught him up and soundly thrashed him. . . . Nor could three or four of his officers prevent it." Further, "Mac challenged the whole crew from Major Wallen down, altogether, or one after the other; but they did not like his style; and he is now awaiting trial for striking a superior officer." Hollister's sympathies were not, by any means, wasted upon the Captain, for—according to the observing Coloradoan—"Lord is——no better than he should be," but McDonold "had a pocket full of Lord's whiskers, torn out in the scuffle." To Hollister "they were interesting as being the relics of a man who hid in the tall grass at val verde." McDonold soon tired of the stone crock and applied to Major Wallen for a release so that he might go to Las Vegas, "there to take the baths at Warm Springs to restore his declining health." Major Wallen reluctantly declined, being under the impression "that no necessity exists for Lieutenant McDonald to go to the warm springs, for feebleness and indisposition, as he has recently given *striking* evidence of his fitness for duty."[10]

Although the Colorado Volunteers had reason to believe from Canby's orders that they were going home, F Company was assigned to garrison duty at Fort Union, later to be joined by Company B. The volunteers found the "West Point dignity" of the post offensive; accordingly, "The small Mexican town called Lome became the rage." Hardly had the Coloradoans taken to that "point of activity" when Major Wallen heard a "riot is going on at Loma Parda." This brought out a "mounted command to investigate the circumstances." The riotous circumstance was "a man by the name of Esther (Alias Curley), a discharged soldier." "Alias Curley" was merely keeping up "his reputation of having killed one or two men," and was now making an "unprovoked attack on a . . . soldier, wounding him severely with a pistol shot." The pistol wielder was placed under arrest, but as he was a civilian, Major Wallen was in a quandary

10 Wallen to Chapin, August 22, 1862, AC, "Fort Union, 1862," File 4, p. 104.

Fort Union Quartermaster's Office and Quarters, 1876.

Arrott Collection

Captain William Rawle Shoemaker, military storekeeper at the Fort Union Arsenal, who retired on June 30, 1882, having been a resident of the fort since its establishment.

Arrott Collection

whether "to retain him in confinement & bring him before the next Military Commission or . . . set him at liberty."[11] The removal of Curley from the scene had little effect, however, for thereafter to the Coloradoans "Loma Linda, Fandangoes, Lome Lightning, and Pecadoras were the attractions, and rows of considerable magnitude. The guardhouse was filled with Lome cadets, and the hospital with Lome patients. The hole was an unmitigated curse to the soldiers but was most generously patronized nevertheless."

During the period of the withdrawal of the Confederates from New Mexico, Canby, "at his own instance through friends in Washington City," secured the issuance of Special Order No. 181, relieving himself of the command of the Department of New Mexico.[12] At Franklin, Texas, Brigadier General James H. Carleton, who had gone "140 miles farther into Texas, to place the national flag over Fort Davis," received Special Order No. 153, directing him to "repair without delay to Santa Fe, for the purpose of relieving Brigadier General Canby in command of the Department."[13] On September 20 and again a week later, *The Santa Fe Gazette* took notice of the departure of Canby "and his estimable lady," feeling that he could not fall "among a people who will place a higher estimate upon his worth . . . than do the people of the Territory."[14] In departing, he felt that he had "restored the sovereignty of the United States in its original integrity."

Carleton came into command of the department fulminating defiance. There were "certain fundamental rules for the government of the people of this Territory" which would be rigidly enforced:

[11] Wallen to Chapin, August 16, 1862, AC, "Fort Union, 1862," File 4, p. 68.

[12] S.O. No. 181, *W. O. R.*, Vol. IX, p. 688; also Heyman, *Prudent Soldier*, 185–86.

[13] *W. O. R.*, Series 1, Vol. IX, p. 567; also Chapin to Carleton, NA, RG 98, Dept. of N. M. Letters, Vol. 12, p. 410.

[14] After leaving New Mexico, Canby commanded in the East and in Louisiana. He was killed in California, April 11, 1873, by the Modoc Indians. His death brought divided opinions regarding his character and services. *The New York Times* rated his assassination with "horrors and indignation," while, understandably, a newspaper from the South printed a headline: "An Indian Massacre—Captain Jack and Warriors Revenge the South by Murdering General Canby, One of her Great Oppressors— Three Cheers for the Gallant Modocs!" (See *Harper's Weekly*, May 17, 1873, p. 441.)

No man would be allowed to reside within the territory who had failed to subscribe to the oath of allegiance. "No words or acts calculated to impair that veneration which all good patriots should feel for our country and Government will be tolerated . . . or go unpunished." Those not pursuing "some lawful calling," or not having "legitimate means of support" would be driven from the territory. In enforcing his will, of course, he had "no thought or motive . . . but the good of the people . . . aiming only to do right." He knew; he had "heretofore resided five years in this country . . . and knows somewhat the character of the people."[15] As far as Confederate prisoners were concerned, there was to be another rule: "Whoever shall violate a safeguard shall suffer death." As to the Indians, he had not had time yet "to promulgate an all-inclusive policy," but so far as the Gila Indians were concerned, the troops might "fight the Indians in that vicinity whenever found." He had "no faith in Mangus Colorado . . . nor confidence in the Mescalero Apaches."[16] And as for the Texans, he had no assurance that they would not come again. If they did come, Forts Union and Craig were "to be defended at all hazards against any force that may be sent." Anticipating trouble both from the Texans and the Mescaleros, he ordered Carson and his First New Mexico Volunteers to report without delay to headquarters.[17]

After revamping Canby's military dispositions, Carleton gave his attention "to the punishment of traitors, and confiscation of their property." His first act was to summon Theodore D. Wheaton, Esquire,[18] United States district attorney for New Mexico. To him he presented his written indictment "of the enemies of the Government,"

[15] "The California Column," *W. O. R.,* Series 1, Vol. IX, p. 562; also G.O. No. 15, August 14, 1862, NA, RG 98, Column of California Orders, Vol. 42 (no p. no.).

[16] Later, Carleton directed Kit Carson "to make war on the Mescaleros, and upon all other Indians you may find in the Mescalero Country. All Indian men are to be killed whenever and wherever you can find them, the women and children will not be harmed, but you will take them prisoners. . . . This severity in the long run will be the most humane course."

[17] Cutler to Carson, September 20, 1862, NA, RG 98, Dept. of N. M. Letters, Vol. 13, p. 6.

[18] Concerning the probable cause of Judge Wheaton's lukewarmness for the New Mexicans, see W. G. Ritch Papers, Archives, Santa Fe, N. M., Box 29: "Theodore

assuring Wheaton that the military would "co-operate in all its power with the civil authorities" in the punishment and control of those engaged in treasonable practices, he being "creditably informed that many persons . . . are enemies to the Government." Furthermore, he thought Wheaton was the proper officer to initiate and carry to conclusion "all cases having for their object the punishment of traitors or the confiscation of their property." In the furtherance of these punishments, he would frown upon "luke warmness from covert sympathy with the traitors themselves." To demonstrate his lack of lukewarmness within the military establishment, Carleton directed Paymaster Martin to discharge his clerk, Charles B. Magruder, because "there was an opinion afloat that Magruder, is not so warm a friend of the Government . . . as a man should be holding his position."

Having encountered no lukewarmness on the part of Judges Hubbel and Kirby Benedict in matters concerning traitors and confiscation, Carleton turned to Chief Justice Benedict for judicial assistance in ridding Fort Union of the ever present threat to health and discipline anchored in Loma Parda. The judge pleaded a lack of jurisdiction, pointing out that "near Mora there lives a gentleman named Judge Knapp, who could —if properly applied to—take measures to have those men [Loma Parda residents] arrested and bound over to the next term of court for selling liquor to enlisted men." Judge Knapp, living within the shadow of the evils of Loma Parda and Fort Union, was notoriously unsympathetic with Carleton's policy of "punish and control." As a result, Carleton dubiously told Captain Plympton, commanding at the fort, that while he preferred that Judge Knapp act, if his "assistance proves to be of no avail . . . then, he [Carleton] would extend the limits of the post as to bring them all within the reach of the military Laws."[19] Before the General could get Judge Knapp's reaction, however, he was apprised of Knapp's decision not to co-operate in any and all things demanded by Carleton.

D. Wheaton—Never was married so far as known—Lived with a Mex [*sic*] woman. He had 17 children, 7 of whom were alive when he died."

[19] Cutler to Plympton, October 31, 1862, NA, RG 98, Dept. of N. M. Letters, Vol. 13, p. 130.

A tragedy took place at Taos, and Carleton called upon Judge Knapp:

Fort Union, Dec. 9, 1862

To the
Knapp, Honorable Judge
at Barclay's Fort, New Mexico,
No. 1116.
Sir:

I learned a week since, unofficially, that an Indian of the Utah tribe was in Taos recently, where certain parties are said to have gotten him drunk, then to have saturated some parts of his garments with spirits of turpentine and set fire to the clothing . . . from the effects of which . . . the Indian died.

The Utah tribe to which he belonged is . . . very much incensed at this inhuman outrage. . . . In your capacity as judge of this district . . . you are the proper person to . . . cause the offenders to be brought to justice. . . . I trust to awaken your zeal to the cause of justice and humanity. . . . I think it never has been my lot to have heard of such horrible barbarity before on the part of white men toward Indians.

Carleton, as he may have anticipated, failed to awaken Knapp's zeal in the cause of justice and humanity. Knapp was being transferred as judge to the Third Judicial District, which included the Mesilla Valley. In order to travel, according to the arbitrary decree of Carleton, Judge Knapp must have a passport, but Knapp refused to apply for it, stating he was a "part of the government." Carleton tendered it, and Knapp refused to accept it. Then Carleton put him in jail when he arrived in Santa Fe, but released him. While the Judge attempted to assume his duties, Carleton connived with the Governor to have military law declared in the Mesilla Valley, this step being necessary "more especially when having as judge such a man as Judge Knapp as the chief law officer. . . . Human life will be held very cheap in that part of the country . . . treason will stalk about unrebuked." Furthermore, Knapp was "the butt and laughing stock of the Territory . . . the ermine is soiled by lying upon his shoulders. If the Attorney General can move him out of the way, the public interest will be greatly served."

Under the semblance of co-operating with Colonel Carson against the Mescaleros and carrying sealed instructions not to be opened until he was well on the road, Captain William H. Backus left Fort Union on October 9, 1862, with Company G, Second Colorado Volunteers, who had expected by this time to be back in Colorado. From Anton Chico he was to turn to the confluence of the Canadian River and Utah Creek. There he was to form a camp "against the fierce cold winds of winter." The purpose: "To watch the road and the country toward Fort Smith and toward Texas, to give timely notice of the advance of any force of rebels." Establishing "a good understanding with the Comanches [would] get a good deal of information." They were not to be "molested or treated unkindly." "Texans or Rebels" were a different matter. Should Backus "have the ability to do so," he was "to fire into their camps at night, shoot their scouts, and the animals . . . stampede their stock . . . burn off the grass in front of them . . . impede their march. . . . Arrest and hold every whiteman who atempts to go either way . . . examine every Mexican and Indian [for] concealed dispatches." If Mescaleros or Navahos came about, he would "always attack them."

Carson's orders were similar; however, he was to "soundly whip, without parley or councils" all Mescaleros "whenever, and wherever" he found them, at the same time, should Confederates be found, "make the country very warm for them and the road difficult." In the meantime, Carleton was to establish a post "at the Bosque Redondo, on the Pecos River [i.e., should the Secretary of War approve] to be known as Fort Sumner, in honor of that staunch patriot and veteran soldier, Major General Edwin V. Sumner, U.S.A., who was formerly the Commander of this Department."[20]

On October 26, Captain Backus learned that "a party had gone down the river," and since he had instructions to arrest all white men going in either direction, the party must be arrested. Therefore, Lieutenant Shoup, with a detachment of Coloradoans, mostly composed of miners turned soldiers, took the trail. After following them

[20] G.O. No. 94, October 31, 1862, NA, RG 98, Dept. of N. M. Orders, Vol. 37, p. 288–89.

nearly 250 miles with the aid of some Comanches (who claimed they were fighting Confederates), they overtook the party. The fleeing party, seeing that the pursuers had their "guns cocked and aimed." dropped their arms without resistance. They identified themselves as the "Green Russell party,"[21] Besides considerable property of value, such as shotguns, rifles, revolvers, mules, horses, and wagons, they had "three well-developed cases of small-pox." That they were, in truth, the Green Russell party was vouched for by several of the soldiers, who recognized Green Russell as their former employer and the discoverer of gold in the vicinity of Denver, as well as a noncombatant Southern sympathizer. They then made it known that besides their camp equipage, smallpox, etc., they were carrying a large quantity of gold dust. No mention was made of the relatively worthless mule shoes carried in a sack: "Mere camp equipage." They were on their way to their homes, Georgia, Arkansas, Missouri, and the Cherokee Nation.

Seeing that the Union troops were merely going to make them prisoners, about one hundred Indians came into camp to protest: They had been out to fight Confederates, and, having captured none, demanded that "they must have a man now . . . to have a war dance." Since furnishing a Confederate for a war dance was not Lieutenant Shoup's idea of disposing of Confederate prisoners, he bargained with his aids and abettors, persuading them to go away and come back tomorrow "to receive their presents." They came, bringing with them "head chief Mouwa and fifty more Indians." The head chief renewed the demand "for a man as well as half the property." After "talking all evening, they separated the best of friends," but not until they had been fed sumptuously.

After the departure of the Indians, Dr. Russell revealed that two of the smallpox patients were too ill to travel. When resting a day did not improve their condition, the afflicted ones were left behind

[21] Other members of the party were Dr. D. I. Russell, J. O. Russell, Sam Bates, John Wallace, Robert Fields, James Pierce, James Whiting, A. S. Rippy, H. M. Dempey, W. I. Witcher, Wm. Witcher, D. Patterson, G. F. Rives, J. Gloss, W. Odem, Isaac Roberts, J. P. Potts, and six children of the Potts family.

with two soldier guards. One of the sick men was named Potts. His motherless children went along with the troops, but not his "possessions." The children were soon fatherless as well as motherless, to say nothing of penniless, for "all the family money [so reported the soldier guards] was buried with him."

Upon arrival at Fort Union, after being searched, the prisoners were found to possess "some treasure—gold dust, watches, chains, rings, etc.," all of which, for the time being, they were permitted to keep. Too, they were noted to be "high toned gentlemen." Their leader, Green Russell, in addition was quite distinguished in appearance "with his two strands of plaited beard stuck down his shirt front." General Carleton took note of the eminence of his prisoner—"well known in California and Colorado as a successful miner"—and also took from him "some $28 000 in gold dust, which he caused to be deposited in the U.S. Depository" in Santa Fe. The men were placed in jail. But as Carleton could not make himself come to "believe that these men have ever given aid and comfort to the enemy, and were only trying to reach their families, which was but natural," they were put on parole at the post to recover "from the smallpox." Finally, with three of the party dead of the disease, the gold dust in Carleton's coffer, and Pott's money buried on the prairie, the orphan children became the object of the largess of kindly disposed New Mexicans, and Captain Plympton served as trustee of the "contributions for the Sick and orphaned children." Since the United States marshal would not proceed against the prisoners, their possessions were released to be "handed to the parties interested."[22] After the departure of the survivors of the party—"all having gone to Colorado under proper care," with the exception of the oldest of the girls, who went away as the wife of a Union officer—a contribution belatedly arrived. Not being able to distribute it according to the wishes of the donor, General Carleton disposed of it by sending it to "S. Seligman, who had

[22] A.C., "Fort Union, 1863," File 1, p. 64; NA, RG 98, Dept. of N. M. Letters, Vol. 13, p. 367; A.C., "Fort Union, 1863," File 1, p. 46; Elma Dill Russell Spencer, "Famous Fugitives of Fort Union," *New Mexico Historical Review,* Vol. XXXII (1957), 1.

collected it with instruction that *it be expended for the purpose of beautifying the Plaza of Santa Fe.*" It was not, however, until after the beautification of the plaza became a reality that it became known that the quantity of mules shoes so carefully guarded in the sack were "shoes and gold coin thrown carelessly" together, so that they might more readily be handled on a pack mule and at the same time be effectively disguised.[23]

[23] "Tales of Early Days," *Santa Fe Daily New Mexican,* January 12, 1886, p. 1, col. 4. The "sack of mule shoes" story is incomplete without notice of the fact that Green Russell, after taking the oath of allegiance and being released, equipped and commanded a Confederate company with "mule shoe money," while Oliver served as his lieutenant. Oliver later moved to Texas, where he became a rich and distinguished cattleman. W. I. Witcher also went to Texas, locating at Hamilton in that newly organized county, where, emboldened with a superabundance of liquor, he bragged of his cattle on the thousand hills. His neighbors, however, noted the number of cattle bearing his burnt monogram far exceeded the multiparous powers of the cattle really owned by him. As a consequence, he was not rated the county's indispensable citizen. Then, when he developed a propensity for disturbing the peace —especially of schools and churches—his career came to an abrupt end one Sunday night when he rode back and forth before the Hamilton Baptist Church shooting and yelling. The deacon of the church paused in his benediction long enough to go to the door and discharge the full contents of his "pepper-box" into the body of the fleeing horseman. The following day the townfolk turned out in mass to view the body of the recent departed lying in state on the public square. (Hervey E. Chesley, "Notes of Hamilton County, Texas," MS now in possession of the author.)

CHAPTER FOURTEEN

THE THIRD FORT UNION

EARLY IN NOVEMBER, 1862, General Carleton visited Fort Union to examine the post. He found the structures erected prior to the war by Colonel Sibley "greatly out of repair." Other buildings were "in a tolerable state of preservation," but all taken together were "not of sufficient capacity" or so located as to meet the wants of the quartermaster. To carry out the rebuilding plans made by Canby would involve authorizing a greater expenditure than Carleton was willing to make; therefore, he directed that roofs be put on walls already standing, the adobes piled "so as to save them from disintegration," and "all employees [discharged] at once whose services can be dispensed with," while awaiting specific instructions from the War Department. He withheld his recommendations when writing the War Department, objecting to the rebuilding at Fort Union, thinking "the site too far from water" but intimating that the entire establishment should go to Albuquerque. "He had no opinion," however, "on the Albuquerque site, for my children are interested in that property."[1]

Rumors "of a circumstantial character" reached Carleton after he had suspended work on Fort Union, discharging all employees. They gave him an excuse "to suspend the movement to Colorado of the

[1] While Carleton was simulating a modesty which prevented his urging the removal of Fort Union to his Albuquerque property, he was at the same time asking the government to reimburse him for burning the houses on the same land during the Civil War, an act made necessary to prevent stores from being taken by the Confederates when the Union forces fled to Santa Fe. In support of his plea, he wrote: "If the United States had vacated and not destroyed the property, it could have been rented to others, but now all my children have to contemplate . . . is a blackened mass of unproductive ruins. . . . This property takes everything I have in the world. I have only my commission—after 20 odd years of hard work! And if I should die tomorrow, my children would be beggars!"

handful of Volunteers belonging to that Territory" while "he waited to learn more of the matter," for, at the moment it was only a rumor that the Texans were returning. But the more he thought about it, the more excited he became, even calling upon the Adjutant General "to give him authority to call for all the troops in Colorado Territory to help repel" the Texans. Moreover, the troops should "be instructed by Telegraph to be ready to march at a moment's notice." While the Colorado troops were coming, he wanted the War Department to "rest assured that, whether we have help or not, we will give the enemy as warm a reception as we can."

The circumstantial rumor was then relayed to Commander Plympton at Fort Union: Baylor had returned from Richmond, Virginia, to San Antonio with orders to march to New Mexico again, to take the territory "and hold it at all hazards." What route Baylor might take, Carleton's rumor did not disclose; but he thought "the country was so extended and so open to attack along its eastern frontier, and has so many avenues of approach from the rebel states of Arkansas and Texas, either of which an enemy can choose, and cover his real designs by diversions" that there must be mature reflection to perfect a plan to repel the threatened attack."

Immediately, however, in preparation for defense at Fort Union, Captain Robb's company of Colorado Volunteers was to go to the Gallinas Mountains, there to remain for four weeks "cutting abattis for Fort Union," while Plympton must complete the defenses "with vigor until done . . . giving his personal supervision to the work." Similar activity must be engaged in at Fort Craig, which, like Fort Union, "is to be held with the old flag flying over it as long as a man . . . can pull a trigger, it makes no difference what force comes against it."[2]

Carleton was of the opinion that Baylor's return to New Mexico would not be by Sibley's route, but would be up the Pecos straight toward Fort Union, but, in his frenzy of directing he included Colonel Riggs in his shower of orders. He was to require all the officers at Fort Craig "to help you." He was himself to "set the example of labor and

[2] Carleton to Riggs, NA, RG 98, Dept. of N. M. Letters, Vol. 13, p. 215.

industry morning and night." Not only were the defenses at the post to be strengthened, but all the grain in the Mesilla Valley was to be bought. If owners refused to sell, "it must be seized and receipts given for it. Under no circumstance will it be left to feed the enemy." Propaganda must be used effectively: "The people living in the . . . Valley should be caused to believe that when the Texans come it will be to fatten upon them without pay." They must be reminded "of how they were robbed before." And the Union officers were "to animate—as you can do"—the *Nuevo Mejicanos* "with a settled determination to attack the enemy from every corner; to shoot down their teams; to stampede their stock when grazing; to destroy the bridges . . . to hover by night around their camps; to set fire to the grass . . . to shoot down their men at night . . . then before day to scatter in all directions." And Carleton admonished Colonel West, while inspiring *Nuevo Mejicanos* to hate, scourge, and impoverish the Confederates, to avail himself of this feeling to get "all good Union men among the Americans to rally around him." Those who did not rally, "all doubtful Americans and foreigners," were to be seized and sent "strongly guarded" to the fort, where, "with the spade, at least, they could help defend the flag." All who belong "to this class of men would suffer their houses and stores to be laid in ashes." Such destruction of necessity would include the mills, but their destruction would not be of great consequence, for the breadstuffs would be removed by the Union forces, and the burning of the mills "would be no serious blow" to the *Nuevo Mejicanos* for "the population who prefer to remain behind can grind their corn on Metates as of old."

At Fort Union, Plympton was to concentrate on making a magazine, none having been provided when the Star Fort was dug. For this necessity the military storekeeper was "to provide the 'plan,'" which he promptly did, it to be "within the entrenched works."[3]

[3] Carleton to Plympton, November 23, 1862, NA, RG 98, Dept. of N. M. Letters, Vol. 13, p. 186. The "plan" specified that the magazine be "within the entrenched works, an excavation 60x28x8 feet, the walls to be formed by upright timbers, lined by rough boards, 14 feet to the plate. The roof . . . boards to receive the earth . . . excavated . . . covered with dirt 3 feet in thickness in order to be bombproof."

While the plans were being evolved, news came from Captain Mills, stationed at Hart's Mills [El Paso] that "The talk of the town is that the Texan troops are at Fort Clark [Texas] and that one Skillman was thought to be the precursor of the approach of the force . . . coming from Texas." Then, realizing that all extra employees at Fort Union had been discharged and that laborers were much in want, Carleton thought he would employ the great confidence the *Nuevo Mejicanos* had in Colonel Céran St. Vrain and through him use their meager talents at Fort Union. Hence, a letter went to St. Vrain:

> We have quite circumstantial rumors that the Texans are coming back, six thousand of them. . . . You know how disastrous this will be to the country. . . . The defenses of Fort Union need a great deal of work . . . I have thought if you would come here in person and would call for one hundred of your good neighbors in Taos to come too, for twenty days, the example would be very great for others to follow. Your social position is such that if you start the movement the whole country would emulate your example. Pray, let me count on you and your hundred fine fellows for twenty days at Fort Union—and right away![4]

Generously, Carleton let it be known that "We will feed them—but we have no money to pay them." But to the assistant quartermaster, at the same time, went orders to "hire thirty first class laborers at once that the magazine may be completed in haste." When that work was done, they could perform "other necessary labor in and about the Field Work."[5]

After Baylor's invasion from Texas did not materialize, Carleton took notice of the fact that the commanding officer's quarters at Fort Union were not in keeping with his position. To correct this deficiency, orders were issued Captain Plymptom to "at once tear down the old house on the hill, known as Col. Sumner's house—which was formerly used as a Hospital at Fort Union . . . and use it to make a set of officer's quarters, say, four rooms and a kitchen, with a yard, complete and comfortable." For the necessary labor, soldiers were to

[4] Carleton to St. Vrain, December 8, 1862, NA, RG 98, Dept. of N. M. Letters, Vol. 13, p. 226.

[5] G.O. No. 209, NA, RG 98, Dept. of N. M. Orders, Vol. 40, p. 209.

be withdrawn from their "regular duties," and to supply their places, prisoners would go from Fort Marcy. They would come "securely ironed and securely guarded—citizen prisoners, Rapp, Munson, Peck and Griffith," as well as Beardsley, who might go without irons. At Fort Union they were "to be put to work on the trenches securely ironed."

Before the old Sumner house could be torn down and made ready for the post commander, Washington's approval to proceed with Canby's plan to rebuild Fort Union arrived.[6] Only two days elapsed before Captain N. S. Davis, acting assistant quartermaster, was on his way to Fort Union to "complete the New Depot and Post of Fort Union in accordance with the approved plans." The work was to be done as soon as possible, not forgetting, however, that "the strictest economy must be observed." In the interest of economy, material was to be salvaged from other buildings. Salvaging must include "the windows and doors, as well as other material in the Quarters in the Demi-lunes of the Field Work . . . as well as that in the storehouses in the Field Work." And so as not to interfere with Davis' construction, Captain Plympton was to vacate his quarters immediately "and occupy the new set of quarters recently erected by the Depot Quartermaster." No one would thereafter occupy "quarters in what is known as Old Fort Union," except the assistant surgeon.[7]

By the third week in April, although Forts Craig and Union were "to be prepared and . . . vigilant . . . and to press the work on the defenses until we have certain intelligence that this rumored advance has no foundation," Carleton believed that Skillman, and perhaps three or four hundred Texan desperadoes, only intended to "raid into the Rio Grande with a view of plunder. But whatever the intention, the commander "had no fears of the honor of the flag while protected by Californians," for "Texans neither love to be killed nor to encounter men who can give them *quid pro quo.*" The soldiers at Fort Union must be "prepared to fight by night or day at a moment's

[6] Carleton to Thomas, April 5, 1863, NA, RG 98, Dept. of N. M. Letters, Vol. 13, p. 410; also, April 12, 1863.
[7] McFerran to Davis, April 6, 1863, AC, "Fort Union. 1863," File 2, p. 4.

notice."[8] All were not of that disposition, however. Cremony must be urged to keep up "discipline and Drill," but he "would fight splendidly." The same could not be said of Lieutenant Bennett; orders were to "look sharp after that Lieutenant. . . . He drinks hard, and in other respects will bear a great deal of scrutiny."[9]

On June 19, a board of officers met at Fort Union to point out the most suitable site for building a hospital. The Secretary of War had directed that they take into consideration "the ground-plan of the post" so that "the position of the Hospital and that of the garrison be adjusted most favorably for the comfort of the patients, and the sanitary condition of the troops."[10]

Captain Davis' construction crews, upon being admonished to complete "the New Depot and Post of Fort Union . . . as soon as possible," interpreted their orders literally, and paid little if any regard to the rights of adjacent property owners. When, after three weeks, complaints to the officers in charge were of no avail, Davis' ruthlessness was brought to the attention of military headquarters by "a most respectable Citizen (Don Juan María Baca) of Las Vegas." He had received "daily and considerable damage from those who are at work near Fort Union, in Supplying the Fort, with wood, and Timbers. The individuals so occupied, with impunity go to the herds of cattle, take what they can find, kill, and appropriate to their own use and benefit, such cattle as they want; and when our pastors go to their Camps, to seek redress, they [the individuals] take hold of their arms, and drive them away."

Another complaint came to the General commanding, this time from the guardhouse, a letter written in red ink and furtively passed through the prison guard so as to avoid the notice of the post commander. Private Eli McJones, a Colorado Volunteer, instead of being on his way home as he had a right to expect, was in the Fort Union

[8] Carleton to Plympton, April 26, 1863, NA, RG 98, Dept. of N. M. Letters, Vol. 13, p. 417.

[9] Carleton to Updegrass, May 3, 1863, NA, RG 98, Dept. of N. M. Letters, Vol. 13, p. 442; also, Carleton to Shinn, May 5, 1863, *ibid.*, p. 449.

[10] S.O. No. 34, NA, RG 98, Dept. of N. M. Orders, Vol. 40, pp. 263-65.

prison, and "had been there three weeks tomorrow." And, although he "had been tried sixteen days for missing two roll calls," his sentence "had not been read out" and he did not "know what it will be," but at the moment all he wanted was to get out. Therefore, he was "under the painful necessity" of addressing General Carleton "a few lines . . . , knowing him to be a man of Sense and Power." The imprisoned McJones thought that, as such, Carleton would want "to look into the way volunteers are persecuted." Coloradans, according to the writer, "have lefte 2 $3.00 per day for to fight for their country and are ready to die in defense of the Union, Sir." Furthermore, they

> had no privileges whatever, only to work on these breastworks, a thing we have done cheerfully, now for two years almost only when on the long sandy desert marching; heretofore, we have been allowed 24 hour passes coming off guard, but here we are not allowed nothing of the kind but kept pened up like so many sheep and worked like a set of negroes. . . . This is not the kind of Soldering I Enlisted for. . . . I am not what is called a guardhouse duck or a louse of the guard. . . . All I want now is to get out . . . .[11]

In early September, 1863, Captain William Craig, depot quartermaster, Fort Union, brought down upon himself the wrath of the department commander when he aligned himself politically with the aspirations of José Gallegos, one-time priest turned politician after refusing to conform to the decrees of Bishop Lamy. Acting under the manipulations of "Dr. Leib and his agency," Quartermaster Craig proposed "to concentrate all the trains and men possible at the Fort by election day—the first Monday in September . . . then discharge them on saturday with the understanding that they shall be re-employed on tuesday," all "these men were to be sent to Mora, or other places to vote for Gallegos." Learning of the political maneuver, Carleton could "not believe that such a gross abuse of power has even been thought of, but to prevent the possible contingency of anything of the sort," he "gave strict orders." To insure no possible interference "of certain parties in Las Vegas with the sacred rights of

[11] AC, "Fort Union, 1863," File 5, p. 77.

the people of all shades of political opinion to go peaceably to the ballot box to vote for whomsoever they pleased," Captain Davis left with "a party of twenty picked men." They were prepared "to arrest any person who shall by bullying, or threats, or otherwise interfere." As he anticipated *"heavy disturbance* and violation of the laws," he made certain that "an officer of discretion and troops were nearby."[12]

An inspection at Fort Union resulted in "charges and specifications against J. C. C. Downing, Assistant Surgeon, U.S.A., and Post Surgeon at Fort Union." The accusation was neglect of duty, failing to attend the sick for three successive days, and four days of neglect to "bestow any attention upon Priv. Yost, in a helpless condition."[13] Upon learning of Dr. Downing's derelictions, another Colorado Volunteer took "the audacious privalege [*sic*] to address" General Carleton, "regardless of military Etiquette to ask a privalege." His request was:

> I am in an infirm condition. Since I came on the Riogrand diseases have followed me thick and fast. My sufferings are intolerable   I have the gravel or stone in the Blader & an obstinate ulser in the er and piles of an agrivating kind   I wish to visit Santa Fe goe before the *medical* directors to see *if* they can doe aney thing for me   if not I want my discharge.[14]

As Baylor's threat to invade came to be known for what it really was, a rumor, the impetuous Carleton employed his energies in "weeding from the service" and confining "traitors, and drunken, dishonest and unprincipled officers."[15] William Craig, rebuffed in his effort to further the election of former priest José Gallegos, tendered his resig-

---

[12] Carleton to Davis, August 30, 1863, NA, RG 98, Dept. of N. M. Letters, Vol. 14, pp. 55–56.

[13] Charges and Specifications *vs.* J. C. C. Downing, AC, "Fort Union, 1863," File 5, p. 62.

[14] Alex S. Adams, Fort Union, to Carleton, AC, "Fort Union, 1863," File 5, p. 83.

[15] Carleton to A. G., Washington, D.C., February 22, 1864, NA, RG 98, Dept. of N. M. Letters, Vol. 14, p. 317. Some other than Fort Union officers to be "weeded" by Carleton are the following:

Lt. Robert Postle, requested to resign from a regiment where he was "not regarded by his brother officers as a gentlemen."

nation as post quartermaster and left the service. Captain Asa B. Carey, successor to Captain Craig, served but briefly until commandeered by Kit Carson to help out in his Navaho war, and Carleton moved Captain Amos F. Garrison to Fort Union to serve as depot commissary in addition to his duties as chief commissary. Garrison registered dissatisfaction, declaring the assignment "quite a hardship." Then he committed lese majesty by expressing the opinion that "Carleton should be removed from command of this department."

Gen. Joseph L. West, charged with lack of courtesy to superior officer and withholding "funds not his own."

Captain Archer, charged with collusion with contractor Angerstein.

Contractor Angerstein, "a notorious secessionist"; collusion with General West and Captain Archer.

Captain J. F. Bennett, "using terms expressive of much bitterness and hatred toward General Carleton, saying the "General had screws loose in his head."

Rev. Damacio Taladrid, chaplain, resigned.

Maj. Arthur Morrison, charged with drunkenness.

Private Coffield, charged with murder and ordered "securely ironed."

Lt. Mortimer, charged with "tarrying about Los Pinos for some unknown and unwarrantable cause." Ordered to "file his resignation."

Lt. John Lewis, dismissed peremptorily.

Lt. Maxwell, resigned on his own accord.

John Murphy, resigned; charges preferred.

Perry J. Eyre, resigned; charges preferred.

Surgeon J. H. Prentiss, resigned; charges preferred.

2d. Lt. E. Depew, resigned.

Private John W. Davis, deserted; arrested; sentenced to be shot. Carleton intervened since the "victim was really penitent"; also, he was "a member of the California Column," and had "lost a brother in battle . . . and would hereafter keep true to the flag."

Col. Geo. W. Bowie, offered to resign, but Carleton tendered appointment "of a two company Infantry post at or near the new Gold Fields," where he could "have a start."

Captain H. N. Enos, acting chief quartermaster, for betting at cards with some friends contrary to disbursing-officer regulations, but Carleton did not consider it to the "interest of the government to discharge him since he was needed to select a site of a post near the Gold Fields."

Capt. A. F. Garrison, imprisoned at Fort Union for ignoring channels of communication and imputing a lack of integrity to Carleton.

Private Canfield, desertion.

Capt. E. Everett, ordered to resign.

Surgeon J. M. McNulty, criticized for overstaying leave.

Secretary of State W. F. M. Arny was Garrison's confidant. Instead of relaying the opinion to Washington "to bring this removal about," Arny repeated it to Carleton, who placed the Captain under arrest at Fort Union, and submitted to the Adjutant General of the army the proposition that "Captain Garrison should at once be removed from this department for what must be considered as a disrespectful act, if not a flippant piece of impertinence," as it was "exceedingly disagreeable to have him serve longer" on his staff.[16]

Capt. William Craig, A.Q., Fort Union, tired of service under Carleton's direction, resigned.

Lt. Archibald McEachran, "drunkenness and other misdemeanors," consisting of shortage in accounts; jailed at Fort Union.

Captain Jules Barbey, "conduct of such a character as nothing could save his commission."

2d Lt. Jesús María Tafolla, promoted from sergeant to lieutenant, then "tried and reduced to ranks account conduct prejudicial to good order and military discipline."

Dr. Lieb, intimidating voters and "exercising his latent talent for gaining the contempt of gentlemen"; driven off the military post.

Lt. Jos. Laughlin, ordered to resign.

Capt. Samuel, A. A. Q.M., "left the department for Chihuahua 'under suspicion of integrity.'"

Maj. Joe D. Sena, resigned after inconspicuous but faithful service.

Private V. Dominguez, deserted, arrested, ordered to be shot; sentence commuted to "remain in the service three additional years."

Antonio Guttierres, same as Dominguez.

Jesús Montoya, same as Dominguez, the three deserters "each to wear ball and chain."

Private Rodriguez, "unceremoniously declared his independence of the army"; landed in jail at Fort Union.

William Sheets, deserted, escaped Fort Union, going as far as Kansas City, under alias Wm. Baker.

Lt. John Ferran, borrowed $600 from his men; "expended it in fit[t]ing himself out, buying a horse etc.; then leaving for parts unknown."

Private Nestor Gallegos, deserted; arrested; sentenced to be shot. At the last moment, at the roll of the drums, reprieved by Carleton as "an example."

[16] General Carleton kept Captain Garrison under arrest at Fort Union for a year, after which he was removed by higher authority from the department to prevent Carleton's having the satisfaction of court-martialing him. See No. 1013, Carleton to Eaton, November 9, 1865, NA, RG 98, Dept. of N. M. Letters, Vol. 16, p. 464.

With his mind yet on the Civil War, trying to weed out from the army ranks traitors, drunks, and dishonest and unprincipled officers, and "detecting traitors who are still plotting to bring this beautiful country under the cloud, and the blight, and the mildew which seems to overshadow as a pall, and attach as a curse to every spot of our beloved land over which this cruel Rebellion has had sway," Carleton was confronted with another kind of disorder. On May 25, 1864, some "40 robbers—supposed to be Texans" waylaid the train of Don Manuel Otero, east of Fort Union, on the Cimarron Route, and took from him eighty American mules and ten thousand dollars in cash. The Don's wagonmaster, instead of reporting his loss to Fort Union, made his accounting to the owner at Peralta, which, of necessity, delayed any effort to apprehend the robbers. When the news was finally received by Carleton, he was not inclined to believe that the Texans "committed the act," having had it from the Comanche chief that there "were no Texans on the plains," and therefore it was "possible the robbers were from *this* Territory." Fort Union was ordered to select fifty cavalrymen "to see what can be learned of the facts . . . and if possible overtake them [the robbers] and recapture the property and money." The general revamping of the military organization, however, had deprived Fort Union of the required number of horses for the scout. Such as were available were pressed into the service, the remainder being borrowed from Mr. Krönig and Lucien Maxwell, to Carleton "an embarrassing case of necessity."[17] This was painfully so, since the commander at Fort Union had "to hire some ox-teams to do the work of the post."

Not waiting for the borrowing of horses and improvising of ox-teams at Fort Union, the robbers struck again, on May 20. This time they pounced upon D. Felix García, a freighter from Santa Fe. García, too, ignored Fort Union as a source of help, calling upon Governor Henry Connelly, instead, saying, ". . . there came upon us a band of rogues of forty-eight in number, all Americans, who killed one of

[17] Carleton to McMullen, C.O., Fort Union, June 4, 1864, AC, "Fort Union, 1864," File 4, p. 11.

the Indian herders and robbed all the rest of the train of the clothing and provisions . . . and the mules and horses they had for riding. . . . They had with them seventy or eighty mules—our oxen, they did not molest. . . . There can be no doubt that this is the same party that robbed Otero at Cedar Springs."

Trailing out of Fort Union, finally, under Special Order No. 107, went forty-eight cavalrymen and infantrymen and two *Nuevo Meji-cano* guides, "all mounted," some on borrowed horses, Captain Nico-las L. Davis commanding, accompanied by Lieutenant D. Cannon. They found "the Wagons of the train that had been robbed . . . but the trail made by the robbers had been obliterated" by intervening rains. The scouts then went "near the head of the Palo Duro," and being convinced that the robbers "did not come from, nor return to Texas," they turned back to Fort Union, not having "seen any Indians but having lost two horses and one mule . . . with all the men in good health."[18]

On May 16, 1864, Governor John Evans, of Colorado, writing from Denver, alerted the Department of New Mexico on the increase of Indian hostilities to the north and east along the Santa Fe Trail.[19] All the consolation Carleton deemed proper to give was, "Be of good cheer, for if Colorado and New Mexico join in hostilities against the Utes," they could be brought to such a state as to make any other campaign unnecessary." So far as furnishing any troops, Carleton could only, at the moment, call attention to the fact that he was "enagaged in the midst of active operations against the numerous hordes of Apaches of Arizona . . . that a band of guerillas had robbed some trains upon the Cimarron Route . . . and he had troops in pursuit from Fort Union." However, he would "try to get some more troops to Fort Union at the earliest practicable day"; then he would "help all we can." With this situation to the north and east of Fort Union,

[18] Davis to Adjutant, Fort Union, July 29, 1864, AC, "Fort Union, 1864," File 4, p. 120.

[19] Carleton to Evans, June 26, 1864, NA, RG 98, Dept. of N. M. Letters, Vol. 4, pp. 529–30.

freighter Charles G. Parker decided to send his wagons to Chihuahua instead of eastward over the Trail. William Krönig, from his ranch adjacent to Fort Union, decided to join Parker in the enterprise. His chief contribution to the Chihuahua-bound train was more of an attraction than a utility. He was to give the people a "free show." The caravan's first stand was at Santa Fe. There Mr. Krönig exhibited his camel, the *New Mexican* advertising it as "the only one remaining of those brought to this section of the country some years ago by Lieutenant Beale." Truthfully, said the newspaper, "It attracted much attention."[20]

The camel-led caravan was on the road but a short time when word came to Fort Union that a party of Indians had come south of the fort and were raiding in the neighborhood of Chaparito. Lieutenants Cannon and Heath, commanding detachments of cavalry and infantry, "took the trail."[21] The situation was further intensified by the arrival of Colonel Berea at the post, who reported the Indians of the plains very troublesome and menacing the safety of trains moving toward New Mexico. To check that menace, Captain Davis again—with his borrowed horses—"fifty Cavalry, Fifty Infantry, and two mountain howitzers" moved eastward along the Trail to "render such aid as in your judgment might be effected . . . to manage the matter as you may deem best." But with Davis only one day on the road, Nesario Gonzales came into the post from Anton Chico reporting "some Indians, probably Apaches, last monday run [*sic*] off 6,000 sheep and killed two herders." Furthermore, he had it from hearsay that "10,000 or 15,000 other stock had been taken by some thirty or forty Indians—all mounted." And then from Lower Cimarron Springs Mr. Allison told of the killing of five Americans and the loss of "cattle from a train of five wagons."[22]

When Lieutenant Heath came in after an absence of six days, all

[20] *Santa Fe New Mexican,* July 29, 1864, p. 2, col. 2.

[21] S.O. No. 127, August 4, 1864, NA, RG 98, Fort Union Orders, Vol. 43, pp. 71–72.

[22] Brigadier General Commanding to Carson, August 15, 1864, NA, RG 98, Dept. of N. M. Letters, Vol. 15 (11-A), p. 89.

he could report was that he had traveled "about one hundred and eighty miles," finding the bodies of nine men killed near Conchas Springs, while "five more were missing." But the "several thousand sheep—some cattle"—were not found. He thought "pursuit on my part unnecessary" since he had been told that "200 Navajo Indians from the reservation" had gone after the depredators. Accordingly he "proceeded in the direction of Anton Chico," but before he got there, one herder had been killed and one boy carried off, so he "took to the hills, but could get no trace of them on account of the heavy rains." The rain hindered him so much that he returned to the post.[23] In the meantime news came to Fort Union that "Mr. Parker has lost his mules near Fort Stanton."[24] That was not all. Mr. Krönig had lost his camel, much to the gastronomical delight of the hungry Indians. Although all of this loss could not be recovered, still Carleton put an "officer and thirteen of the California Cavalry, with pack mules going light . . . to rescue the mules and destroy the Indians. . . . *Every man must be a Cossack!* and a hero when the Indians are come up with!"[25]

By the end of August, 1864, Fort Union found itself practically encircled by marauding Indians. The fort was no longer a strong point of defense; it had turned into a reservoir of supplies. Its importance was chiefly as a place of safety for trains carrying all the supplies for the Army of the West. To provide necessary storage, and in compliance with the War Department plan, Captain Enos, A.Q.M., had 420 civilian employees engaged in erecting the necessary buildings. Captain Shoemaker added "thirteen hired men, at a salary of (average) $44.74 per month, to protect the arriving arsenal stores."[26] On September 7 orders went to Fort Canby "to send at once to Fort Union three of the weakest companies. Every man able to travel—

[23] Heath to Smith, August 10, 1864, AC, "Fort Union, 1864," File 5, p. 14.

[24] Brigadier General to C.O., Fort Stanton, August 12, 1864, NA, RG 98, Dept. of N. M. Letters, Vol. 15 (11–A), p. 78.

[25] Brigadier General to C.O., Fort Craig, August 12, 1864, NA, RG 98, Dept. of N. M. Letters, Vol. 15 (11–A), pp. 112–13.

[26] Enos to McMullen, August 31, 1864, AC, "Fort Union, 1864," File 5, p. 59; also, Post Returns, August, AC, File 5, p. 60.

prisoners and all—must be sent." They were to "go on foot, and as quick as possible." They were "greatly needed on account of the hostilities of the Indians of the Plains."

After calling in three of the weakest companies for service out of Fort Union, the department commander directed Kit Carson to meet him at Tecolote "next Friday night." After the conference, Carson went on to Taos, there to talk with Lucien Maxwell, who was reporting "some two hundred or more Indians (Utes) were willing and anxious to go to the plains and attack the Kiowas." Their anxiety, however, presupposed that the army would "furnish some rations, ammunitions—perhaps a blanket apiece—and that they would have whatever stock or other property they might capture." It was agreed that the terms of the Indians were acceptable and that Colonel Carson would proceed to Fort Union with his Indian warriors, the "main object being to have the Utes commit themselves in hostility to the Indians of the Plains," for in that way there would be less chance for them to join against the whites.

To his assistant adjutant general the commander confided that Carson's recruitment of Indians was "really a feint." He really did not want "Carson to be fitted out with an extensive expedition *now;* but wished this: If he can get—say—not less than two hundred or more than three hundred Utes to go—starting at once, he can have the help of the twenty-five cavalry from the California Company at Fort Union, and the help of the troops already on the plains . . . he is to have rifles (old and worn) and powder and ball, and a blanket apiece, and rations for the Utes. This movement is intended mainly to cripple the Indians of the Plains and commit the Utes to our side meantime."[27]

At the end of August, 1864, Carleton had succeeded in concentrating at Fort Union seven hundred troops. Under the rule of seniority, Colonel J. Francisco Cháves, a favorite among the New Mexican people, was entitled to the command. Instead of permitting him the

[27] Brigadier General to DeForrest (unofficial), September 24, 1864, NA, RG 98, Dept. of N. M. Letters, Vol. 15 (11-A), pp. 152–53.

choice post (as it was considered), Carleton sought to place him at the out-of-the-way station of Fort Bascom, whereupon Chávez submitted his resignation. The Santa Fe *New Mexican,* understanding that Carleton was but pursuing his policy of discrimination, came to his defense under a headline:

LIEUTENANT COLONEL CHAVES

Lieutenant Colonel Chaves was this week mustered out of the service, his term having expired. We regret the government loses his services. He is one of New Mexico's favorite sons and likes military life and duties; and no officer has more faithfully done his duty than he has; and at the same time he has been so persecuted by General Carleton by every means in his power. It seems that he exerted more than common his own activity to see how he could harass Colonel Chaves, and if possible to humiliate and crush his spirit. He would put him on service and drudgeries, try to degrade him in the eyes of officers and soldiers, and among the New Mexican people. But for these things the colonel would have remained in the army. He will not further risk General Carleton's power to oppress, persecute and humiliate him among his friends and countrymen.

Then, to blunt this outspoken public condemnation of the Brigadier General commanding, there was connivance between Carleton and Governor Connelly. Since the Carleton-launched Gila campaign had come to a close, the two publicity seekers thought to inspire plaudits from the people. *The New Mexican* was also taking cognizance of the close of the war, commenting facetiously, "This Apache expedition has lightened our paternal uncle's breeches pocket of at least one or two million dollars."[28] Connelly and Carleton, thereupon, in true *Nuevo Mejicano* style, decided upon a *promulgación.* But in New Mexico legal announcements, when sanctioned by the church, were *ex concesso*—or so accepted by *Nuevo Mejicanos* generally; therefore, it was valuable to have the participation of the Bishop. But the editor of *The New Mexican* being neither of the Church nor an apostle of Carletonism, took the occasion to report *"The Whys and the Wherefores* ... of Carleton ... Anti-Lincolnite ... malignant

[28] *Santa Fe New Mexican,* December 9, 1864.

partisan of McClellan . . . Yankee peddler . . . who gives army contracts only to McClellanites," particularly stressing the connivance of the Governor and the department commander and their use of the church to foster their purpose:

> He even profanes the sanctuary of the Most High to disseminate a lie. The Governor [Connelly], it is well known, is troubled semi-occasionally with symptoms of piety and a weak back. Here is a glorious opportunity for Major Pomposa to make a point—and he made it. Satan-like he sat "squat like a toad at the ear of Eve" in the executive office until he convinced His Excellency that the Indians were all subdued; that the powerful enemy was completely subjugated and lies prostrate at our feet. And what—said he in his blandest tones—would be more fitting than a proclamation, appointing a day of thanksgiving for the peace and tranquility of the Territory!! The Bishop, unfortunately, was absent on his California visit at the time, and the vicario, in the innocence of his heart, unsuspectingly granted the use of the church for a Te Deum to be sung on the occasion.
>
> The day came: all soldiers that could be mustered into line were ordered out; the band of music took its place at the head of the columns with brand-new instruments; and a procession was formed. His Excellency, enjoying a heavenly frame of mind, took part; and the crowd moved on.
>
> Inside the tabernacle in inconspicuous positions might have been seen one captain seeking promotion; two lieutenants whose applications for furloughs were on file in the adjutant's office; three contractors seeking relief; two hungry fellows seeking contracts: and the general's translator —eternal sunshine settled on his head; in fact, his head assumed a more sanguinary hue than ever—for never before had it found itself in such a situation since it was christened.

But the Commandante Himself Was Not Present.

And for what was the Church desecrated, but for buncombe? Was not this proclamation based upon a falsehood; known to be at the time; known to be so now. In what direction from Santa Fe can a man travel twenty miles without being armed to the teeth! . . . Are not robberies and murders by Indians of daily and nightly occurrence? and yet in the face and eyes of these facts, this man Carleton inveighed the Governor

into issuing a thanksgiving proclamation for his buncombe purposes.—
Eight thousand Indians
whose untutored minds
Don't know enough
to cover their behinds.[29]

In mid-March, 1865, the behavior of Captain W. R. Kemp, then serving as provost marshal, was such that Fort Union Assistant Surgeon J. W. Shout felt called upon to report to headquarters "the condition and capacity of Captain W. R. Kemp." The post commander immediately came to the Provost Marshal's defense, avowing that he had known the Captain "since his joining the Service and I have never yet seen him so much under the influence of Alcoholic Liquor as to incapacite him for any duty." Of this assurance, Carleton was skeptical, thinking it better "that a Board be requested."[30] Investigation of internal conditions at the post brought to the post commander's attention "that great nuisance to the post and depot at Fort Union, viz: Loma Parda." The chief quartermaster was thereupon ordered "to take a lease from the proprietors of the ground," after which destruction of the village "would be legal."[31] Of particular importance was the acquisition of a lease, at the moment, since members of Company G, New Mexico Infantry, had pointed out Loma Parda as the cache for thefts from Fort Union, accusing Captain José Beneficio Romero as the thief who had caused to be deposited there "three hundred pounds of flour . . . and four sacks of bacon."[32]

Disclosure of the thief's cache brought about a general inspection of the post. Inspector General Nelson H. Davis softened his criticisms, knowing as he did that most of the peculations had occurred under

[29] When the attack was made on General Carleton, eight thousand Mescalero and Navaho Indian prisoners at Fort Sumner were being given passes to leave the prison to go on hunts.

[30] Abreu to Cutler, March 15, 1865, AC, "Fort Union, March, 1865," File 2, p. 18.

[31] Carleton to Enos, March 31, 1865, NA, RG 98, Dept. of N. M. Letters, Vol. 16, p. 239.

[32] Affidavit, Members of Co. G, N. M. Inf., April 5, 1865, AC, "Fort Union, April, 1865," File 2, p. 62.

the command of Major Henry R. Selden, "who had suffered an extended period of illness and had but recently died, the command falling to Colonel Abreu. To Carleton the inspector surmised "from indications and reports" that the military affairs at Fort Union had been "indifferently attended to . . . military duty and inspection had been neglected . . . there was no manifestation of a proper zeal and spirit therein." Officers exhibited "apathy and lethargy." There was "too much interest in personal ease and indulgencies . . . deficiencies and surpluses were found." The post was "improperly policed and inspected . . . the ditches of the fieldworks were used as substitutes for suitable sinks." Some of the men "in the Mexican Companies look as if they were recruited to make the required number, and were available only for the consumption of rations."[33]

Carson's expedition finally took definite form, Carleton agreeing that the strength might be increased to three hundred men, but some "Apaches from Fort Sumner will have to be included." Supplies were to go from Fort Union to Carson at Maxwell's ranch. The shipment was to contain "one hundred and twenty blankets and one hundred and twenty shirts." The quartermaster must choose "red shirts and gray blankets as they are for the Indians." Special consideration must be given to Kau-i-at-ay, the head chief of the Utes." He was to have a horse to ride; and Fort Union's quartermaster must "retain one for him: a good one."

On November 10, having marched eastward from Maxwell's ranch, Carson, "with seventy-five Ute and Apache Indians," was in Fort Bascom, where he found "all the companies comprising the expedition." From Fort Bascom he moved to "a point known as the Adobe Fort, about two hundred miles east . . . on the Canadian," where he formed a depot.[34] Scouts were sent forward, who soon reported to Carson that "he would have no difficulty in finding all the Indians he desired." This proved to be true, for soon came the cry, "Bene-aca, bene-aca." Indians had been encountered. The Indians retreated to

[33] Carleton to C.O., Fort Union, March 22, 1865, NA, RG 98, Dept. of N.M. Letters, Vol. 16, p. 229.

[34] See Dr. Courtwright's *Reminiscences;* also Carson's Report, December 4, 1864.

the vicinity of the Old Adobe Walls. Within, Dr. Courtwright prepared a corner for a hospital. From this vantage point the doctor watched the battle: "Some twelve or fourteen hundred [Indians] with a dozen or more chiefs riding up and down their line haranguing . . . a finer sight I never saw." But when Carson put his howitzers into action, the scene changed: "Those, a moment before riding backwards and forwards, those that were standing in line, rose high in their stirrups and gazed a single moment with astonishment, then guiding their horses' heads away from us, and giving one concerted, prolonged yell, they started in a dead run." This precipitous retreat deceived Colonel Carson; he thought the battle was over.

During the fight before the Adobe Walls a young *Nuevo Mejicano* soldier of Carson's command was bitten on the finger by a rattlesnake. Fearing *crotalus atrox* more than Comanche arrows, he suspended participation in the battle to retire to Dr. Courtwright's emergency hospital, where the doctor "dressed his hand and gave him a stiff drink of whiskey, also heart stimulants." This ministration "made him very bold." So, when the Indians renewed the attack (which they did with great fury), the snake-bitten *Nuevo Mejicano* returned to the skirmish line, where soon "a Comanche rode up in a cloud of smoke." Then a gust of wind left the Comanche completely exposed. The Indian fired and missed, but the soldier was a better marksman and the Comanche fell dead from his horse. Instantly, the slayer "rushed forward to secure his scalp," but ten or more Indians interceded to bear away the body. This brought the *Nuevo Mejicanos'* comrades into the melee, they keeping "the enemy at bay while he finished the scalping operation." Then, having established his prowess, he gave the scalp to the doctor in appreciation of his kindness and the potency of his ministrations; but the doctor disclaimed any "use for it, and was just then more concerned about his own scalp," so he passed it along to Carson's scouts, who used it in their ceremonial scalp-dance. Before there was an opportunity for a scalp-dance, however, Carson, seeing that the Kiowas and Comanches were concentrating a formidable force and knowing that victory surely would soon turn into defeat, "marched into darkness for three hours . . .

and that ended the day's work." Carson had suffered 2 killed and 21 wounded, two of whom died later, while the Kiowas and Comanches suffered a loss nearly 100 killed and 150 wounded. After getting back to Fort Union, for a Christmas present to intensify their celebration, each man was issued "1 Gill of Whiskey." Three weeks later Carson disbanded his expeditionary force as the head chief of the Comanches came in "making overtures of peace."

Since many of the Fort Union soldiers had not been paid for eighteen months, Paymaster Marston, as 1865 drew to a close, was ordered to draw the necessary funds from the Santa Fe depository and make the trip to Fort Union. At the end of his third day of travel, the paymaster admitted "a little shock as he arrived at the fort." He found "a *Baile* in full blast . . . they were giving the most brilliant *baile* of the season . . . in one of the largest rooms of the Q.M. Department . . . *Senoritas* gorgeously arrayed— after their style—and gallant *Senors* ready to do or die, were tripping the light fantastic toe beneath the protecting folds of the star spangled banner." Sensing the dignified Marston's chagrin at "such hilarity," the participants gave as their excuse *New Year's Day,* although it was one day gone.

Finishing his duties at Fort Union, the paymaster left on January 3, being entertained at "the house of Mr. Krennic,[35] the largest farmer in the territory." The next day he started toward Chaparita, encountering "one of the steepest and most rugged hills. . . . To keep right end up was a problem for a philosopher," but he "overcame it—or came over it, as you please," the escort thereafter placing "themselves in the charge of the Govt. Agent, and were delivered to the hospitalities of a young mexican for the night." His "fare was chiefly *Chile-Colorado,* a combination of red pepper and lard, its component parts, red pepper, about one pint, ground with small pieces of beef -fried. . . . *the* dish of New Mexico—a rather warm dish for a novice." The paymaster, however, "skirmished with it a little, and made fair progress in its demolition." He was fed another "delectation . . . called *Tortele,* made of corn meal and water, spread over the knee instead of rolling pin and board, and baked on a flat

[35] Krönig, once owner of the camel.

stone. As the knee of the mexican is none of the cleanest, nor the stone of the neatest," all that the disconsolate paymaster could do was "consider the result." The following day, however, "furnished delicious meals . . . numerous herds of antelopes." But it also developed "a game of another stripe . . . a lot of Comanche Indians" who began to collect on every knoll "to dispute their passage and play a desperate game of scalps." The California scouts—"old hunters: hence it was greek against greek—charged with such vigor that the Indians wavered, then *better time was never made by Indian:* It was: *Run! Mr. Red Skin for your life."*

And while Paymaster Marston disputed access to the plains with "Mr. Red Skin," Mr. William Davis, "a Texas refugee," made his way to General Carleton to tell of the "assembling of an armed party near Gainesville and Fort Belknap in Texas . . . under the leadership of one Spruce M. Baird, who was formerly a lawyer in this Territory." It was "a marauding expedition" with New Mexico as destination. Informant Davis was not able to tell Carleton whether Judge Baird knew that "the *quasi* Confederate Govermanent had dissolved and scattered," Davis having left Texas before Richmond and Mobile had fallen, "nor had Lee and Johnson [*sic*] and Mosby surrendered." Under the conditions, Carleton gleefully directed his subordinates[36] that, if Baird knew of the status of the Confederacy, he and his followers "could not perform without putting themselves in the position of freebooters and pirates; for they represent no political nationality, and can not march under not even the flag of the so-called Confederate States." The consequence was, "Those men, wherever found, must be considered as outlaws, robbers and highwaymen for whom nothing awaits in prospect but a halter."

To insure a sufficient number of halters, Carleton sent out his familiar call for help. This time it was a plea to Washington for "two regiments of Infantry and one of Cavalry." These additional troops "should in my humble judgement [so he wrote] be ordered at once to meet the pressing demands of the service, and . . . occupy the proper

---

[36] Since it was surmised that Baird would move by way of the Pecos or Río Grande, orders were dispatched to Franklin (El Paso), Texas.

points along the frontiers of Texas and Mexico, which adjoins this Department." To the scare over the approach of Judge Baird, Carleton added the menace of "the Indian hostilities upon the plains." The Plains Indians, he admitted "require more troops than are here, properly, and speedily to bring them to a successful issue." It was, of course, "with reluctance" that he called upon the War Department for assistance, but "If superadded to these troubles the Territory is to be menaced by large bands of lawless ruffians, who flee from the great theatre of war to portions of the country so sparsely settled as to offer but a feeble resistance to their efforts at robbery and bloodshed . . . and New Mexico is one of them . . . timely and sufficient succor and protection should be forthcoming . . . now."[37]

The appeal to Washington was supplemented by a circular letter directed to Fort Union[38] disclosing the rumor that "a band of marauders and bushwhackers has been formed at, and near, Fort Belknap, Texas," to raid New Mexico. Should the Texans come, "they must be fought from the jump" and every man must do his utmost to destroy them. All must "fight like devils against these worse than devils." To avoid "a stampede if they come," the fight "must be a quiet business until it is accomplished." Then, in an effort further to inflame the prejudice of the *Nuevo Mejicanos* against the Terrible Texans, Carleton confirmed statements—"by another party—these being Mexicans"—that the Kiowas were very much aggrieved by the attack made on them by Colonel Carson, and were seeking revenge, "and being—as they say—*backed by the Texans*—will make a good thing of it this summer." Next, Carleton addressed to the editor of the *Gazette* a double-purpose diatribe, intended to influence the New Mexicans—"In order that they may know the matter as it is known at these headquarters"—pleading for "all good citizens to unite . . . to let by gones be by gones," now that the war was over (and at the same time inveighing against Judge Baird's brand of followers)—

[37] Carleton to A.G., U.S.A., Washington, D.C., May 9, 1865, NA, RG 98, Dept. of N. M. Letters, Vol. 16, p. 266.

[38] Fourteen copies were dispatched to various points in New Mexico, one being directed to Colonel Carson at Cold Springs Camp, the camp not even then established. NA, RG 98, Dept. of N. M. Letters, Vol. 16, p. 268–69, May 11, 1865.

"such men as would bring discredit upon any cause and disgrace any flag."

Then, having made a public record of his sentiments, Carleton passed along a copy of the newspaper to Brigadier General Connor, U.S. Volunteers, at Denver, indicating the necessity he was under to "call for some help from you, should the rumored raid into this country by bushwhackers and ruffians . . . spoondrift from the ocean of troubles . . . of the Quantrell and Anderson stamp" materialize. He could but presume "that these raiders would advance up the Pecos toward our depots at Fort Union."

CHAPTER FIFTEEN

POW-WOWS, SPEECH-MAKING, THIEVES, CUTTHROATS, DESERTERS

UNITED STATES SENATOR J. R. Doolittle wrote from Fort Lyon on June 11, 1865, advising officially that a Congressional committee was on its way to the Department of New Mexico "to inquire into Indian matters." General Carleton turned immediately to Colonel Carson, then at Cedar Bluffs, Cimarron route, hastily directing that the command be turned over to Major Pfeiffer and that Carson report to Santa Fe "at once." The committee would be in Fort Union "on Wednesday next." The investigation group "comprised, Major General McCook, Honorable J. R. Doolittle (Chairman), Vice President Foster, Mr. Ross (of the House), Doctor Davis and others." They were due to leave "Fort Union *direct* to visit the Bosque Redondo . . . to start from Fort Union next Thursday."[1]

Of first importance to the department commander was "the salute, due to the Vice President, Mr. Foster, i.e. seventeen guns," which would be fired upon his arrival at the fort.[2] As a precautionary measure, directions went to Fort Union to insure that Mr. Foster "receive the salute due his rank both by the troops at Fort Union and at Union Arsenal," and that the General "have everything . . . which may be required by him." While Major McCleave was making certain that all Indians were at the Bosque when the committee arrived and the guns at Fort Union were being primed for the Vice-President's salute, with General Carleton on the road to greet his guests, a private letter arrived from Captain Henry B. Bristol giving the very kind of news the General least wished to hear: Ganado Blanco, Barboncito Blanco,

---

[1] Letter No. 409, NA, RG 98, Dept. of N. M. Letters, Vol. 16, p. 295.
[2] Letters Nos. 411, 412, NA, RG 98, Dept. of N. M. Letters, Vol. 16, p. 295.

and some ten or twelve Navahos with their herds of horses and sheep had left the reservation for Chusca, their place of abode before they were made prisoners at Bosque Redondo. In fact, Captain Bristol "could not ascertain positively the number gone . . . but nearly all had taken leave who had stock to carry them." Forty cavalrymen had taken up pursuit. They had orders "to capture or destroy them wherever found." An alarm went out to the people "to have their herds brought in and carefully guarded until this matter is cleared up or adjusted." Don Ambrosio Armijo was to be importuned "to raise one hundred picked men, well mounted, Americans and Mexicans" and proceed to Galisteo . . . or in the direction of Anton Chico where he could get an idea of the whereabouts of the run-aways." Other citizens should be induced "to get out and attack these Indians"; their reward was to be "all the stock they can recover." Carleton, having tarried long enough to deliver himself of comprehensive instructions, "would continue to Fort Union . . . see the Congressional Committee . . . go on to the Bosque as soon as possible."

Major Fritz with his forty-five cavalrymen, "found a small trail leading south, some fifteen or eighteen horses," followed it to the "Tanks at the foot of the Oscura," and coming upon a rancheria, "captured four horses, one mule, and one burro, and one child about three years old." The troops contented themselves by "destroying everything in the village, broke up some twenty-five bows and a great many arrows." The soldiers drank some water left by the Indians in the camp, then "started for the Rio Grande" to water their horses.

A party of *Nuevo Mejicanos,* encouraged by Carleton's offer of "all the stock they could recover," had more success than the troops. A woman had been captured at the house of Juan C. Ysidro, brother of the *alcalde* at Bernalillo. She, with several others, had but recently escaped from the reservation. The "party of Mexicans captured herself but killed her husband and several others." After her capture, the brother of the *alcalde* "bought her for a cow and ten goats." Thereafter "she wanted to go back to the Bosque." More pleasing news was soon to come to the Bosque: The run-aways were returning to the reservation; they "got out of provisions and suffered greatly for want of water." It was "doubtful "if a single one had been able to cross the river." Those who were not captured "died from starvation or want of water." The final accounting showed: missing— "not exceeding twenty-eight or thirty."

Carleton explained to the committee: "It is believed by many officers here that these Navajos have been tampered with by men, who, for political purposes, have opposed the reservation and would be willing to see the interests of the country suffer, provided, they could advance their own."[3] *The Gazette* appraised the situation differently, in its query: "Can one eivine [divine?] a reason for the *Gazette*'s desire to stuff the public ear with the story that the Indians have all returned? May not the proximity of the Congressional Committee to Carleton's elbow be the true one!"[4]

The Doolittle committee, not waiting for General Carleton at Fort Union (who delayed at Tecolote to order scouts out after the runaways), took testimony there, then journeyed on to the Bosque Redondo, to Santa Fe, and finally to Denver, Colorado. From Denver the committee announced that the Commissioner of Indian Affairs "had a *carte blanche* to make treaties with all the Indians of the Plains."

Since such a delegation of authority would interfere with Carleton's military plans, Carleton immediately communicated his opinion to General McCook. Fearing that the General might misunderstand his voluntary officiousness, he hastened to declare it "merely a thought," but he "had no faith in treaties with Indians and think none should be made as a rule." However, since the committee thought "it to be the best plan to make treaties with the Indians of the Plains," he was decidedly of the opinion that "Mr. Dole and Colonel Leavenworth (not being men who understand Indian character as Colonel Carson and Mr. Bent do) should . . . retire from the treaty-making business." It was his "object to state [so he told General McCook[5]] . . . that if

[3] Cutler to Lewis, Santa Fe, June 25, 1865, NA, RG 98, Dept. of N. M. Letters, Vol. 16, p. 304.

[4] *Santa Fe New Mexican,* July 21, 1865, p. 2, col. 1.

[5] Carleton to McCook, July 17, 1865, NA, RG 98, Dept. of N. M. Letters, Vol. 16, p. 329.

Mr. Dole is charged with such extraordinary powers, and if Colonel Leavenworth is also clothed with treaty-making powers as an itinerary plenipotentiary, and then Colonel Carson and Mr. Bent are sent to talk with the same Indians, so many diverse and independent parties with so many diverse views, and encountering the Indians for talks and smokes at such unexpected times and places, may lead to some little confusion from the cross-purposes in which the parties may act." The Indians would "look upon such proceedings as a practical joke of their Great Father; as the result of some policy, which, being unable to fathom, they will charge to the general credit of a Big Medicine; or, abandoning all these grounds, will receive such proceedings with their accustomed gravity and revolve over and over again their probable purpose with an assumed, yet baffled, sagacity."

Carleton's unsolicited evaluation of the abilities of the treaty-makers resulted in Carson's receiving direct from Mr. Doolittle dispatches assigning him to a special mission on the plains. Complying with army punctilio, Carson relayed the correspondence to his commander. Carleton thereupon issued Special Order No. 22, authorizing him to co-operate with the committee. He was to accept the assignment and go on "Special Service upon the Plains for the purpose of seeing if the Comanches, Kioways, and other Indians living on, and South of the Arkansas River, cannot be induced to stop their acts of hostility."[6] To Colonel Carson (who had Mr. Doolittle's communications for guidance) Carleton felt himself "precluded from giving special instructions," but since he had no confidence in treaties with Indians, he wanted Carson "to look well to the country you pass over with an eye to the site of a large post *to be built in the place where the Kioways and Comanches spend their winters.*"

On July 12, 1865, the jail at Fort Union was closed as a place of confinement for all persons except "employees of the military departments of the government for crimes punishable by military law" and "persons from the so-called Confederate States who do not give a satisfactory account of themselves, or who do not shew undoubted

[6] S.O. No. 22, August 5, 1865, NA, RG 98, Dept. of N. M. Orders, Vol. 41, pp. 50–54.

evidence of having taken the oath of Allegiance to the United States."[7] Prior to the order reserving Fort Union's prison facilities for military offenders and Confederate miscreants, Private Charles W. Squiers, Second Colorado Volunteers, murdered Captain S. S. Soule, provost marshal, at Denver. Escaping arrest, he was "seen with a train below Pueblo en route to New Mexico . . . his arm bandaged and in a sling." Later, he was located by the commander at Fort Union "and caused to be followed." His pursuers were Lieutenant James D. Cannon and Captain Morton (himself under technical arrest for peculations at Fort Sumner), who took him into custody at Las Vegas. Although the Fort Union jail was full, room was found for him while awaiting orders to Lieutenant Cannon to "take the prisoner to Denver City with an escort." Being much in the favor of the commanding general, he prophetically surmised upon taking leave of his Fort Union and Fort Lyon companions that he would "be detained Sometime before I get back to Fort Union."[8] In this he was correct, for he died at the Tremont House in Denver, July 14, 1865, "Cause of death—Congestion of the Brain . . . the Lieutenant has been using liquor very freely." But Private Squiers, tiring of his restraint, escaped again, this time being very careful not to admit his identity.[9]

On September 11, the commander at Fort Union was told of the inadequacy of the jail at Mora, the civil authorities making a desperate call upon Colonel Willis to hurry a detachment from the fort to Mora "for the protection of the Moro [*sic*] jail from a threatening mob." The population there was "in open revolt against the civil authorities."

As the military responded to the call, the newspapers at Santa Fe nonplused the department commander by announcing that the Department of New Mexico had been abolished, that New Mexico had been assigned to the Department of California, and that Carleton

[7] Circular, Carleton to C.O., Fort Union, July 12, 1865, AC, "Fort Union, July, 1865," File 4, p. 50.

[8] Cannon to Colonel, Fort Lyon, July 3, 1865, AC, "Fort Union, July, 1865," File 4, p. 18.

[9] AC, "Fort Union, 1865," File 4, pp. 64–65.

would thereafter report to Colonel Richard C. Drum, assistant adjutant general at San Francisco.[10] Instead, the reduced commander bided the time he would receive General McDowell's order assuming command of New Mexico as a district of the Department of California. Then he wrote "as a matter of duty," he said, "having had service enough to form a judgment with reference to the military status of New Mexico as a command." He objected to New Mexico's being other than a department (not that he "should command it"), for it "could not be judged by a rule applicable to any other portion of the United States." So far as communications were concerned, "it should be regarded as an Island, with a prairie on the east . . . and a desert on the west." If the New Mexico Territory could not continue to form a department, then "the officer commanding it should be vested with the powers of a Department Commander, and be one of sufficient judgment to manage the details here without the embarrassments consequent upon delays and interruptions in his communications with higher authorities. If, then, he should have a Division Commander between himself and the headquarters of the army . . . that Division Commander should be on the shortest line between himself and Washington. In this case, New Mexico would belong to General Sherman's Division."[11]

Carleton sent Colonel Drum a photographic copy of a map of the Department of New Mexico, now defunct, for "future reference . . . to enable him to understand the position of the posts," describing Fort Union as the Number One Post, "near the western limits of the great plains which extend uninterruptedly from Fort Leavenworth to the Rocky Mountains. Here there is a defensive earthwork with temporary quarters in the demilunes for eight companies . . . the depot for quartermaster stores and the depot of subsistence are building . . . and new and permanent quarters for the four companies are also in process of erection." The ordnance stores, so he said, "were also at Fort Union . . . in the confused group of log and adobe buildings

[10] G.O. No. 1, NA, RG 98, Dept. of N. M. Orders, Vol. 38, pp. 283–85.

[11] Carleton to A.G., Washington, D.C., September 16, 1865, NA, RG 98, Dist. of N. M. Letters, Vol. 16, p. 416.

. . . erected from time to time since 1851." And although authority for erection of an arsenal had been approved for Fort Union, he recommended that it be built "near the junction of the Mora and Sapello Rivers, seven miles south of Fort Union."[12]

With official notice that the Department of New Mexico had been absorbed by the Department of California and the likelihood of a general inspection, Carleton informed General Eaton at Washington that large quantities of supplies shipped over the Santa Fe Trail were "not arriving at the fort." This shortage was in addition to spoilage. This loss, Carleton thought, was attributable to employees "who depredate on the stores entrusted to them, and sell many of the stores en route, and take the risk of deceiving Boards of Survey. If they have, now and then, a few articles charged to them at cost-price they lose nothing. . . . For example: A contractor deficient on flour would be obliged to pay only four dollars . . . while this staple is now selling in the vicinity of Fort Union, say, $18 per hundred pounds." But shortages at Fort Union, so Carleton hastened to disclose, were not limited to goods stolen in transit. One lot of 2,500 cattle received at Fort Union, after being weighed the second time, "had a difference of weight ascertained at Fort Union . . . of 180 000 pounds."

On October 10, the War Department acceded to Carleton's request, changing the jurisdiction of New Mexico and attaching it to the Department of the Missouri. Concurrently General Pope directed the return to California of the California Volunteers. Carleton immediately responded that this was "utterly impracticable" and made an effort to have the order rescinded, for he "could not dispense with the services of any company till more troops come." The commander's reaction to the removal of the California troops was prescient. On the very day that he objected there was a mass flight of the Mescaleros from Bosque Redondo,[13] with consequent orders for Fort Union to have "thirty-five or forty horses, which are doubtless fit for remounts for cavalry . . . at the Quartermaster Depot at Fort Union . . . care-

[12] Carleton to Drum, September 5, 1865, NA, RG 98, Dist. of N. M. Letters, Vol. 16, p. 409.

[13] NA, RG 98, Dist. of N. M. Letters, Vol. 16, p. 461.

fully shod at once," as well as Captains Henderson's and Fox's companies put on the road to Big Hill, "prepared at all points to fight." Those to go out after the run-aways were admonished, "It is no boy's play now; those Indians have got to be recaptured or killed." But if there was to be "dilly dallying, and talk, and no energy on the part of the troops and the people, that part of the country might as well be given up to the Indians first as last."[14] But despite the orders for two companies to move to the fight, Fort Union could find "only sixty-four men for duty." Captain Fox was not one of the number."[15]

The command at Fort Union was strengthened immeasurably during the last days of December, 1865. Colonel Christopher ("Kit") Carson, having completed his special services upon the plains and at St. Louis, came into Fort Union. Immediately orders were published assigning him to command.[16] Three days after Carson had assumed command at Fort Union, Carleton had to submit to the humility of forwarding to the Secretary of War "a Memorial to the President and Secretary of War, enacted by the Council of the House of Representatives of New Mexico, praying . . . that General James H. Carleton be relieved from this command." Defensively, Carleton avowed he had been "scurrillously condemned," that the memorial contained "foul aspersions," that the very men who had originated the slanders should be caused "to make good their words."[17]

Pleasing news, however, came to Carson. On January 2, 1866, he received a letter, one month in transit from the Secretary of War, informing him that the President had been pleased to appoint him a brevet brigadier general of United States Volunteers. This appointment Carson accepted with "grateful pleasure, though unsolicited by

[14] Carleton to Fritz, November 12, 1865, NA, RG 98, Dist. of N. M. Letters, Vol. 16, p. 462.

[15] DeForrest to C.O., Fort Union, November 12, 1865, NA, RG 98, Dist. of N. M. Letters, Vol. 16, p. 462.

[16] S.O. No. 13, December 8, 1865, NA, RG 98, Dist. of N. M. Orders, Vol. 41, pp. 91–92; also, G.O. No. 57, December 24, 1865, NA, RG 93, Fort Union Orders, Vol. 38. The order relieving Colonel Willis, Carson assuming command.

[17] Carleton to Secretary Stanton, December 27, 1865, NA, RG 98, Dist. of N. M. Letters, Vol. 16, p. 479.

me," and he did so "as a memento that during the late rebellion the exertions of the New Mexican Volunteers, though restricted in its sphere of usefulness to their own Territory, have not been overlooked by the United States Government." On January 13, 1866, General Carson opened the doors of the Fort Union jail "to all deserters from *volunteer* organizations," immediately discharging them from the service.[18] On the same day that General Carson was releasing imprisoned deserters forty men of the Seventh Cavalry, stationed at Fort Morgan, Colorado Territory, "deserted in a body, taking with them their horses and arms." Although they went in the direction of Denver, information existed to the effect that Mexico was their destination. Consequently, it was to be presumed they would pass through Fort Union; and Carleton told General Carson "to kill or capture every man in the party that can be found within the limits of your command."[19]

Within less than a month after assuming command at Fort Union, General Carson came under General Carleton's displeasure. It came to the commanding General's attention that P. G. D. Morton, convicted of irregularities connected with feeding the Basque Redondo Indian prisoners and serving out his sentence at Fort Union, was permitted the limits of the post, even going "as far away as Las Vegas." Such laxity on Carson's part was reprehensible to Carleton; consequently, General Carson was "to see the sentence and orders in the case." After seeing, he would "at once confine Morton in a room under a sentinel who belongs to the guard." Furthermore, Carson's officer-of-the-day was to be made "as responsible for him as for any other prisoner ... and he *under no circumstances* would be permitted to leave his place of confinement—except to answer calls of nature— when he would be accompanied by a sentinel. *This* will not be allowed after retreat at night until reveille next morning." Then, as a bitter rebuke to General Carson (striking through the helpless Cap-

[18] Circular letters, NA, RG 98, Dist. of N. M. Letters, Vol. 16, p. 488. This was done in conformity with an announced policy of the Secretary of War.

[19] To C.O., Fort Union, January 14, 1866, AC, "Fort Union, January, 1866." File I, p. 14.

tain Morton), Carleton concluded: "Should I find that the rule here laid down is violated by any sophistry which runs counter to its spirit, I shall order Captain Morton to be confined in the ordinary prison room of your guardhouse as other prisoners are confined [with] . . . no further consideration than the most humble of your prisoners."[20]

Three other "humble prisoners," confined in the ordinary prison room at Fort Union were to fare better at the review of their cases by the War Department. The day following Carleton's criticism of Carson for leniency toward Captain Morton, he passed along to Fort Union a headquarters order to release three privates of infantry, viz: James Dolores Espanosa, who was doing "hard labor in charge of a guard, forfeiting ten dollars per month of his pay, since August 5, 1865"; Pedro Archuleta, "confined at Hard labor in charge of the Guard . . . wearing a 24 pound ball attached to his left leg by a chain three feet long," under such restraint since September 5, 1865, and sentenced to "serve two more years," at the end of which he was to have "his head shaved and be drummed out of the service"; and Juan de Jesús Trujilla, "incarcerated since November 7, 1865, for desertion, but against whom no formal charges had been filed." On April 14, Judge John P. Slough appealed to Carson, "the Commandante, Fort Union," to relieve the sheriff of Taos of the responsibility of keeping "safely two soldiers LaCrux and Olivers who are charged with the crime of murder . . . because of the condition of the Jail and finances of the Country." Despite the order that Fort Union's jail would be limited in use, Carleton directed Carson to accept the Taos prisoners to prevent them from "escaping & desertion from service, [holding them] carefully *guarded* and ironed on legs."[21]

As General Carson tired of his position as military sheriff, he, on February 14, 1866, asked General Carleton if he might be mustered out of the service "on the last day of the present month." He wanted, so he said, "to avail himself of the first opportunity which offers

[20] Carleton to Carson, January 17, 1866, NA, RG 98, Dist. of N. M. Letters, Vol. 16, p. 490.

[21] AC, "Fort Union, April, 1866," File 1, p. 63.

itself for the purpose of agriculture." But instead of turning to agriculture, he took a leave from Fort Union, March 5, "to visit Taos, for the purpose of removing my wife and family."

On May 1, 1866, Carleton read in a newspaper Order No. 23, bearing the date of April 10, providing that James H. Carleton "be honorably mustered out of the service of the United States to date from April 30, 1866 . . . [account] services no longer required." In frustration, he sent a messenger with a note to General Carson still at Taos, reading: "I have been mustered out of the service as a Brig. General of Volunteers, and . . . the command devolves upon yourself. I would suggest that you come at once to Santa Fe and take charge of Headquarters, and publish an order assuming command. Meantime I will do the best I can to keep the current business running." For three days, awaiting the arrival of General Carson, he did the best he could, but before Carson could make his appearance, another order came: He would remain on duty in New Mexico according to his brevet rank, and Carson would transfer to Fort Garland, while Major John Thompson would command at Fort Union. In addition, the importance of Fort Union was to be enhanced: an ordnance reservation was ordered to occupy "the site of the Old Fort." Captain Shoemaker would remain in charge.

Post Commander Thompson, immediately upon succeeding General Carson, was introduced to the ever present disorder at Loma Parda. He sent Sergeant Martínez with three enlisted men "to arrest and send to the Post of Fort Union any and all soldiers who may visit the Loma Parda."[22] Three days later he supplemented this order by prohibiting "any and all enlisted men belonging to the Post of Fort Union from even visiting the Loma Parda, N.M., under any pretext whatever."[23] The penalty for 'infringement' was to be "severe punishment." The decision to place Loma Parda off limits had arisen from a breach of the peace on the night of the tenth of May, when two soldiers were brought into post badly wounded.[24] The sight of

---

[22] S.O. No. 56, May 25, 1866, NA, RG 93, Fort Union, N. M., Orders, Vol. 43, p. 239.
[23] S.O. No. 57, May 28, 1866. *ibid*.
[24] AC, "Fort Union, July, 1866," File 2, p. 32 (July 3).

the wounded men caused the Major to go to Loma Parda "to hear how it occurred." There he learned that "the attack was made by citizens of the place without any provocation on the part of the soldiers." Upon receiving this information the Major made "application to the Alcalde to have the parties arrested." Instead of complying, the *alcalde* "made requisition upon the commander for a number of soldiers charged with having committed a breach of the peace," a counteraction "made for the purpose of shielding the *Guilty* parties," since it was "a notorious fact that a majority of the residents of that place are *thieves* and *Cut-throats* subsisting entirely upon what they can procure from the soldiers and do not hesitate to resort to any means, however infamous, to procure it."

Fearing to clash with the civil authorities and "endeavouring to treat all persons with courtesy," Thompson "duly considered the requisition," passing it along to Santa Fe headquarters with the request that he be informed whether he must "accept the statement of these notorious characters, charging soldiers with offenses, and permit them to be taken to Loma Parda for trial by the Alcalde. . . ." Thompson warned that if such must be done, then "this post will be largely represented at that place, and the soldiers will be detained so long as a dollar, or a Dollar's worth of property can be gleaned from them." While Thompson hesitated, the *alcalde* acted. He arrested, disarmed, and held as hostages the very detachment sent by the Major to arrest and return Union soldiers from Loma Parde; and Sergeant Martínez, Privates Apodaca, Baca, Gonzáles, Cordero, Jesús Paz, and Polonio Paz found themselves "detained by the civil authorities" as hostages. Thereupon Lieutenant Thomas Clancy (acting under verbal instructions) proceeded to the "City of Hostages" to ask the *alcalde,* "Why these men are detained from their proper station?" The *alcalde* replied, "That is my business. I will keep them until I see fit to try them." Furthermore, he deemed it proper and timely to pay his disrespects to the inquisitive lieutenant, stating, "I do not care a damn for you, the commanding officer or any other military authority, and I will turn them loose when I get through with them, and after that they can go where they damn please."[25]

During the latter part of July, 1866, Fort Union had a very much excited and unexpected visitor. Casimer Sais came in from a sheep ranch beyond Red River asking "to live for safety some days in the guardhouse at Fort Union." He explained his unusual request by relating this story: He was at his sheep ranch "when two Indians came to my herd and killed three sheep. Of these I gave them one whereof to eat. An hour later another Ute came and wanted some meat. I gave this Ute some of the sheep already killed. The Ute said he would not have that sheep and would kill from the herd." This Sais would not permit, whereupon the Indian not only made it known that he would not only kill from the herd but he would kill Sais himself, and to show his resolution, "he drew an arrow and shot me through the coat." Sais then "fired a pistol twice at the Ute and killed him." The slain Ute was a son-in-law of Kaniatzi, the head chief.

The dead Ute's companions "waited for their companion for a long time, but he did not come. They went back and found him dead, with a bullet through his body and with one arm mangled." This made "The whole Ute tribe . . . very angry, and assumed a threatening attitude," all of which was sufficient to cause Sais to run away to the protection of Fort Union. But the Utes followed, demanding that the post commander surrender the Mexican to them. General Carleton, who was a Fort Union visitor at the time of the Utes' arrival, refused their request, telling them Sais "would be tried at Mora: that they could go there and tell their story." Though far from satisfied, they agreed and left for Maxwell's ranch. Carleton then directed the post commander to send Company F, Third U.S. Cavalry, to Maxwell's ranch in anticipation of more trouble.[26]

Lying alongside Casimer Sais in Fort Union's jail was another, involuntary, prisoner, who had quarreled with a teamster "while in a state of intoxication," and firing his pistol, had missed the teamster,

[25] Thereafter the obliging *alcalde* released the hostages. They returned to Fort Union, where Thompson arrested them for being "absent without leave."

[26] Carleton to Slough, Chief Justice, from Fort Union, August 19, 1866, AC, "Fort Union, August, 1866," No. 227.

but "the spent ball struck one of the soldiers . . . on the ankle, producing a slight contusion." This slight contusion, however, was sufficient cause for finding himself, four days later, in jail, now sober and penitent and appealing to the post commander for release. For justification he asserted, "Had I not been under the influence of liquor such an occurrence would not have happened." As for the future, he would "endeavor to conduct himself, were he set at liberty, in such a manner as to shew that the commander's favor was not improperly bestowed."

Another, by no means penitent, inmate of the lockup was Lieutenant Joseph I. Ennis, who had been guilty, not only of neglect of duty as an officer-of-the-day, but had "talked Grossly Disrespectful to the Commanding Officer, taking off his Sword & telling Colonel Marshall to place him under arrest." Colonel Marshall was an accommodating man.

After evading the demand of the Utes to surrender Sais to them for the murder of their chief's son-in-law, Carleton followed Company F, Third Cavalry to Maxwell's ranch, overtaking Lieutenant George J. Campbell at Cimarron. There he conveyed this message to the Lieutenant:

> I find that the Ute and Apache Indians who reside near this place are wholly destitute of food; the game has entirely gone; and they are forced to kill the stock of the people or starve. . . . killing the people's cattle and sheep leads to collisions. Already blood has been spilled. . . . In this matter the Indians cannot be blamed. The Indian Department does not feed them; and there is really left but one alternative for the Indians; that is, to kill stock, let the consequences be what they may, or perish . . . and now to kill them for committing depredations solely to save life cannot be justified. We have but one alternative. We have either got to feed the Indians, or let them kill the stock of the people. . . . I have therefore directed that some wheat meal and fresh meat be purchased to feed the Indians . . . until further orders. You will, therefore, receive from Mr. Maxwell . . . these articles. . . . The bounty of the government can only be bestowed upon those who behave themselves."[27]

[27] Carleton to Campbell (present), Cimarron, August 25, 1866, NA, RG 98, Dist. of N. M. Letters, Vol. 16, pp. 571-72.

With the Indians accepting the bounty bestowed upon them and Carleton determined that he "would not be *forced* into a war until I am right as well as ready," the Utes were quiet in the Maxwell region (with the exception of Colonel Alexander's clash—"chasing some Utes up the Purgatoire River") until "Lieutenant Campbell being drunk at Maxwell's . . . drew a pistol on Kaniatz." After that Carleton confessed "that the matter looked a little mixed." But the flare-up was of short duration, Kaniatz going into Fort Garland and surrendering himself and his hostile Ute followers to his friend, Kit Carson.

On October 27, 1866, *The New Mexican* with bold headlines was first to spread the news: *Carleton Removed*. Although the general had "heard" that this fate was soon to be his, the newspaper was first to obtain the details: so, editorially it said:

Carleton Removed

On the 19th of September an order was issued by the Secretary of War directing the commander of this Department to relieve Lt. Col. James H. Carleton . . . from duty in New Mexico and ordered him to join his regiment in the Department of the Gulf. It thus appears that our Territory will be relieved of the presence of this man Carleton who has so long lorded it over us. For five years . . . he has accomplished nothing for which he is entitled to the thanks or gratitude of the people or the confidence of the War Department. He has, however, gained for himself detestation and contempt . . . publicly and privately. The community at large will rejoice at his removal. With the means at his disposal, such as no other commander had, he has signally failed in giving peace. . . . Instead of placing troops where they were needed . . . he has stationed them where it would be most lucrative to speculators and favorites. . . . his administration . . . has been a most ignominious failure.

Now that it was public information that Carleton was to be sent away from the territory, General Hancock gave him advance notice that he would receive instructions to remove his troops "from the towns in New Mexico," and furthermore, he was "to make his permanent Headquarters at Fort Union." To the first proposal General

Carleton made prompt and explicit reply: "There are no troops stationed in any *towns* in New Mexico, except the towns of Albuquerque and Santa Fe." So far as Albuquerque was concerned, instead of
removing the troops, more should be placed there. As to Santa Fe,
there was no comment. And to the latter proposal, moving the headquarters to Fort Union, "while the quarters are on the eve of being
completed [it] would be *like a shot between wind and water.*" Then
the commander obligingly suggested, "Better wait until you come
and see for yourself."[28]

General Hancock failed to accept General Carleton's invitation,
but Dr. William A. Bell, an English physician with a bent toward
speculations in railroad building and land development, tarried long
enough at Fort Union in his quest for easy money to observe the fort-
building and the opportunities afforded there for peculations. He
saw Fort Union as "a bustling place . . . the largest military establishment to be found on the plains . . . the supply center from which
the forty or fifty lesser posts scattered over the country within a radius
of 500 miles or more are supplied with men, horses, ammunitions of
war, and often with everything needed for their support . . . a vast
collection of work-shops, storehouses, barracks, officer's quarters, and
officers of all kinds . . . a large settler's [*sic*] store . . . at which the
daily sales average 3 000 dollars. . . . Over 1 000 workmen" were kept
there "constantly employed, building and repairing wagons, gathering in and distributing supplies, making harness, putting up buildings, and attending to the long train of goods and supplies constantly
arriving and departing."

The immensity of these activities was enhanced in the doctor's mind
when he realized that everything had to be brought hundreds of
miles "by a slow and expensive mode of conveyance—600 miles by
wagon from the end of the railway, and nearly 1,500 by rail from St.
Louis." "Even a traveller," wrote the traveling doctor, "can not help
being amazed at the enormous expenditure of money necessary to
maintain so large an establishment in such a locality. The millions
of dollars which are yearly absorbed by such a place as Fort Union

[28] Carleton to Hancock, NA, RG 98, Dist. of N. M. Letters, Vol. 43, pp. 5-6.

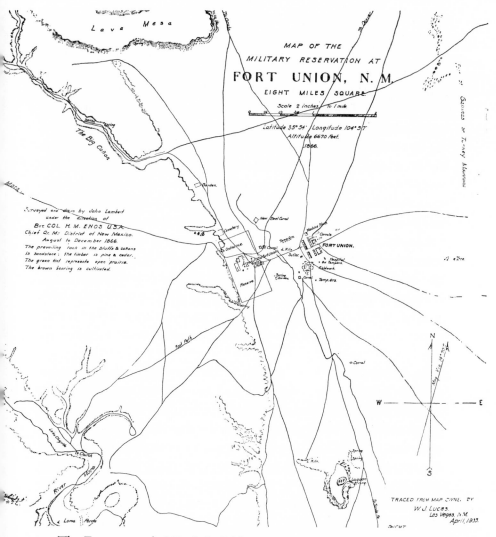

The Enos map of 1866 of the Military Reservation of Fort Union

must be something enormous; and the opportunity for peculation and growing fat by the misappliance of public money, by exorbitant charges, if not by actual fraud, are probably greater here than any other branch of the public service."[29]

[29] Dr. William A. Bell, *New Tracks in North America*, I, 120–35.

Even before attention was called to the Fort Union peculations by the observant Dr. Bell, Captain Andrés Tapia's activity had come under the observation of post commander Kit Carson. In mid-January, 1866, it was observed that he had "purchased such a large amount of subsistence stores" during the previous month that he was precluded from additional purchases until "he had satisfactorily accounted for the amount purchased in December." Furthermore, he was to be placed under arrest by Carson "should he not satisfactorily account" for his action.[30] But thefts were not always perpetrated with finesse. Even the military storekeeper, Shoemaker, had a brush with the thieves so blatantly that he was unable to defend himself and had to call upon the post commander for assistance. He had suffered the loss of a horse, and having found the horse, *demanded* it, but the man who had the horse "took it away again."[31] And while Captain Shoemaker was unsuccessfully demanding the return of his horse, it came to light that James Hegan, one of the Captain's employees, had succeeded in getting "more money from the quartermaster's department than he was justly entitled to," whereupon Shoemaker was precluded from paying "Hegan any wages . . . until further orders from headquarters."[32] At the post it became known that the baker had his "hands in the dough": he had stolen "bread and Flour to the amount of $200.00." Carleton, directing details as usual, ordered the bread thief tried by a garrison court. To this Major Marshall, commanding Fort Union, registered positive objection. He must be brought before the highest court as an example to other post bakers who might be guilty of the same offense. Furthermore, Major Marshall believed Private Snyder's case "a most aggravated one." With the proceeds of his thefts he had been "supporting two mexican women and playing at monte. . . . He requires a severe example."[33]

[30] DeForrest to Carson, January 14, 1866, AC, "Fort Union, January, 1866," File I, p. 13; also p. 18.

[31] AC, "Fort Union, 1866," File I, p. 89.

[32] Carleton to Shoemaker, May 19, 1866, NA, RG 98, Dist. of N. M. Letters, Vol. 16, p. 252.

[33] Marshall to A.A.G., Dept. of Mo., November 26, 1866, AC, "Fort Union, November, 1866."

Another situation at Fort Union was regarded as insupportable by the post commander. A practice had developed by "officer's servants [citizens] and government employees of both sexes to 'jump their contracts' and transfer to other employers to obtain higher wages." This freedom to choose employment, ruled Major Marshall, "needed thwarting." As a result, a circular posted at Fort Union, December 8, 1866, declared: "Hereafter officers' servants (citizens) and government employees of both sexes, who leave or are discharged from their places, will be sent immediately off the reserve, unless they obtain in writing a recommendation of good character. No person, so discharged, will be harbored at the post, coming from the Arsenal or Q.M. Depot. . . . The necessity of this order [is] for the mutual protection of the community. Often have officers brought at great personal expense their servants from the States, and immediately upon their arrival here, without even a warning, have them leave to obtain higher wages."[34] Almost immediately Fort Union's post adjutant notified both Captain Shoemaker and Captain Henry Inman, A.Q.M., that "a Colored Woman, named Cielia, has been ordered off the reservation for immoral conduct."[35] Cielia's departure was followed by another of Marshall's circulars. This time it was Annie McGee, "a vagrant and notoriously drunken and bad character," who had been "prowling around the garrison and entering officer's quarters." With Annie was to go "Coruz Benner, a Mexican Woman, late a Laundress . . . she having been discharged for being a woman of bad repute."[36]

And when Post Commander Marshall sought to banish "a certain servant girl" in the employ of Captain Henry Inman, the employer registered a protest, believing that "her Character has been misrepresented." Chaplain Woart came to her assistance, certifying "that during the trip across the Plains her conduct was excellent." As an added reason, for her retention, Captain Inman cited the "sickness of my Servants," leaving his household in a "very disorganized state,"

[34] Circular, December 8, 1866, Fort Union Headquarters, NA, RG 93, Fort Union Orders, Vol. 40, pp. 49–50.

[35] AC, "Fort Union, December, 1866," File 5, p. 51.

[36] Circular, December 12, 1866, NA, RG 93, Fort Union Orders, Vol. 40, p. 51.

so that he "would take it as a *personal favor*" if Marshall would rescind his order "so that no obstacle will remain in the way of my keeping her." To Marshall granting the request was "impossible," for the "woman was turned out of the Welches [*sic*] for talking too freely about officers and their families." Also, "Officers of the 5th have reputed her bad conduct since her arrival here and demanded action." Therefore, the decision was, "No *personal favor* can excuse a disobedience of my orders!"[37]

Thefts from the government were not limited to the commissary department. On January 18, 1866, Captain James R. Kemble, after inspecting his company, filed a requisition for fifty-five Remington revolvers to supply the deficiencies in his company. Since originally eighty-eight pistols had been issued, it was obvious that "the pistols had been sold by the men," for pistols of that manufacture cost the government (and the soldier, if he lost it) twelve dollars, while the selling price in New Mexico was fifty dollars.[38]

Commander Marshall attempted to refurbish the physical aspects of the post, also. In making a trip "along the road connecting the Post with the Arsenal," he found "police matter" of such a character "as to be extremely disagreeable to Ladies and Officers [who] come to church and visit the Post." As a consequence, it was ordered that thereafter refuse "must be thrown below the old post" and any "train must be required to encamp at a respectful distance so as not to annoy those passing."[39]

In February, 1867, Commander Marshall had General Carleton's enthusiastic co-operation in disposing of one of General Carson's favorite officers, Lieutenant Thomas W. Smith, of the newly formed battalion of New Mexico Volunteers. The Lieutenant's neglect of duty had caused him to tender his resignation direct to the Department of the Missouri. The department deemed it inappropriate to

[37] Inman to Marshall and Marshall to Inman, AC, "Fort Union, January, 1867," File 1, p. 7.

[38] Letter No. 54, January 26, 1867, NA, RG 98, Dist. of N. M. Letters, Vol. 43, pp. 70–71.

[39] S.O. No. 5, January 15, 1867, NA, RG 93, Fort Union Orders, Vol. 40, p. 55.

allow him to leave the service by resignation, so the matter was referred to Carleton, who ordered Carson to "file charges against this lieutenant" and muster him out of the army, "his services being no longer required. . . . He is nearly all the time drunk—and it is doubtful if he can keep sober long enough to try him. He has become a perfect sot ond seems lost to all sense of shame. He has done no duty to date from January 1 1867, and is now lying drunk, doubtless. . . . He is not worth the trouble or expense of a sentinel over him and a set of quarters; Nor is he worth the expense of a trial."

On January 20, 1867, Brevet Colonel Elisha G. Marshall retired as commander of Fort Union, after which he appeared before the Retiring Board and was permitted to leave the service "in consequence of very severe wounds received . . . at the Battle of Fredericksburg." Carleton wished him the "happiness and prosperity" which he had so well earned in the cause of his country, and at "the sacrifice of his health and his blood in sustaining the supremacy and honor of the National Flag." Brevet Colonel W. B. Lane relieved the Fredericksburg veteran as Fort Union's commander.

Immediately Colonel Lane became aware of "a nuisance at the post." The adjutant pointed out Lieutenant Speed as that "nuisance," stating that "the conduct of Speed is such that he has become such to the officers . . . by his habit and drunkenness." And even as he was being reported, he was "laboring under a fit of Delirium Tremens and Captain Henderson had been obliged to stay with him from 2 A.M. until daylight." The new commander attempted to shift the responsibility to Dr. DuBois, who asserted he was "well aware of the Lieutenant's condition, having treated him for two other attacks," and now he could only recommend that he be placed in charge of a "trusty non-commissioned officer" with admonition to forestall all visitors, "as well as prevent any stimulants being brought in." In such a way "alone [said the doctor] can the nuisance be abated." This attempt to control the officer resulted in "the dangerous character disturbing the whole neighborhood" and attempting to shoot Captain Henderson. Even now Dr. DuBois remained adamant: Speed was not to be admitted to the hospital. He did provide "a competent nurse . . . proper medicines . . . and put him in a tent," after which all the officers of the post signed a complaint specifying "habitual drunkenness, becoming a nuisance, and an attempt to shoot one Thomas Henderson." Thereafter, "This miserable man was . . . dismissed upon charges of the most disreputable character." After dismissal, "it leaked out . . . that he was also guilty of visiting the Town of Loma Parda, and gambling with Qr. Mr. Employees and Enlisted men, being absent without leave and returning [from Loma Parda] without Hat, coat or Pants, in almost a nude state to his quarters in the post."[40] Furthermore, it now became known that "Lieutenant Speed was in the habit of receiving supplies from the acting quartermaster Sergeant Gillon."

On October 13, 1866, a man applied "for the security of the military jail" at Fort Union. Albuquerque citizen George Withers, who admitted having "escaped from the jail in Mora, indicted for murder in that county" declared that he was "afraid to return to Mora and be placed in the Common Jail for the reason that there is danger of being hanged by the Mob." He would like to be "allowed to remain at Fort Union's jail until time for the Mora Court," certain that if placed "in the Mora Jail, I will be murdered."[41]

If conditions at Mora when Withers applied for the protection of Fort Union were similar to those of a decade later, then Withers' longevity was questionable. The clerk of the Mora District Court, in lieu of minutes, made the following official entry:

Fall Term Mora District Court 1876, Palen Judge
Atty. Gen. on a big drunk. Important Criminal Case pending. Judge Says atty gen'l must straighten for the next day. The bar—(that is, two of them including the U.S. Atty & a Subsequent Ch.J.) with the Clerk, found the Atty Gen. took him to his room & put him to bed take his cloth[es] except undergarments with them & lock the door. A subsequent examination in the evening find the window open & the Atty Gen gone. Suspecting his whereabouts the party meandered to proceed

[40] AC, "Fort Union, 1867," File 1, pp. 82–83.

[41] George Withers to Carleton, October 13, 1866, AC, "Fort Union, 1866," File 4, p. 53. The application was granted.

to an adjacent bagnio the Escaped in Company with an old one Eyed hag and her daughter. The Atty Gen. made an Excuse to change base—real object an opportunity to get a drink. Clothed in shirt & drawers he started holding the girl by one and and the old hag by the other. Coming to a Saloon he proposed to enter but his friends council NOT to be outdone seats himself in the road, holding tightly to them, the dame and the *"one eye."* The U.S. Atty & Sub Chief J., the clerk, then pick him up by main force by arms & legs, and car[r]y him to his room, he clinging to the Whorse Etc. Reaching the room it was found impossible to retain him unless he was furnished with Whiskey, So a bottle of Whiskey was procured and the three together lock up in the rooms & morning found him where he had been left. Subsequently one of the friends of the Atty. Gen. settled the bill of the *dove* $2.00. On Enquiring what Kind of a time she had, She replied: "Mui borracho!"[42]

In mid-February, 1867, Colonel Lane became distressed over the condition of the guardhouse at Fort Union. "The large number of men in confinement required a place of greater security.... Prisoners were constantly escaping." He called upon the quartermaster to put men to work on a new guardhouse without interfering with the completion of other buildings already being constructed.

A War Department directive forbidding the use of soldiers to apprehend violators of civil law, "whether white or Indian," had served to increase the number of robbers in the vicinity of Fort Union. One of their sources of loot was the government paymaster. Then, on March 2, 1867, a daring attempt was made to rob Paymaster Watts, while at San José en route to Fort Union, carrying $300,000. Upon his arrival at San José, Watts entered the post office, leaving the corporal of escort outside. A party of seven men approached, boldly disclosed their intention to rob the paymaster, and asked the corporal's cooperation. Pretending to acquiesce, thus getting the robbers off guard, he suddenly fired three shots at them, putting them to flight and saving the payroll.[43] They tried again at Hatch's ranch, their number having been increased to eleven, but they were again repulsed and "incontinently fled." A third effort was made in "the neighbor-

42 W. G. Ritch Papers, Archives, Santa Fe, Box 25.
43 *Santa Fe New Mexican,* March 2, 1867, p. 2, col. 1.

327

hood of Calhoun's Ranch." This time their luck ran out: two of their number were killed, "both Americans."

Next horse thieves made off with Fort Union's cavalry horses. Sergeant Young discovered them as he passed through Cherry Valley "down the river below the Fort." This discovery so incensed General Carleton that he suspended the War Department's instructions and ordered Fort Union's commander to "take a suitable party of men and go down the Mora River . . . and have all public animals brought to Fort Union." Should the thieves resist, the officer in charge was "to destroy all of them." Carleton would not "sit down and have a set of thieves run off our stock with impunity. The Civil authorities seem to be powerless to cope with them, and they gain in numbers and audacity all the time."[44] Colonel Lane chose to lead the detachment in person. After a narrow escape from ambush and assassination, the Colonel brought back five men, who were thrust into the overcrowded Fort Union jail with no probability of escaping, for they were "doubly ironed."

While the jail filled with thieves, cutthroats, deserters, and nondescripts, the Reverend Mr. Woart, post chaplain, had Colonel Lane's reminder that "the law . . . makes it the duty of the Chaplain to perform the duty of schoolmaster." Mr. Woart found such a duty "insufferable." "The reading of the document occasioned him *sorrow of heart.*" He had entered service with the impression that "Congress had placed chaplains in the army in a dignified & independent position as *Ministers of Christ.*" He would gladly supervise the schools, "as he could then continue his ministry, but if chaplains had to teach school, his views & feelings . . . would be different." At the moment he was in "doubt as to what to do . . . but he would advise with judicious Christian friends—trusting to Divine Providence. . . . But O! who can calculate the importance of ministerial duty & influence at our Military posts!"[45]

The post commander immediately became the friend-at-court to the Reverend Mr. Woart, pointing out that the chaplain not only

[44] NA, RG 98, Dist. of N. M. Letters, Vol. 43, p. 118.
[45] Post Chaplain to Lane, July 23, 1867, AC, "Fort Union, 1867," File 3, pp. 83–84.

was "doomed by orders to the indignity of a schoolteacher," but, because of the negligence of the government, he had to perform his ministerial duties "in quarters borrowed from The Templars." To correct this inadequacy, he forwarded direct to the Quartermaster General, at Washington, "Plans and Specifications for a Chapel for this Post, the basement to be used as a schoolroom for the enlisted men." He pressed his point, citing the fact that the post was in "process of construction" and that it was the intention of the War Department "to move the Hd Qrs of the District here." Furthermore, he emphasized the fact that "The Chaplain of the Post is the only Protestant in the Country, and often have the different denominations in the States endeavoured to obtain a footing here, but without success. Fort Union is the only place where such footing may be obtained, from which point other churches may in time Spring!"[46] He suggested construction be of stone, costing $17,987.

[46] Marshall to Q.M.G., Washington, D.C., AC, "Fort Union, 1867," File 1, p. 23. The Quartermaster General snuffed the dream of Marshall and the chaplain by ordering "quarters for troops first."

CHAPTER SIXTEEN

EXPANDED FORT UNION SUPERVISION

THROUGHOUT SEPTEMBER and two weeks of October in 1866 the weather was rainy at Fort Union, and as a result there was an increase in "Intermittent Fever and Rheumatism with heart complications due in great part to the casemated barracks occupied by the troops"; then, on the night of October 16, a rainstorm flooded the "Old Garrison," depositing in the underground quarters from eight to twelve inches of water. This brought a demand from the post commander that Assistant Quartermaster Inman turn over the new construction at the post for the use of the troops. However, since but one set of the new quarters were completed, the troops had to be moved out into tents.

Despite the insufficient housing, orders came from the Department of the Missouri to remove district headquarters from Santa Fe to Fort Union.[1] Colonel Marshall promptly demurred, stating, "There are no quarters at the Post for the Hd. Qrs. of the District." Furthermore, he did not "have stables for the use of the cavalry horses" and was contemplating turning over "two sets of Co. Quarters of the Old Garrison for that purpose . . . so there is no room at the post for the headquarters of the District." While refusing to provide quarters for the headquarters staff, Captain Inman announced "a set of Quarters in the New Post, designated for the Commanding Officer . . . ready for occupancy, and I officially turn them over to you." Two days later Commanding Officer Marshall indignantly rejected them: "I return to you the possession of the building . . . as not being *habitable,* and positively refuse to occupy the same unless the obstacles are over-

[1] Marshall to DeForrest, November 21, 1866, "Fort Union, November, 1866."

come. Three fireplaces or Chimneys smoke so that a man's life would
be endangered in occupying same!"[2]

While the Fort Union garrison tried to dry out its quarters, a band
of Utes and Apaches "passed through the town of Upper Las Vegas
driving thirty or forty head of horses and mules which had been
stolen from the neighborhood." Secretary W. F. M. Arny relayed the
information, which came to him from the probate judge of San
Miguel County. One man had been killed, one wounded, and two
children stolen. Later reports listed three men killed, three wounded,
"and five herders missing—as well as a considerable amount of stolen
stock." After this information came "officially" to the commander
at Fort Union, Colonel Bankhead "proceeded the same day to Los
[*sic*] Vegas." His instructions from General Carleton were to "investigate and report the facts in the case." This he did by "obtaining
the depositions of Juan Maria Baca and Simon Baca . . . represented
as responsible men," and he also "visited Simon Baca's herder, Manuel
Hanojos, finding him suffering from nine arrow and lance wounds."
Too, he found a twelve- or fourteen-year-old boy, "who was suffering
so much from his wounds" that he could obtain no information from
him.[3] Also from the Valley of St. Geronimo came the news that
Ramón Sánchez, near Tecolote, had been killed by thirty Indians,
having been "shot with a ball through the breast and through the
arm with an arrow."[4]

Then, before the Las Vegas investigation could be completed, Mr.
Tipton, from a few miles southeast of Fort Union, reported that
there was a raiding party "between Fort Sumner and Fort Union"
moving southward "with their booty." Mr. Tipton's herders had
accosted them, whereupon "they commenced to abuse and curse the
herders in the Mexican language," and the herders had fired at them.
At that "about 30 or 40 in number arose with their Arms in hand."
At the second fire Tipton's chief herder fell, mortally wounded, and

[2] AC, "Fort Union, December, 1866," February 5, pp. 66–68.
[3] AC, "Fort Union, October, 1866," File 4, pp. 93–94.
[4] *Ibid.*, pp. 95–96.

Mr. Watrous' chief herder was wounded. With this information, General Carleton closed the incident, expressing to Mr. Tipton "exceeding regrets that your people have been killed and wounded . . . but the Indians were fired upon first." For future protection, however, a company was sent to Fort Bascom "with orders to destroy all Indian *men* in that neighborhood . . . and those Indians found about Mr. Tipton's herds, who have no right there."[5]

In January, 1867, the Fort Union Hospital had twenty cases of scurvy. The disease was disabling the soldiers "to alarming extent," and Dr. DuBois, lacking sufficient quantities of fresh vegetables, prevailed upon Carleton to order the Commissary of Subsistence "to infringe upon War Department instructions and purchase fresh vegetables which were urgently needed for the health of the command."[6]

By March, 1867, the inundated Star Fort had deteriorated so much that post commander W. B. Lane directed Lieutenant Granville Lewis to make a thorough inspection and report concerning the propriety of demolishing it so as "to preserve the lumber . . . and promote discipline of the garrison." Taking advantage of the unoccupied underground quarters were "those who have authority to occupy them, and those who have not." As a disciplinary measure, "All citizens, male and female, having no employment under government, or any other person not having the authority of the post commander to remain on the Reservation will at once be removed from it," he ordered.

It took Lieutenant Lewis but one day to report his findings:
The *Old Post* or Earthwork, consists of three rows of partially underground frame structures in a very delapidated state, fast falling to decay and ruin [Portions of them are] occupied by citizens Employed in the Depot Quartermaster's Department who have Mexican women whom

[5] Carleton to Tipson, December 27, 1866, NA, RG 98, Dist. of N. M. Letters, Vol. 43, p. 37.

[6] Captain McClure complied with Dr. Du Bois' appeal. The Commissary General refused to honor McClure's accounts until appealed to by Commander Marshall, saying, ". . . a just government will agree that the issue should have been made and the small amount of funds employed does not compare with the loss . . . which would have occur [*sic*] by no issue."

they represent to be their wives. . . . [Besides the quartermaster's employees and their consorts, there are] a lot of Mexicans and unknown Americans harbored around these buildings—Gambling, Drinking and Prostitution seem to be the principal use to which many of the rooms are appropriated,—and soldiers of the garrison are enticed and harbored there to carouse all night. To such an extent have these orgies been carried on, drinking and fighting at all hours of the night, that the Guard have been compelled to make a descent upon and arrest the inmates and conduct them beyond the Military reservation and forbid them to return. . . . No doubt deserters are harbored in these places, and schemes concocted to Rob the Government.

In addition to Privates Judge, Jasper, Housebourn, Brushes, and their wives, employed as laundresses, the Lieutenant made a "List of Unauthorized Persons":

2 Rooms occupied by a carpenter in Depot Qm. Dept. Mexican woman Pictures of Rebel Generals & indecent subjects.

2 Rooms occupied by Painter in Depot QM. Dept. 2 Mexican women.

3 Rooms occupied by Tinner in Depot Qm. Dept. 2 Mex. women & 1 Man   Pictures of Rebel Generals.

2 Rooms occupied by a woman kept by a Mr. Magruder, Clk in Sutlers Store—others in rooms.

1 Room occupied by a Colored woman (Cecelia). [Note that Cecilia, or Ciella, was back from banishment.]

2 Rooms occupied by One Muggins, in Depot Qm. Dept. has a Mex. woman.

2 Rooms occupied by a Printer, in Depot Qm. Dept. has a Mex. woman.

1 Room occupied by a Carpenter in Depot Qm. Dept. 2 men & two Mex. Women.

2 Rooms occupied by Taylor—2 men & ? women Mex.

1 Room occupied by five Mexican men, have no occupation ? Mex. Woman, Gambling.

1 Room occupied by Teamster in Depot QMD 1 Mex Woman.

1 Room occupied by Mexican and woman.

On March 15, 1867, General Carleton received Special Order No. 46 relieving him from command of the department, but not before he had directed post commander Marshall not to tear down the buildings of the Star Fort. The new commander, however, countermanded the order, putting out of existence "Carleton's Star Fort—the den of rascals and crime."

On April 3, 1867, General Sykes had notice that the Commissary General of Subsistence had charged against him "certain issues" originating at Fort Union. One was molasses, thought by Dr. DuBois to be an "indispensable necessity to prevent the spread of scurvey"; the other was whisky. The issue of whisky came about as a result of the commander's putting five companies to work "gathering ice," of which they had "put up between three and four hundred tons . . . much needed where for six months the heat is oppressive, ranging above 100°." In doing the work, the soldiers had walked in "slush and water, many wet from head to foot, and all underwent an exposure that warranted the issue of a few gallons of whiskey." Sykes thought these considerations should be "sufficient to relieve him of the charges."[7]

On April 8, 1867, Dr. DuBois accepted the "Post and Depot Hospital with five separate wards and eighty-four beds." It had, however, "an inadequate detail of nurses." To alleviate the shortage, Dr. DuBois asked that he be allowed to detail Private Thomas King, still an inmate of the hospital, not requiring treatment but not fit for duty, as a nurse. This he deemed expedient, since he could do so "without placing white and black patients and Contagious Cases in the same wards." Recognizing the expediency, Commander Lane directed the post adjutant to "make the detail and file the papers."[8]

Unexpectedly a boon came to the hospital. John Smith and Andrew Cameron, emboldened by consumption of their own wares, invaded the Fort Union reservation, where they were caught selling whisky. The post commander forthwith issued Special Order No. 111, under which "their whiskey, and other property—mules, pony, burro, wagon and harness—was confiscated, the whiskey being turned over to the . . . Post Hospital . . . the other property to the Post Quartermaster,

[7] Sykes to Eaton, April 3, 1867, NA, RG 98, Dist. of N. M. Letters, Vol. 43, p. 134.
[8] AC, "Fort Union, 1867," File 2, p. 7.

and the men to the Guard House." Before delivery was made to the quartermaster, however, "there was goods stolen [from the prisoners' wagon] by the Soldiers . . . to the amount of about fifteen hundred dollars," which, the prisoners complained, "has in a pecuniary sense quite ruined us."[9]

On April 26, General Sykes was superseded by General George W. Getty, who reported, "All is quiet within the limits of the command."[10] Conditions remained so until June 4, when a premature discharge of an old six-pounder gun blew off one of Lieutenant Campbell's arms at Maxwell's ranch. Dr. DuBois hurriedly left the Fort Union hospital to care for the injured officer.[11] Then came news from General Custer that the Pawnees were killing whites "ten miles west of Fort McPherson" and that the "Cheyennes have turned south intending to go south of the Arkansas." Since these events promised trouble, General Getty called the Third Cavalry into Fort Union by "the shortest practicable route . . . prepared for field service." In an abundance of precaution, masters of wagons thereafter must "travel in groups large enough, and well armed, to protect themselves." William McLaughlin, quartermaster sergeant, Third U.S. Cavalry, was to "group the freighters." The rendezvous was to be König's ranch. With surprising rapidity the freight trains arrived: The first day, McLaughlin reported "12 teams here"; that evening, "20 more will reach here, having in all over 40 men." On June 19, Bonita Baca with a party of thirteen arrived. They were to go to Red River and wait there, after loading with wool, for about "40 teams . . . en route for the States." Then a Mr. Roole "reached here from Albuquerque" and went along with the Baca train. Four days later, "27 mule teams with 36 men came to Koenig's"; S. L. Luna was "the owner of the greater part of this train." Following close behind Luna's train "was a train of 46 teams (oxen)." McLaughlin had "some trouble with a Mexican in charge of the 10 first wagons of this train." The Mexican

---

[9] *Ibid.*, pp. 55–56 (February).

[10] Getty to Enos, April 27, 1867, NA, RG 98, Dist. of N. M. Letters, Vol. 43, p. 170.

[11] AC, "Fort Union, 1867," File 3, p. 4.

in charge wanted to go on alone, and McLaughlin was "having him brought back when 36 more came up." They waited as "more [are] expected tomorrow."[12]

While measures were being put into effect to guard against raids upon trains traveling the Santa Fe Trail, other news, of more immediate import, spread fear at Fort Union. Troops moving into New Mexico were bringing with them the scourge of cholera. The post surgeon at Fort Lyon, writing to Fort Union, "spoke of the prevalence of Cholera in two companies of the 38th Infty En route" to Fort Union. Post commander Lane immediately conferred with post surgeon Peters, who ordered a quarantine established near the post. Passing the responsibility to General Getty, Lane asked for "another company and more medical officers." Supplementing the order for quarantine, commander Lane appointed a board of health with instructions that "they be obeyed and respected accordingly." With the intention of having the post properly policed, the Board of Health "visited the Corral, used for slaughtering the Beef Cattle . . . found it in a most horrible Condition. Offal, filth, hides and hogs Scattered about in a miscellaneous manner . . . the whole Sufficient to produce and generate disease of any type." Furthermore, the corral was so situated that the drinking water used by the post and depot was contaminated.

After hearing that cholera-infected troops were moving toward Fort Union, Dr. DuBois left to intercept the battalion of the Thirty-eighth Infantry. General Getty hastened to Fort Union to co-operate with the doctor and ordered the troops to be halted "upon reaching Ocate Creek and await there for further orders." Further orders required them to go into camp at a point nine miles from Mr. Calhoun's ranch, with none of the command being permitted to come to the post—"either officers, Citizens, Soldiers, or Teamsters." The encampment pleased the travel-weary soldiers. They found it "one of the most beautiful and healthful . . . in a pine grove . . . more like a park . . . wood, fine grass, and pure mountain water in abundance." Occupying the quarantine encampment were "220 Enlisted men . . . 22

[12] McLaughlin to Lane, AC, "Fort Union, 1867," File 3, p. 43.

Civilians, employed as teamsters and herders, 3 officers (two married and their wifes [*sic*] . . . and six laundresses."

On August 12, 1867, the ban was lifted, and the cholera-quarantined Thirty-eighth Infantry moved on to Fort Union; but on August 20 another infected detachment appeared at the inspection point, which was forthwith "furnished a person to guide and point out the Quarantine Camp on the Ocate." It was then learned that Colonel Brown, sutler from Fort Sumner, had avoided the quarantine on the Ocate and had moved "within the environs of Fort Union with a party of nine, including two small children," intending to go on to Fort Sumner. Before moving, however, Brown's party was inspected by Dr. Peters, who did not find they "had anything like cholera," but he ordered them off the reservation without delay "as they are Citizens who have shown very little regard to Quarantine regulations."

By taking advantage of the lull in activities at Fort Union as a result of the cholera quarantine, Cherry Valley horse thieves came into the post and left with five government mules. When the loss was discovered, two soldiers were sent out to bring them back. Tracking them as far as Cherry Valley, they found the mules with "the U.S. brand already burned out and other brands put on them." The soldiers, after recovering the newly branded mules, "put off at a gallop for fear of being overtaken and killed." At Fort Union they reported "quite a number of fine mules in the herd supposed to belong to the government." Commander Lane, despite this information, did not dispute ownership, "as it was impossible to send after them, for it was with the greatest difficulty that he could mount a guard of six at his post and "carry on the other necessary duties." He therefore begged for "at least another Company of Cavalry . . . to prevent the almost daily stealing of mules." Too, he called the attention of the commanding general to the fact that "as the case now stands, I have some notoriously bad men in the guardhouse, and they outnumber the guard."[13]

Mules were not the only things stolen from the post. On August 29, "twenty-seven or twenty-eight Kegs of powder" were found to

[13] Lane to DeForrest, August 4, 1867, AC, "Fort Union, August, 1867," File 4, p. 5.

be missing from the magazine. In criticising Lane for this loss, DeForrest thought it "a sizeable quantity of powder to be exposed to Fort Union thieves over which no sentinel was posted."[14] And from Frank Weber of Las Golondrines came the complaint that, although he had furnished twelve men of Company A, Third U.S. Cavalry, with forage for their horses and had also provided them a place to sleep, they left "about three hours after all had gone to sleep, stealing and taking with them three turkeys, which they took from the roof of the stables," turkeys which he had "brought from the States under great Expenses for the purpose of raising stock"; and Mr. Weber demanded "Satisfaction."[15] The day following the turkey thefts, Fort Union's commander had thefts of greater magnitude to consider. Captain G. O. McMullen became one of the post's inmates under conviction of selling government property—flour, vinegar, bacon, and corn, soap, and coffee, to say nothing of one barrel of Bourbon whisky.[16]

But while the post commander puzzled over the method of recovering embezzled government property, a group of hostiles, this time a mixture of Mescalero Apaches and renegade Navahos, appeared "near Fort Union, and killed several Mexicans" who were herding their animals. A party of Third Cavalry under a captain "went out . . . but with no results." This so angered General Getty that he sent them back again, telling them, "Follow the trail until they are overtaken and punished."

On October 22, 1867, Lieutenant Deane Monahan placed Private McLaughlin in jail and kept him there for eight days without filing charges against him. To this action the post commander took exception, calling upon the Lieutenant for a full explanation. Monahan replied that the explanation was simple: he had put McLaughlin in jail "because of being continually drunk, and were it not for his

[14] DeForrest to Lane, August 29, 1867, NA, RG 98, Dist. of N. M. Letters, Vol. 43, p. 267.

[15] Frank Weber to Col. Lane, Fort Union, September 17, 1867, AC, "Fort Union, September, 1867."

[16] A.A.G. to P. H. Sheridan, March 27, 1868, AC, "Fort Union, March, 1868," File 1, p. 112.

being an old soldier I would prefer charges against him for *worth-lessness*." He would like to have him remain in jail until he could send him away from the post.[17]

By mid-September, 1867, Colonel Lane had information that the Cherry Valley thieves had removed from the vicinity of Fort Union to make their headquarters across the Raton Mountains and ply their trade in southern Colorado. Lieutenant Scott H. Robinson was directed to follow them to their new rendezvous. He soon learned of a "set of men on the Purgatory River who were stealing Government Stock," the citizens of the area being afraid to say anything about them as the thieves proclaimed openly that they would kill anyone who reported them. In substantiation of their threat, one man was killed the very day he indicated he would report them to the military authorities. Among those identified as members of the gang were "I. Smith . . . generally called 'Esquire Smith'; John Jackson . . . under sentence of death for murder . . . at Mora, but the citizens are afraid to arrest him; James Wadsworth who lives . . . at Union; . . . another one who sirname [*sic*] was unknown, but the thieves call him 'Dick' . . . an intrepid thief if not braggard . . . who boasted that about six weeks since he drove off twenty-nine head of Government mules from Fort Union . . . this theft accomplished by an arrangement with the man who had them in charge." Although the Lieutenant had discovered the identity of the thieves, he admitted his inability "to recover a single animal," nor had he attempted to capture the men, believing it "inopportune to attempt to take prisoners," not because of any doubt of their guilt, but because "they would in all probability escape." Therefore, he recommended "placing a party of soldiers . . . in the neighborhood as secretly as possible . . . lay around on the hills close to their headquarters and watch for them . . . and kill at least several of the leading ones."[18]

While Lieutenant Robinson "lay around on the hills" hoping to "kill at least several of the leading ones" north of the Raton Moun-

[17] Monahan to Wightman, October 30, 1867, AC, "Fort Union, October, 1867," File, 6, p. 66.

[18] Robinson to Lane, September 17, 1867, AC, "Fort Union, September, 1867," File 5, pp. 41–42.

tains, rustlers who came south into the Cimarron region to prey upon the miners of Elizabethtown were being stalked by Lieutenant Campbell, who had gone out of Fort Union under Colonel Lane's direction. Lieutenant Campbell had moderate success. He surrounded a house and arrested "a man named Cole," taking from him "4 Guns and a quantity of powder." He threw the powder in the river but appropriated the guns. He also found a mare "having the brand of L. B. Maxwell, Esquire, one mule branded L. M. and one having numerous brands, which he believed was a government mule." Cole plead for an opportunity "to vindicate his character" and "professed innocence" of being a horse thief, declaring that his being connected therewith was "only malice and originated principally from a man in Gov't Employ at Fort Union Depot, and who is a very doubtful character, named Fairchild."[19]

In addition to the horse thieves in the vicinity of the Cimarron, there was the ever perplexing problem of the Ute Indians. On September 23 the Department of Subsistence at Washington ruled that General Carleton's agreement with L. B. Maxwell to furnish supplies for the Utes would terminate on November 1, 1867, that any subsistence furnished thereafter must be through advertised bids. This decision made General Getty feel that it was necessary to keep troops in the region or remove the Indians. To the latter proposal both the Utes and Jicarillas presented an obstinate refusal, claiming the land by right of inheritance and refusing to move elsewhere without compensation. They had previously stated:

> We are separate and have never made any treaty with the Great Father; we travel over no lands but this: we know no other land, and want to stay here. Sometimes we go off but come back to this land again. The roads here have no blood on them, but the roads east and north are all bloody. On *our* roads who have been killed? On the Old Santa Fe road no one travels ... when do you see blood in our tracks. ... and we claim from the Arkansas.

Knowing that this amounted to a declaration of war if an attempt

[19] Fairchild, a one-time government employee, was at the time acting deputy sheriff at Mora, AC, "Fort Union, 1867," File 5, p. 67.

should be made to remove them and, furthermore, "that he could feed them cheaper than fight them," General Getty acquiesced, announcing that hereafter "contracts for subsistence for these Indians will be awarded to the lowest bidder" and that a detachment of Fort Union troops would remain in the vicinity of Maxwell's on the Cimarron.

On February 4, 1868, Acting Assistant Surgeon Longwill called on Fort Union's post adjutant for assistance at the hospital. One Private London, a prisoner, was beastly drunk and was being very abusive. If the adjutant would furnish the force, the doctor thought he could effect a cure: he would "tie him up by the hands for six hours, then put him in irons, thinking this *inducive to sobriety*."[20] The hospital had another unwelcome patient, Private Charles Lane, who was ushered out of the hospital into the guardhouse "for disorderly conduct," after which the doctor prescribed "the most potent medication." He was returned to his company "as fit for *full* duty."

On the night of June 23, 1868, two solitary prisoners, confined in the newly completed stone jail, made their escape. Prisoner Hardinger used the ruse of having the supernumerary of the guard "take him out for exercise a short time before tattoo." Once out, he fled into the darkness, "although fired on." And as Hardinger exercised himself in eluding the searching party, prisoner Ellis, having "in some manner become possessed of a skeleton key," walked calmly to freedom. In thus taking his departure, he did not mar a previous reputation of being "adept at burglary and housebreaking."[21] Another, not yet in the new stone prison but soon to find himself there (provided restraint, at the moment, suited him) was Private Charles McMann. He was to acquire the undisputed title of "Chief Obstructionist and Non-conformist Prisoner." His behavior came to the attention of department headquarters, after which Fort Union's commander, upon request, detailed the prisoner's diabolism:

I have the honor to acknowledge receipt of communication . . . calling

[20] Longwill to Post Adjutant, February 4, 1868, AC, "Fort Union, 1868," File 1, p. 40.

[21] Brooks to Hunter, July 2, 1868, AC, "July, 1868," File 3, p. 3.

for . . . facts in the case of prisoner Charles McMann, particularly as
to the necessity of ironing him. This man is of gigantic physical strength,
a horsethief, deserter, Sneak thief and hypocritical scoundrel in general.
His career . . . not withstanding the fact that he has been a prisoner,
has been one of drunkenness, violence and crime. With few exceptions
the enlisted men were completely cowed by him.

When he desired to leave the post, which he did from several days
to several weeks at a time, he did so without let or hindrance, on several
occasions breaking his way through the walls, sometimes of the guardhouse, sometimes of the Military Prison, and escaping in that manner.
Just previous to the departure of Major Alexander . . . he broke through
the walls of the Military Prison and partly succeeded in breaking down
the wall of the Cavalry corral appeariently [sic] endeavoring to Steal
horses; not succeeding in this he left the Post unhindered. At about
Revielle Major Alexander, Commanding, had a Cavalry company
mounted . . . and I heard him express his determination to pursue,
Capture and Kill McMann. It was not done, however. WHY, I do not
know. A few days [later?] McMann came back into the Post with an
insolent swagger and delivered himself up. A few nights afterwards,
he broke through the side of the guardhouse and escaped again. At
daylight, the ground being soft, I struck his trail and sent a Sergeant
and some Mounted men in pursuit. They captured him at a Mexican
town some ten miles from here in a state of semi-nudity, he having sold
his clothes. He was brought back to the Post when he attacked and
nearly succeeded in overpowering the entire Guard, and would have
done so had he not been brought to submit by repeated blows by the
butt end of their pieces.

A few days after this the Sergeant of the Guard reported . . . that he
had escaped from the Sentinal [sic] while cutting wood . . .; that night,
between ten and twelve o'clock the Post was startled by the most frightful yells . . . and McMann was discovered . . . executing a war dance and
swearing vengeance upon the officers of the Post. On the approach of
the Guard he attacked in a savage manner, but patience had ceased to
be a virtue with the long suffering men of the Garrison, and he was
promptly pulpified into quiet and placed in jail. The next morning . . .
he again aroused the Post by his diabolical yells, as his great strength
prevented a sufficient number of men from entering the cell to iron

342

him: he was again pulpified into silence. Violent conduct and brutal threats toward the Ladies and children of this post and his publicly expressed determination to set fire to the Quarters and Stables of the Post Surgeon, and Stables and Hayricks of the Depot Quartermaster, and to murder myself and Dr. Gardner immediately upon his release from confinement, I concluded to securely iron him. . . .

McMann became very abusive when getting measured for his Manacles; stating that I did not dare to put irons on him: that no commanding officer had dared to; that he would cut off any irons I could put on him . . . all this in the sight and hearing of the Guard.

When the Irons were made they were brought to my Quarters and examined and approved by Dr. Gardner, the Post Surgeon, and his assistant, Dr. McLain. I instructed to have them put on the Prisoner the next day; but that evening just before Retreat Dr. Gardner came . . . and earnestly recommended that they be put on immediately, as he had been told that McMann intended to break out of the Guard House that night and put his threat of murder and arson into execution: the irons were at once put on by candlelight.

Some days afterwards he went on Sick Report, and Dr. McLain informed me that he was trying to get an inflammatory action set up in his hands by causing the irons to fall with undue pressure on his wrists. I asked if the irons should be removed, to which the Doctor answered, "Decidedly not." When he found that he could not humbug the doctor, as he repeatedly boasted he had done at other posts, telling the men that Doctors and Chaplains were his pet game, no more complaint was heard from him.

A few days afterwards while passing the Guard House I met him going to the rear—with one hand he drew a pocket-handkerchief from his pocket and waved it at me in a insolent manner, at the same time placing the thumb of the other hand upon his nose, he gyrated the rest of the fingers in the air in a manner usually intended to be particularly exasperating. I merely mention this latter circumstance to show that the sturdy vagabond did not seem to be at all inconvenienced by the weight of his irons.

The above are but samples of his everyday life. . . . I think this man's character has been sufficiently made plain; and on several occasions Butcher Knives, files, duplicate keys of the prison Locks and duplicate keys of Patent Shackles have been taken from his person and from among his Blankets. I, myself, discovered and removed a large axe. . . ."[22]

Since a profusion of hirsute adornment was in vogue with both officers and men after the Civil War, in July, 1868, Fort Union's post adjutant moved to encourage a touch of pulchritude by standardizing the post barber charges. A bulletin was posted regulating "the charges both to Commissioned Officers and Elisted men," the specifications being:

> Shaving per month (Not more than three times per week), $1.50:
> Single Shave . . . $.15:
> Hair Cutting . . . $.30.
> Attendance exclusively upon Officers . . . 7 o'clock AM until 8 o'clock A.M. and 5 O'clock to 7 P.M.[23]

And as "an aid to the convenience of the officers," Sergeant Adolph Greisinger, whose term of military service was expiring, sought permission to establish at Fort Union "a Restaurant connected with a Bowling Alley." In this enterprise, he said, he had "the promise of support of friends in anything he would begin." Furthermore, since he was leaving the military service, he was "desirous to engage into respectable business," and what he had in mind "would greatly add to the comfort of the officers of Fort Union and for those passing through it." Exactly one week before Sergeant Greisinger determined to engage in a respectable business, however, the officer of the day registered a complaint against the extra-contract activities of the post trader, J. E. Barrow, doing business on the reservation under the name of Barrow & Barnard, demanding that the "drinking Sub-connected with [the] Billard Saloon at J. E. Barro's C. S. Store be closed immediately." The reason: ". . . liquors is sold there to soldiers by the drink . . . daily . . . [which] tends to keep men in the Guard House." The complaining officer also understood that "the Saloon pays better than the Store"—of this he "had no doubt!"

[22] Ellis to A.A.G., October 23, 1875, NA, RG 98, Fort Union Letter Books, Letters Sent, Vol. 16, pp. 382–86.

[23] Monahan to Post Barber, AC, "Fort Union, July, 1868," File 3, p. 37.

Upon being forbidden to sell "liquors of any description," partner Barnard quietly dissolved the partnership, being careful, however, to retain his position as post trader, no public mention being made of the dissolution until it was revealed incidentally when the *Daily New Mexican* reported "A Distinguished Visitor in New Mexico." By "private letter," it was made known that the distinguished visitor was Colonel John C. Dent, who was visiting his brother-in-law, W. D. W. Barnard, Esquire. That the distinguished visitor was a brother of Mrs. General Grant, wife of the President-elect of the United States, did not detract from his eminence. And thus the *New Mexican* could say, "We understand that Colonel Dent is a true gentleman and worthy of the close relationship with the President-elect." Moreover, it was "gratifying to learn that a prospect exists that the Colonel may make New Mexico his future home." This he did by forming a partnership with his brother-in-law, making Post Traders, Fort Union, New Mexico, thereafter Barnard & Dent.[24]

On February 10, 1869, for reasons of economy, it was decided to return the cavalry stationed at Cimarron and replace it with infantry from Fort Union. The exchange did not disturb the Indians in the vicinity. Then during August, J. J. Ennis, the Indian commissary agent was thrown from his horse and killed, Captain A. S. B. Keyes replacing him. When Keyes arbitrarily told the Indians that annuity goods which they had been accustomed to receive at Maxwell's ranch would be withheld pending their consent to removal to a reservation in Colorado, Mr. Maxwell, always alert to Ute and Jicarilla thinking, called upon Fort Union to send a cavalry force of not less than one hundred men. The Indians were prepared to hold their homeland.[25]

During the first week in June, 1869, there was trouble between the Negro soldiers at Fort Union and the resident *Nuevo Mejicanos*. On Saturday night, June 5, so reported the Santa Fe *Daily New Mexican,* "A serious fight occurred . . . between some Mexicans and 'darkies,'

[24] *Daily New Mexican,* November 30, 1868, p. 1, col. 4; "Colonel John C. Dent," December 4, 1868; April 2, 1869, p. 1, col. 4.
[25] Kobbe to Grier, December 13, 1869, NA, RG 98, Dist. of N. M. Letters, Vol. 44, pp. 432–33.

in a *baile* room at La Junta ... six or seven miles from Fort Union, in which two of the natives were severely handled, one being cut accross [*sic*] the abdomen and wrist and the other receiving slight cuts. Several shots were fired but no one was injured by them." Fort Union's Dr. Peters, however, who complained at having to furnish hospital supplies and services in such quantity, added more details to the racial clash:

> ...two negroes Jim Lawson and Johnson came to the Hospital badly wounded today. The wounds of the former are quite serious, and may result in the loss of the use of the left hand, even if it is not eventually to be amputated. The attendants at the Hospital is too limited for me to give him nursing, therefore request that some action be taken to compell [*sic*] the negroes (male) around the garrison to nurse this man. There are a number of negroes apparently loafing about the garrison without any visible means of support, and it appears to me that they should be made to thus assist one another, as I find they will not do it voluntarily. Many of these negroes carry weapons, such as razors, pistols, etc., which I have learned from experience in dressing wounds, they use freely in fracases occurring generally in the neighboring towns. I respectfully request that these negroes be put under restrictions in carrying arms at will, and that they be detained [restrained?] in engaging in further rows. The last row was between the negroes and the Mexicans, and the result, no doubt, of molestation on the part of the former.[26]

On Sunday night, after Dr. Peters had pleaded that the Fort Union Negroes be "detained from further rows," the doctor's skills were again in demand. A reporter for the *New Mexican* gave the story to his paper:

> Last night, while two or three darkies were coming here [Fort Union] from La Junta, one of them named Richard Henderson, a barber here, when within a few hundred yards of the post drew his pistol, saying: "I am going to have some fun to myself," fired and shot himself through the head just above the left eye. He is still insensible and not expected to recover.[27]

[26] AC, "Fort Union, 1869," File 2, p. 23.

[27] *Daily New Mexican,* June 8, 1869, p. 1, col. 4 (telegram of June 7, 1869).

All trouble makers, however, did not reach Fort Union environs. The *New Mexican* reported the continued absence of one intended prisoner, stating, "The constable and the prisoner disagreed as to which was the best route, *and as the prisoner has not been heard from since, it is supposed that he took the wrong road!*"

In 1866, President Andrew Johnson had appointed James L. Collins United States depositary with headquarters at Santa Fe. For recommendation he was "a so-called Santa Fe Trader," being a familiar figure "all the way from Independence to Chihuahua, Mexico." He also laid claim to "conspicuous service at Val Verde." Further, he had gone over the mountain into Apache Cañon with Colonel Slough in the action which enabled the Union detachment to destroy the Confederate supplies, thus effecting the retreat of the Texan-Confederate Army from New Mexico. He had been pension agent in New Mexico, although he was not indicted, as was his sub-agent, William Breeden, when a Civil War widow's pension failed to reach her in full. After Grant's election, Captain E. W. Little, "an ardent, earnest republican," taking a leave of absence, went East to visit friends and attend the inauguration. He returned with an appointment as Collins' successor. His arrival at Santa Fe was followed by an announcement that on "Thursday last [had been] delivered to the Depositary (Colonel James L. Collins) in sealed packages four hundred thousand dollars in greenbacks." Captain Little thereupon announced that he would assume the duties of his new office on Monday, June 7, "and receipt for the government money." On Sunday morning, however, a girl of the Collins household "discovered the dead body of Col. Collins . . . on the floor in a pool of congealed blood with a pistol bullet through the heart. . . . All over the floor were scattered various sealed packages of fractional currency and sundry piles of same in small quantities, while the money vault and iron safe showed they had been broken open and all the bills of large denominations extracted and carried away." According to the *New Mexican* there was a shortage of "probably $100,000.00." Attention was directed to "two suspicious persons who had left Santa Fe, taking the trail over the mountain eastward toward Fort Union." Fort Union's commander was forthwith instructed "by all means in your power to capture and retain the supposed murderers and robbers and recover the money."

Colonel Collins' funeral took place on Tuesday, June 8, from the residence of his son-in-law, James M. Edgar. He was buried in the Masonic Cemetery, the rites attended by a large number of people, including the "military, Federal and Territorial officers, carriages with families, and citizens generally. The *Santa Fe Weekly Gazette* (at one time owned and edited by the deceased) "lamented the fate of the brave old man who laid down his life at the post of duty which he was to surrender to his successor, refusing to be diverted from the palpable facts, in another day."

In the meantime, General Getty rigorously investigated the shortage from the depositary, discovering all but $33,000, some of it, said the *Daily New Mexican,* being discovered "in the privy of an unoccupied house belonging to Mr. J. M. Edgar," and the newspaper gladly wrote "finis to the robbery and murder of that man of so many good, generous and christian qualities which ornamented his nature."

The Honorable William Breeden, however, had his day in court, having been tried four times for embezzlement of the widow's allotment, and was adjudged "Not Guilty." To celebrate the event, he went to Fort Union, from whence came the information that "the late U.S. Assessor for the Territory of New Mexico and Miss Baker of Jamestown, New York, were married. The interesting ceremony was performed at the residence of the Rev. Mr. Woart in the presence of most of the military officers on duty at the post and a number of other guests of the officiating clergyman. . . . At the conclusion, the party partook of an excellent supper prepared by the estimable wife of the chaplain, and then repaired to the residence of Colonel Dent where the beauty and chivalry of Fort Union chased the glowing hours with flying feet."[28]

[28] *Daily New Mexican,* June 15, 1869, p. 1, col. 3. This was Rev. Woart's last marriage ceremony at Fort Union. He was relieved soon thereafter by Rev. J. A. M. LaTourette.

CHAPTER SEVENTEEN

ILLICIT TRAFFIC

DURING THE LATTER PART of September, 1869, General Grier absented himself from the Fort Union command to attend to business in Santa Fe. Captain G. W. Bradley, depot quartermaster, took advantage of the general's absence to apprise the Postmaster General of the "delays, confusion or inattention to business at the Fort Union Post Office," attributing these shortcomings to the "frequent drunkenness of Mr. Edward Handren, the present incumbent." When the General returned, he confirmed the accusation, adding that "Mr. Hendren's conduct and management . . . has been growing worse and worse" and asked for his immediate removal, recommending that "Mr. Richard Dunn, a civilian of good character, reliable, and of strictly sober habits, be appointed in his place." Nine months passed, however, before there was a new postmaster, but he was not Dunn. He was Edward Shoemaker, son of the military storekeeper.[1]

On May 25, 1870, General Pope suggested abandoning Fort Union entirely. Tactfully, General Getty demurred. He would give it "most earnest consideration," but there had "been a gradual but decided change in affairs" in New Mexico so that abandonment would "result in a great additional expense" which he wished to avoid. He did, however, acquiesce to restaurateur Greisinger's request to banish an assortment of Mexicans who had hedged him in, now that he was engaged in his "respectable business." According to Greisinger, they were "nothing more than thieves [who] made it a practice to steal everything" he had; therefore he wanted the "market for Mexicans" adjoining his house "dispersed with or broken up." As evidence of the necessity for immediate action he related that only that afternoon

---

[1] *Daily New Mexican,* July 29, 1870, p. 1, col. 3.

he had seen one Mexican stealing some of his chickens—"in fact, caught him in the act." Furthermore, he had previously "lost about fifty chickens besides several other articles." Dr. Peters confirmed the complaint, adding, "The market next to Krissinger's [*sic*] Restaurant (between Moore and Dent's Store) is the resort of thieves, vagabonds, and the worst class of prostitutes, who ply their various avocations, contaminate the garrison, and drive out the industrious Mexicans who would otherwise bring in articles to sell." He called upon the post commander to have the guard "visit the place daily and cause these bad characters to leave as a sanitary measure."

As a result, one William Carter (Negro) found himself "under charge of a guard," leaving the post with a warning "never again to come upon the Reservation." Also expelled were "Citizen Charles and Mrs. Charles, the latter a Laundress . . . the former for selling whisky, and the latter for allowing women of bad character in their quarters."[2]

Colonel Céran St. Vrain died at Mora on October 28. Funeral services were conducted at Mora "by the Masonic fraternity with military honors." Captain Starr, Eighth Cavalry, with his troop acted as escort. The regimental band furnished the music; General Gregg and his staff were pall bearers. Nearly all the officers at Fort Union attended, as did some two thousand other persons. The *Daily New Mexican* reported "the services very impressive . . . the surroundings of a very romantic character . . . nothing equal to it was ever seen in New Mexico."[3]

In May, 1870, raids in the vicinity of Fort Bascom proved to be by Cheyennes and Arapahos. Since cavalry was more effective than infantry against the prairie raiders, the Eighth Cavalry was ordered out from Fort Union to be *"constantly* in the field and *on the move."* The cavalrymen were to go down toward Texas and the Indian Territory. This detachment interpreted the General's instructions literally, and while scouting forsook the prospect of encountering Indians to desert toward Colorado. There they were apprehended by Sheriff

[2] NA, RG 93, Fort Union Orders, Vol. 44, p. 246.
[3] October 29, 1870, p. 1, col. 2; October 31, 1870, p. 1, col. 3.

W. G. Riffenburg, who reported to Fort Union that he had put them "under guard day and night." But after three days of rest they again moved, this time "taking to the mountains." Although the sheriff followed "after them all day," he could not overtake them, and dejectedly informed the army that "all he had left for his pains was a government carbine, the only thing the thoughtless cavalrymen left behind." The success of their escape he attributed to "no Jail and Citizen guard cannot be depended on." He promised, however, "The next I take will not get away."[4]

A detachment of recruits for the Fifth Cavalry and Fifteenth Infantry arrived at Fort Union under the command of Captain Alfred Hedberg. Awaiting was Special Order No. 88 directing the Captain to continue toward the south, distributing the replacements to their proper stations.[5] Rumors were rife at Fort Union regarding Captain Hedberg's inhumane treatment of his charges before he left with them, and for some three months thereafter, allegations of mistreatment drifted into headquarters. Lieutenant Colonel August V. Kautz was directed to "investigate the allegations." This he did "by an examination of a few of the most intelligent men at each post" through which the recruits had been conducted. "The first act of barbarism [as reported by the Colonel] transpired on the march before leaving Fort Lyons, C. T. The march was a long one and many of the men gave out and dropped by the wayside and were urged on by Capt. Hedberg by abusive language and by riding at them with his mule and by trying to ride over them. A waterwagon came out to meet the command, and all those who had continued with the main column were supplied with water, and the stragglers, who probably needed it most, were refused, and the remaining water was thrown away by direction of Captain Hedberg. On this occasion Pvt. Shafer, who had given out for want of water, was berated by Captain Hedberg with abusive language, and when Pvt. H. Cornwell . . . asked for water

4 W. G. Riffenberg to Gregg, July 17, 1870, AC, "Fort Union, July, 1870," File 2, p. 50.

5 S.O. No. 88, September 3, 1870, NA, RG 98, Dist. of N. M. Orders, Vol. 153, pp. 139–40.

for Shafer and was refused, and when he tried to catch some which leaked from the water tank, he was attacked by Captain Hedberg and kicked over. (This affair became aggravated by . . . the death of Shafer after arrival at Fort Union.)

"After leaving Fort Lyon two men were tied up near Bent's Fort . . . Miller, for disobeying a noncommissioned officer . . . Storey for threats to shoot Lieutenant Boyd. . . . The next event . . . was near Iron Springs. Private Dooley, having become intoxicated and lost his carbine, was required to carry a knapsack on the March. Captain Hedberg came up and ascertaining that he had no firearm, directed that he carry the carbine of a sick man, which he refused to do; then the Captain proceeded to strike him with his fist . . . then drew his revolver and struck him a number of times; then took him to the rear and caused his hands to be tied behind his back with a rope around his neck tied to the wagon—thus compelled to march the rest of the day. He was put in charge of the guard until leaving Fort Union, and then released, but he deserted a few days after."

A more intensive investigation by the Colonel disclosed that "Nearly all complain of long hard marches, and many of being refused to ride in the wagons when unable to march from sore feet. . . . Quite a number of [them] being refused to leave the ranks on necessary occasions, and two state instances of relief by holding their excrement in their clothing."

All the recruits arriving at Fort Union were not, however, restrained under guard or tied behind a wagon. The day following their arrival happened to be Sunday, so, being off duty and "joined by a few of the Non-commissioned officers and private soldiers of the garrison," they went off limits to Loma Parda, and there, to the disgust of General Gregg, engaged in "disgraceful and unlawful proceeding," which brought forth from the commander the wrist-tapping edificatory admonition:

It is the duty of the soldiers at all times to uphold the laws, not to violate them: to protect the citizens, not to outrage and maltreat them: and when he permits himself to be hurried into such excess of outrage and cruelty as that of Sunday night, he justly loses the respect of all good citizens and the confidence and sympathy of his officers.[6]

With Loma Parda off limits to Fort Union soldiers, Colonel Gregg attempted to impose additional restrictions. First, the guard was to improve sanitation by taking up all hogs found running loose around the post, charging a fee for their release. Dutiful guards soon had eight unclaimed hogs in the corral. Then, as it was found that the post commander had no authority to issue rations for their hogs, the post adjutant turned them over to the public auctioneer. The restraint of the loose pigs was followed by a regulation that thereafter there would be no smoking "except on the porches of the Officer's Quarters within the limits of the parade grounds." Neither might men walk across the parade ground but must use one or the other of the walks; and on Sunday all "places of business and amusement would be closed, with officers and soldiers required to repair to their quarters, reading room or chapel, as their inclinations might prompt."[7]

In late February, 1871, word came to headquarters that Mexican traders were out early in the Indian country trading "large quantities of sheath-knives, powder, lead, caps, bayeta cloth, *and perhaps spiritous liquors.*" No longer was trading limited to a venturesome *Nuevo Mejicano*. They traveled in large groups, well provided for from inside New Mexico with articles desired by the Indians, and the accepted medium of exchange was invariably Texas cattle. In other words, sporadic trading between the Indians and *Nuevo Mejicanos* had developed into a well-financed system of cattle stealing, the *Nuevo Mejicanos* (and at times a few New Mexico Indians) being the catspaws for the backers, the Indians of Texas stealing the cattle. As a consequence, when the trade was renewed in earnest when the weather became such that cattle might be put on the trail, General Gregg reverted to orders of 1869—"break up and punish these bands of traders"—and ordered out to Fort Bascom 150 cavalry horses and

---

[6] NA, RG 93, Fort Union Orders, Vol. 44, pp. 222–23.
[7] Order No. 127, NA, RG 93, Fort Union Orders, Vol. 44, p. 236.

54 mules, with the proper complement of men "to look out for Indian signs." The troops were to make temporary camps "near the
eastern line of New Mexico . . . and intercept all parties going in or
coming out of the Indian Territory."

On March 16, a sergeant returning to Fort Union reported "burros
and oxcarts passing toward Comanche Springs in considerable numbers every day." One settler had lost four thousand sheep, which
"were subsequently recovered." Specific instructions went to Fort
Union: The country between the fort and Fort Bascom would be
patrolled; all Indian trails would be pursued; all persons—"Mexicans
and others"—found roaming through the country would be seized.

On April 28, 1871, General Granger came into Fort Union with
orders from General Pope to relieve Colonel Gregg as commander
in New Mexico. After reaching the fort, he had suffered a humiliating
loss: twelve government mules for which he was responsible had been
stolen by a party of armed citizens at Cow Creek on April 30, the
mules having been left behind with two teamsters near Cimarron
in his haste to reach his destination. The only information he had
was that "parties were in pursuit, but it is doubtful if the thieves can
be overtaken." At Santa Fe, the *New Mexican* introduced him to the
people as the man who "won distinguished honors during the late
war," adding that the newspaper had "no doubt that in the administration of military affairs . . . he would be guided by the same soldierly
instinct which impelled him at Chickamauga to move his division to
the point where the roar of the muskets revealed the fact that his
comrades-in-arms were sorely pressed without waiting for orders from
the commanding general." Instead of displaying such initiative here,
however, he turned to the secretary of state—the governor being
absent—and requested "a personal interview with the gentleman who
represents Governor Pile . . . with a view of devising means by which
the civil authorities, aided by the military, may inaugurate an active
crusade against these marauders and horse thieves, who infest all sections of the Territory, in order that they may be promptly captured
and brought to trial." The *New Mexican,* cynically speaking for the
absent governor, gave lip-service to the laudable purpose of the new

354

general, thinking "it high time that the nest of thieves and outlaws on the Cimarron be broken up," adding "that if the civil authorities were powerless, let the military take hold!"[8] Obviously the *New Mexican's* faith in the military was also at a low ebb since its conclusion was, "Hanging would do good here."[9]

At this stage of the stalemate, a well-informed "one Mr. Smoot" came into the General's headquarters with the suggestion that if he would send a detachment to the vicinity of Red River Station, "the three men could be captured," whereupon Mr. Smoot "took off in a buggy with one black and one bay horse" stating that he would pass through Fort Union "about the 19th instant." This information Granger relayed to Major Clendenin, directing him to "detail a Lieut and 10 men" at Fort Union and disguise them "in such manner as to avoid suspicion and accompany Mr. Smoot . . . and arrest the three thieves" and bring them into Fort Union. But while General Granger furtively tried to retrieve his property, citizens in the Conejos region of Colorado, northwest of the New Mexico hangout of thieves, devised their own method of brigand disposal. Instead of acting covertly and with disguised military forces, they organized publicly the "Conejos String Band." And when the hempen strings began attuning the region to a higher pitch of morality, some forty Coloradans, in an effort to avoid the stridulous disharmony of stretching hemp, fled to New Mexico. Once out of Colorado, they began reverting to type, and—in the language of the *New Mexican,* which had not welcomed their arrival—"some of the wretches in the southern part of Rio Arriba County began selling whiskey to Indians." This "brought threats by settlers of an encore serenade by the Conejos String Band" —all of which the *New Mexican* approved.

Turning attention from mule thieves to *Comancheros* on the eastern plains, General Granger gave Fort Union explicit instructions to keep troops "moving out toward Fort Sumner as far as may be necessary . . . as far as the boundary line of Texas," with no idea of "going into garrison . . . and no patrols would be sent into Fort Union unless

[8] *Daily New Mexican,* May 5, 1871, p. 1, col. 3.
[9] *Ibid.,* May 11, 1871, p. 1, col. 3.

compelled to touch there for rations."[10] Scouting Sergeant George
Ferrari was the first to report "evidences of the operations of Comancheros."[11] He captured "5 loose animals—1 Horse, 3 mules, and
I Burro—the mule being packed with old Blankets—a few pounds
of Gun Powder and a few Boxes of Gun Caps." Capturing the animals had involved no difficulties: "The owner or driver . . . escaped
before the detachment came up." Taking his loot along, Sergeant
Ferrari continued his scout, discovering a "Person mounted, running
his animals on the prairie." The Sergeant overhauled him, whereupon
he sought to explain his singular presence upon the prairie by declaring he was a member of a party of buffalo hunters. In proof of his
assertion he led his captors to "7 more (all Mexicans) with a Train consisting of 12 Horses and wagon loaded with Buffalo Meat Provisions
&c." With eight prisoners claiming they were catching *mestanas,*
although they had "no license to show," the Sergeant released one
"to go to Caloniam, a town 60 miles from the Camp in order to
obtain the license." A week later the paroled prisoner rejoined the
detachment bearing a certificate from a justice of the peace avowing
that to the best of his knowledge Ferrari's prisoners "went out on the
plains for the purpose of catching mestanas." Thus fortified against
criticism from his commanding officer, Ferrari released the prisoners
and marched back to Fort Bascom, noting as he went "fresh trails
of Cattle, Horses or Mules," to report "5 captured animals viz: one
horse (a Comanche poney, three mules . . . in a very poor condition
. . . a very inferior animal . . . the mules with sore backs . . . the Burro,
a fine Specimen of her Kind." General Gregg, having assumed command at Fort Union to permit Major Clendenin to go in search of
Comancheros, received the Sergeant's report with complete disapproval, for no civil officer had authority to permit buffalo hunting in
the Indian country.

After Lieutenant A. P. Caraher moved away from Fort Union
toward Fort Sumner, a band of about one hundred Kiowas moved

[10] Glendenin to C.O. Troops in the Field, April 30, 1871, AC, "Fort Union, 1871,"
File 2, p. 66.
[11] AC, "Fort Union, 1871," File 3, p. 5, May 3, 1871.

into "the ranch or establishment of Simon Baca . . . near the Dry Cimarron," taking "twenty American mules and two saddle horses," a loss estimated at four thousand dollars. The owner further reported: "Also there was killed at the same place two Major Domos of the herd . . . both residents of the village of upper Las Vegas."[12] As the Kiowas raided, Caraher "met and arrested a Mexican who acknowledged to be a guide for Indian Traders." With the assistance of the prisoner he was measurably successful, finding "a packtrain of loaded Buros [*sic*] moving toward the Indian country." Accompanying the burros were "Texans, Comanche Indians, and Mexicans to the number of about 50 men, 21 being mounted." An attack was made, but the *Comancheros* proved "too strong and well armed," and when they attempted to surround the soldiers, Caraher decided to withdraw and come back to camp." At camp Caraher "mounted every available horse, also the mules from his wagon," and made another sally—this time chasing the *Comancheros* about fifty miles—coming upon two herds of cattle. When the soldiers "came to an aim," the *Comancheros* "dropped their arms and surrendered," all except the mounted men, who succeeded in making their escape leaving the soldiers as custodian of "21 Indians, including two chiefs . . . and 700 herd of horned cattle, 12 horses and ponies and 17 Buros with their packs." On the way to Fort Union, two hundred cattle and six ponies became so worn out that Caraher shot them, finally going into Fort Bascom with 450 head of cattle.[13] There he received orders to bring the cattle and prisoners into Fort Union.

On May 24, 1871, the *Daily New Mexican* took a position on the situation east of Santa Fe. It had up-to-date information, so it said, "from a gentleman but recently arrived from San Miguel and from all portions of the Rio Pecos where the Comancheros do most congregate." In that region "the most intense excitement prevailed amongst all those interested, and their name is legion." The immediate cause of the excitement seemed to spring from the fact that the soldiers were doing good work; they had captured a great many

[12] Romero to Pile (translation), May 12, 1871, AC, "Fort Union, 1871," File 3, p. 18.
[13] AC, "Fort Union, 1871," File 3, pp. 24–25, May 14, 1871.

cattle and had "prevented the Comanche traders from passing." Having blocked the way for the *Comancheros* to deliver their stolen cattle, they had "fortified themselves at a place known as Portales . . . erected works of defense [in] preparation to fight." Some of the parties had "escaped barely with their lives, leaving their cattle behind. Some thousand head of cattle had been captured, but for some cause or other, most of them had been lost, either intentionally or otherwise." The "lost" cattle mysteriously had "been picked up by different parties and sold to the Colorado traders of whom the country is full." In fact, according to the newspaper's information, "The trade has become so immense there is, at this time, more than a thousand persons engaged in this illicit and reprehensible traffic. The Texans are suffering severely, not only from the loss of their stock, but many of them being killed and their helpless children made captive."

With this evaluation of the situation, the *New Mexican* took its stand: "This damnable and outrageous traffic must be stopped, and we cannot sufficiently thank the military for their laudable efforts in this direction. The best Mexican citizens are most fervently opposed to this trade and are doing their best to stop the same. Horses and mules from New Mexico are stolen and taken to the Comanches to trade for cattle. The people on the Pecos have almost entirely neglected their ranches for this more profitable traffic. . . . *in the last three months more than 30,000 head of cattle have been brought to this country from that source alone!*"

As the stepped-up military activities against the *Comancheros* netted more prisoners, the post commander at Fort Union complained that there was "no convenient building at Fort Union for the custody of the Indian prisoners." In fact, he needed to have the jail "both strengthened and enlarged." The guardhouse only "consisted of ten Stone Cells, originally designed for the Accommodation of one prisoner Each, and which cannot with any regard to humanity be made to accommodate more than two prisoners." The prison reports showed he was attempting to hold "forty-five prisoners . . . sentenced for infamous crimes . . . and Safe Keeping," and he had just been apprised that four more were coming.

As the post commander complained, Dr. Peters inspected the jails, being thoroughly displeased with what he saw. There was not enough food, and what there was contained "very little solid ingredients"; even the soup was "of a very inferior quality" and the "Bread and meat insufficient in quantity." What was even worse, there was no tobacco allowance. That tobacco was a necessity, he "would cite from history: Men long accustomed to this weed become, as it were, slaves to its want. Popes and Kings have issued edicts against its use—still it sways—in the Placer and Mine—it carries its power—and I believe in our General Prisons (Civil Life) it is granted. If it was a degenerator of our Race, it would long since have exterminated us, to say what you will—used *pro re nata*—it is a boon both to the poor and rich." He would, therefore, ask "this favor for these prisoners as a slight comfort to their lot—Fort Union being . . . a General Penitentiary."[14]

Colonel Gregg, anxious to resolve the *Comanchero* problem, on February 25, 1872, proposed locating troops at the source of cattle supply. But on April 13, orders from Fort Leavenworth confirmed previous instructions; there would be no change in the haphazard *Comanchero*-chasing. The troops would again go out east of Fort Bascom "with the same duties as . . . during the last summer."[15]

During the "off-season" for *Comanchero* activities, many of the more daring cattle thieves congregated in the vicinity of Fort Union, making headquarters at Loma Parda. Since the addition of a few more lawbreakers did not change the general character of Loma Parda citizenry, no attention was paid to their presence until the *Daily New Mexican* received a letter from Fort Union stating that "quite an affray occurred among a lot of cattle thieves at Pardita: one was dangerously hurt, while another had his horse killed from under him." The correspondent thought that "the affair is not settled, and people in the vicinity are praying that the next row will clean them all out." For a time prayers were ineffectual, but the thieves, lacking Texas

---

[14] AC, "Fort Union, May, 1871," File 3, pp. 58–59, May 24, 27, 1871.

[15] R. Williams to C.O., Dist. of N. M., April 13, 1872, NA, RG 98, Fort Union Letter Books, Letters Received, Vol. 2, p. 185. Received April 28, 1872, at Fort Union.

cattle to steal, turned their activities toward herds of sheep. This prompted a neighboring *alcalde* with a sense of humor to render this verdict in a homicide case: "Cause of death—Sheep-i-cide in the first degree."[16]

Having failed to get permission to take troops to the source of the cattle thievery because of overlapping military jurisdictions and consequent jealousy of commanders, Colonel Granger concluded to Mohammedanize his army: He would bring the mountain to him; he would "enlarge the freedom of use of government arms by civilians —even Texans—to help break up the raids and thefts of the Comancheros." He would invite "the assistance of the owners of the cattle being stolen." Consequently, on July 18, 1872, Colonel Granger dispatched a letter to Colonel Gregg vouching for "Mr. John Hittson of Palo Pinto, Texas, and Mr. James Patterson of Denver, Colorado, who are engaged in the cattle trade." In explanation, attention was called to "some fifty prairie men" accompanying the bearers of the letter, who could give "information regarding the country." It was highly probable that these fifty prairie men might need arms. Should such be the case and should Gregg "have any surplus," he "might loan them to the party"; otherwise, they were authorized to "make arrangements to get some from Captain Shoemaker." Further, scouting parties were instructed "to co-operate with these gentlemen."

During August, 1872, the *Daily New Mexican* renewed its attack on behalf of the Texas cattlemen. This time it went to the source in New Mexico. It said:

> There is a species of stealing and robbery more contemptible and cowardly than the midnight depredations of the common burglar. *We allude to the practice of certain capitalists,* who, by the potency of the funds they control, enlist the aid of the savages, the scalping knife and the faggot, in adding yet more to their ill-gotten wealth, while they, lying about fashionable hotels, smoking cigars, and enjoying all the comforts of security, smile in gloated satisfaction at the murder and theft and Indian horrors that are the inevitable concomitants of their illicit business. These remarks apply to that class who encourage the Co-

16 *Daily New Mexican,* April 16, 1872, p. 1, col. 3.

manches . . . to steal cattle from Texas . . . with the offer to buy from them all they can obtain. These men hire ignorant creatures to go out and meet the Indians on the plains and bring . . . the stolen stock to market where bona fide purchasers become the sufferers. This kind of traffic is what has led to the Texas raids in San Miguel and other counties . . . . The people of Texas . . . have risen to protect themselves. They are retaking their stock wherever they find it. . . . We cannot deny the justice of the Texan's claim . . . all [of us] condemn and curse the men who are at the bottom of these troubles, and if they could be caught the reported hangings would soon be true . . . they would meet their just deserts if swung by the neck from the limb of the nearest pine. . . . We think the Texans should be encouraged and protected . . . to get back their own."[17]

Four days after attacking the New Mexico capitalists, the *Daily New Mexican,* although refraining from making mention of the "visiting" Texans, dispensed news from Loma Parda: "Within the past three weeks the town of Loma Parda . . . has lost four of its citizens by violence. They became too intimately associated with their neighbor's stock and were strung up by the sufferers, who had more faith in a stout lariat than stone walls."

These effective dispositions of *Comancheros* prompted Colonel Granger's headquarters to warn military commanders out on scouts that "certain parties, supposed to be Texans, are . . . forcibly taking the stock of citizens under the claim that said stock is stolen from parties in Texas, and it is probable that there will be a collision: therefore, *take no part in the matter."*

During the early days of September, the "collision" came. One morning "Hittson's men came to town [Loma Parda], looking for Texas cattle: found seven head, and started to drive them off. They were resisted; whereupon they retired from the town, returned the next morning and brought with them about twenty men." After that there was total confusion, punctuated by volley after volley of gunfire. One onlooker described the aftermath thus: "The murderers with their party now moved down the street like Indians, shooting

[17] *Ibid.,* August 9, 1872, p. 1, col. 3.

up the street and into houses." When the smoke had drifted away and quiet had been restored, Sam J. Seaman and Toribio García lay dead, the *alcalde* was seriously wounded. The Hittson and Patterson "fifty prairie men" moved to the Red River Station, where Mr. Patterson reviewed the incident, as he said, "in the language of reliable men who were present"—admitting that Mr. Childers was in charge of the party. Mr. Childers, however, chose not to remain with his prairie companions, not being heard from until December 27, when he was arrested in Los Ranos and thereafter brought to Las Vegas. The accommodations at Las Vegas, however, were not to his liking, and on January 2, 1873, he was reported as "having already escaped," the *New Mexican* venturing to state, "... it is safe to say he will never be heard of again in this Territory." And as Mr. Childers vanished, so did the zeal of *Comancheros* dwindle in the illicit cattle trade.

CHAPTER EIGHTEEN

THE HATCH REGIME

WITH THE HITTSON INVASION of New Mexico over, there was little demand for Fort Union troops to scout the plains, the Comanches finding fewer and fewer customers for their stolen cattle. The Navahos, formerly prisoners at Fort Sumner, now had the attention of the military authorities, who were demanding that the government comply specifically with the treaty. Former Governor W. F. M. Arny became Navaho agent in 1873. The *Daily New Mexican* considered him "one of New Mexico's truest and best friends" and wished there "were many others like him in the territory."[1]

The new agent, finding a treaty stipulation that the government should provide a schoolhouse and a teacher for every thirty pupils and discovering that no effort had been made to comply with it, brought to his new task a missionary's zeal plus an earnest desire to meet the obligation. To give impetus to his conception of Indian education, he loaded four stagecoaches with Indians and departed for the East. No extra coaches were available for regular passengers, and service had to be suspended since "all the seats were engaged for the time with the party and baggage."[2] Soon Arny and his charges were reported as being in Washington. From there a side trip was made to Boston to attend a re-enactment of the Boston Tea Party, but the sight of Indians dumping boxes of tea into the harbor was incomprehensible to Navahos. Then Arny started west, stopping off for several days in St. Louis to lecture on the progress of the Western Indians.[3] This, said the *Daily New Mexican,* which had been following the tour, he had been doing "in the principal cities through

[1] February 1, 1875, p. 1, col. 3, "Governor and His Braves Returned."
[2] *Ibid.,* January 19, 1875, p. 1, col. 3.   [3] *Ibid.,* January 25, 1875, p. 1, col. 3.

which he has traveled during his absence, beyond doubt enlightening the people about New Mexico and correcting many false impressions about the country." The newspaper could say also that the Governor's efforts "in this behalf, and in behalf of the Indians . . . were worthy of high commendation, and will largely and creditably add to the already voluminous record of good things he has done for his adopted home."[4]

S. N. Goodale pulled away from the returning Arny-Indian tourists at Fort Union with one coach and four Indians to come into Santa Fe on January 30 and introduce himself as "the master mechanic of the Navajo Nation." Following several hours behind was the Governor's party, including "Miss Cook, a niece of [Indian] Commissioner Smith, who comes out to instruct the Navajoes in the use of the loom." The master mechanic of the Navaho Indians proudly informed the Santa Feans that the Governor had purchased modern looms while in the East. Arny, who did not arrive until night, was "in fine spirits with large hopes for the future advantages to accrue to the Navajo nation by reason of the many sights, novelties and associations with which the Navajo has been brought in contact in his extended trip to the capital, and through the Western, Middle and New England States." Navaho Chief Manuelito, too, was in fine spirits, but for a different reason: he was pleased to be "back in the free open air of the plains and mountains." His first thoughts upon viewing the many sights, were that "he would like to live East, but [he] finally came to the conclusion that too many people are there already." Now that he was back, "New Mexico was best for him and his people after all." Miss Cook modestly admitted that she had had "several years experience with different tribes of Indians in the north in learning [sic] them the use of the loom. Now, she had volunteered to do the same service for the Navajo people." Her attitude, proclaimed the Daily New Mexican, indeed reflected a "self-sacrificing and missionary spirit for which it took pleasure in paying a tribute of respect," bespeaking for her while in the city "the kindly atten-

[4] Ibid., February 1, 1875, p. 1, col. 3.

364

tions of our people, *the ladies especially,"* she and the Governor being "registered at *The Exchange."*

On February 4, a *New Mexican* reporter witnessed the departure of "King Manuelito with his *consort* and suit [*sic*]" for the Navaho Reservation, using "transportation furnished by Col. McGonnigle, Chief Quartermaster." The "King" "likewise was accompanied by Dr. Whitney, the interpreter and master-mechanic," while the Governor and Miss Cook remained in Santa Fe receiving the "kindly attentions" of the people, though announcing their intention to follow the "King" within three days.

At Cañon Bonito, Manuelito's party came upon the body of a man freshly murdered. Their information was that he had been killed by "two California Spaniards and an Irishman," so "no effort was made to apprehend them."[5]

Five days after the "King" had returned to his reservation, the Governor and Miss Cook followed "in this morning's western coach." The Governor did not return to Santa Fe until two months later; then he came "in search of sundry unsanctified whiskey venders," whose "whiskey selling had increased" during his lecture tour. "Too, more *squaw men* had moved in to live with the Navajo women, who were notorious for their libidinous orgies." The fact that the military authorities had "refused to intercede" indicated to the distraught Arny that the "military was favoring prostitution." In addition, there was discord regarding the schoolteacher. More time elapsed before Arny was able to forward "the machinery, looms, etc., which had finally arrived from the states . . . and a train of nearly a dozen wagons left the warerooms."[6]

On June 5, 1875, Colonel J. Irving Gregg returned to Santa Fe from sick leave, remaining at headquarters, however, for several days before displacing Colonel Devin.[7] He was little more than back in

[5] *Ibid.,* February 8, 1875, p. 1, col. 4; February 9, 1875, p. 1, col. 4.

[6] See H. H. Bancroft, *History of Arizona and New Mexico,* 734, n. 1: "The looms were introduced with prospects of success which were never realized."

[7] Gregg to A.A.G., Leavenworth, Kansas, NA, RG 98, Dist. of N. M. Telegrams, Vol. 125, p. 132.

command when news came that Arny's Indians were "becoming restive."

On July 23, Captain H. A. Ellis, commanding at Fort Union, received word that General John Pope, commanding the department, intended to visit the fort. Immediate orders went to Captain Shoemaker to "furnish two Field pieces or Howitzers and Twenty two rounds of blank Cartridges for the purposes of firing the required salute." Two days later Pope arrived amid resounding volleys from the largest guns on the post. The General, accompanied by twenty-five infantrymen and his staff of four, spent the night at the fort, leaving at six the next morning, but not before a telegram had informed Santa Fe headquarters that the visitors would be there in due time.[8]

Steps were immediately taken to "have the Field Pieces at the Post hauled to the top of Old Fort Marcy . . . to be fired from that point" on Pope's arrival in Santa Fe. About noon on the following Saturday, General Pope made his appearance "at the outskirts of the city. There he was met by a detachment of the 8th Cavalry and escorted in Salvos of artillery" to the accompaniment "of the Cavalry band playing in the pagoda." The reporter for the *Daily New Mexican* was particularly impressed by the music: ". . . selections . . . not of the slam bang order that fills the plaza with rabble, but . . . refined, chaste, artistic—arresting the attention of the artistic ear." For the edification of the General the "refined, chaste, artistic" mellifluence was repeated the next day, Sunday, in a "fine programme." To this display of military homage there was raised at least one discordant note: One patron wrote that he "should object to being held by the ears even to listen to this fine programme."[9]

Another discordant note of more serious portent came to General Pope's ear as he visited with his old Santa Fe army acquaintances: A petition arrived from Fort Wingate asking for the removal of Indian Agent Arny. General Pope evaded a decision, stating that "the Mili-

[8] Dunn to C.O., July 27, 1875, NA, RG 98, Dist. of N. M. Telegrams, Vol. 125, p. 183.
[9] *Daily New Mexican,* August 9, 1875.

tary authorities have nothing to do with the Navajoe Indians and their Agents. The matter pertains entirely to the Department of the Interior." However, he suggested to Fort Wingate's commander that "If the dissatisfaction of the Indians with their Agent is likely to culminate in outbreaks on their part detrimental to the quiet and safety of the settlers on the Navajo Reservation, the fact should be reported to the Commanding Officer."[10] Ending his Santa Fe visit on August 16, General Pope camped that night at Tesuque on his way to Fort Garland, much disturbed by an article in the *New Mexican* disclosing that the Utes also were discontented and had prevented surveyors from making a survey "west of Pagoso, which included their valleys."[11] Thus there was a probability of trouble with both the Utes and the Navahos.

On August 25, dispatches came from both Fort Wingate and Fort Defiance that the Navahos were "in a great state of excitement." Indian Agent Arny had gone to St. Louis, leaving Dr. Whitney in charge, and the Indians had driven off all the employees of the agency, making it necessary for Colonel Gregg to be called on for assistance. The bad news was passed along to General Pope, who by that time had reached Denver. With the relay of news went the suggestion that there was no enthusiasm for Agent Arny. As for the cause, the *Daily New Mexican* had it that the Navahos "became somewhat restive under an inequitable distribution of rations and Indian goods and the introduction of looms, agricultural instruments and schoolteachers, and other items of civilization." Taking advantage of the objections to changes, the Indians held a "whiskey-inspired pow-wow with the squawmen," whereupon the "mal-contents were ordered off the reservation." Before the Indians adjourned their powwow, however, they "came to the conclusion that rations and annuity-goods could be best distributed through *their* chiefs, and that the dirty white villains could be better served if they had some other than Governor Arny as agent." Then the Navahos gave notice "that there would be

[10] Letter No. 217, NA, RG 98, Dist. of N. M. Letters, Vol. 51, p. 167.
[11] "The Utes Outraged," *Daily New Mexican,* August 7, 1875, p. 1, col. 4.

another dead agent, if Arny returned; that the women folks would be included if there was not a change."[12]

Anticipating that Colonel Gregg would move troops from Fort Union to the Navaho disturbance, Pope telegraphed him to do everything practicable, although too few troops were in New Mexico "to do anything by force." He was to "avoid hostilities—confine yourself to protecting public property and people at the Agency & make no military movements." Further, he was to tell "King" Manuelito that he would at once see that Agent Arny was removed; that he must not commit any depredations—to do so would ruin his cause and "force the troops to take part against him." This information was sufficient for Miss Cook. On September 15, she passed quietly through Santa Fe, "returning to the States." No notice was taken of her leaving except by the *New Mexican,* which thought it "a subject of regret."[13] Before Miss Cook could take her departure, General Pope telegraphed, "Arny is relieved . . . ."[14]

In mid-August news reached Fort Union that former President Andrew Johnson had died. Orders were issued for all posts to fire appropriate commemorative salutes in his honor on the evening of August 20, and Fort Union's old fieldpieces were again hauled out for service. The honor of firing the salute fell to Sergeant Summers of Captain McKibbin's company, Fifteenth Infantry, the Sergeant having had twenty years in the army and "counted one of the best men." A premature explosion during the preparation of the charge "horribly mutilated [the Sergeant] lacerating the flesh of the face and hands, necessitating the amputation of both hands." The doctor pronounced his condition "precarious, although hopes are entertained for his recovery . . . he may lose the sight of both eyes."[15]

---

[12] "Will There Be an Indian Outbreak," *ibid.,* October 4, 1875, p. 1, col. 3.

[13] *Ibid.,* September 15, 1875, p. 1, col. 3.

[14] Pope to Gregg, August 30, 1875, NA, RG 98, Dist. of N. M. Telegrams, Vol. 125, p. 206–207.

[15] *Daily New Mexican,* August 21, 1875, p. 1, col. 4; October 13, 1875, p. 1, col. 3. The last news account reported him "fearfully shattered, and losing his arms, recovered his sight and general health as far as possible; able to be about. To be transferred to a soldier's home at Washington."

The Arsenal, about 1880. Demolition began in July, 1882.

Arrott Collection

Colonel Henry M. Black, commander of Fort Union, October 16, 1882, to July 12, 1883, and from August 5, 1883, to June 6, 1884.

Arrott Collection

Of grave concern to the commander of Fort Union was Indian Agent Irvine's report from Cimarron of "considerable excitement" there over the "cold-blooded murder of Reverend Mr. Tolby." Tolby, as Irvine had the facts, had left Cimarron for Elizabethtown with only two dollars in his pocket. He was seen to enter a cañon and two days later was reported dead. "There was no clue to the murder," but suspicion was rife. Amid the growing excitement the Masonic fraternity "offered a $500 reward for the cowardly villian," but the Tolby murder remained a mystery, producing an alarming mass of speculation and accusation. The "Santa Fe Ring," not disdaining an increase in the control of the Elizabethtown gold mines, came in for criticism by local aspirants to wealth. Arrests were made; forced confessions and involvements were extracted. One man was shot; another was hanged. High on some lists of suspects were Dr. Longwell, Probate Judge W. M. Mills, and a Mr. Donaghue.

Troops were called for. Lieutenants Lafferty and Cornish went up from Fort Union. They found feeling very bitter against Longwell, "but not so bitter against Mills"; however, a large number of Texans had arrived, "all armed." Dr. Longwell refused to surrender to the so-called civil authorities, as did Mills, both declaring that, if they did so, they would be hanged. There was little chance to hang the doctor, however, for, as the Lieutenant rendered his report, Dr. Longwell, "with Mr. Mezick of San Jose," was arriving in Santa Fe, telling the *New Mexican* reporter that he had passed a "detachment of Cavalry, 20 in number" on its way to Cimarron.[16] At Santa Fe, Dr. Longwell placed himself "under directions of the United States Marshall [*sic*]," while Lieutenant Cornish, at Cimarron, considered the probable consequences of trying to arrest Mills, seriously taking into account that "the Texans might put seventy-five men under arms to resist." He believed, however, that he could "get the men before they knew it."[17]

He thought that the Texans were "bent on violence, lawlessness, and ruling to suit themselves." They declared they were "assisting

[16] "Anarchy at Cimarron," *Daily New Mexican,* November 9, 1875, p. 1, col. 3.
[17] NA, RG 98, Dist. of N. M. Telegrams, Vol. 125, p. 253.

the civil authorities," but from all the Lieutenant could learn, they were compelling the civil authorities "to do as they see fit." As a result, the citizens were terrified, and many had left "to save their lives." Mills and Donaghue, charged with complicity in the murder of Tolby, were "in the hands of the mob," and the Lieutenant did not think they would be surrendered "even on a Writ of Habeas Corpus." In fact, as he viewed the situation, that portion of the territory was "in anarchy . . . without adequate means of protection; and the sheriff seems powerless to do anything except by permission of the mob."[18]

That the so-called civil authorities were powerless to do anything was evident from developments. On November 10, there was a preliminary examination before the justice of the peace. Mills was set at liberty; Donaghue was bound in twenty-thousand-dollar bail; the Mexican, Cárdenas, while being conveyed to jail, was killed "by a shot by someone of a party of 15 to 20 men who had concealed themselves near the jail." Immediately, there was the "local presumption" that the fatal shot had been fired "by a party from out of town, as the citizens were all at home." Lieutenant Cornish with his troops was five minutes late getting "on the ground, but [by then] everybody had disappeared." Too, the Texans began leaving town, and he deemed that there was "very little use staying any longer."[19] On November 24, "The honorable W. M. Mills arrived [at Santa Fe] on this morning's coach, and looks smiling and fresh, and unscathed from his recent ordeal under the eye of the regulators of Colfax County."[20]

On January 10, 1876, Colonel Granger visited several of his friends, went to his office, then back to his residence, where at three o'clock he had a stroke, dying three hours later. Major J. F. Wade, at Fort Union, received orders to proceed at once to Santa Fe and take temporary command, Captain Francis Moore assuming command at Fort Union. But before Major Wade left Fort Union, he called Captain

[18] *Daily New Mexican,* November 10, 1875, p. 1, col. 3.

[19] NA, RG, 98, Dist. of N. M. Telegrams, Vol. 125, p. 253; "Report of Hanging a Mexican," *Daily New Mexican,* November 4, 1875, p. 1, col. 3.

[20] *Daily New Mexican,* November 24, 1875, p. 1, col. 4.

McCleave in from Cimarron, leaving Lieutenant Cornish behind.

Meantime Indian Agent Irvine went to Fort Defiance, trusting the Indian stores at Cimarron to a clerk. This was injudicious, Cornish soon thereafter reporting the clerk "on the verge of Delirium Tremens," so that it was necessary to "shut the store & put on guard." Cornish wanted someone sent "authorized to take charge of it." Instead, he got welcome orders: ". . . remove all troops from there."[21] Acting with great haste, Cornish bade farewell to Cimarron, but before he could reach Fort Union, Governor Axtell was asking for help again.

"I have received communication from the Sheriff of Colfax County [telegraphed the Governor] stating that he cannot enforce the civil law. I have to request that you instruct Lieut. Cornish to remain at Cimarron . . . to protect the lives and property of citizens."[22] Although Fort Union's command did not have authority to comply with the Governor's plea, still General Pope telegraphed: "By command of the President, you will furnish a company of Cavalry . . . to aid the civil officers of Colfax County . . . the Commanding Officer of the Detachment to act under the orders of the proper Territorial civil officers."[23]

Before action could be taken under martial law, Colonel Hatch, arriving in Santa Fe, telegraphed: "I report for duty, and assume command of this District." Wade went back to Fort Union only to find that some unknown incendiary had, the night before Hatch's arrival there, burned the fort's planing mill, engine house, and several thousand feet of much-needed lumber.[24]

Colonel Hatch's first consideration upon assuming command of the district was the strength of Fort Union. He notified the War Department that "the Post of Fort Union requires two companies of

[21] *Ibid.*, January 11, 1876; also, Blair to A.A.G., January 10, 1876, NA, RG 98, Dist. of N. M. Telegrams, Vol. 126, p. 76; G.O. No. 5, January 14, 1876, NA, RG 93, Fort Union Orders, Vol. 41, n.p.

[22] S. B. Axtell to Wade, Fort Union, January 24, 1876, NA, RG 98, Dist. of N. M. Telegrams, Vol. 126, pp. 34–35.

[23] NA, RG 98, Dist. of N. M. Telegrams, Vol. 126, pp. 44–45, February 4, 1876.

[24] Fort Union Post Returns, AC, "Fort Union, February, 1876," File 1, p. 22.

Infantry, owing to the details required at the Post, the large Quarter-master Depot . . . and guard duty." He proposed that the fort be "kept as strong as possible," especially in view of the civil troubles about Cimarron "and the usual Indian troubles." He did not "consider it advisable to do without a general Depot," and should the post be broken up (as General Pope seemed to be inclined), "it would only compel the creation of another at some post under the control of a Post Commander." Furthermore, it was Hatch's intention "to repair trains, recuperate animals, and hold a reserve of Transportation in case of an emergency." For these purposes he knew of no place "preferable to Union."[25]

On March 14, thirty enlisted men of the Ninth Cavalry left Fort Union for Cimarron to comply with the Presidential edict. After ten days, half of the detachment under command of Captain Moore was ordered back to Fort Union, where the Captain was "to witness the Payment of his company." Before the order could be executed, however, it was rescinded by Colonel Hatch, who was listening to rumors of renewed disorder in Cimarron. Captain Moore, being in closer communication with the sources of these rumors, rated the actual facts as almost inconsequential, saying that only three cavalrymen had been killed, viz: "Privates George Small, Anthony Harvey & John Hanson," their deaths having taken place in "a sort of Bar-room fracas, [which] only lasted a few minutes." To the Captain's chagrin, he was unable to make any arrests, "after making a thorough search for the killers," and his efforts were "without avail," despite the fact that it was common knowledge that "it was David Crockett and Gus Hefron that did the shooting." Not being able to arrest the two murderers, he had the dead soldiers' bodies taken to Fort Union for interment. After the funeral, Colonel Wade ordered "the remainder of L Company, 9th Cavalry, to rejoin those left at Cimarron, who had not had an opportunity to receive their pay." This last draft on Fort Union reduced the garrison to 159 men, "only two officers of the regular garrison being present."

[25] Hatch to A.A.G., March 9, 1876, NA, RG 98, Dist. of N. M. Letters, Vol. 51, pp. 275–76.

Before Lieutenant Cornish could get back to Cimarron, more violence occurred. The disturber of the peace this time was William Breckenridge, a Negro belonging to the small detachment that had not been permitted to go to Fort Union with the bodies of their murdered comrades and consequently not privileged to draw pay. Breckenridge, finding himself short of cash, undertook to replenish his purse by murdering William Maxwell and his son, Emmett, his acts netting him $58.50.[26]

At this stage of anarchy Governor Axtell got assistance from the legislature: Colfax County was attached to Taos County for judicial purposes. In support of this novel effort to restore law, the *Daily New Mexican* took a firm position:

> This legislation was demanded by reason of the lawlessness and anarchy that is well known has existed in that county for several years, and has assumed a somewhat chronic form, and counts for its harvest the deaths of some dozen persons, or more, from violence. . . . the perpetrators have enjoyed an immunity from any prosecution for their villainies and cheated the gallows and penitentiary of several able bodied occupants. By reason of their lawlessness and aggressiveness in that community, and among the people who go to make up the grand jury, the petit juries and the witnesses, a terror has been created which has subverted all power and rendered the community helpless in the maintenance of law and order. It has become to be unmistakably the fact that it is as much as a person's life is worth in that county to either inform on or convict anyone of murder. . . . The fact remains that all the controlling element is bad, is vicious in the last degree. The change will probably be for the better; it certainly cannot be worse. Indictments can be secured in Taos; and indictments are bad things to have laying around loose. Those whom the indictments are against will eventually have to stand trial or leave the county for their country's good.[27]

In April, 1876, news trickled out of Taos that "there were a great many people attending court"; "everything was quiet and orderly."

[26] *Daily New Mexican*, April 13, 1877, p. 1, col. 3; "Execution of the Murderer, Breckenridge," *ibid.*, May 9, 1877, p. 2, col. 2.

[27] "Colfax attached to Taos for Judicial Purposes," *Daily New Mexican*, January 17, 1876, p. 1, col. 3.

On April 10, Dr. Longwell came into Santa Fe saying that he had been to Taos, where he had been wanted as a witness, and that "the business of the court was progressing." Captain McKibbin was sent "to bolster the civil government," and he, too, found "everything lovely as it should be." Judge Waldo had made "a very brief allusion to some of the things" which would necessarily come before the grand jurors. He called to their attention that "during a period of time dating back no further than the first of November last, no less than eight homicides had been committed in the town of Cimarron or iť immediate vicinity, and since the beginning of the year 1875 at least 16 or 18 men had come to their deaths in brawls or assassinations, to say nothing of the numerous shootings . . . of which little note has been taken." Then, hoping to provoke action by the passive jurors, he pronounced the situation "a matter of shameful and horrid notoriety, at which all decent men will stand shocked, that one room in the village of Cimarron can boast that no less than six men have been killed within its walls during the last six months, besides having been the scene of many furious and bloody encounters not ending in death." Not content with this recital, he thought it "no exaggeration to say that there is hardly a plank in its floor but, could it speak, tell some fearful tale of blood." To the Judge—if not the indurate jurors —"such a record of crime was appalling to the imagination and a disgrace to the civilization of the age . . . . More especially was it a disgrace for yet no indictments have been found."

Then, in an effort to atone for the disgrace by causing indictments to be returned, the judge declared it to be "his duty to refer particularly to three instances of violent taking of life," the first being the murder of the Reverend T. J. Tolby. It was murder, he said, "because the manner of his death can bear no other description . . . one of the most cruel and brutal murders of which the annals of crime give an account." Two other murders mentioned by the judge were of "Cruz Vega, by hanging, and Cardenas, by shooting, at the hands of mobsters." The perpetrators of these "diabolical crimes . . . should be brought to the bar of justice and upon the scaffold forfeit to the offended majesty of the law their wretched lives."

The Taos grand jury "no-billed" Longwell, Mills, and Donaghue; whereupon the *Daily New Mexican* reported "everything in that interesting locality—Cimarron—lovely, with the most profound peace and perfect order prevailing. The mere anticipation of such an ecstatic condition of affairs in Cimarron is heavenly in the extremest sense." Since David Crockett and Gus Hefron had been implicated in the deaths of the three Fort Union soldiers and since Judge Waldo had said that "no innocent man should be allowed to rest under a cloud," the justice of the peace took notice of the undissipated cloud and proceeded with a hearing. The "evidence, however, failed to show any reason for holding them and they were accordingly discharged."[28] After their discharge for lack of evidence, the Taos court administered "a slap on the wrist—mind your Ps and Qs—in the case of The Territory *vs.* David Crockett," fining him fifty dollars for carrying arms.

During its deliberations the Taos court indicted William Breckenridge, the Fort Union soldier, murderer of William and Emmett Maxwell. He was speedily tried and convicted, Chief Justice Waldo sentencing him to "be hung at Cimarron on May 8, next." "May 8, next" came, and so did Sheriff Burleson with the doomed William Breckenridge to the place of execution. Four hundred people also came to watch as he mounted the scaffold at 1:10 P.M. Among those present were the Reverend S. D. Loughreed, there to "attend the murderer on the scaffold," Dr. Ludlum, official hangman's physician, and Dr. Tipton, volunteer aide to Dr. Ludlum, with a purpose of his own.

When Breckenridge was asked if he had anything to say, he began to talk. Not wishing to terminate the proceedings, he "spoke about an hour, confessing the crime, robbed his victims, getting only fifty-eight dollars and a half." Becoming weary, at two-thirty-one, the sheriff brought the spectacle to a close: "The drop fell . . . breaking his neck, and at 2:59, Doctors Ludlum and Tipton pronounced life extinct, and the body was cut down." Whether the Reverend Mr. Loughreed interred the body is not clear from the record, but Dr.

[28] Cimarron, N. M., *News & Press,* August 11, 1876; also, *Daily New Mexican,* August 16, 1876, p. 1, col. 4.

Tipton lingered for other observations and purposes. The doctor's father had it that "the young doctor took advantage of it and *resurrected* him and brought him home [to Tiptonville, six miles southeast of Fort Union] and *dissected* him."[29]

During Carleton's tenure as commander, he consolidated at Fort Union the positions of assistant quartermaster and post quartermaster, making that officer responsible, not to the Fort Union post commander, but to headquarters at Santa Fe. When Hatch assumed command, this order was not rescinded, much to the annoyance of the post commander since it left the post quartermaster in a measure independent of the post command. When Colonel Nathan Augustus Monroe Dudley on November 19, 1876, entered upon his duties as Fort Union commander, he inherited the growing feud between the post commander and the Quartermaster Department. To Dudley it was a most welcome inheritance. In fact, he came boasting that he had been "fighting quartermasters twenty-odd years . . . and would continue to fight them." In this instance, however, Dudley's antipathy was not restricted to quartermasters. He had brought with him the yeast of an eight-year-old personal feud, which, since 1869, had been leavening unrestrained—from the time of the clash with Hatch down in Texas. And the barm had accelerated now that he had developed a predilection for "taking a glass of whiskey or wine."

The story, as it filtered out of Texas, was this:

> In 1869, a Mr. Smith, formerly an officer of an Ohio Reg't was murdered in Jefferson in this State [Texas] and with hired (five) negroes. The cause of the killing was that his murderers were in debt to him. . . . A military commission was appointed to try the murderers, who were members of the leading families of Jefferson. As soon as the commission reached Jefferson, Col. Hatch, who was Pr-st [*sic*], was taken to the house of one of the murderers, and other members of the commission were offered similar courtesies by the kinspeople of the parties under arrest. Colonel Dudley was one of the officers who declined to be *used*. This made bad blood between Hatch and Dudley; in fact, made them enemies, and they remained so.

[29] "Court Martial of Col. N. A. M. Dudley," AC, File 3, p. 275.

Two weeks after assuming command of Fort Union, Colonel Dudley, through an inadvertence of headquarters, Department of Missouri, found an opportunity to complain of the consolidated quartermastership. Headquarters, Department of Missouri, overlooking the fact that Hatch maintained jurisdiction of the assistant quartermaster–post quartermaster (and that his own post quartermaster was not accountable to Dudley), called upon Dudley for a report. All that he could furnish was a statement that "the Post Quartermaster makes no returns . . . . All government transportation, as well as all other property at Fort Union is on the papers of the Depot Quartermaster . . . independent of the Post Commander. He has neither the approval or revision of the papers. . . . therefore I can not inspect the means of transportation."

Hatch then took advantage of the situation to lay emphasis on his intention to withhold authority from Dudley over the post quartermaster, issuing Order No. 114:

> The additional duties of Captain A. S. Kimball, A.Q.M., U.S. Army, Depot Quartermaster, Fort Union, as Post Quartermaster of that Post, are hereby defined. . . .
>
> He will be subject to the orders of the Commanding Officer of Fort Union so far as issuing upon proper requisitions such supplies as are authorized . . . when on hand at the Depot. . . . He will furnish transportation when required for official business upon the order of the Post Commander and for the ordinary daily routine of supplying the Post from stores. He will not be subject to drills . . . etc., by order of the Post Commander. . . . Enlisted men [drawn from the post] will be under the control and command of Captain Kimball.

These limitations Dudley furiously protested, classing them "a violation of the rules and customs of the service, [to] say nothing of the discourtesy to the Post Commander."[30]

After receiving Order No. 114, Dudley decided to satisfy himself regarding the transportation that belonged to the post as distinguished from that under the control of the assistant quartermaster. He there-

---

[30] The main source on the feud between Hatch and Dudley is AC, "Dudley Court Martial Proceedings," consisting of several hundred pages of testimony.

fore informed Captain Kimball that on May 30 he would inspect the post transportation, and for that purpose Captain Kimball would "call it out and display it." To test Captain Kimball's reactions and determine for himself whether Kimball intended to obey the order to display, Dudley, in company with President Grant's post-sutler brother-in-law, John C. Dent, made a social call upon the post quartermaster. During the conversation Dudley made inquiry about the character of fuel available to the post and available upon Dudley's orders. Instead of answering verbally, Captain Kimball passed over his desk to the post commander a status report. After making an effort to read the missive, Dudley gave it back to the Captain: "He could not read it. . . . he had been drinking and was very much intoxicated."

Inspection day came. Promptly Captain Kimball displayed the transportation. Colonel Dudley became "very much excited." He had noticed that the transportation displayed was not the identical transportation previously presented and represented as belonging to the post. Kimball attempted to explain that it had been drawn from the pool, that nothing specific belonged to the post. Dudley became enraged; he charged Kimball "with conducting the Depot in a corrupt and fraudulent manner," declaring that his authority had been taken from him by Colonel Hatch so that "I may not detect the fraud: General [sic] Hatch knows . . . and shields you: I do not know what the arrangements between you and the District Commander are, but I will find out if I have to send to the Secretary of War. . . . You can prove anything from the records of the Depot."

The inspection ended on that unhappy note. A few days later the post commander was seen "to pass into the Mechanic's Corral." He was "staggering and had every appearance of a drunken man." Not wishing to encounter Colonel Dudley in that condition, Kimball left his office "to avoid an interview with him."

At Fort Union, with no larger issues confronting the post, petty quarrels were carried to higher authority. In June, 1877, charges and countercharges flew between Dr. Carvallo, of the hospital, and the Reverend Mr. George Simpson, the post chaplain. The altercation began when Dr. Carvallo wrote Colonel Dudley that he "felt obliged to request the post commander to direct the post chaplain to refrain from speaking to his patient, L. T. Emery," as what the chaplain said "had the tendency to depress him." The Reverend Simpson countered resentfully that Dr. Carvallo's request stemmed from religious intolerance, that it had "an air of religious presumption on account of Catholic bigotry." This charge drew a rejoinder from the doctor that there was absolutely no foundation for the statement.[31] Colonel Dudley did not support the chaplain; instead, he issued General Order No. 56, "suspending Divine Services until September 1." He gave no reason for his unusual order, only explaining to Colonel Hatch two weeks later.[32]

On July 4, the "101st Anniversary of Independence," there was a "Federal salute at dawn of day, a national Salute at retreat, a rocket in the evening, suspension of labor, foot- wheel-barrow, and sack races," and from the salutes from the Arsenal, "the ceilings of the quarters of the officers" came tumbling down. The destruction was almost complete one week later "as the morning and evening gun ... rendered them in a dangerous condition." While the Arsenal guns were shaking down the plaster, preparations were in progress for a fandango at Tiptonville, "to which only the elite were bidden." Invitations were at the instance of Dr. W. R. Tipton, S. B. Watrous, Jr., S. E. Shoemaker, and J. C. Fritzlen. The committee selecting the élite took notice of the allurements of Miss Lizzie, daughter of the post chaplain, the Reverend Mr. Simpson, and, to make certain of her attendance, placed the invitation in the custody of the young doctor for her "to attend a party at the residence of Mr. S. B. Watrous, on Wednesday evening, July 4th, 1877." Since the doctor was the custodian of the young lady's invitation, he made it known that it would afford him "the greatest pleasure to have the honor of your company"; and, anticipating acceptance, he would "endeavor to secure an outfit" and call at her home.

Prior to the Tiptonville party, however, Colonel Dudley had ob-

[31] AC, "Fort Union, 1877," File 2, pp. 122–23.
[32] AC, "Fort Union, 1877," July: No. 56.

served that Miss Lizzie "had been flirting with an enlisted man." For this flaunting of military convention Colonel Dudley "took action in regard to it with her father." No action, however, was taken with Lieutenant Humphrey, who was rather free in his facetious talk about "an improper conversation which she had with him regarding her past conduct with him." This added to the general rumors about the post that "Miss Simpson's character was not good."

The young doctor, having secured "an outfit," attended Mr. Watrous' *baile* accompanied by Miss Lizzie; and after the élite had gone, Miss Lizzie spent the remainder of the night at the residence of the Reverend McHowland at La Junta. The next morning, still in possession of his outfit, the young doctor and Miss Lizzie drove to Tiptonville, thence to Boonville, before returning to Fort Union. Several "rides" followed, until July 23.

During the interim Miss Lizzie had acquired several epistolary commitments from the doctor which she thought might be useful in influencing him to consent to having her father "read the marriage ceremony." When her threat, "If you hear of my death, you may know it is on your account," failed to accomplish her purpose, the letters were delivered to Colonel Dudley. Forthwith, he notified Santa Fe headquarters that he had mailed Chaplain Simpson's application for sick leave. The circumstances underlying the chaplain's desire to leave Fort Union were "peculiar" and painful." His daughter had been "seduced and she had sworn it on Dr. Tipton." She had been "on a visit at the Reverend McHowland's house at the time." The chaplain had been out of health for some time, "unable to preach, and this affliction has prostrated both him and his wife." He would like to apply for a change of station.

After completing his letter to Colonel Hatch, Dudley called in several of his brother officers and told them, ". . .a villain [Dr. Tipton] has seduced the daughter of a fellow officer. It is our duty to go there and try to prevail upon him to make reparations or restore the good name of the girl." All except Dr. Martin agreed. Then the Colonel's ambulance appeared, and they were on their way to Tiptonville. But their enthusiasm soon waned. They "stopped and fortified themselves with a drink . . . and shortly after that another one." Emboldened now, Dudley volunteered "to be the spokesman." Just at the close of day Dr. Tipton peered out of a window of the residence of his Tiptonville uncle, and seeing an ambulance-full of military men, hid in a near-by cemetery. While the officers harassed the Tipton family concerning the whereabouts of the doctor, Dr. Tipton concluded that he, too, needed fortification, but he chose less vaporous means. He left the cemetery and found his friend Bennington, who provided a rifle and a shotgun and insisted upon accompanying the doctor to his father's home at Boonville. When the two finally reached Boonville, they found that the ambulance had preceded them. Enoch Tipton, the doctor's father, disarmed both parties, and "the doubly fortified Fort Union Post Commander" again made his speech: He was responsible for the good name and reputation and actions of all Fort Union inhabitants; he had come to "accuse you, Dr. Tipton" of having "seduced the daughter of a fellow officer."

Thus accused, Dr. Tipton faced Dudley, deliberately sneering, "Whoever says I seduced that girl *lies.*"

Enoch Tipton, upon hearing the denial, announced his intention to return the rifle and shotgun, whereupon Dudley told his companions, "I don't see that anything more can be done. Let us go home." They did, not waiting upon ceremony of farewells.

At Tiptonville there was great excitement. The appearance of the ambulance-load of military men gave rise to the rumor that the Negro soldiers from Fort Union would soon follow their officers to wreak vengeance upon all the friends of Dr. Tipton who had "resurrected and dissected" the executed William Breckenridge.

The young doctor made certain that both Colonel Hatch and the Department of Missouri heard what had happened. Hatch made a statement: "The matter at Tiptonville and Boon Valley was entirely unauthorized, and a gross violation of his [Dudley's] duty as an officer. The citizens whose domiciles he violated are wealthy and influential men. . . . I consider this officer has thrown such reproach upon the good name of the army that it is extremely important that he be brought to trial. The interests of the service demands it." The grand jury at Mora thought likewise, and the civil authorities filed charges against all the offending officers. Neither the grand jury nor reports to the War Department mentioned the possible deductions to be made from Lieutenant Humphrey's facetious talk regarding Miss Lizzie's "past conduct with him."

Three weeks passed while Captain Kimball kept Hatch informed of Dudley's behavior. Then Hatch decided to bring the Colonel "to an account for his conduct." Taking his wife with him, he left for Las Vegas, where he was met by Captain Kimball, who told the commander that, in addition to making charges of connivance and fraud, Dudley was also accusing Dr. Carvallo of embezzlement of donated hospital funds through the connivance of Hatch. Further, Dudley planned to fire a major general's salute in Hatch's honor when he appeared at the fort. This information caused Hatch "to remain away and arrive in the night time," thus avoiding the embarrassing courtesy.

Since Colonel Dudley had not been told of the night-time arrival of the Colonel, he was not in his office when Colonel Hatch arrived. Brusquely Hatch sent a message: "With my compliments to Colonel Dudley. I want to see you at the office." Arriving a few minutes later, Dudley started to salute, but was checked with an abrupt, "Never mind, sir. You are under arrest for making false charges." Colonel Dudley replied, "Those are grave words and must be proven." Then, dropping his sword on the desk and straightening himself to look the Colonel squarely in the eyes, he declared himself: "I will make your depot stink, Sir. I will made it red hot for some officers here if that is the course you are going to pursue!" Issuing Special Field Order No. 5, "Lieutenant Colonel N. A. M. Dudley, 9th U.S. Cavalry, is hereby placed in arrest with the limits of Fort Union," Hatch called Captain Whittemore and passed the command of the post to him.

A few days later, Colonel Dudley countered, filing "charges and specifications" against Colonel Hatch connecting him with numerous and sundry connivances at fraud upon the government, even "playing poker in violation of regulations with subordinate officers." After reading the charges and specifications against Hatch, General Pope intervened: "Dept. Comdr directs that Lieutenant Col. Dudley be released from arrest assuming however no functions of military command until report of Inspecting Officer is received."[33]

Finally, on November 23, 1877, the court-martial met at Fort Union. Colonel Dudley presented as counsel W. T. Thornton and Thomas B. Catron. The latter was dubbed by the *Optic,* "Tom Catron, the grass-fed Webster of the New Mexican bar, who would never be mistaken for a dude. . . . Brusque, burly, and brainy . . . three adjectives that fit Catron's character like the paper on the wall, and when he is observed sitting around the courthouse it is safe to assume that there is litigation of some magnitude to be disposed of. Mr. Catron is a conspicuous figure in New Mexico, not only for his standing at the bar and the extensive area of his real estate, but because of the extra-ordinary and almost phenomenal fact that the prizes of politics to which lawyers are seldom indifferent, and most of them are crazy for, Tom Catron would have rather been Warwick than Edward IV —the kingmaker than the king."[34]

Testimony at the court-martial proceeded slowly. To begin with, Dr. Carvallo announced the presence of smallpox at the home of a quartermaster employee. Although a limited quarantine was imposed, the court continued in session.[35] After assembling seventy-eight witnesses, Colonel Hatch gave his testimony, leaving the stand in the afternoon of November 27. Upon adjournment the court announced that Captain Kimball would be the next witness on the following day. The next day Dr. Carvallo made an entry in his meticulous diary: "The office of Captain Kimball, Asst. Qr. Mr., U.S.A., post and depot Qr. Mr. was destroyed by fire on the morning of Nov. 28. It was an extremely cold morning." But, as announced, Captain Kimball began his testimony, no reference being made to the destruction of his office or to the loss of any documents.

Taking of testimony continued into the third week of December.

[33] NA, RG 98, Dist. of N. M. Telegrams, October 27, 1877.

[34] *Daily New Mexican,* March 2, 1886, p. 1, col. 5, quoting the *Las Vegas Optic.*

[35] Medical history, Dr. C. Carvallo's Diary, AC, "Fort Union, November, 1877," File 4, p. 146–47.

The smallpox scare intensified. Dr. Carvallo said "the contagion [was] brought to the reservation by Sylvia Francisco, Lt. Col. Dudley's servant, who visited Loma Parda." Since Colonel Dent had testified that Colonel Dudley had been drunk while on duty, Dudley was not displeased when it became a part of the record that one "J. D. Davis, the colored servant of the post trader . . . had contracted the disease from his concubine, a mexican woman who visited Loma Parda...with frequency." But irrelevant accusations stopped when the parish priest came up from La Junta "to inform the post surgeon that one hundred and thirty-four deaths in his parish had taken place . . . 250 in the parish of Las Vegas . . . 300 in the vicinity of Mora." So, fully aware of the danger of the epidemic, the trial was speedily brought to a close, but not until Dudley had made strenuous efforts to connect Colonel Hatch with some frauds and many irregularities in the Fort Union quartermaster's department. The most troublesome accusation directed at Colonel Hatch was the presence, under Captain Kimball's charge, of some eight hundred cords of wood. The records showed that this wood had been "issued," but a survey showed it as "present," and there was testimony that it was being "sold."

On December 19, the court adjourned, announcing no decision but leaving behind a trail of rumors, unsupportable by any accessible fact, that Dudley had been convicted on every specification and charge— that he had been dismissed from the service. He was, however, again under arrest, enduring "the slanders, awaiting action of the court," while he thought himself "as free from blemish as . . . any officer of his own grade in the service." On January 17, 1878, the verdict came: Of all the numerous charges leveled at Dudley by Colonel Hatch, he was guilty only of "defaming" Captain Kimball by "villifying and prejudicing Colonel Hatch" and of conduct to the prejudice of good order and military discipline [intrusion into the privacy of the Tiptons]." For these malefactions he was "to be suspended from rank and command and forfeit his pay for three months." In due time General Pope approved; but the President of the United States did not. Interceding, the President ordered that "the unexecuted portion of the court-martial be remitted." Again Colonel Dudley was free for assignment.

Colonel Hatch, acting under superior orders, published Special Order No. 28, placing Dudley in command of Fort Stanton, New Mexico.[36]

On January 26, 1878, anticipating the arrival of the railroad in New Mexico, which would render obsolete many of the transportation vehicles at Fort Union, the Department of Missouri indicated its intention to abandon Fort Union's quartermaster depot. Hatch promptly sought to avert this. The transportation of supplies was "but a part of the usefulness of the depot." It was difficult to "estimate its value," but teams, wagons, etc., were fitted up there. Worn-out wagons were turned in for repairs; all animals requiring recuperation "are sent there." It was the only "reservation furnishing good grazing." It was "absolute economy to continue it." But despite his plea that it was economy to continue, on February 25, positive instructions came "to, as rapidly as possible, reduce the Q.M. Depot to a mere place for repairing. "Goods would be shipped "to posts as will need them." Again, on May 29, 1878, headquarters announced its intention, this time to abandon Forts Union, Craig, Selden, and Garland.[37] To District Commander Hatch this was "not practicable at present." It was not safe to abandon Fort Union "as long as the Arsenal remains at that point." It would be unthinkable "to leave so much valuable property without the protection of a small garrison."[38]

By act of Congress approved June 20, 1878, the removal of both the Utes and Apaches from Cimarron to their respective reservations was directed. As superintendent of the undertaking, Special Inspector E. C. Watkins with a purse of five thousand dollars was sent to Cimarron to pay the expenses of the removal. Colonel Hatch was to "furnish the necessary assistance, provided he had force enough." Pending the concentration of troops at Cimarron, the Indians became aware of the fact that they were to be uprooted. A man "unknown" told them "not to go to Fort Union or they would be killed." To test the ac-

---

[36] S.O. No. 28, NA, RG 98, Dist. of N. M. Orders, Vol. 4, p. 622.

[37] Hatch to A.A.G., June 4, 1878, NA, RG 98, Dist. of N. M. Letters, Vol. 54, pp. 193–94.

[38] NA, RG 98, Dist. of N. M. Letters, Vol. 54, pp. 193–94.

curacy of this information, "on July 13, at 7 P.M. three Utes came into the post at Fort Union to ask Captain Whittemore who this man was and what he knew about it." To pacify the inquisitive Utes, he disclaimed any information concerning the man unknown, telling them also that he himself had no orders to remove them from Cimarron. The Indians then insisted that he "write it on a paper," which he did. With their paper they were ordered to leave the fort. This they refused to do. They would wait until morning. When morning came, they left quietly. Arriving at Cimarron, they presented their paper to Inspector Watkins, who became much alarmed lest "the unauthorized statements of Captain Whittemore at Fort Union might defeat his movements." Whittemore, as a consequence, was ordered to Cimarron to correct the impression, but before he could leave, the "same Chief and three other Utes came into the Fort again." They had traveled all night from Cimarron, and now wanted to know if the paper was correct. Fort Union's adjutant sought to placate them by explaining that the situation had changed: "Big Man[39] was Washington Agent and his orders must be obeyed." Since Watkins was "Big Man from Washington," the Indians were thoroughly satisfied and began retracing their steps to Cimarron. Three days later word came to Fort Union that all the Indians were "now en route to their agencies." They had seen Captain Whittemore at Cimarron; he had told them they should go, and they decided they should.

In early September, 1878, the *Cleveland Leader* took notice of the failure of Governor Axtell to suppress outlawry in both Cimarron and Lincoln counties, and reported that "a Mr. Fred W. Angell, of New York City, has been conducting a curious sort of *investigation* of Gov. S. B. Axtell of New Mexico under a commission from the President and Secretary Schurz." The *Daily New Mexican* added that it appeared that Angell had gone "around the Territory picking up all the gossip and slander of sore-heads and removed officials, which he finally embodied into a bill of indictment against Governor Axtell ... putting himself in the position of the Governor's accusers." These accusations had been caused "by the machinations of a party

[39] "Big Man" was Inspector Watkins.

in our Territory he has persistently and energetically opposed [and] ... in many instances [they] were highhanded criminals."

Not unexpectedly, Governor Axtell received notice of his dismissal. Before leaving the territory, he prepared for release to the public his "Respects to the Angel." It was in substance a vigorous attempt to align attorney Frank Springer with the outlaw element in Cimarron, directly accusing him of being, at the time of the murder of the Negro soldiers from Fort Union "present and consenting to the murder." The *New Mexican* expanded on the theme, making a more invidious attack citing an undercover cause:

How the Cattle Kings Seek
to Crush Out the Small Cattle Growers

An intelligent and reliable Santa Fe correspondent writes to *The Times*[40] that the removal of Governor Axtell has been effected by a speculative combination that centers in the National Bank of Atchison, Missouri. The great cattle ring of the Territory has failed in its mob law and violence policy, owing to the fidelity of Governor Axtell and the ring want [*sic*] a governor who will serve their interests and crush out the small stock-growers. It is stated that Mr. Barrett, Cashier of the Atchison Bank, has been most active in concentrating the opposition to Axtell, and Mr. Springer, Attorney for the Cattle ring, has been active in manufacturing evidence to damage the late Governor. Collum of Illinois, and Secretary McCrary, of Iowa, would do well to tell the President all they know about it.[41]

Opponents of Mr. Axtell, the followers of Mr. Springer, alleged to be attorney for the cattle ring, got as the ousted governor's successor Lewis [who always signed his name "Lew."] Wallace. His appointment by President Rutherford B. Hayes carried the admonition that nothing be left undone in New Mexico to bring that territory out of chaos. The *New Mexican* credited Wallace with a "national reputation," and, should any other reputation be needed, he was "an earnest republican."

[40] The *Philadelphia Times*.
[41] *Weekly New Mexican,* September 28, 1878, p. 1, col 5, copying from the *Philadelphia Times*.

On March 2, 1879, Governor Wallace and Colonel Hatch conferred at Santa Fe. After the conference Hatch wrote General Pope (in an effort to banish Colonel Dudley, then commanding at the scene of the Lincoln County War): "The Governor believes if an Officer, not possessed with the peculiarities of the present Post Commander were in Command at Fort Stanton, and entrusted with restoring quiet, that matters would have reached a better state sometime since. . . . I am under the impression, the present Commander is unfit for the Command. . . . Where to send Colonel Dudley is a question."

Five days after Hatch declared Colonel Dudley unfit for the Command, Governor Wallace lent his assistance, declaring in writing: ". . . it is charged here that Lt. Col. Dudley is responsible for the killing of several people in Lincoln County. I have information also connecting him with the recent murder of H. J. Chapman to the effect that he knew that the man would be killed and announced it the day of the night of the killing, and that one of the murderers stated publicly that he had promised Col. Dudley to do the deed."

With this charge over the signature of the Governor, Hatch promptly relieved Dudley from command and ordered him to Fort Union to await developments. Although protesting vigorously, Colonel Dudley left for Fort Union, arriving, much to the amusement of his fellow officers, "with a large escort." General Pope was amused neither by "the large escort" nor by Dudley's banishment from Fort Stanton; therefore, Dudley was ordered back again, while Fort Union's commander was reminded, "When changing Stations Mounted Men are not used for Escort. . . . When you deem it necessary to provide Escorts for Lieutenant Colonel Dudley, you will furnish them from the Infantry . . . not to exceed Six enlisted Men."

Back again at Fort Stanton, Colonel Dudley invoked his right to a hearing before a court of inquiry, but before there was time to be heard, through Governor Wallace's influence he and Sheriff Peppin were indicted for burning the McSween residence. After they were arraigned, the indictment was dismissed, while the court of inquiry completely exonerated the Colonel. Again Dudley moved to Fort Union, to assume command, January 14, 1880, during the temporary absence of Captain Whittemore. His garrison consisted of "110 Regular, 12 Attached."[42]

In command once more at Fort Union, Colonel Dudley renewed his attacks upon the Quartermaster Department: The mule assigned for use by the post was "totally unfit for a cart-mule, being to [*sic*] small by nearly one-half for any such purpose"; stray stock were running loose upon the reservation. "After this date they will be picked up and placed under a herder to be held subject to paying damages." Too, the spring from which the garrison got its drinking water was receiving the run-off water "filled with manure of the loose stock." The Reverend La Tourette was failing to perform his duties "relating to Post Schools." It was the duty of the post chaplain "to instruct enlisted men in the English Branches." There were "some twenty children at or near the post who should be required to attend school." And the quartermaster had drawn from his command so many guards that he had left "only eight men for duty." The depot of Fort Union was drawing rations for more teamsters "than the Post of Fort Union has for duty." Too, the post quartermaster had "more teamsters than mules."

During the latter part of June, 1880, because of illness in Dudley's family in Kansas City, Dudley left, only to find upon his return that he was ordered "forthwith to Fort Cummings." He learned that "the Garrison [Fort Union] had been broken up—only three men left to care for the buildings—during my absence." The changes at Fort Union, however, were not the result of abandonment. All the available force at Fort Union had been utilized in a full-scale war which had developed with the Chiricahua Indians in southern New Mexico.

To Dudley's regret at being unceremoniously ordered away from Fort Union was added another regret: During his absence a request for use of one of the large guns by the citizens of Las Vegas to fire a salute for visiting former President Grant had been overlooked.[43] In Dudley's absence the Grant party passed on from Fort Union to

[42] Post Returns, Fort Union, AC, "Fort Union, January, 1880," File 1, p. 3.

[43] Dudley to G. W. Prichard, chairman of the Grant Committee, July 6, 1880, NA, RG 93, Fort Union Letter Books, Vol. 18, n.p.

Las Vegas and thereafter to Santa Fe, where General G. A. Smith and Colonel Edward Hatch, acting as co-chairmen of a committee, tendered "a reception at the Palace and thereafter a collation." Since the visitor was known to "collate salubriously," this was a pleasing gesture. After the collation the party visited the placers south of Santa Fe, returning to the "house tendered by the military," a final courtesy being "a reception by General [sic] and Mrs. Hatch."

In mid-October, Fort Union was again to miss the opportunity of honoring a celebrity. This time it was President Rutherford B. Hayes, who chose to travel from California by way of the Southern Pacific to its terminus (yet to be completed), thence north by way of the Atchison Topeka and Santa Fe, into Santa Fe, where Colonel Hatch was again holding himself in readiness to provide a "collation." This gesture failed to excite Mrs. Hayes's highest approbation since she was an ardent prohibitionist. To Lehman Spiegelberg fell the honor of playing host to the President and the First Lady, so, after they "were made comfortable . . . they drove about in hacks." At the plaza the President spoke briefly to the citizens, disclaiming any facility in the art of public speaking, choosing "to let others of the party do the talking who made greater pretensions in that regard." Thereupon the President presented General William Tecumseh Sherman, who—so he said—had been here before and was "glad to be back." He knew the people; they had much to look forward to, but they "must learn by contact with the Americans to improve . . . and acquire wealth." They must "get rid of their burros and goats and make the most of their resources; they must go to work and develop the country or they would be crowded out by the Americans who were a stronger and superior race. New Mexico has a bad name. I have said very hard things about her myself, though I am kindly disposed toward her. Their people have sat eating their garlic in idleness, and abusing General Sumner, General This-and-that, and lastly General Hatch. . . . They want the soldiers to do everything. They must help themselves and the people must not expect the soldiers to run down every Indian."[44]

[44] "Honors to Hayes—Party at Santa Fe," *Daily New Mexican,* October 29, 1880,

When Colonel Dudley took his departure from Fort Union, that post was definitely on the wane. The Indians had retreated from the contest in eastern and central New Mexico, now only striving to hold territory in the south and west. The *Comancheros* had reason to remember the Hittson invasion. Supplies were bypassing Fort Union on the railroad. At the end of July, 1880, post commander H. S. Weeks had little more than token strength to report: "White 19—Colored 2." Five of the whites were officers, as was one Negro. In addition, Weeks had "five whites and 1 Colored in prison and nine enlisted men available for duty but one was sick."[45]

In August, 1880, the situation changed for the worse. On the twenty-fifth there was a furious rainstorm, accompanied by considerable hail. The near-by railroad washed out, and almost all of the post buildings leaked badly. The school was closed; a detachment returned from Santa Fe "from their trials at Fort Marcy" to find three inches of rain flooding the post. Only one of the returning detachment had cause for happiness: he had been acquitted. Three of the other prisoners and one Negro were remanded to jail; and the month finished with eighteen in garrison, five of whom were officers, "two colored."

The ensuing winter was marked by "unusual inclement weather. During December eleven enlisted men went into the hospital "in addition to six prisoners" and a "destitute person" who came into the fort "suffering from frozen feet." Captain Whittemore had no choice but to "care for him at army expense." In January (1881) Sergeant Hugh Walker died "of inflammation of the lungs"; and other unwelcome visitors arrived in February. A band of forty Jicarilla Apaches came to encamp in the Turkey Mountains. They were friends of Captain Shoemaker. They were both hungry and cold. They asked their friend for a permit "to go to the buffalo country," but Shoemaker, "entirely unprepared to cope with the situation," directed them back to their camp. They were back the next day hungrier than before.

p. 1, col. 2. At this stage of Sherman's diatribe the *New Mexican* reporter ended his report, observing that "much more of a like nature was said by the general which did not warrant recording."

[45] AC, "Fort Union Medical History, July, 1880," File 4, p. 47.

Since the post commander had no guards, he did not arrest them, but they were fed and made happy.[46]

Conditions at Fort Union during the next six months became public information. The *Las Vegas Daily Optic,* on September 6, 1881, made a public bid for the removal of the fort to Las Vegas. Editorially it advanced arguments for abandonment and removal:

A Military Move
How Union Will Not "Hold the Fort"

In August, Captain Whittemore (who had been relieved at Fort Union and was merely idling away his time so that Major Van Horn might have quarters and not go to Fort Wingate) received a letter from Colonel Hatch introducing "Mr. M. T. Conway who was starting from Fort Union to certain portions of the Territory upon public business." It developed that his public business had to do with "instructions of the General of the Army" who had commissioned him "to decide upon the location for a colony of colored people." This public business was to be conducted at the expense of the Fort Union facilities, "the necessary escort, one spring wagon and one Escort wagon." In order that Captain Whittemore's connection with the colonization scheme should be strictly legal, he was directed to "make a joint report giving his opinion of the region visited for the purpose required." Two weeks of travel brought the inspectors to Embudo. There Conway declared himself as preferring that site over Fort Union.

And on October 3, 1881, Hatch telegraphed from Santa Fe for twenty days' leave: "My wife [*sic*] death in Washington requires my presence." Promptly General Pope granted the request. Hatch left Santa Fe, October 4, 1881, not to return.[47]

---

[46] NA, RG 98, Fort Union Letter Books, Vol. 18, n.p.; S.O. No. 5, Whittemore, February 5, 1881, NA, RG 98, Fort Union Orders, Vol. 46, p. 84.

[47] NA, RG 98, Vol. 145, pp. 433–34; No. 1083, 1085, October 3, 1881, NA, RG 98, Vol. 134, p. 414; Vol. 134, p. 417.

CHAPTER NINETEEN

MISSION ACCOMPLISHED
—DETAIL DISMISSED

As President Hayes's administration drew to a close, the President, urged by the First Lady, filed "his famous temperance Manifesto" prohibiting the sale of intoxicating liquor at military posts and stations. There would be no more "collations." The *Military Review* rated it the *"farewell shot,* conceived in fanaticism and executed in ignorance, spurred on by his Bed-Room Cabinet." The *Daily New Mexican* prophesied that "under the new regime each military post will be surrounded by a score of low groggeries under the control of disreputable fellows...dealing out liquors as vile as man can concoct." Fort Union's commander ordered that no more sales be made there while he inquired whether or not beer was considered an intoxicating liquor. Following the inauguration of President Garfield, representative prohibition advocates appeared at the White House with a commemorative gift—a portrait of Mrs. Hayes, a reminder to the new President of the former First Lady's aid to the cause. In accepting the portrait, Garfield gave little encouragement regarding his "wine-policy" in the White House. "There is a sovereignty of the family [spoke the President], the absolute right of each family to control affairs in accordance with the conscience and conviction of the head of the family." As he was not only head of the family but head of the army, he announced that "he and his family would drink wine or let it alone as they happened to feel inclined." It took until November 1, 1881, however, for the liquor ban to be lifted at Fort Union.[1]

During January, 1882, the weather ranged "from a maximum of

---

[1] Weeks to Jaeger, October 18, 1881, NA, RG 98, Fort Union Letter Books, Vol. 19, p. 50.

66° to a minimum of 11 below," during which time "some of the recruits, who arrived at the post a few months ago had been allowed but one blanket . . . insufficient for health and comfort." Colonel Haller, commanding, protested to headquarters that the situation needed "immediate remedial action." At the same time he recommended that use of the fort as a prison headquarters be discontinued. This latter suggestion brought a sharp reprimand from the district commander. Instead of transferring the prisoners, Haller was "to allow them to be taken out to work, but with great care to prevent them from escape," for no "change in their place of confinement can be made, except by higher authority."[2]

Three months later,[3] in an effort to economize as directed by General Sheridan in an order of February 24, 1882, McKenzie, then commanding the district, seized upon Haller's proposal as an economy measure and ordered the military convicts transferred from Fort Union to Fort Leavenworth. Lieutenant Patch, who had an artificial leg much in need of repairing and refitting, which could not be done in Fort Union, was selected to accompany the convicts to Leavenworth.

As prisoners started for Fort Leavenworth, word came from Fort Wingate that Indian prisoners were being taken there. General Pope thereupon ordered them to Fort Union, despite the post commander's objection that he already had Indian prisoners who "needed clothing very badly" and he had "no authority to issue it to them." Furthermore, the Indians were "full of vermin & it is impossible to keep them clean without cutting their hair & giving them an entire change of clothing. Orders were issued just the same, and Fort Union was advised to be prepared to receive "two men and 19 Women and Children." They were to be guarded and fed "until further instructions." Since Fort Union did not have enough men for guard duty, the In-

[2] Dorst to C.O., Fort Union, January 28, 1882, NA, RG 98, Dist. of N. M. Letters, Vol. 60, p. 184.

[3] MacKenzie to A.A.G., Fort Leavenworth, March 11, 1882, NA, RG 98, Dist. of N. M. Letters, Vol. 60, pp. 230–32.

The Military West, 1883

dian men were "to be shackled and put in the guardhouse proper."[4]

On June 30, 1882, Captain William Rawle Shoemaker, military storekeeper at the Arsenal, announced his retirement. He asked permission to retain the quarters theretofore occupied by him. In return he "volunteered to keep general supervision over all the buildings at the Arsenal." Permission was granted. The Arsenal remained without

[4] Smith to A.A.A.G., Santa Fe, May 22, 1882, NA, RG 98, Fort Union Letter Books, Vol. 19, p. 133; Dorst to C.O., Fort Union, May 24, 1882, NA, RG 98, Dist. of N. M. Letters, Vol. 60, pp. 296–97.

an officer in charge until July 14, 1882, when A. H. Russell, first lieutenant of Ordnance, appeared with district headquarters instructions
to abolish the Arsenal. Demolition began, as did persistent rumors
that "certain citizens had government arms for sale." Chief of the
arms vendors was the firm of Browne and Manzares of Las Vegas.
Colonel Mackenzie directed Lieutenant Russell "to investigate the
matter," and report to him, after which he "would act on the information."[5]

On July 17 an alarm went out, spreading all the way from Whipple
Barracks, Arizona, to Fort Union, New Mexico. A large band of San
Carlos Indians had left the reservation, attacking "a wagon-train,
killing one man, and stealing the wagon-train stock." As Colonel
MacKenzie was preparing to move Fort Union troops to Cimarron,
he "contented himself to await developments and orders." The reason
for Mackenzie's apathetic approach to engaging in the search for
the San Carlos raiders conceivably may be found in the Lordsburg
operator's telegram to the *Santa Fe Daily New Mexican*:

Lordsburg, N. M.

July 27 [1882]

Exterminate Them

A courier just arrived from Clifton reports a large party of Indians
attacked a wagon-train 3 miles this side of Clifton, yesterday morning
killing two men. The teamsters, 7 in number, stood the Indians off for
two hours, and mortally wounded one of the Indians. The teamsters . . .
rushed out and dragged the wounded Indian into camp, and after the
fight was over, *scalped him and roasted him alive*. The party who saw
him says he was "well done, nice and brown" . . . .[6]

On August 1, 1882, the strength of Fort Union was ninety-five enlisted men and nine officers, Captain Brady in command. Once the

[5] NA, RG 98, Dist. of N. M. Letters, Vol. 60, p. 335; see also Russell's Report
(of 1882), L.R. 3573 and 3137.

[6] Details concerning the "roasted" Indian are to be found in the *Santa Fe Daily
New Mexican*, July 28, 1882, p. 1, col. 4; July 30, p. 2, col. 1; and August 4, p. 2,
col. 4. No one could say, however, whether the Indian was dead or alive during the
process, although there was "ample proof" that the five brave men "traveled up and
down the valley for 90 miles exhibiting proof (scalp) of their valor."

"roast Indian" scare had subsided, Brady moved out to the Cimarron country to observe the Jicarillas, taking with him three officers and sixty-five men. To the reduced garrison of the fort fell the responsibility of guarding twenty-seven Indian prisoners, six general convicts, and two garrison prisoners. Before the year was out, all were "without sufficient clothing for the preservation of health." In fact, the prisoners had had "nothing of clothing since their arrival at post; their Mocassins [*sic*] were entirely worn out, and they were unable to procure any material with which to make new ones." Only twenty blankets were held "among the whole number . . . and those so worn as to be very little protection."

On November 2, 1882, Private James Gray went into Loma Parda, which was off limits, for an evening of gaiety. His social frivolities, however, were suddenly terminated when he was ambushed and assassinated. Twelve days later the *Optic* wrote the concluding chapter in the story:

A Regular Hanging Bee

The murderer of the soldier, James Gay . . . mysteriously shot and killed at Loma Parda last week, has been sought, found, and lynched, the affair taking place last evening. The soldiers of Fort Union were greatly incensed over the dastardly murder of their comrade and decided to avenge his death. Last night a *baile* was gotten up at Loma Porda [*sic*] and a number of the boys in blue at the post disguised themselves and took it in, dancing and drinking with the guests. They singled out their man, caught him, and were not long in swinging him into the air—where he strangled to death.[7]

From "A Regular Hanging Bee" the soldiers of Fort Union turned to "that manly art under the rules of the London Prize ring." On Fort Union's October pay-day there was a new arrival, named O'Reilly, "fresh from the *auld* sod," who, in consonance with Irish predisposition, "began drinking freely and was sadly under the influence of liquor." In such condition, he encountered one Seiner, "weight about 180 pounds . . . who had a good record and had whipped some good men . . . never having suffered a defeat in a fistic affair." Of him his

[7] *Las Vegas Daily Optic,* November 14, 1882, p. 4, col. 1.

friends said, "He was as good a man as stood in New Mexico." That claim became questionable when the hard-drinking O'Reilly appeared. Induced by drink and taunts, O'Reilly "agreed to a fight to see which was the better man." Seiner was the taller "but not so well built," while the Irishman had the disadvantage of "free drinking." Upon squaring away, Seiner violated the rules of fair play, threw O'Reilly, and "beat him unmercifully while he was down," conduct "unheard of in Ireland."

Although whipped, O'Reilly challenged Seiner "to fight for sport ... under the rules of the London prize ring." Seiner refused "unless there was money in the affair." Immediately a friend of O'Reilly's posted fifty dollars for a fight on November 19.

When the two confronted each other again, O'Reilly presented a better appearance. He also presented Seiner "with a *daisy* on the cheek which brought the blood freely," but O'Reilly himself "took a terrible blow ... which laid him on the grass ... but he came to his feet in a twinkle." Then the fight continued for "one hundred and one rounds," Seiner's seconds throwing in the sponge to bring the affair "to a bloody close ... one of the longest battles on record ... a battle of endurance versus skill" which changed the ownership of "about fifteen hundred dollars," at the same time "modulating" the prowess of the bully of Fort Union.[8]

As a follow up to this violence, nature dealt Fort Union a stunning blow on January 29, 1883, from which it was unable to recover. A terrific windstorm struck, beginning at 10:00 A.M. and continued through the morning of the following day. The flagstaff came down, making a gaping hole in one of the quarters. The sheds of the quartermaster's corral were partially unroofed, the roof of the post trader's dwelling was blown off, and chimneys were leveled to the ground. "The violence of the storm surpassed anything known to the old inhabitants—it was simply terrific, and the sand and dust was blinding." Unfortunately there was no appropriation available for repairs.

Six months after the storm, the Secretary of the Interior made an effort through the Secretary of War to have the post buildings (or

[8] *Las Vegas Gazette,* November 22, 1882.

such as were left of them) "turned over to the Department of the Interior under the Act Approved July 1, 1882, to provide additional industrial training schools for Indians, authorizing use of unoccupied barracks for such purpose." The effort was unsuccessful, Colonel Mackenzie claimed that the buildings were still "needed for military purposes."[9] On November 8, 1883, the superintendent of Indian schools made another unsuccessful effort to acquire the old Arsenal buildings. He wanted to establish an Indian manual labor school.[10]

On the night of December 24, 1883, Fort Union suffered more destruction from a damaging fire. Investigation disclosed nothing except that "the fire was an act of an incendiary, cause unknown." Again, there was no appropriation to take care of the damage.[11]

When he took command at Fort Union, Colonel Mizner discovered that the post "had no artificial illumination." He promptly requisitioned oil lamps and posted a "schedule of Hours during which lamps and oil lanterns may be kept lighted." Artificial illumination thereafter might be had in the reading room, schoolroom, office of the post adjutant, hospital hall, water closet, and guardhouse for a period of two hours. "7 P.M. to 9 P.M." In addition, "one oil lantern might be lighted occassionally during the night in posting sentinels even though nine oil lanterns would be used for illumination of grounds, walks, etc."[12]

Fort Union was the scene during January, 1885, of both social and military activities to which it had not been accustomed for some years. In mid-January, Major James A. M. La Tourette, chaplain, announced the forthcoming marriage of his daughter Mary to Lieutenant J. M. Stotsenburg. Another daughter, Genevieve, had previously married Major Joseph H. Collins, assistant Fort Union surgeon. The current wedding was set for February 5. But then, "out of the clear sky . . .

[9] AC, "File of Reservation," Department of Fort Union, 1883, File 2, p. 8, item No. 163.

[10] Smith to Worth, supt. of Indian schools, Watrous, N. M., November 19, 1883, NA, RG 98, Dist. of N. M. Letters, Vol. 64, p. 65.

[11] Stanley to Logan, January 21, 1884, NA, RG 98, Dist. of N. M. Letters, Vol. 64, pp. 99–100.

[12] Letter No. 103, July 6, 1884, NA, RG 98, Fort Union Letter Books, Vol. 20, n.p.

the general assembly was sounded by the buglers." The call: All at the post "who could be spared" were to leave at sunrise for the Strip in Oklahoma.

After working all night, finally, at 6:45 P.M., instead of at sunrise, the detachment "started marching the nine miles to Watrous." They left behind "six enlisted men, two surgeons and Chaplain La Tourette." The band went away playing "The Girl I Left Behind Me," "which started many a tear to flow."[13]

After the troops had gone north by train from Watrous, the telegraph receiver at Fort Union "began to tick." No one could read the message until the bride-to-be found a "young nephew" who had come to attend the wedding, who was familiar with Morse code. He reported that the troops were to return, "not needed." Then "great joy" again burgeoned forth, for there would be a wedding as planned. At sundown the returning band again played, this time, "Out of the Wilderness." Then all assembled for the ceremony. "The entire hall [was] attractively draped with flags . . . festoons of green . . . wedding marches . . . gay music . . . officers wearing their full uniforms . . . relatives and friends . . . visitors from Las Vegas . . . Bishop Dunlap of New Mexico, officiating," and the newly married couple left, "amid playing of the band, shoes and plenty of rice."

On January 31, 1885, Colonel Mizner, accompanied by an inspector "not a member of Fort Union," arrived to inspect the post. With the officials came "a down pour of rain . . . the worst rainstorm . . . ever experienced at the post. The women made the most of the situation: as their roofs leaked, they went around in their quarters with umbrellas." With the facts thus starkly before the inspector, Colonel Mizner pronounced "this post the most dilapidated of any I have ever seen in the army."

In August, 1885, Colonel Douglas replaced Colonel Mizner, who immediately was asked by army headquarters, "What posts, if any, may be discontinued or retained with decreased . . . garrisons?" The query was forwarded to Colonel Bradley, who unhesitatingly said,

[13] Genevieve LaTourette, wife of Major J. H. Collins, to James W. Arrott, November 12, 1850, *New Mexico Historical Review,* Vol. XXVI, pp. 277–86.

The sitting room of Chaplain La Tourette's quarters about 1885.
The Chaplain, his wife, and his daughter are shown.

Arrott Collection

Soldiers of Company H, Tenth U.S. Infantry, photographed at
Fort Wingate, N. M., in 1892, transferred from Fort Union.
Left to right, lower, Privates Roser, Miner, and Powell;
upper, Bell, Forsyth, and Brown. Alexander Forsyth
claimed that he was the "last man to leave Fort Union."

Arrott Collection

"Fort Union . . . can be discontinued with benefit to the service."[14]

On September 16, 1886, Captain W. R. Shoemaker died, succumbing from "general senile debility." At the time of his death he was still volunteer custodian of the unoccupied Arsenal buildings, having served most of his lifetime in the army.[15]

On June 26, 1887, Benjamin F. Butler, who had acquired the land adjacent to and surrounding Fort Union, complained to the Secretary of War that the officers at Fort Union were interfering with the grazing of his cattle "on the immediate environs of Fort Union." Colonel Douglas sarcastically replied that he was not "aware that Governor Butler owned the land," but if he did, it would be "detrimental to the interests of the government" not to drive off his cattle.[16]

In September, 1888, Fort Union's commander again had cause to complain of the necessity of "confining so many prisoners in the small prison rooms of this post." They were "too much crowded for good health." One convict, however, he was willing to hold, one who had made application for commutation "of a portion of his sentence." For "character" his former captain stated:

> Mil. Convict Charles E. Gray . . . Previous to his trial . . . by General Court Martial . . . had been convicted four times by Garrison Court. . . . He was a habitue of the Yellowstone Park, a disreputable ranche . . . the chosen resort of whores, thieves and gamblers, and his reputation in his troop was bad, being generally regarded as a swindler. . . . I regard Gray as a perfectly unreliable, unscrupulous man and his statements are unworthy of consideration or belief.[17]

On January 1, 1889, Major Morrow, now commanding at Fort Union, got orders to suspend repairs on the hospital. The reason assigned was: "superfluous, in consequence of reduced garrison." Post surgeon Henry Lippincott interceded, however, requesting per-

[14] Martin to C.O., Santa Fe, August 27, 1885, NA, RG 98, Dist. of N. M. Telegrams Received, Vol. 138, p. 269; also Vol. 148, p. 292.

[15] AC, "Fort Union Medical History, 1886," File 2, p. 41.

[16] Douglas to A.G., U.S.A., July 17, 1887, NA, RG 98, Fort Union Letter Books, Vol. 21, pp. 233–35.

[17] September 17, 1888, NA, RG 98, Fort Union Letter Books, Letters Sent, Vol. 22, pp. 123–25.

mission at least to "finish the repairs of the roof" in preference to letting "the walls be ruined by the storms."[18] Following Dr. Lippincott's
appeal, General Grierson asked Colonel Carr to return to Fort Union
and "re-examine the quarters, etc and examine the Indian prisoners."
This assignment he completed on August 1, 1890, pronouncing the
fort "totally unfit for habitation. The roofs were of tin, corroded and
cracked, . . . only three rooms did not leak." The walls were of adobe,
and the windows and doors had become loose, and "during a blizzard
sand came in . . . a foot deep on the floor. The privies were old and
bad . . . there is no sewer . . . only open drains." Dr. Lippincott "has
sixteen leaks in his bed room." The roofs of the horse sheds had been
blown off. "The snow fills the mangers three feet deep where the
horses stand." The contractors were furnishing "only swamp grass,
where meadow-grass is in the vicinity." The "old mule sheds at Fort
Wingate were more comfortable than the quarters at Union." The
post was no longer of any strategic importance: "It serves but one
purpose—a prison for captured Indians . . . and those Indians might
be located at some other post."

He counted sixty-eight Indian prisoners at Fort Union. For interpreter, he "selected *Stovepipe,* who, with Kin-de-lay, the principal
chief, spoke some English." He heard their tales of imprisonment.
Kin-de-lay "don't like Fort Union." He wanted to tell the head chief
that "the Indians here like to work"; at San Carlos, they "have lots
of wagons, cattle, horses . . . make good crops, have good cattle, good
houses. . . . Here, Fort Union, no work, no money, nothing to do.
I like money. No got any money . . . no blankets, quilts, hats, shoes,
anything. All worn out. At San Carlos, work heap, buy more. Captain put me in calaboose for makin tizwin—me no fight—me make
tizwin. Don't know why they send me here. Me no kill white man:
these all good men. We all good men."
Stovepipe doffed his hat to explain that he did not know why they
had sent him to Fort Union. It was true that he was a brother of Kid,
who had caused trouble at San Carlos, but he did not "like his broth-

[18] NA, RG 98, Fort Union Letter Books, Letters Sent, Vol. 22, pp. 175, 176, 182.

er." He would like to see him suffer for "bringing trouble on the other Indians." Captain Jack, chief of the band, "disliked his Fort Union imprisonment": it "disturbed his farming." At San Carlos he had "good crops, plenty of barley, wheat, corn, ponies, money . . . here have nothing. . . . Would like to go back to San Carlos: There all time feel good, would kill no white man, no white squaw."

In tendering his report on the imprisoned Indians, Colonel Carr pointed out the fact that the chains had been removed from the Indians. They were no longer in the jail, but in camp "about a half-mile from the post toward the Old Arsenal." There was no guard over them. They were allowed to hunt with guns and ammunition. Some had taken trips and returned, some to the mountains, others to Santa Fe to visit their children in the Ramona Indian School, always without guard. They could take to the mountains any time they wished to do so. They were badly in need of clothing. They had to eat "the usual Indian ration." Other Indian children had been invited to the Ramona School, but the parents "bitterly opposed parting with any more."

Then, even with Carr's report in hand and Fort Union's appeal for blankets—"The temperature registered six above yesterday morning" —it took until December 27 for authority to be granted to draw "fifty-four pairs of blankets for issue to Indian prisoners."[19]

On May 23, 1890, Colonel Morrow informed the soldiers at Fort Union that he "had been officially notified that the post would be abandoned." No date had been indicated, but ennui, resulting from a lack of purpose, reduced the morale of the men to a low ebb. Lieutenant Shullenberger suggested that a canteen be established. The Colonel and the Council of Administration approved. Soon there was a noticeable and "marked effect on the discipline of the post." "Philo," a self-appointed soldier-scribe, who found satisfaction in reporting facts, rumors, and an abundance of fiction to neighboring newspapers under the caption "Faberings from Fort Union," announced the canteen "doing nicely under the jurisdiction of Lieutenant Shalenburger

---

[19] Whittemore to A.A.G., Los Angeles, Calif., December 27, 1890, NA, RG 98, Fort Union Letter Books, Letters Sent, Vol. 23, p. 131.

[*sic*]. Beer is sold freely to the men; nothing stronger. The men are more content now than previous to its establishment. The canteen includes the bar-room, billiard-room and lunch counter."

About the time it became known that abandonment of Fort Union was imminent, a news dispatch arrived from Denver, Colorado, presaging General Butler's taking over his Fort Union property. Butler had arrived in Denver, October 14, 1890, "accompanied by a large party of notables." He refused to be interviewed "when surrounded by a party of ladies and gentlemen." He did let it be known, however, that this was his first trip "west of the Missouri River," that he was on "business and pleasure," that he would view his "Craig Ranch below Pueblo, consisting of one hundred thousand acres," and "three fourths of a ranch in New Mexico—the Mora Grant." He also had extensive mining interests.[20]

On December 2, 1890, the *Santa Fe New Mexican* learned that Fort Union would lose some of its troops immediately. "They are ordered to leave at once for the Indian Territory, and will take station among the red skins there who are said to be whooping up the 'ghost dance' in anticipation of the Messiah's coming and threatening to lift the scalps of a few of the inoffensive guards stationed about the Agency."[21] At the same time Sergeant Patrick Kelly relinquished his sinecure as commissary sergeant at the old fort and proceeded under orders to Whipple Barracks, Arizona.[22] Forty-seven others—Lieutenant Peterson, ten enlisted men, and thirty-six Indian prisoners (as a result of Carr's report) "took the cars" for Fort Grant. And on February 5, 1891, "Philo" favored the *Las Vegas Optic* with more faberings: At the post, among the soldiers, "there were mutterings, good and bad." For a month they had been "victims of terrible storms and piercing cold weather. The temperature registered as low as 13° below. Soldiers, while on guard, found it almost unbearable, especially when night came." Some people thought "soldiers have a *soft thing*. Yes: when he walks hours in a terrible gale and blinding snowstorm:

[20] *Santa Fe Daily New Mexican*, October 15, 1890, p. 1, col. 4.
[21] *Ibid.*, December 2, 1890, p. 4, col. 3.
[22] *Ibid.*, December 19, 1890, p. 1, col. 5.

Yet, it would be a *little softer* in a nice room, nice fire, feather-beds, pillows and down." The writer was authorized to pass along the rumor that Fort Union is recommended for abandonment: It was "high time . . . leaky quarters . . . not very agreeable." Too, "Fort Union troops anticipate . . . a great transfer and mighty transformation. . . . all expect to become angels—not because of immaculateness, but because the chances are they will be transferred to Angel Island, Cal."[23]

A loss to be regretted by the transferring soldiers, according to "Philo," was their benefactor, the post chaplain, the Reverend G. S. Seibold, who conducted services twice each Sunday. "He preaches some fine sermons, but possibly pours theology into unwilling ears." The post trader was "already running before the storm—selling out his stock of goods . . . expects to move in the near future."

Then as "Philo's" fabering rolled off the press,[24] his "bad weather turned into a fearful storm . . . roaring and raging characteristic of caged, mad lions." General Butler's off-limits cattle broke the bounds: "Hundreds of them gathered around the buildings . . . dead cattle everywhere. . . . The mournful groans of the almost frozen cattle was fearfully sad."

Pay-day preceded the blizzard by two days. "As usual the boys celebrated the day by drinking to the health and luck of their individual selves, their comrades and Uncle Sam." Chaplain Seibold went off to Watrous to conduct a service. The weather held him there. Free from "church-call . . . no service at the chapel . . . no murmurs of discontent." Instead, there was "speculation, Eden-like Dreams . . . glorious anticipations . . . as to the fate of the Tenth Infantry." Some would "go to California! O, land, fairy land where the flowers shed their sweet fragrance on every hand, where the *water-millions grow all de yeah*, where the soldier sits near the window and gathers golden oranges. . . . Others . . . ."

Speculation was short-lived. On February 12, 1891, the Fort Union

[23] *Las Vegas Optic,* February 7, 1891, p. 1, col. 41.
[24] "Philo" dated his "faberings" February 5; the *Optic* printed them October 7, 1891.

detachment was relieved from duty and ordered to "proceed to Fort Wingate, N. M., and take station." Then came the final word: *Fort Union is entirely abandoned.* Added was: "The 24 Indians will be taken to the same station." First Lieutenant John H. Shullenberger would "remain at Fort Union to ship government stores and property." Assigned as a detail were the following:

Comp. C., 10th Infantry	Comp. H., 10th Infantry
1. Sergt. John W. Lambert	1. Private Richard van Schranendyk
2. " George B. Adams	2. Martin Miller
3. Private Peter Meyer	3. Daniel Foster
4. " Edwin L. Miner	4. James Riley
5. " Wm. L. Adams	5. Franklin Marker
6. " Henry Herule	6. John W. Meyer
7. " Danial Callaghan	7. August Fitting
8. " Jerry Collins	8. Michael Curtis
9. " Mark Murphy	9. Alexander Forsyth
10. " William Joyce	10. Frederick Methys

For the comfort and security of the loading squad, "full arms and equipment" would be issued, "30 rounds of ammunition per man," as well as "the necessary bunks, bunk-bottoms and matresses."[25]

Before the order assigning the twenty-man detail arrived, scribe "Philo" saw "everything in running order"; thereafter, things were upside down and inside out. "A stranger at the post might have imagined that he was nearing the World's Fair. Scores of teams, great and small—drivers also—could be seen in and around the post . . . soldiers busy, packing government property. They were having a 'picnic' . . . sleeping anywhere . . . exhibiting their cleverness and ingenuity in inventing places to rest their somewhat weary bones . . . beds made out of tables . . . hard beds . . . all blankets shipped. Some soldiers made hammocks, yes, bad luck if someone were to cut the ropes in the night when the soldier was dreaming of his sweetheart

[25] Order No. 12, February 18, 1891, NA, RS, Records of U.S. Commands, Fort Union; AC, "Fort Union, 1891," File 1, p. 2.

'way-back-East' or some great battle in which he had engaged and lower him to the floor not too gently!"[26]

On February 21, Lieutenant Shullenberger, now by orders in charge of Fort Union as commander, called the roll. He noted Captain John Drum's status and marked him AWOL from February 19, he having been on leave since the previous June 19—this despite orders for his company to change stations.

On February 18, despite "somewhat weary bones," there was a mass march of Fort Union soldiers upon near-by Watrous. They went without formation, chanting:

> *Yes, Dolly, there was a grand wedding*
> *In the gray church under the hill;*
> *A beautiful trail and shimmering veil,*
> *A bride-lady, dainty and still:*
> *Sunshine and flowers, O, my Dolly,*
> *With plenty of goodies to eat.*
> *A wedding is always the happiest thing,*
> *And a bride-lady is always sweet.*

The "bride-lady, always sweet" was Miss Annie Calhoun; the groom, John B. Rice. Elder S. L. Barker officiated.[27] The music—Captain W. B. Brinton's "string band . . . dispensing sweet music during the ceremony and afterwards at the supper." At the supper "only a few of the elite . . . ." The bridesmaids "vying with the bride in good looks . . . hoping soon to cast off their 'single blessedness.' "

Moving on schedule—11:30 o'clock, A.M., February 21, 1891— Major E. W. Whittemore with his Fort Union soldiers, left for Watrous, thence for Fort Wingate. "He was gazing on Fort Union for the last time. . . . The march was a very pleasant and easy one . . . only nine miles to the railroad station. Accompanying the troops were officers, Davis, Wooley and Crawford. While awaiting the ar-

[26] "Philo's" letter to the *Optic,* dated February 18, 1891, printed February 21, 1891, p. 1, col. 4.

[27] Rev. S. L. Barker was the father of S. Omar and Elliot S. Barker, well-known writers.

rival of the train at Watrous Captain Drum arrived," two days late, A.W.O.L. At 5:00 P.M., the train came from the east drawing three special coaches, "one for each company and one for the Indians. . . . It was quite a large train and heavily loaded, yet the old iron horse with a little puffing, snorting and blowing, pulled out of Watrous and sped onward and reached Wingate without the crack of a whip or a weary limb."

On board the train and relaxed, "naturally the 'boys' began to feel good. Some sang with vim and power, and *sometimes* melodiously: *I'se gwine back to Dixie,* and *No More I'se gwine to wander:* other songs: *There's a Land that is Fairer than This and We'll Reach it bye and bye."* At Lamy there was an agreeable surprise. The Tenth Infantry Band was there to board the train. "More laughter . . . more handshakes."

At Albuquerque the band "broke the stillness of the night reverberating everywhere . . . six select pieces." As the music started, "clouds were hanging heavy and black"; then they disappeared, and "the shining stars looked down with amazing wonder; the pale moon, the Queen of the Night, was bewitched and almost stood still. . . . methinks the angels were struck with awe and wonder at the unexpectedness of the joyful sound and left their shining abodes and came halfway to earth, but possibly they did not hover long," for they were moving westward again.

On reaching Wingate Station, "the troops were almost paralyzed at the first sight . . . on second sight, they were entirely paralyzed." Looking at the government wagons there to transport them, they "imagined the wheels were made of mud, wheels proper invisible." They wondered what was in store for them on the road to the fort. Then the snow began to fall "from yonder world . . . it became very cold" but the troops "began to take the bold steps toward the post." So, then and there, "Philo" made his last announcement: "Ladies and Gentlemen of the Universe: By the stars, Mars and Jupiter, by all the undiscovered worlds floating in endless space, such a spectacle and exhibition of mud and clay as met the wondering and bewildered eyes of the 10th Infantry from Wingate Station to the post

. . . was never paralleled in the history of the Constitution of the United States! The soldiers said: 'Instead of going to Fort Wingate, We are going to Fort Mudgate.' "

At Fort Union, Commander Shullenberger received instructions to be ready to withdraw the detachment "not later than May 15." To facilitate complete abandonment, he recommended discharge of all civil employees as of April 30, 1891. Then, on May 9, he performed a sad duty, notifying Fort Wingate that "Private Richard van Schranendyk, Company H, 10th Infantry, died at this post at 11:30 A.M., this day from Bronchial Pneumonia from La Grippe." The deceased "had very few effects outside of several checks and a small amount of money," which Shullenberger would "bring to Fort Wingate."

On May 15, post commander Shullenberger posted this notice:

Fort Union, N.M.

Orders No. 25:

In compliance with instructions Hdqrs Dept of Arizona, April 10, 1891 the detachment of the 10 Inf. now at this Post will be withdrawn tomorrow, May 15, 1891.

The Quartermaster's Department will furnish the necessary transportation and the Subsistence Department travel Rations & funds for the purchase of liquid coffee for one day.

John H. Shullenberger
1st Lieut. 10 Inf.
Comndg Post.[28]

On the morning of May 15, 1891, having accomplished their mission, the surviving nineteen members of the detail, accompanied by post commander Shullenberger, hesitated at the newly made grave. There they placed a marker while the words of "Old Philo" echoed in their ears: "Fort Union! May the pale moon and shining star look down upon thee until thou shalt, by unseen power, sink into everlasting oblivion!" A marker to Private Schranendyk—a symbol to all who had served before. Then they marched stolidly away.

[28] Order No. 25, May 14, 1891, NA, RS; AC, "Fort Union, 1891," File 1, p. 1.

COMMANDING OFFICERS, FORT UNION
FROM ITS FOUNDING IN 1851
TO ITS ABANDONMENT IN 1891[1]

1. Capt. and Bvt. Lt. Col. Edmund B. Alexander, July, 1851, until April 22, 1852.

2. Capt. and Bvt. Maj. James H. Carleton, April 22, 1852, until August 3, 1852.

3. Capt. and Bvt. Maj. William Brooks, temporary, from August 3, 1852, until December 18, 1852.

4. Maj. Gouverneur Morris, December 18, 1852, to June 30, 1853.

5. Capt. and Bvt. Col. Horace Brooks, June 30, 1853, to August 3, 1853.

6. Capt. Nathaniel C. Macrae, August 3, 1853, to November 4, 1853.

7. Lt. Col. Philip St. George Cooke, November 4, 1853, to March 11, 1854.

8. Capt. Nathaniel C. Macrae, March 31, 1854, to May 7, 1854.

9. Lt. Col. Philip St. George Cooke, May 7, 1854, to September 17, 1854.

10. Col. Thomas T. Fauntleroy, September 17, 1854, to January 25, 1855.

11. Capt. Nathaniel C. Macrae, January 25, 1855, to February 20, 1855.

12. Capt. Joseph Whittlesey, February 20, 1855, to July 20, 1855.

13. Col. Thomas T. Fauntleroy, July 20, 1855, to January 17, 1856; relieved by Lt. William T. Magruder, February 15, 1856; reassumed command from March to April 29, when Magruder was again in command until June 16, when Fauntleroy returned. Capt. and Bvt. Maj. William N. Grier, July, 1856, to August 21, 1856, when he was relieved by Lt. H. B. Critz, who in turn was relieved by Col. W. W. Loring, September 27, 1856.

14. Col. W. W. Loring, September 27, 1856, until April 19, 1857. Capt. F. Jones, April 19, 1857, to September 27, 1857; Loring, April 8, 1858, when Capt. Andrew Lindsey assumed command.

15. Capt. Andrew Lindsey, April 8, 1858, until August, 1858, when he was

---

[1] This compilation and the numbering have been taken from NA, War Department microfilm of Fort Union Post Returns, in AC.

temporarily relieved by Capt. Robert M. Morris, who remained until September 20, 1858, when Col. Loring returned.

16. Col. W. W. Loring, September 20, 1858, to January 31, 1859. Capt. John Walker, temporary, January 31, 1859, to February 8, 1859, continuing as permanent commander until April 23, 1859; relieved by Maj. John Simonson.

17. Maj. John Simonson, May 31, 1859, relieved temporarily by Capt. Robert M. Morris, June 7, 1859, until October 22, 1859, when Maj. Simonson rejoined the post. Relieved by Maj. Charles Ruff, August 15, 1860, and relieved by Lt. Col. George B. Crittenden, September 17, 1860.

18. Lt. Col. George B. Crittenden, September 17, 1860, until December 27, 1860; Lt. Herbert Enos, temporary. Col. Crittenden returned January 8, 1861, and commanded until February 28, 1861; Capt. Thomas Duncan, temporary, until May 18, 1861, when Bvt. Maj. W. W. Sibley joined the post, temporary, until relieved by Col. William Chapman, June 13, 1861.

19. Lt. Col. William Chapman, June 13, 1861, until December 6, 1861. Post Returns are missing for August, September, October, and November, 1861, at the National Archives. See Fort Union Letter Book correspondence of those months, and December 6, 1861, when a letter from Headquarters, Department of New Mexico, is addressed to Lt. Col. J. F. Chavez, First New Mexico Volunteers, as commanding officer. See also Special Order No. 210 designating Col. Gabriel R. Paul as post commander. Post Returns for December give Chavez as commanding officer.

20. Col. Gabriel R. Paul (commanding officer of Fort Union and Eastern District of New Mexico), December 9, 1861, by Special Order from Headquarters, Department of New Mexico, December 9, 1861, until April 6, 1862. Relieved by Capt. Asa B. Carey, temporary, until June 4, 1862; relieved by Capt. P. W. L. Plympton.

21. Capt. P. W. L. Plympton, June 4, 1862, until August 1863; Maj. H. D. Wallen, temporary, August, 1862, to September 25, 1862. Plympton was relieved August 12, 1863.

22. Col. William M. McMullin, approximately August 12, 1863 (Post Returns missing for August), to September 1, 1864.

23. Col. Henry R. Selden, September 1, 1864, until January, 1865, when relieved because of illness.

24. Lt. Col. Francisco Abreu, January, 1865, until August, 1865.

25. Lt. Col. Edward B. Willis, August, 1865, until December, 1865.

26. Col. Christopher ("Kit") Carson, December 23, 1865, until April 21, 1866.

27. Maj. John Thompson, April 22, 1866, to August 12, 1866.

28. Col. Elisha Marshall, August 12, 1866, to February 20, 1867. During this period Bvt. Col. H. C. Bankhead was on duty at Fort Union and apparently the commanding officer of the attached garrison. Post Returns from January to October, 1866, are missing, but November and December, 1866, and January, 1867, show Col. Bankhead as commanding officer of the post, although all correspondence during the period is signed by and addressed to Col. Marshall as commanding officer. Cullum assigns the position to Col. Marshall.

29. Bvt. Col. William B. Lane, February 20, 1867, until October, 1867.

30. Bvt. Brig. Gen. John R. Brooke, approximately October 15, 1867, to July 12, 1868. During his absence in May, 1868, Charles J. Whiting acted as temporary commanding officer.

31. Bvt. Brig. Gen. William Grier, July 12, 1868, until June 1, 1870.

32. Bvt. Brig. Gen. Irvin Gregg, June 1, 1870, until February 25, 1871.

33. Maj. D. R. Glendenin, February 25, 1871, until December 17, 1871. During this period Col. Gregg was relieved as commanding officer of the district and served as commanding officer at Fort Union, July 1, 1871, to July 13, 1871. Col. Gregg became commanding officer at Fort Union in March, 1872, and was on detached service from June, 1872, until November 2, 1872, when he was again at Fort Union until June 3, 1873, after which he became commanding officer of the District of New Mexico.

34. Capt. Horace Jewell, temporary, June 10, 1871, to July 4, 1871, while Maj. Glendenin was on detached service.

35. Col. J. Irvin Gregg, September 30, 1871, to October 5, 1871, when Maj. Glendenin became commanding officer.

36. First Lt. H. H. Humphreys, temporary, June 12, 1872, until July 4, 1872.

37. Capt. Henry A. Ellis, temporary, July 4, 1872, until November 2, 1872.

38. Capt. Charles Hobart, temporary, April 28, 1873, to May 4, 1873.

39. First Lt. John Eckles, temporary, August 25, 1873, to ?

40. Maj. A. J. Alexander, September 15, 1873, to July 9, 1875, when he was transferred to Texas.

41. Capt. Henry A. Ellis, temporary, July 9, 1875, to November 21, 1875.

42. First Lt. James Roper, temporary, November 21, 1875, to December 20, 1875.

43. Maj. James F. Wade, December 20, 1875, to January 13, 1876.

44. Capt. Francis Moore, temporary, January 13, 1876, to February 10, 1876.

45. Maj. James F. Wade, temporary, February 10, 1876, to April 29, 1876.

46. Capt. Francis Moore, temporary, April 29, 1876, to June 5, 1876.

47. Capt. Edward W. Whittemore, June 5, 1876, to August 2, 1876.

48. Maj. James F. Wade, temporary, August 2, 1876, to October 24, 1876.

49. Capt. Edward W. Whittemore, temporary, October 24, 1876, to November 18, 1876.

50. Lt. Col. N. A .M. Dudley, November 18, 1876, to August 23, 1877, when he was placed under arrest and court-martialed.

51. Capt. Edward W. Whittemore, temporary, August 23, 1877, to September 3, 1877.

52. Maj. A. P. Morrow, September 3, 1877, to November 26, 1878. He commanded an Indian campaign April 3, 1878, to September 9, 1878, during which time Edward W. Whittemore temporarily commanded Fort Union.

53. Capt. Edward W. Whittemore, temporary, November 26, 1878, to January 14, 1880.

54. Lt. Col. N. A. M. Dudley, temporary, January 14, 1880, to June, 1880.

55. Capt. Edward W. Whittemore, June, 1880, to July, 1880.

56. First Lt. Harrison S. Weeks, temporary, July, 1880, to December 9, 1880.

57. Capt. Edward W. Whittemore, temporary, December 9, 1880, to February 25, 1881.

58. Maj. Nathan W. Osborn, February 25, 1881, to June 11, 1881.

59. Capt. Edward W. Whittemore, temporary, June 11, 1881, to August 15, 1881.

60. Maj. James J. Van Horn, August 13, 1881, to September 4, 1881.

61. Lt. Harrison S. Weeks, temporary, September 4, 1881, to October 21, 1881.

62. Col. Granville O. Haller, October 21, 1881, to February 8, 1882.

63. Capt. George K. Brady, temporary, February 8, 1882, to April 29, 1882.

64. Capt. Thomas M. K. Smith, temporary, May 29, 1882, to July 12, 1882.

65. Capt. George K. Brady, July 12, 1882, to October 16, 1882.

66. Col. Henry M. Black, October 16, 1882, to July 12, 1883.

67. Capt. George K. Brady, temporary, July 12, 1883, to August 5, 1883.

68. Col. Henry M. Black, August 5, 1883, to June 6, 1884.

69. Lt. Col. Henry R. Mizner, January 6, 1884, to August 10, 1885.
70. Col. Henry Douglas, August 10, 1885, to October 5, 1885.
71. Maj. Charles C. Davis, temporary, October 5, 1885, to November 15, 1885.
72. Lt. Col. Henry R. Mizner, November 15, 1885, to December 2, 1885.
73. Col. Henry Douglas, December 2, 1885, to May 24, 1886.
74. Capt. Joel T. Kirkman, temporary, May 24, 1886, to June 8, 1886.
75. Col. Henry Douglas, June 8, 1886, to September 25, 1886.
76. Lt. Col. Henry R. Mizner, September 25, 1886, to February 9, 1887.
77. Col. Henry Douglas, February 9, 1887, to June 29, 1888.
78. Capt. Charles Davis, temporary, June 29, 1888, to July, 1888.
79. Col. Henry Douglas, July, 1888, to December 31, 1888.
80. Lt. Col. A. P. Morrow, December 31, 1888, to December 2, 1890.
81. Maj. Edward W. Whittemore, December 2, 1890, to February 21, 1891.
82. First Lt. John H. Shullenberger in charge of the post and detachment at Fort Union until it was abandoned and the detachment was transferred to Fort Wingate (May 15, 1891).

BIBLIOGRAPHY

The Arrott Collection

The Arrott Collection, located in the Rogers Library, Highlands University, Las Vegas, New Mexico, consisting of approximately 53,000 pages of historical material—original, photocopies, microfilm, and compared copies—is the source from which much of this book has been drawn. The collection focuses chiefly upon Fort Union, but it contains much that is incidental thereto. Where the Arrott Collection files show the place of origin or present depository of the material, that is indicated in my text; where such is not available, the Arrott Collection file-folio is given. No effort has been made to list the Arrott Collection items separately in this bibliography because of immense amount of space it would occupy.

Other Archival and Manuscript Collections

Highlands University, Las Vegas, New Mexico:
Blanchard, Charles A. "Account of a Wagon-trip between Las Vegas, New Mexico, and the Missouri River, 1868." Personal reminiscences.
Lucas, W. J. "Las Vegas, New Mexico." Personal experiences.
New Mexico Archives, Santa Fe:
37th U.S. Infantry Company Order Book, 1868–69.
Alvares, Manuel. Papers.
Bent, Charles. Papers.
Chapman, W. A. Raton, New Mexico, Scrapbook.
Dryden, William G. Testimony at Chihuahua, Mexico, November 18, 1841. (Copy.) Gift of W. E. Bard, Dallas, Texas.
Fordyce, Kenneth. "Northern New Mexico's Bad Man and His Gang, Black Jack Ketchum." W.P.A. File 5, D # 4, Folder 6.
Martínez, Juan B. W.P.A. Project File.
Martínez, Luis. "Padre Martínez of Taos." Manuscripts, W.P.A. File S–240, Folkways.

Moore and Mitchel vs. *G. E. Huntington*. Lawyer's brief, accounting of partnership, Fort Union Trading Company.

Pfeiffer Papers.

Schearer, Mrs. Mabel. "Fort Union."

Thompson, A. W. "The Story of Fort Union–Camp Nichols." 1865. Folder.

Vigil Papers.

Whitemore, James E. Diary, 1861–64.

W.P.A. File, Drawer 4, Folder 6.

University of New Mexico, Albuquerque:

Rich Papers (William Gillett Rich).

Texas State Archives, Austin:

Texan–Santa Fe Papers.

Unpublished Theses

Cason, Ina Wilson. "The Bent Brothers on the Frontier." University of New Mexico, 1939.

Espinosa, G. A. "The Curate of Taos: The Story of Padre José Martínez and His Times." University of New Mexico.

Johnson, Emmet E. "New Mexico in the War of the Rebellion." Highlands University, Las Vegas, N. M., 1934.

McLaughlin, Thomas J. "History of Fort Union." University of New Mexico.

Nutt, Willie Larriett. "Texas–New Mexico Boundary Controversy, 1836–1859." University of Oklahoma, 1933.

Pearson, Jim Berry. "A New Mexico Gold Story—Elizabethtown." University of Texas.

Government Documents and Publications

Abert, James William. "Report of Lt. J. W. Abert on His Examination of New Mexico in the Years 1846–47," 30 Cong., 1 sess., *House Exec. Doc. No. 41.* Washington, Wendell and Van Benthuysen, 1848.

Calhoun, James S. *The Official Correspondence of . . . .* Ed. by Annie Heloise Abel. Washington, Government Printing Office, 1915.

Emory, Lt. Col. W. H. "Notes of a Military Reconnoissance . . . Made in 1846-7 with the Advance Guard of the 'Army of the West,'" 30 Cong., 1 sess., *House Exec. Doc. No. 41.* Washington, Wendell and Van Benthuysen, 1848.

Bibliography

Heitman, Francis Bernard. *Historical Register and Dictionary of the U.S. Army.* 2 vols. Washington, Government Printing Office, 1903.

Laws of the Territory of New Mexico, 1860–1861. Santa Fe, 1861.

U.S. Congress, *Senate Executive Documents:*

    22 Cong., *No. 43.*

    22 Cong., *No. 90.*

    28 Cong., 1 session., *No. 1.*

    31 Cong., 2 sess., *No. 26* (McCall's Report).

    32 Cong., 2 sess. (Sibley's Report on Fort Union).

    47 Cong., 1 sess., *No. 142* (Land Grants).

    56 Cong., 1 sess., *No. 442* (Report of Sterling Price).

U.S. War Department. *The War of the Rebellion: A Compilation of the Official Records of the Union and Confederate Armies.* Four series, 128 vols. Washington, Government Printing Office, 1880–1901.

Newspapers

The New Mexican, Santa Fe, New Mexico.

New Mexico Press, Santa Fe, New Mexico.

The New York Tribune, New York City.

Niles' Register, Washington, D.C.

The Optic, Las Vegas, New Mexico.

The Republican, Santa Fe, New Mexico.

Rio Abajo Weekly Press, Río Abajo, New Mexico.

The Santa Fe Gazette, Santa Fe, New Mexico.

The Weekly Examiner, San Francisco, California.

Books

Anderson, George B. *History of New Mexico, Its Resources and People.* 2 vols. Los Angeles, Pacific States Publishing Co., 1907.

Andrade, Vincente de P. *Noticias biográficas sobre los ilustrísimos prelados de Sonora, de Sinaloa y de Durango.* Mexico, D. F., Imprenta del Museo Nacional, 1899.

Athearn, Robert T. *William Tecumseh Sherman and the Settlement of the West.* Norman, University of Oklahoma Press, 1956.

Austin, Mary. *The Land of Journey's Ending.* New York, The Century Co., 1924.

Baca, Manuel C. de. *Vicente Silva and His Forty Bandits.* Trans. by Lane Kauffmann, Washington, D.C., Edward McLean, Libros Escogidos, 1947.

Bailey, Jessie Bromilow. *Diego de Vargas and the Reconquest of New Mexico*. Albuquerque, University of New Mexico Press, 1940.

Bancroft, Hubert Howe. *History of Arizona and New Mexico, 1530–1888*. Vol. XVII of *Works*. San Francisco, History Publishing Co., 1889.

Bell, Major Horace. *Reminiscences of a Ranger*. Santa Barbara, Calif., William Hebberd, 1927.

Bell, William A. *New Tracks in North America*. 2 vols. London, Chapman and Hall, 1869.

Benavides, Fray Alonso de. *Fray Alonso de Benavides' Revised Memorial of 1634*. Ed. by F. W. Hodge, G. P. Hammond, and Agapito Rey. Albuquerque, 1945.

Bennett, James A. *Forts and Forays: A Dragoon in New Mexico*. Ed. by Clinton E. Brooks and Frank D. Reeve. Albuquerque, University of New Mexico Press, 1948.

Binkley, William Campbell. *The Expansionist Movement in Texas, 1836–1850*. University of California *Publications in History,* XIII. Berkeley, 1925.

Bolton, Herbert E. (ed.). *Athanaze de Mézières and the Louisiana-Texas Frontier, 1768–1780*. Cleveland, Arthur H. Clark, 1914.

Bravo Ugarte, José. *Diócesis y obispos de la iglesia mexicana. 1519–1939*. Mexico, D. F., "Buena prensa," 1941.

Brayer, Herbert O. *William Blackmore: The Spanish-Mexican Land Grants of New Mexico and Colorado, 1863–1878*. 2 vols. Denver, Bradford-Robinson, 1949. Brevoort, Elias. *New Mexico: Her Natural Resources*. Santa Fe, the author, 1874.

Callon, Milton, W. *Las Vegas, New Mexico*. Las Vegas, N. M., Las Vegas Daily Optic, 1962.

Campa, Arthur L. *Spanish Folk Poetry in New Mexico*. Albuquerque, University of New Mexico Press, 1946.

Carroll, H. Bailey, and J. Villasana Haggard (trans. and eds.). *Three New Mexico Chronicles*. Albuquerque, Quivira Society, 1942.

Chittenden, Hiram M. *The American Fur Trade of the Far West*. 2 vols. New York, Pioneer Press, 1935.

Cleaveland, Agnes Morley. *Satan's Paradise*. Boston, Houghton Mifflin, 1952.

Cleland, Robert Glass. *A History of California: The American Period*. New York, Macmillan, 1922.

———. *This Reckless Breed of Men*.

Coan, Charles C. *A History of New Mexico*. 3 vols. Chicago, American Historical Society, Inc., 1925.

Connelley, William Elsey (ed.). *Doniphan's Expedition and the Conquest of New Mexico and California.* Topeka, Crane and Co., 1907.

Cook, Philip St. George. *The Conquest of New Mexico and California.* New York, G. P. Putnam's Sons, 1878.

Conrad, Howard Louis. *Uncle Dick Wootton.* Chicago, W. E. Dibble and Co., 1890.

Copeland, Fayette. *Kendall of the* Picayune. Norman, University of Oklahoma Press, 1943.

Cornish, Dudley Taylor. *The Sable Arm: Negro Troops in the Union Army.* New York, Longmans, Green and Co., 1956.

Craig, Reginald S. *The Fighting Parson: The Biography of Colonel John M. Chivington.* Los Angeles, Western Lore Press, 1959.

Davis, W. W. H. *El Gringo, or New Mexico and Her People.* New York, Harper and Brothers, 1857.

Defouri, Rev. James H. *Historical Sketch of the Catholic Church in New Mexico.* San Francisco, McCormick Brothers, 1887.

De Shields, James T. *Border Wars of Texas.* Tioga, Texas, The Herald Co., 1912.

Drannan, Capt. William F. *Thirty-one Years on the Plains and in the Mountains; or, The Last Voice from the Plains.* Chicago, Rhodes and McClure, 1908.

DuBois, Colonel John Van Deusen. *Campaigns in the West—1856–1861; The Journal and Letters of Colonel John Van Deusen De Bois.* Ed. by George P. Hammond. Tucson, Ariz., Arizona Pioneers Historical Society, 1949.

Edwards, Frank S. *A Campaign in New Mexico with Colonel Doniphan.* Philadelphia, Carey and Hart, 1847.

Estergreen, M. Morgan. *Kit Carson: A Portrait in Courage.* Norman, University of Oklahoma Press, 1963.

Ewell, R. S. *The Making of a Soldier: Letters of General R. S. Ewell.* Ed. by Capt. Percy Gatling Hamlin. Richmond, Va., Whittet and Shepperson, 1935.

Falconer, Thomas. *Letters and Notes on the Texan Santa Fe Expedition, 1841–1842.* New York, Dauber and Pine Bookshops, 1930.

Favour, A. H. *Old Bill Williams, Mountain Man.* Chapel Hill, University of North Carolina Press, 1936. New edition, Norman, University of Oklahoma Press, 1962.

Fergusson, Erna. *New Mexico: A Pageant of Three Peoples.* New York, A. A. Knopf, 1951.

Fergusson, Harvey. *The Conquest of Don Pedro.* New York, Pocket Books, 1955.

French, William. *Some Recollections of a Western Ranchman, New Mexico, 1883–1889.* New York, Frederick A. Stokes, 1928.

Garrard, Lewis H. *Wah-to-yah and the Taos Trail.* New edition, Norman, University of Oklahoma Press, 1957.

Garrison, George P. (ed.). *Diplomatic Correspondence of the Republic of Texas.* 3 vols. Vol. I published as Vol. II of the *Report of the American Historical Association for the Year 1907* (Washington, 1907). Vols. II and III published as Vol. II of the *Report of the American Historical Association for the Year 1908,* in 2 parts (Washington, 1908).

Grant, Blanche C. *100 Years in Old Taos.* Taos, N. M., 1925.

——. *Taos Today.* Taos, N. M., 1925.

——. *When Old Trails Were New, the Story of Taos.* New York, Press of the Pioneers, 1934.

Gregg, Josiah. *Commerce of the Prairies: The Journal of a Santa Fe Trader.* Dallas, Southwest Press, 1933.

——. *Diary and Letters.* Book First: *Southwestern Enterprises, 1840–1847.* Ed. by Maurice Garland Fulton. Norman, University of Oklahoma Press, 1941.

Griffin, John S. *A Doctor Comes to California: The Diary of John S. Griffin, Assistant Surgeon with Kearny's Dragoons, 1846–47.* Ed. by George Walcott Ames, Jr. San Francisco, California Historical Society, 1943.

Hafen, LeRoy, and W. J. Ghent. *Broken Hand: The Life Story of Thomas Fitzpatrick, Chief of the Mountain Men.* Denver, Old West Publishing Co., 1931.

Hall, Martin Hardwick. *Sibley's New Mexican Campaign.* Austin, University of Texas Press, 1960.

Hamlin, Percy Gatling (ed.). *"Old Bald Head" (General R. S. Ewell): The Portrait of a Soldier.* Strasburg, Va., Shenandoah Publishing House, 1940.

Harris, Gertrude. *A Tale of Men Who knew Not Fear.* San Antonio, Alamo Printing Co., 1935.

Hayes, Augustus Allen, Jr. *Unwritten Episode of the Late War.* London, C. Kegan Paul and Co., 1881.

Hayes, Jesse G. *Apache Vengeance.* Albuquerque, University of New Mexico Press, 1954.

420

Hewett, Edgar Lee, *Pajarito Plateau and Its Ancient People*. Albuquerque, University of New Mexico Press, 1938.

Heyman, Max L., Jr. *Prudent Soldier: A Biography of E. R. S. Canby, 1817–1870*. Glendale, Arthur H. Clark, 1959.

Hollister, Ovando J. *Boldly They Rode: A History of the First Colorado Regiment of Volunteers,* Lakewood, Colo., Golden Press, 1949.

Howlett, Rev. W. J. *Life of the Right Reverend Joseph P. Machebeuf*. Pueblo, Colo., Franklin Press Co., 1908.

Horgan, Paul. *Great River*. 2 vols. New York, Rinehart, 1954.

Hulbert, Archer B. (ed.). *Southwest on the Turquoise Trail*. Denver, Denver Public Library, 1933. (Becknell Journal.)

Hunt, Aurora. *James H. Carleton, Frontier Dragoon*. Glendale, Arthur H. Clark, 1958.

Keleher, William A. *The Fabulous Frontier*. Santa Fe, Rydal Press, 1945.

———. *Maxwell Land Grant*. Santa Fe, Rydal Press, 1942.

———. *Turmoil in New Mexico, 1846–1868*. Santa Fe, Rydal Press, 1952.

———. *Violence in Lincoln County, 1869–1881*. Albuquerque, University of New Mexico Press, 1957.

Kendall, George Wilkins. *Narrative of the Texan Santa Fe Expedition*. 2 vols. New York, Harper and Brothers, 1844.

Ladd, Horatio. *The Story of New Mexico*. Boston, D. Lothrop, 1891.

Lamar, Mirabeau. *The Papers of Mirabeau Lamar*. Ed. by Charles A. Gulick, Jr., and others. 6 vols. Austin, Texas State Library, 1920–27.

Lane, Lydia Spencer. *I Married a Soldier*. Philadelphia, J. B. Lippincott, 1893.

Lavender, David S. *Bent's Fort*. Garden City, N. Y., Doubleday, 1952.

Look, Editors of. *The Santa Fe Trail. (A Look at the Opening of the West.)* New York, Random House, 1946.

Loomis, Noel M. *The Texan–Santa Fé Pioneers*. Norman, University of Oklahoma Press, 1958.

Loring, W. W. *Confederate Soldier in Egypt*. New York, Dodd, Mead, 1884.

Lowe, Percival G. *Five Years a Dragoon*. Kansas City, Mo., The Franklin Hudson Co., 1906.

McWilliams, Carey. *North from Mexico*. Ed. by Louis Adamic. Philadelphia, J. B. Lippincott, 1949.

Magoffin, Susan Shelby. *Down the Santa Fe Trail and into Mexico: The Diary of Susan Shelby Magoffin*. Ed. by Stella M. Drumm. New Haven, Yale University Press, 1926.

Malkus, Alida Sims. *Caravans to Santa Fe*. New York, Harper and Brothers, 1928.

Martínez, Antonio José. *Historia Consisa del Cura de Taos*. Taos, N. M., [probably Jesús María Baca, printer], May 4, 1861.

Meline, James F. *Two Thousand Miles on Horseback*. New York, Hurd Houghton, 1867.

Marshall, Thomas Maitland. *A History of the Western Boundary of the Louisiana Purchase*. University of California *Publications in History, II*. Berkeley, University of California Press, 1914.

Mowry, Silvester. *Arizona and Sonora: The Geography, History, and Resources of the Silver Region of North America*. New York, Harper and Brothers, 1864. 3d ed., revised and enlarged.

Nevins, Allan. *Frémont: Pathmarker of the West*. New York, Appleton-Century, 1939.

Peters, Dewitt Clinton. *Pioneer Life and Frontier Adventures: An Authentic Record of the Romantic Life and Daring Exploits of Kit Carson . . . .* Boston, Estes and Lauriat, 1881.

Pike, Zebulon M. *The Southwestern Expedition*. Ed. by Milo Milton Quaife. Chicago, The Lakeside Press, 1925.

Prince, L. Bradford. *Historical Sketches of New Mexico from the Earliest Records to the American Occupation*. Kansas City, Mo., Ramsey, Millett and Hudson, 1883.

Raine, William McLeod. *Famous Sheriffs and Western Outlaws*. Garden City, N. Y., Doubleday, Doran, 1929.

Read, Benjamin M. *Illustrated History of New Mexico*. Santa Fe, New Mexico Printing Co., 1912.

Reid, Jesse Taylor. *It Happened in Taos. Albuquerque,* University of New Mexico Press, 1946.

Richardson, Albert Deane. *Beyond the Mississippi: From the Great River to the Great Ocean. Life and Adventures on the Prairies, Mountains, and Pacific Coast, 1857–1867*. Hartford, Conn., American Publishing Co.; Newark, N. J., Bliss and Co., 1867.

Riddle, Kenyon (Comp.). *Records and Maps of the Old Santa Fe Trail . . . .* Raton, N. M., Raton Daily Range, 1948.

Russell, Marian. *Land of Enchantment: Memoirs of Marian Russell Along the Santa Fe Trail*. As dictated to Mrs. Hal Russell. Ed. by Garnet M. Brayer. Evanston, Ill., The Branding Iron Press, 1954.

Ruxton, George Frederick. *Life in the Far West*. Edinburgh and London, Blackwood and Sons, 1881.

———. *Ruxton of the Rockies*. Collected by Clyde and Mae Reed Porter; ed. by LeRoy R. Hafen. Norman, University of Oklahoma Press, 1950.

Sabin, Edwin LeGrande. *Kit Carson Days, 1809–1868*. 2 vols. New York, Press of the Pioneers, 1935.

Sahagún, Bernardino de. *General History of the Things of New Spain*. (Florentine Codex.) Trans. by Arthur J. O. Anderson and Charles E. Dibble. Santa Fe, School of American Research, 1950.

Sanchez, George I. *Forgotten People: A Study of New Mexicans*. Albuquerque, University of New Mexico Press, 1940.

Saunders, Lyle. *Cultural Differences and Medical Care: The Case of the Spanish-speaking People of the Southwest*. New York, Russell Sage Foundation, 1954.

———. *A Guide to Materials Bearing on Cultural Relations in New Mexico*. Albuquerque, University of New Mexico Press, 1944.

Segale, Sister Blandina. *At the End of the Santa Fé Trail*. Milwaukee, Bruce Publishing Co., 1948.

Shirley, Glenn. *Toughest of Them All*. Albuquerque, University of New Mexico Press, 1953.

Sonnichsen, C. L. *Ten Texas Feuds*. Albuquerque, University of New Mexico Press, 1957.

Stanley, F. (Father Stanley Crocchiola). *Fort Union*. Denver, The World Press, 1953.

———. *The Las Vegas Story*. Denver, The World Press, 1951.

———. *One Half-Mile from Heaven: The Cimarron Story*. Denver, The World Press, 1949.

Streeter, Floyd Benjamin. *Prairie Trails and Cow Towns*. Boston, Chapman and Grimes, 1936.

Stephens, H. M., and H. E. Bolton (eds.). *The Pacific Ocean in History*. New York, Macmillan, 1917.

Thompson, Albert W. *They Were Open Range Days: Annals of a Western Frontier*. Denver, The World Press, 1946.

Twitchell, Ralph Emerson. *The History of the Military Occupation of the Territory of New Mexico, 1846–51*. Denver, Smith-Brooks Co., 1909.

———. *The Leading Facts of New Mexican History*. 5 vols. Cedar Rapids, Iowa, The Torch Press, 1911–17.

————. *Old Santa Fé*. Santa Fe, The New Mexican Publishing Co., 1925.

Tyler, Daniel. *A Concise History of the Mormon Battalion in the Mexican War, 1846–47*. Salt Lake City, n.p., 1881.

Vaughan, John H. *History and Government of New Mexico*. State College, N. M., the author, 1921.

Vestal, Stanley. *Mountain Men*. Boston, Houghton Mifflin, 1937.

Wallace, Lew. *An Autobiography*. 2 vols. New York, Harper and Brothers, 1906.

Warner, Louis H. *Archbishop Lamy*. Santa Fe, The New Mexican Publishing Co., 1936.

Whitford, William Clarke. *Colorado Volunteers in the Civil War*. Denver, The State Historical and Natural History Society, 1906.

Westerners' Brand Book, Denver Posse, 1950. Includes "Sidelights on Santa Fe Traders, 1839–46," by Harold H. Durham. Denver, University of Denver, 1951.

Williams, Albert N. *Rocky Mountain Country*. New York, Duell, Sloan and Pearce, 1950.

Wilson, James Harrison. *The Life and Services of Brevet Brigadier General Andrew Jonathan Alexander, U.S. Army*. New York, n.p., 1887.

Young, Otis E. *The West of Philip St. George Cooke*. Glendale, Arthur H. Clark, 1955.

Periodicals

Allison, W. H. H. Articles in *Old Santa Fe,* October, 1914; April, 1915.

Anthony, Bro. Claudius. "Kit Carson," *New Mexico Historical Review,* Vol. X (1935).

Binkley, W. C. "New Mexico and the Texan–Santa Fe Expedition," *Southwestern Historical Quarterly,* Vol. XXVII (October, 1923).

Bloom, Lansing B. "New Mexico Under Mexican Administration," *Old Santa Fe,* Vol. I (1913–14); Vol. II (1914–15).

"Bulletin—Creswell Taylor," *Missouri Historical Society Bulletin,* Vol. XI (1954).

Carroll, H. Bailey. "The Texan–Santa Fe Trail," *Panhandle-Plains Historical Review,* 1951.

"Charles Autobees," *Colorado Magazine,* Vol. XXXV, p. 102.

"Development of Irrigation," *Colorado Magazine,* Vol. X, p. 3.

"Fort Union," *Freemasons* (Santa Fe), n.d.

"Gertrudis Barcelo," *El Palacio,* Vol. LVII, No. 8.

Bibliography

"Guide to Western Historical Manuscripts Collection," University of Missouri *Bulletin No. 7, 8* (1956).

Hafen, LeRoy R. Article in *Colorado Magazine*, Vol. XXIX, pp. 241–55.

——. "The Early Fur Trade Posts on the South Platte," *Mississippi Valley Historical Review*, Vol. XII, pp. 334–41.

——. "Fort Jackson and the Early Fur Traders on the Platte," *Colorado Magazine*, Vol. III, No. 4.

——. "When Was Fort Bent Built?" *Colorado Magazine*, Vol. XXXI (April, 1954), 105–69.

"Indian Attack on St. Vrain's Train," *Harper's Magazine*, 1857.

Kansas State Historical Society Transactions, Vol. IX (1905–1906), 556.

"Luciano Maxwell: Beaubien, a complete family record," *El Palacio*, Vol. LXIV, Nos. 9–10, p. 317.

"Letter from General James McKinley to Senator Sam G. Britton . . . ," *El Palacio*, Vol. LVIII.

Manson, Laura C. "Albert H. Pfeiffer," *Colorado Magazine*, Vols. X–XI.

"Manuel Alvares," *New Mexican Quarterly*, Vol. II (1932).

New Mexico Historical Society Bulletin, Vol. XIII.

Old Santa Fe, Vol. I, pp. 176ff.

"Protection of Trade as Far as the Arkansas River," *Niles Register*, Vol. LXI.

"Red, the Indian Wife," *Colorado Magazine*, Vol. XXIII, pp. 63–64.

Santa Fe Employe's Magazine, Vol. VI, No. 10.

"Secret Treaty," *Niles Register*, Vol. LXIX (May 23, 1829), 199.

Sonnichsen, C. L. "Major McMullen's Invasion of Mexico," *Password*, Vol. II (May, 1957).

"Spanish-speaking Culture in the Early 1870's," *Harper's New Monthly Magazine*, June, 1876.

Spicer, Edward L. "Worlds Apart," *Arizona Quarterly*, Vol. XIII, No. 3 (Autumn, 1957).

"Texans Invited to Take Over to Rio Grande," *Niles' Register*, Vol. LXIV (August 26, 1843), 406.

Thompson, Albert V. "Insurrection at Taos," *New Mexico Magazine*, Vol. XX, No. 4.

"Treaty with Santa Ana," *Niles' Register*, Vol. I, pp. 413–14.

Wallace, William S. "Forgotten Army Post—Las Vegas," *New Mexico Magazine*, Vol. XXXIII, No. 9 (September, 1958), 21.

INDEX

Fort Union and the Winning of the Southwest has been printed on paper expected to last not less than three hundred years, bearing the watermark of the University of Oklahoma Press. The type chosen for the text is Granjon, a twentieth-century machine face derived from the classic French Garamond type.

UNIVERSITY OF OKLAHOMA PRESS

NORMAN